Praise for *The Hundred-Year Marathon*

"China's ambition to become the world's dominant power has been there all along, virtually burned into the country's cultural DNA and hiding, as [Pillsbury] says, in plain sight.... The author is correct to assert that China constitutes, by far, the biggest national challenge to America's position in the world today."   —*The Wall Street Journal*

"This is a highly engaging and thought-provoking read. It does what few books do well, and that is to mix scholarship, policy, and memoir-style writing in an accessible but still intellectually rich fashion.... Pillsbury ... draw[s] on his extensive knowledge of Chinese historical military writings and theory as well as his interactions with Chinese defectors and senior military officers to develop a compelling analytical defense of this thesis.... In the end, whether you agree with Pillsbury or not, the book is well worth a careful read."

—Elizabeth Economy, Council on Foreign Relations

"Despite dealing with a weighty subject, Pillsbury says everything that he wants to say ... [in] this highly readable book. It deserves to be widely read and debated."   —*The Christian Science Monitor*

"Pillsbury's scholarship is buttressed by an eye-popping amount of declassified material.... Pillsbury's key claim [is] that China ... is methodically undertaking a 'hundred-year marathon' strategy to displace the United States as the global hegemon.... The time is ripe to examine the trajectory of American relations with the world's second-largest economy [and] the marathon is hardly over."

—*The Weekly Standard*

"Following the Communist victory in the Chinese civil war, Americans agonized over 'Who lost China?' If we do not recognize the Chinese party-state for the predatory animal that it is, in twenty years the question we will be asking ourselves is 'Who lost the world?' The answer will be 'We did.'"   —*The Washington Times*

Award. It is a fascinating chronicle of his odyssey from the ranks of the 'panda-huggers' to a principled, highly informed, and lonely stance alerting us to China's long-term strategy of achieving dominance. He shows that we face a clever, entrenched, and ambitious potential enemy, suffused with the shrewdness of Sun Tzu conducting a determined search for the best way to sever our Achilles' heel. We have vital work to do, urgently."

—R. James Woolsey, former Director of Central Intelligence and chairman of the Foundation for Defense of Democracies' Leadership Council

THE HUNDRED-YEAR MARATHON

ALSO BY MICHAEL PILLSBURY

China Debates the Future Security Environment

Chinese Views of Future Warfare
(editor)

THE HUNDRED-YEAR MARATHON

CHINA'S SECRET STRATEGY TO REPLACE
AMERICA AS THE GLOBAL SUPERPOWER

MICHAEL PILLSBURY

ST. MARTIN'S GRIFFIN ⋒ NEW YORK

www.stmartins.com

Designed by Kelly S. Too

The Library of Congress has cataloged the Henry Holt edition as follows:

Pillsbury, Michael.
    The hundred-year marathon : China's secret strategy to replace America as the global superpower / Michael Pillsbury.
        p. cm.
    Includes bibliographical references and index.
    ISBN 978-1-62779-010-9 (hardcover)
    ISBN 978-1-62779-011-6 (e-book)
    1. Strategic planning—China.   2. China—History.   3. National security—China.   4. China—Politics and government.   5. China—Foreign relations.   6. United States—Foreign relations—China.   7. China—Foreign relations—United States.   I. Title.
    JZ1734.P55 2014
    327.1'120951—dc23

                                                                                            2014012015

ISBN 978-1-250-08134-6 (trade paperback)

Our books may be purchased in bulk for promotional, educational, or business use. Please contact your local bookseller or the Macmillan Corporate and Premium Sales Department at 1-800-221-7945, extension 5442, or by e-mail at MacmillanSpecialMarkets@macmillan.com.

First published by Henry Holt and Company, LLC

First St. Martin's Griffin Edition: March 2016

20 19 18 17 16 15 14

For Susan

CONTENTS

AUTHOR'S NOTE

The CIA, the FBI, the Office of the Secretary of Defense, and an agency of the Defense Department reviewed this book prior to publication to ensure that there was no disclosure of classified information. I appreciate the work of the reviewers to remove any sensitive operational details that might jeopardize methods used in the field.

THE HUNDRED-YEAR MARATHON

WISHFUL THINKING

"Deceive the heavens to cross the ocean."
—*The Thirty-Six Stratagems*

At noon on November 30, 2012, beneath a clear late-autumn sky, Wayne Clough, the white-bearded, affable secretary of the Smithsonian Institution, appeared before a collection of cameras and microphones. As he spoke, a cold wind blew across the National Mall. The audience stood bundled in their overcoats as a representative of Secretary of State Hillary Clinton held aloft a mysterious gold medal. The Smithsonian's honored guest that day was the famed Chinese artist Cai Guo Qiang, who had been feted the night before at a tony gala inside the Sackler Gallery of the Smithsonian's National Museum of Asian Art—an event cohosted by my wife, Susan. Some four hundred guests, among them House minority leader Nancy Pelosi, Princess Michael of Kent, and the seventy-four-year-old widow of the shah of Iran, clinked glasses to celebrate the Chinese-American relationship and to catch a glimpse of Cai, who had won international acclaim for his awe-inspiring fireworks display during the opening ceremony of the 2008 Beijing Olympics. Cai was known to celebrate Chinese symbols with performance art, and had once used lighted fires to extend the Great Wall by ten kilometers so it could be better seen from space. Our evening gala raised more than $1 million for the Smithsonian and made the social pages of various newspapers and magazines.[1]

The following day, as Cai was introduced, he was dressed in a

Western-style suit, gray overcoat, and orange-red scarf. A trim, handsome man with graying hair, he looked out upon the Mall and the subject of his latest piece of performance art, a four-story-tall Christmas tree decorated with two thousand explosive devices.

As Cai twisted a handheld trigger, his audience watched the tree explode before their eyes, with thick black smoke emerging from the branches. Cai twisted the trigger again, and the tree exploded a second time, then a third. The five-minute display sent pine needles across the vast lawn in all directions and dense black smoke—symbolizing China's invention of gunpowder—billowing up the façade of the Smithsonian's iconic red sandstone castle.[2] It would take two months to clean up the debris and residue left by the explosion.

I don't know if any of the guests contemplated why they were watching a Chinese artist blow up a symbol of the Christian faith in the middle of the nation's capital less than a month before Christmas. In that moment, I'm not sure that even I appreciated the subversion of the gesture; I clapped along with the rest of the audience. Perhaps sensing the potential controversy, a museum spokesman told the *Washington Post*, "The work itself is not necessarily about Christmas."[3] Indeed, the museum labeled Cai's performance simply, "Explosive Event," which, if one thinks about it, is not much more descriptive than what Cai called it on his own website: "Black Christmas Tree."[4]

Secretary Clinton's aide waved the gold medal for the press corps to see, as Cai smiled modestly. He had just been given the State Department's Medal of Arts, the first of its kind, which was presented to the artist by Clinton herself, along with $250,000, courtesy of the American taxpayer. The medal was awarded, she said, for the artist's "contributions to the advancement of understanding and diplomacy."[5] Cai seemed to agree with the sentiment: "All artists are like diplomats," he said. "Sometimes art can do things that politics cannot."[6]

I was a little suspicious and mentioned Cai the next day during a secret meeting with a senior Chinese government defector. He was incredulous at the award and explosion. We scoured the Internet. I wanted to investigate Cai and his works of art a little more closely. I didn't bother reading the English articles proclaiming Cai's genius, but rather what the Chinese were saying on various Mandarin-language websites about one of their most acclaimed citizens.

Cai, it turned out, has quite a large following inside China. He was and remains arguably the most popular artist in the country, with the notable exception of Ai Weiwei. Many of Cai's fans were nationalists, and applauded him for blowing up Western symbols before a Western audience. China's nationalists called themselves *ying pai*, meaning "hawks" or "eagles." Many of these *ying pai* are generals and admirals and government hard-liners. Few Americans have ever met them. They are the Chinese officials and authors I know the best because since 1973 the U.S. government has instructed me to work with them. Some of my colleagues wrongly dismiss the *ying pai* as nuts. To me, they represent the real voice of China.[7]

Cai and the hawks appear to be very supportive of the narrative of the decline of the United States and the rise of a strong China. (By coincidence, his given name, Guo Qiang, means "strong country" in Mandarin.) Cai's earlier exhibits featured variations on this theme. For instance, while American soldiers were coming under nearly constant assault by IEDs in Afghanistan and Iraq, the artist simulated a car bomb explosion to ask "his viewers to appreciate some kind of redeeming beauty in terrorist attacks and warfare."[8] The artist raised eyebrows when he said that the terrorist attack of September 11, 2001, was a "spectacle" for the world audience, as if it were—in some twisted sense—a work of art. Shortly after the attacks, an Oxford University professor reported that Cai Guo Qiang proclaimed that his favorite book[9] was *Unrestricted Warfare: War and Strategy in the Globalization Era*, a work of military analysis in which two Chinese colonels recommended that Beijing "use asymmetrical warfare, including terrorism, to attack the United States."[10] Even now, Chinese bloggers were enjoying the spectacle of their hero destroying a symbol of the Christian faith only a stone's throw from the U.S. Capitol. The joke, it appeared, was very much on us.

Only later did I learn that the U.S. officials responsible for the payment to Cai had not known about his background or his dubious artistic strategy. I couldn't help but feel that my wife and I had also been caught unawares—happy barbarians gleefully ignorant of the deeply subversive performance taking place before us. This wasn't much different from U.S. policy toward China as a whole. Chinese leaders have persuaded many in the West to believe that China's rise will be peaceful and will not come at others' expense, even while they adhere to a strategy that fundamentally rejects this.

We Americans still don't see China the way it sees us—a condition that has persisted for decades. Why else would the Smithsonian Institution and the State Department pay a famous Chinese artist $250,000 to blow up a Christmas tree on the National Mall? The answer lies, at least in part, in an ancient proverb that says, "Cross the sea in full view" or, in more practical terms, "Hide in plain sight." It is one of the *Thirty-Six Stratagems,* an essay from ancient Chinese folklore.[11] All of these stratagems are designed to defeat a more powerful opponent by using the opponent's own strength against him, without his knowing he is even in a contest. Perhaps unwittingly, Cai alluded to this idea in remarks he delivered later to an audience at the State Department. "Everyone," he said, "has their little tricks."[12]

It is generally understood among those of us calling ourselves China experts that our life's work is devoted to reducing misunderstandings between the United States and China. We have our work cut out for us. Americans have been wrong about China again and again, sometimes with profound consequences. In 1950, the Chinese leadership believed that it had given a clear warning to the United States that its troops should not come too close to the Chinese border during the Korean War, or China would be forced to respond in kind. No one in Washington got that message, and in November of that year Chinese troops surged across the Yalu River into North Korea, engaging U.S. troops in numerous battles before the war was halted by an armistice in 1953, after more than thirty thousand American soldiers had died. The United States also misunderstood China's relationship with the Soviet Union, the reasons for its overtures to the Nixon administration in the 1970s, its intentions regarding student protesters at Tiananmen Square in 1989, its decision to treat an accidental U.S. bombing of a Chinese embassy in 1999 as an act that Chinese leaders equated with the atrocities of Hitler, and more.

Many of us who study China have been taught to view the country as a helpless victim of Western imperialists—a notion that China's leaders not only believe, but also actively encourage. When I was studying for my PhD at Columbia University in 1967, my political science professors emphasized how the West and Japan had mistreated China, with the implication that my generation needed somehow to atone for this. Many of our textbooks contained similar arguments.

This perspective—the desire to help China at all costs, the almost willful blindness to any actions that undercut our views of Chinese goodwill and victimhood—has colored the U.S. government's approach to dealing with China. It has affected the advice that China experts offer to U.S. presidents and other leaders.

It even has influenced our translations. One of the first things a student of the Chinese language learns is its essential ambiguity. There is no alphabet, and Chinese words aren't formed by letters. Rather, words are formed by combining smaller words. The word for *size* combines the character for *large* with the character for *small*. The word for *length* combines the words for *short* and *long*. Chinese use dictionaries to organize thousands of characters, which must be filed under approximately two hundred so-called radicals or families, all sorted according to relatedness. Under each category of relatedness, the dozens of characters are again sorted in order of the total number of strokes required to write a character, from a minimum of one to a maximum of seventeen strokes.

Adding to this complexity are the tones and pitches that delineate words. The effect of tones is to give a single word four possible meanings. A classic example is *ma*. In the first tone, *ma* means *mother*. The second tone is a rising tone, so *ma* then means *numb*. The third tone for *ma* means *horse*, and the fourth tone for *ma*, which falls sharply, means *to scold*. The Chinese must talk loudly to make the tonal differences audible. Another ambiguity is how few sounds the Chinese language uses for syllables. The English language uses ten thousand different syllables, but Chinese has only four hundred. Thus, many words sound the same. Puns and misunderstandings abound.

The language's very complexity is like a secret code. A foreigner has to make important decisions about how to translate Chinese concepts, which can inherently lead to misunderstandings.[13] I had to decide how to translate unusual, elliptical Chinese phrases that were used by Deng Xiaoping in 1983 to a Senate delegation in Beijing, then ambiguous comments in 1987 by Zhu Rongji in Washington, then again in 2002 to decipher what Hu Jintao meant to convey during his visit to the Pentagon. My colleagues often share our translation decisions with each other. Unfortunately, the vast majority of so-called China experts in the United States do not speak Chinese beyond a few words—enough to feign competence in the presence of those who do not speak the language fluently. This fact makes it easier for the supposed China "experts" to interpret Chinese messages subjectively in ways that conform to their own beliefs. What we all must do better is to look not just at speeches but also at the context of those speeches, and we need to look for larger hidden meanings. For well over a half century, Americans have failed to do this. Until recently, the sometimes vaguely phrased expressions of the Chinese hawks were obscure references to ancient history, so their input to Chinese strategy was hidden from most foreigners.

Ever since President Richard Nixon's opening to China in 1971, U.S. policy toward the People's Republic has largely been governed by those seeking "constructive engagement" with China to aid its rise. This policy has remained in effect, with only marginal changes, for decades, across eight U.S. presidential administrations. Democratic and Republican presidents have had different foreign policy visions, but all agreed on the importance of engaging with China and facilitating its rise. The constructive engagement crowd, populated by prominent academics, diplomats, and former presidents, has held significant sway over policymakers and journalists covering China. I should know—I was a member of this group for many decades. In fact, I was among the first people to provide intelligence to the White House favoring an overture to China, in 1969. For decades, I played a sometimes prominent role in urging administrations of both parties to provide China with technological and military assistance. I largely accepted the assumptions shared by America's top diplomats and scholars, which were inculcated repeatedly in American strategic discussions, commentary, and media analysis. We believed that American aid to a fragile China whose leaders thought like us would help China become a democratic and peaceful power without ambitions of regional or even global dominance. We underestimated the influence of China's hawks.[14]

Every one of the assumptions behind that belief was wrong—dangerously so. The error of those assumptions is becoming clearer by the day, by what China does and, equally important, by what China does not do.

FALSE ASSUMPTION #1:
ENGAGEMENT BRINGS COMPLETE COOPERATION

For four decades now, my colleagues and I believed that "engagement" with the Chinese would induce China to cooperate with the West on a wide range of policy problems. It hasn't. Trade and technology were supposed to lead to a convergence of Chinese and Western views on questions of regional and global order. They haven't. In short, China has failed to meet nearly all of our rosy expectations.[15]

From thwarting reconstruction efforts and economic development in war-ravaged Afghanistan to offering lifelines to embattled anti-Western governments in Sudan and North Korea, China has opposed the actions and goals of the U.S. government. Indeed, China is building its own relationships with America's allies and enemies that contradict any peaceful or productive intentions of Beijing.

Take, for example, weapons of mass destruction. No security threat poses a greater danger to the United States and our allies than their proliferation. But China has been less than helpful—to put it mildly—in checking the nuclear ambitions of North Korea and Iran.

In the aftermath of 9/11, some commentators expressed the belief that America and China would henceforth be united by the threat of terrorism, much as they had once been drawn together by the specter of the Soviet Union. These high hopes of cooperating to confront the "common danger" of terrorism, as President George W. Bush described it in his January 2002 State of the Union address, by speaking of "erasing old rivalries,"[16] did not change China's attitude. Sino-American collaboration on this issue has turned out to be quite limited in scope and significance.

FALSE ASSUMPTION #2:

CHINA IS ON THE ROAD TO DEMOCRACY

China has certainly changed in the past thirty years, but its political system has not evolved in the ways that we advocates of engagement had
hoped and predicted. A growing minority of China experts is beginning
to appreciate this. Aaron Friedberg of Princeton University has observed
that instead of being on the verge of extinction the Chinese Communist
Party may survive for decades.[17] The author James Mann, who has
reported on China for more than thirty years, points out that what he
terms the "soothing scenario," which predicts that China will somehow
evolve smoothly into a liberal democracy, could prove to be a fantasy.
Twenty or thirty years from now, he warns, China will likely be far richer
and stronger than it is today, yet it may still be ruled by a Communist
dictatorship that remains "hostile to dissent and organized political opposition," supportive of other oppressive regimes around the world, and
sharply at odds with the United States.[18] A 2009 assessment by the European Council on Foreign Relations, a leading center-left think tank,
describes as "anachronistic" the belief that contact with the European
Union will cause China to "liberalize its economy, improve the rule of
law and democratize its politics."[19] Rather than the emergence of an
American-style free market economy, scholars are increasingly noting
the emergence of a system termed "authoritarian capitalism."[20] Andrew
Nathan of Columbia University, writing in *Journal of Democracy*, calls the
transformation "authoritarian resilience."[21]

Nonetheless, the idea that the seeds of democracy have been sown at
the village level became the conventional wisdom among many China
watchers in America. With patience but no pressure from the United
States, the argument went, local elections in Chinese cities and towns
would eventually be followed by regional and national elections.

Like many working in the U.S. government, I had heard the democracy story for decades. I read about it in countless books and articles. I
believed in it. I *wanted* to believe in it.

My faith was first shaken in 1997, when I was among those encouraged to visit China to witness the emergence of "democratic" elections in
a village near the industrial town of Dongguan. While visiting, I had a

chance to talk in Mandarin with the candidates and see how the elections actually worked. The unwritten rules of the game soon became clear: the candidates were allowed no public assemblies, no television ads, and no campaign posters. They were not allowed to criticize any policy implemented by the Communist Party, nor were they free to criticize their opponents on any issue. There would be no American-style debates over taxes or spending or the country's future. The only thing a candidate could do was to compare his personal qualities to those of his opponent. Violations of these rules were treated as crimes.

One candidate I spoke to asked me if this was how democratic elections worked in the West. I didn't have the heart to tell him the truth. China's hawks had already done away with true elections.

FALSE ASSUMPTION #3:
CHINA, THE FRAGILE FLOWER

In 1996, I was part of a U.S. delegation to China that included Robert Ellsworth, the top foreign policy adviser to the Republican presidential nominee, Robert Dole. Shrewdly playing to the possibility that Dole might win the presidential election and tap Ellsworth as secretary of state, the Chinese offered us what appeared to be an unprecedented look at their country's inner workings and problems. Some of our escorts were military officers who called themselves *ying pai*.

In what appeared to be a forthright exchange of views with Chinese scholars, we were told that China was in serious economic and political peril—and that the potential for collapse loomed large. These distinguished scholars pointed to China's serious environmental problems, restless ethnic minorities, and incompetent and corrupt government leaders—as well as to those leaders' inability to carry out necessary reforms. Considering the well-known secretiveness of the Chinese Politburo, I was astonished by these scholars' candor and startled by their predictions, which only underscored my support for efforts to provide U.S. aid to a supposedly fragile China.

I later learned that the Chinese were escorting other groups of American academics, business leaders, and policy experts on these purportedly "exclusive" visits, where they too received an identical message about

China's coming decline. Many of them then repeated these "revelations" in articles, books, and commentaries back in the United States. For example, a study published by the influential RAND Corporation listed ten factors that would cause China's slowdown or even collapse in the imminent future.[22] This trend would continue to characterize the China debate for years afterward. The title of an article published in *Commentary* magazine in 2003 referred to China's "sickness,"[23] and a best-selling book published in 2001 referred to China's "coming collapse."[24] Many expressed the worrisome view that if the United States pressed China too hard to have elections, to free dissidents, to extend the rule of law, and to treat ethnic minorities fairly, then this pressure would lead to the collapse of the Chinese state—causing chaos throughout Asia.

For decades, we have seen such arguments in op-ed pieces, news stories, and books that have dominated our national discourse about China. Yet the hard fact is that China's already robust GDP is predicted to continue to grow by at least 7 or 8 percent, thereby surpassing that of the United States by 2018 at the earliest, according to economists from the International Monetary Fund, the Organisation for Economic Cooperation and Development, and the United Nations.[25] Unfortunately, China policy experts like me were so wedded to the idea of the "coming collapse of China"[26] that few of us believed these forecasts. While we worried about China's woes, its economy more than doubled.

FALSE ASSUMPTION #4:
CHINA WANTS TO BE—AND IS—JUST LIKE US

In our hubris, Americans love to believe that the aspiration of every other country is to be just like the United States. In recent years, this has governed our approach to Iraq and Afghanistan. We cling to the same mentality with China.

In the 1940s, an effort was funded by the U.S. government to understand the Chinese mind-set. This culminated in several studies, including one in which 150 Chinese emigrants in New York's Chinatown were shown Rorschach inkblot cards. The researchers, who included the scholars Nathan Leites, Ruth Benedict, and Margaret Mead, also analyzed the themes of popular Chinese books and films. One conclusion that emerged was that the Chinese did not view strategy the same way Americans did. Whereas Americans tended to favor direct action, those of Chinese ethnic origin were found to favor the indirect over the direct, ambiguity and deception over clarity and transparency. Another conclusion was that Chinese literature and writings on strategy prized deception.[27]

Two decades later, Nathan Leites, who was renowned for his psychoanalytical cultural studies, observed:

> Chinese literature on strategy from Sun Tzu through Mao Tse-tung has emphasized deception more than many military doctrines. Chinese deception is oriented mainly toward inducing the enemy to act inexpediently and less toward protecting the integrity of one's own plans. In other cultures, particularly Western, deception is used primarily with the intention of ensuring that one's own forces can realize their maximum striking potential . . . the prevalent payoff of deception for the Chinese is that one does not have to use one's own forces. . . . Chinese tend to shroud their means in secrecy and not publicize the day-to-day activities of those in power; for surprise and deception are assumed to be vital.[28]

Chinese literature often highlights the role of deception, and the need for the "sage"—that is, the wise statesman—to penetrate the deception around him to find the hidden signals in reality. There is an emphasis in many classic Chinese stories of heroes using cunning to manipulate others. The heroes of many popular novels, films, and television programs are those who prove adept at concealing their motives, misleading enemies, and veiling their true intentions until the end. Those artists considered the most skilled convey deceptive signs that require a reader's effort and intelligence to decipher and understand before the plot reaches a conclusion.[29]

The results of the original 1940s study—the idea that an ethnonational group viewed the world differently—proved controversial and politically incorrect, and they were never published. The sole existing copy rests quietly in the Library of Congress.[30] It would not be until 2000 that I learned from Chinese generals that the study's conclusions were essentially correct. The Chinese value highly the importance of deception stratagems. They are proud of their cultural uniqueness. Two hawkish generals formed a "Chinese Strategic Culture Promotion Society" to broadcast this view. Their national media influence has risen since I first met them twenty years ago. My colleagues mistakenly ignored them until some of their recommendations recently became Chinese policy.

FALSE ASSUMPTION #5:
CHINA'S HAWKS ARE WEAK

In the late 1990s, during the Clinton administration, I was tasked by the Department of Defense and the CIA to conduct an unprecedented examination of China's capacity to deceive the United States and its actions to date along those lines. Relying on intelligence assets, unpublished documents, interviews with Chinese dissidents and scholars, and Chinese writings that I read in the original Mandarin script, I began to see the secrets that the Chinese had been hiding—in plain sight—from people like me.

As I assembled clues contradicting the conventional narrative about China that I had always believed, I starting connecting the pieces of an alternative narrative of roughly the past four decades. Over time, I discovered proposals by Chinese hawks (*ying pai*) to the Chinese leadership to mislead and manipulate American policymakers to obtain intelligence and military, technological, and economic assistance. I learned that these hawks had been advising Chinese leaders, beginning with Mao Zedong, to avenge a century of humiliation and aspired to replace the United States as the economic, military, and political leader of the world by the year 2049 (the one hundredth anniversary of the Communist Revolution). This plan became known as "the Hundred-Year Marathon." It is a plan that has been implemented by the Communist Party leadership from the beginning of its relationship with the United States. The goal is to avenge or "wipe clean" (*xi xue*) past foreign humiliations. Then China will set up a world order that will be fair to China, a world without American global supremacy, and revise the U.S.-dominated economic and geopolitical world order founded at Bretton Woods and San Francisco at the end of World War II. The hawks assess that China can only succeed in this project through deception, or at least by denial of any frightening plans.

When I presented my findings on the Chinese hawks' recommendations about China's ambitions and deception strategy, many U.S. intelligence analysts and officials greeted them initially with disbelief. They had not seen the evidence I found. (Thankfully, George Tenet, the director of Central Intelligence, was not among them, and in 2001 he awarded me the Exceptional Performance Award for this work.) I can understand my colleagues' skepticism. The Chinese government had long portrayed itself as a backward nation in need of assistance for its "peaceful rise." The Chinese have denied any desire to exercise global leadership—or to clash with the United States. Indeed, written into the Constitution of the People's Republic of China is language that prohibits the nation from becoming a hegemon.[31] Chinese leaders routinely reassure other nations that "China will never become a hegemon."[32] In other words, China will be the most powerful nation, but not dominate anyone or try to change anything. We don't have a copy of the plan. Indeed, the Chinese say there is no plan. They merely want to restore China to its former global position of three hundred years ago, when it commanded roughly a third of the world economy. That apparently means becoming at least twice as strong as the United States by 2049, the hawks say.

These notions of the more peaceful and less nationalist China have been confirmed by ideological allies in the West who populate academia, think tanks, financial institutions, and government. Advancing the notion of a China that is more interested in economic growth than global dominion serves to advance their self-interest, whether it be a private equity fund manager making investments in Chinese companies or a think tank scholar whose funding, access, and ability to facilitate studies and conferences with her Chinese counterparts depends on advancing the rosy scenario. This predominant school of thought among our foreign policy experts, economists, and businessmen is well meaning and not without evidence. There exist in China moderates and those who genuinely seek cooperation with the United States. Indeed, Chinese government officials usually echo those views and are eager to promote them as the authentic voice of China.[33]

But the more benign view of China held by those derisively called "panda huggers"—a term I wore as a badge of honor for decades—also requires suppressing reams of countervailing evidence and dismissing the many hard-line nationalist voices within China, from the highest levels of politics and military institutions to the conventional wisdom of the masses, as "fringe" and "marginal." They are hard-liners labeled as "out of touch" and as relics of a past that has been obliterated by globalization and information technology.

Dismissing Chinese nationalism as out of the mainstream is what most Western experts on China have done for decades. The bias of wishful thinking has created a blind spot to what is likely to emerge as America's thorniest national security challenge in the next twenty-five years. There are moderates and hard-liners in China, doves and hawks, who are locked in a fierce debate over the shape of China's future within the halls of government in Beijing and in frequent conferences. But increasingly, the more hard-line and nationalist worldview is winning out and indeed has far more influence in the inner circle of China's new president, Xi Jinping. The hawks' government-sponsored newspaper *Global Times* has become the second or third most popular source of news, and its editor, Hu Xijin, makes clear how China's hawks see the moderate doves: they are "the cancer cells that will lead to the demise of China."[34]

For the past three decades, as a China expert who has worked in the Congress and in the executive branch for every administration since Richard Nixon's, I have arguably had more access to China's military and intelligence establishment than any other Westerner. Representatives from the People's Liberation Army and the Ministry of State Security have opened the doors to their most secretive institutions and given me documents and writings that no other Westerner has read. The hardliners among them saw me as a useful tool to promote their views, even if I caused discomfort among those in Beijing and Washington who were invested in the image of a peaceful, docile China. In 1998 and 2000, I published two academic books called *Chinese Views of Future Warfare*[35] and *China Debates the Future Security Environment*,[36] which translated many of the documents I had collected on my visits to Beijing or that had been given to me by Chinese military leaders and defectors. I included documents from both sides of the internal Chinese debate about the nation's role in the world, what I called the "orthodox" (hard-line) and "revisionist" (moderate) perspectives at the time. The generals and foreign policy experts I quoted in my two books expressed gratitude that their views had been translated accurately and were receiving some attention, at least among a small clique of national security experts in Washington, and proceeded to grant me more access in the years following.[37]

After decades of studying China closely, I am convinced that these hard-line views are not fringe, but are very much in the mainstream of Chinese geostrategic thought. They are the unvarnished views of senior policymakers who represent hundreds of millions who want to see China rise to global preeminence. Dating back to the beginnings of the Cultural Revolution, there is indisputably also a long line of liberal thinkers who seek integration within the global free market and evolution toward a more democratic system of governance. Just as America has its camps of hawks and doves, its so-called neoconservatives, interventionists, realists, and isolationists, Chinese elites are divided. The difference, of course, is that those debates rarely occur in view of the Chinese public and the Western press. There is no Congress of elected representatives or truly open forums to discuss such matters.

The challenge for Western policymakers, intelligence analysts, and scholars in the coming decade is to penetrate the cloak of secrecy in which these debates occur and to determine the level of influence these different camps have. Until now, it has largely been taken for granted among Western policy and business elites that China seeks a peaceful rise and will gradually evolve to more resemble America. The explosive growth in China of consumer brands such as Starbucks, McDonald's, and Apple serves only to reinforce this view. Only recently have there been disturbing signs that a more militaristic China may be ascendant, which has caused some to question the wishful thinking that has prevailed for more than forty years.[38]

What is indisputable, even for those who continue to advocate for closer ties between the United States and China, is that not only has China's rise happened right under our noses, but also the United States, and the West more broadly, have helped the Chinese accomplish their goals from the beginning. One key source of such assistance was the World Bank. Meeting with Chairman Deng Xiaoping in 1983, World Bank executives secretly agreed that a team of economists would study China intensively and, looking ahead twenty years, recommended how China could catch up to the United States.[39] But this wasn't the only means of assistance. For decades, the U.S. government has freely handed over sensitive information, technology, military know-how, intelligence, and expert advice to the Chinese. Indeed, so much has been provided for so long that Congress complained in 2005 that there is no full accounting. And what we haven't given the Chinese, they've stolen.

The strength of the Hundred-Year Marathon, however, is that it operates through stealth. To borrow from the movie *Fight Club*, the first rule of the Marathon is that you do not talk about the Marathon. Indeed, there is almost certainly no single master plan locked away in a vault in Beijing that outlines the Marathon in detail. The Marathon is so well known to China's leaders that there is no need to risk exposure by writing it down. But the Chinese are beginning to talk about the notion more openly—perhaps because they realize it may already be too late for America to keep pace.

I observed a shift in Chinese attitudes during three visits to the country in 2012, 2013, and 2014. As was my usual custom, I met with scholars at the country's major think tanks, whom I'd come to know well over decades. I directly asked them about a "Chinese-led world order"—a term that only a few years earlier they would have dismissed, or at least would not have dared to say aloud. However, this time many said openly that the new order, or rejuvenation, is coming, even faster than anticipated. When the U.S. economy was battered during the global financial crisis of 2008, the Chinese believed America's long-anticipated and unrecoverable decline was beginning.

I was told—by the same people who had long assured me of China's interest in only a modest leadership role within an emerging multipolar world—that the Communist Party is realizing its long-term goal of restoring China to its "proper" place in the world. In effect, they were telling me that they had deceived me and the American government. With perhaps a hint of understated pride, they were revealing the most systematic, significant, and dangerous intelligence failure in American history. And because we have no idea the Marathon is even under way, America is losing.

1

THE CHINA DREAM

"There cannot be two suns in the sky,
nor two emperors on the earth."

—Confucius

As President Xi Jinping took office in March 2013, China watchers in America did not yet know what to make of him. China's hawks admired him, but the prevailing sentiment among Western observers was that Xi, a rather harmless-looking man of sixty with thick black hair and a genial smile, was a Gorbachev-like reformer intent on displacing China's old guard and finally realizing these observers' long-held conviction that China would become the free market–style democracy of their dreams. But Xi soon demonstrated that he had a dream of his own—one of a resurgent China that would reclaim its rightful place atop the global hierarchy. This has been a Communist Party ambition since Mao took power in 1949, the date commonly understood by China's leaders as the beginning of the Hundred-Year Marathon. President Xi had picked up a slogan from the hawks, *fuxing zhi lu*, which roughly means "the road to renewal." An expression confined to the nationalistic fringe had become the new president's signature issue. It would not be long before the implications became visible.

On the edge of Beijing's Tiananmen Square stands a ten-story obelisk, built on Mao's orders in 1949. Official tour guides, licensed and monitored by China's government, tend not to take foreigners to it. Even if Western-ers do find their way there, they likely won't understand what it depicts, since the site does not offer English translations of the Chinese charac-ters etched in marble and granite. And yet the obelisk spells out the thinking that has governed the Marathon from the beginning.

The mammoth object is described online, rather generically, as a "Monument to the People's Heroes."[1] What the monument actually sig-nifies is the airing of China's grievances, which are perceived to be the products of a "century of humiliation" at the hands of Western powers, beginning in 1839 with the First Opium War, when the Royal Navy laid waste to Chinese ports over a trade dispute with the Qing dynasty. The text and carved images on the monument describe the subsequent one hundred years of Chinese history—at least as the Communist govern-ment sees it—as a time of popular resistance, Western occupation, and guerrilla warfare that culminated in the triumphant ascension of Chair-man Mao Zedong in 1949 to end China's humiliations by the West.

American tourists walk by the obelisk every day, often taking pictures from a distance, and yet remain oblivious to the message it conveys—a message directed at them. That the obelisk has become a centerpiece for patriotic demonstrations among the Chinese people sends another signal that we have also missed: China's day of justice is coming. In short, the obelisk is a perfect symbol of the relationship between China and the United States—the former nursing grievances, the latter completely in the dark.

The notion of China's special position in the hierarchy of nations long predates the rise of the Chinese Communist Party.[2] In the late nineteenth century, the European powers labeled China "the Sick Man of East Asia," a phrase mirroring the "Sick Man of Europe" moniker given to the decaying Ottoman Empire. To many Chinese intellectuals, the term rankled, justi-fying a sense of grievance against Western powers and other outsiders. "Foreigners call us the 'Sick Man' of East Asia," the revolutionary Chen Tianhua bitterly wrote in 1903, "a barbaric, inferior race."[3] This festering wound could never be healed until China reclaimed its proper place at the top of the global hierarchy.

At the dawn of the twentieth century, Chinese writers and intellectu-als developed a fascination with the works of Charles Darwin and Thomas

Huxley. The Darwinian concepts of competition and survival of the fittest struck a chord as a way to avenge the humiliation that the Chinese felt at the hands of the West. The translator, scholar, and reformer Yan Fu is believed to be the first person to translate Huxley's *Evolution and Ethics* into Mandarin. But Yan made a key error—translating the phrase *natural selection* as *tao tai*, or "elimination," which would come to dominate the Chinese understanding of Darwin's thought.[4] Thus, not only would those on the losing end of the competition be considered weaker, but also they would be eliminated from the natural or political world altogether. "The weak are devoured by the strong," Yan Fu wrote, "and the stupid enslaved by the wise, so that, in the end, those who survive . . . are most fit for their time, their places, and their human situation."[5] He wrote further that the West assumes that "all members of an inferior race must be devoured by a superior one."[6] In 1911, China's modern founding father, Sun Yat-sen, based his program explicitly on racial survival. Sun imagined China's struggle against foreign powers as a form of resistance against the threat of "racial extinction" by the white race, which sought to subjugate or even obliterate the yellow race.[7]

The theme was adopted again in 1949. Mao's writings were filled with Darwinian ideas. One of the two translators who most inspired Mao concluded that only two races, the yellow and the white, formed the future struggle in which the whites "had the upper hand" unless the yellow could change its strategy. Even before they discovered the writings of Karl Marx, Mao and his comrades believed that China's survival would depend on a long-term, radical strategy that highlighted the unique traits of the Chinese people.[8] Chinese Communist strategic thought came to be dominated by the idea of struggle for survival in a harshly competitive world.

During Mao's famous Long March—in which his Red Army sought to evade capture by the ruling government in the 1930s—he brought only one book with him, a statecraft manual with lessons from history that have no Western counterpart. The most important component of the book, translated into English as *The General Mirror for the Aid of Government*, centers on stratagems of the Warring States period in China and includes stories and maxims dating as far back as 4000 BC.[9] One in particular, attributed to Confucius, fit nicely with the Darwinian concepts of which the Chinese had become enamored: "There cannot be two suns in the sky."[10] The nature of world order is hierarchy. There is always one ruler at the top.

One of the biggest mistakes made by American experts on China was not taking this book seriously. It was never translated into English. Only in 1992 did we learn from Harrison Salisbury, a *New York Times* reporter, that not only did Mao love this book's lessons in 1935, but also that he read it over and over until his death in 1976.[11] Deng Xiaoping and other Chinese leaders read it, too. Chinese high school students even learn to write from a textbook of selections from *The General Mirror* that includes many of the same lessons from the Warring States era about how to use deception, how to avoid encirclement by opponents, and how a rising power should induce complacency in the old hegemon until the right moment. We missed all this.

"Socialism, in the ideological struggle," Mao said, borrowing a clear Darwinian phrase, "now enjoys all the conditions to triumph as the fittest."[12] In the 1950s, Mao and others in the Chinese leadership spoke often of dominating the rest of the world—phrases dismissed by Westerners as mere delusions of grandeur or harmless efforts to stoke nationalist fervor, not unlike exhortations in the United States by Eisenhower, Kennedy, Truman, or Nixon portraying America as the greatest nation on earth. As the Chinese Communist Party issued slogans proclaiming that China would "overtake Britain and catch up with America" during a period known in China as the Great Leap Forward,[13] few appreciated the seriousness of the espoused intent.

Throughout Mao's tenure, American intelligence officials succumbed to their own biases and prejudices. Most viewed the Chinese as a reclusive, almost primitive people being led by a collection of radicals. The country's streets were filled with bicycles instead of cars. Chinese manufacturers couldn't build electric fans. There was little foreign investment. Chairman Mao's bizarre nationalist schemes were sources of amusement to the West: he withdrew all of China's ambassadors from overseas. To help farmers, Mao ordered the military to kill all the sparrows that were eating the crops. Yet the Great Leader did not seem to appreciate that the sparrows also kept harmful insects away. As a result, China's crops suffered from widespread infestation.

U.S. intelligence officials had trouble believing the reports that China was not satisfied being the junior partner to the Soviet Union. Americans considered the idea laughable that such a supposedly backward nation might one day rival the Soviet Union, much less the United States. But there was one group of people who weren't laughing—the leaders of the Soviet Union. They saw what China was up to long before the Americans did. The first clues about the Marathon came from Moscow.

In the 1950s, China publicly deferred to the Soviet Union as the leader of the Communist bloc. The Chinese feigned weakness and sought aid and assistance from the more technologically advanced Russians. But second fiddle was not a role that suited Mao. The Soviets knew this. And as much as they feared and mistrusted China, they feared a Sino-American alliance even more. So they sent the Americans a false message.

At the end of 1961, a man named Anatoliy Golitsyn approached the CIA station chief in Helsinki and expressed his desire to defect from the Soviet Union. The CIA helped him board a flight from Helsinki to Stockholm with his family.[14] The Ukrainian-born Golitsyn was a forty-five-year-old KGB major who had worked in the agency's strategic planning division before being dispatched to the Soviet embassy in Finland, under the name Ivan Klinov. From Stockholm he boarded a flight to the United States, carrying with him intelligence files on Soviet operations in the West. Dubbed "the most valuable defector ever to reach the West"[15] and later a model for a character in the hit TV series Mission: Impossible, Golitsyn also brought an understanding of the Sino-Soviet relationship that would drastically influence the U.S. diplomatic and intelligence communities for the next several years.

From the outset, American intelligence officials were inclined to trust Golitsyn. He demonstrated his credibility by providing the names of a number of known Soviet spies in the West. His most crucial assistance was to confirm that the British intelligence officer Kim Philby was actually a double agent for the KGB.

Golitsyn was also something of a conspiracy theorist and would later claim that British prime minister Harold Wilson was a KGB informant. One of his conspiracy theories concerned growing rumors of a serious rupture between the Chinese Communists and the Soviet Politburo, each fighting for control of the Communist world. These rumors were unfounded, Golitsyn assured the Americans, a hoax orchestrated by the KGB to deceive the United States so that the Chinese could steal valuable U.S. intelligence. Golitsyn offered an additional warning—at some point, he claimed, another Soviet defector would come to the Americans claiming to have proof of a Chinese-Soviet split. This defector, whenever he arrived, was not to be believed. A little more than two years later, Golitsyn's prophecy came true.

In January 1964, a KGB agent by the name of Yuri Nosenko made contact with a CIA officer in Geneva, and soon thereafter he defected. He had been playing a role with the Soviets as a double agent for the West, and his treachery had been discovered. Nosenko had been recalled to Moscow, where he believed he faced certain imprisonment—and likely worse—so he defected instead to the United States, where he made a number of claims that contradicted much of the received wisdom regarding Sino-Soviet relations. He brought news of a serious Sino-Soviet rift—directly contradicting Golitsyn's assurances that rumors of such an emerging divide were baseless. In fact, this supposed rift was so serious that it had led to border clashes and the threat of full-scale war between the two countries.[16] He claimed that it was Golitsyn, not he, who was planted by the KGB and was deliberately feeding misinformation to the United States to stave off a Sino-American alliance—an alliance that China would use to get even more powerful. Perhaps most ominously, he reported that Mao sought dominance not only of the international Communist system, but also of the entire world order.

The competing views of these two informants put the U.S. government into a quandary. On the one hand, the idea of a split between the two powerful Communist nations was almost too irresistible not to explore and, hopefully, exploit. On the other hand, the Americans believed that one Communist country was ideologically bound to support another and that together they would resist any attempt by the West to drive a wedge between them. A consensus slowly developed within the U.S. intelligence community—and, as would often be the case when it came to China over the ensuing decades, it was the wrong one. They decided not to believe Nosenko.

Nosenko was placed in solitary confinement, where he was expected to remain until he recanted his story. After three years of confinement, however, he did not budge in his story or his confidence. Eventually, some American analysts dared to hope that what Nosenko was dangling before them—the tantalizing prospect of a Sino-American alignment against the Soviets—was real. The CIA and the FBI started a global effort to collect intelligence to get to the bottom of the issue. That was where I came in.

In 1969, there were two things on the U.S. intelligence community's wish list that would resolve the debate. The first was an asset in the KGB's counterintelligence division. The second was an individual with high-level access to members of the Soviet Politburo. Unfortunately, neither was available. So instead, to unboggle the Sino-Soviet conundrum, U.S. intelligence had to settle for what was available. At the time, that was a lowly graduate student who happened to be working at a Soviet-packed organization in New York, the UN Secretariat.

I was twenty-four years old and working as a political affairs officer in the secretary-general's office, having obtained the job with the help of one of my professors at Columbia University. Though in a junior position, I was the only American assigned to any spot in the division. Since I had a security clearance (from a previous government job) and regular access to top UN officials from around the world, I was an obvious target for recruitment by the FBI and the CIA.

At 8:35 a.m. on a slightly overcast Monday in April, I stood on the corner of First Avenue and Forty-Second Street, waiting for traffic to dissipate. Black limos with diplomatic plates lined the entire block, much to the ire of New Yorkers. I had made this trek many times since starting as a political analyst at the UN Secretariat two months earlier. That day, however, my job had changed. I had agreed to work as a spy for the U.S. government.

My two interlocutors, "Peter" of the CIA and "Agent Smith" of the FBI, were tasked by the U.S. national security adviser, Henry Kissinger, with gathering intelligence from any Soviet sources available on the possibility of a Sino-Soviet rupture. There was little interest in what kind of partner China might turn out to be—reliable, erratic, or even dangerous. The single-minded focus of my American colleagues was on how we might use Beijing as a wedge against Moscow. This whole process was building up to an August 1969 meeting to discuss the future of Asia, to be hosted by President Nixon at the so-called Western White House in San Clemente, California.

If espionage conjured notions in my head of John le Carré thrillers and James Bond films, I soon confronted reality. My code name was not something suave and mysterious like 007.[17] On the Sino-Soviet question, the most in-depth reports were lengthy CIA studies called ESAU and POLO.[18] Evidence was mixed. Henry Kissinger's NSC staff was evenly divided about whether to try to improve relations with China. Most supported sticking with President Nixon's view, as expressed in a February 1969 conference, that China was a more dangerous threat than the Soviet Union, and so we needed missile defense against China. By November 1969, what is known today as the famous opening to China was still being opposed by Kissinger's advisers in memoranda to him and the president. Kissinger had been told Nixon might try to visit China, and replied, "Fat chance."[19]

I spent hours reading these reports—and what they said about Chinese ambitions proved astonishing. I learned that from 1960 until 1962, thousands of pages of classified Soviet documents had been secretly photographed with a Minox camera in a series of operations that the CIA called IRON BARK. Incredibly, the documents revealed that Moscow's military leaders already saw China as a military threat as dangerous as the NATO alliance. I also learned that the FBI in New York had been running three espionage operations, code-named SOLO, TOP HAT, and FEDORA, that had demonstrated very reliable and high-level access to the inner workings of the Soviet Politburo.[20] But the FBI and the CIA wanted me to amplify this intelligence by asking questions that came from Kissinger and his advisers.

The Secretariat offices occupied the thirty-fifth floor of the UN building. The most impressive Soviet official I encountered there was a plump, white-haired extrovert named Arkady Shevchenko. I got to know him well. Then thirty-nine years old, Shevchenko was a heavy drinker—martinis were his drink of choice—and he would hold forth regularly at a French bistro in Manhattan called La Petite Marmite. I attended many lunches with him, where he joked about the phony protocols at the United Nations, such as those that discouraged employees from giving the appearance of consorting with officials of their home countries. All the Russians employed at the United Nations, he noted with a laugh, came to his office at the Soviet Mission every day to share intelligence and receive instructions.

In April 1969, as I gained his trust and friendship, he told me the details of atrocities committed by the Chinese at two clashes on the Sino-Soviet border that had taken place a month earlier, which were then unknown to most American intelligence officials. China, he said, had deceptively started the fight by ambushing Soviet troops. Shevchenko also told me that the Soviet leadership hated and feared the Chinese, believing that China was planning to take control of the Communist world and eventually assert global dominance. For decades, the Chinese had so skillfully played the part of weaklings dependent on Soviet assistance that the Soviets were shocked that the Chinese would challenge them so directly.

I remember one particular meeting with Shevchenko over coffee in the North Delegates Lounge of the UN headquarters building. I laughed perhaps too loudly at Shevchenko's revealing joke about China's future. In the joke, the Soviet leader Leonid Brezhnev calls President Nixon on the telephone.

> "The KGB tells me you have a new supercomputer that can predict events in the year 2000," Brezhnev says.
>
> "Yes," Nixon replies. "We have such a computer."
>
> "Well, Mr. President, could you tell me what the names of our Politburo members will be then?"
>
> There is a long silence on Nixon's end of the line.
>
> "Ha ha!" Brezhnev exclaims to Nixon. "Your computer is not so sophisticated after all."
>
> "No, Mr. General Secretary," Nixon replies, "it answers your questions, but I can't read it."
>
> "Why not?" Brezhnev demands.
>
> "Because it is in Chinese."

The joke was funny because it was so absurd. The idea that the future could belong to a Marxist backwater that couldn't even feed its people seemed ridiculous. But to the shrewd Russians, they saw something that had been lost on us. I also had a number of exchanges with the other

Russians in my unit—Yevgeny Kutovoy, Vladimir Petrovski, and Nicho-lai Fochine—all of whom repeated the same joke to me on different occasions. I thought it was funny, but not for a moment did I consider the serious underlying message being conveyed.

I spent most of my time with Kutovoy, who worked in an office down the hall from me in the Political Affairs Division.[21] Petrovski, our boss, would go on to become a Soviet deputy foreign minister. Kutovoy would become the Soviet ambassador to Yugoslavia. Like Shevchenko, they seemed to enjoy answering my questions. Both were then in their thirties. They even jovially tutored and lectured me about the history of Sino-Soviet conflict and the deviousness of the Chinese. Kutovoy told me that the Soviet Union had essentially built the modern Communist Chinese state, with Soviet advisers placed in every key government bureau. Weapons transfers, military training, and technical advice had all been pro-vided in an attempt to modernize the Soviets' Chinese ally. But in 1953, upon the death of Joseph Stalin, the relationship had begun to sour.

Kutovoy said that Soviet leaders now believed that the Chinese had secret dreams of surpassing the Soviet Union, and that they would not just stop there—their next target would be the Americans. China wouldn't play second fiddle. China would follow its own playbook, and that meant doing everything possible to become the dominant actor on the global stage. The United States, Kutovoy warned, was going to get more than it bargained for if it took China's bait. The main Soviet message was that the Chinese were guided by their own historical ambition to restore their position atop the global hierarchy of nations. He and his colleagues told me that lessons learned from Chinese history advised the Chinese to become the most powerful nation and to conceal their intentions until the opportune moment. He warned me that the worst error the United States could make would be to provide military aid to China. He gave me two books by Russian scholars on ancient Chinese history to illustrate his points. A CIA report in 1971 quoted some of my findings, such as my conclusion that the Soviets anticipated that President Nixon would open ties with China and that they would not overreact to purely diplomatic contacts.[22] By 1973, Moscow directly warned Nixon that the Soviet Union would use force if the United States went beyond pure diplomacy and actually formed a military relationship with China. Kissinger's team would debate this option, and I argued in favor of direct aid in a memo that Kissinger implemented in great secrecy.[23]

I liked Kutovoy and found him credible. But it was 1969, and I was just twenty-four years old. He sounded to me like a boyfriend talking about his ex-girlfriend, warning that she'd break my heart like she broke his. At the time, the Chinese economy was languishing at about 10 percent of America's GNP.[24] It seemed unrealistic that the Chinese would dare to dream about truly surpassing the United States. All official Washington heard was that China wanted a new dance partner. President Nixon would have to decide whether to cut in. Thus began a relationship with consequences far more profound than any of us at the time dared to consider.

The Chinese planned to use the Americans as they had used the Soviets—as tools for their own advancement, all the while pledging cooperation against a third rival power. This was how the Marathon was conducted throughout most of the Cold War—China using the Soviet Union's rivalry with America to extract Soviet aid and then, when that faltered, shifting to the Americans by offering to help against the Soviets. In doing so, the Chinese were reflecting another ancient stratagem—"kill with a borrowed sword"[25]—or, in other words, attack using the strength of another.

Four decades later, shortly after Xi Jinping assumed office as general secretary of the Communist Party of China (a precursor to his becoming president), he provided a greater glimpse of China's underlying intentions. In his maiden speech in his new role, Xi used a phrase that no Chinese leader had ever used in a public speech, *qiang zhongguo meng*, or "strong nation dream."[26]

The comment was remarkable. China's leaders are extremely careful with their language, especially in public, far more so than Western politicians. They avoid words such as "dream" or "hopes" in their public remarks. Such emotion-laden sentiments are considered a flaky, Western eccentricity. However, Xi has since made repeated references to the "China dream" in his speeches. According to a front-page story in the *Wall Street Journal*, Xi referred to 2049 as the date the dream will be realized—one hundred years after Mao Zedong's ascension in China and the formation of the Communist state.[27]

Xi's reference was neither casual nor inadvertent. A veteran of the People's Liberation Army and a former secretary to the defense minister, Xi is closely connected to the nationalist "super hawks" in the Chinese military. As I discovered from my own conversations with some native Chinese speakers in Xi's audience, those educated in the country's universities and members of the military understood Xi's reference to the "strong nation dream" immediately.

By invoking the "strong nation dream," President Xi was referring to a once-obscure book—obscure, that is, in the West—published in China in 2009 called *The China Dream*. The book was written by a colonel in the People's Liberation Army named Liu Mingfu, then working as a leading scholar at China's National Defense University, which trains future generals of the People's Liberation Army. It was there that I first spotted a specific written reference to "the Hundred-Year Marathon."[28]

The China Dream became a nationwide best seller. The book, only parts of which have been translated into English, outlined how China will become the world's leading power, surpassing and then replacing the United States. It analyzed how the Soviet Union had failed to supplant the United States, and an entire chapter was devoted to the eight ways China's effort would be different.[29] The phrase Liu adopted as his own—"the Hundred-Year Marathon"—held resonance across China, though the word *marathon* itself is borrowed from English. The concept is more readily referred to in Mandarin as China's "rejuvenation" within a "just" world order or, in keeping with the book's title, "the China Dream." The word for rejuvenation or restoration (*fuxing*) seems to be synonymous with Marathon, assuming it takes a century counting from 1949. China is both secretive and sensitive about the end state of the Marathon. It has never spelled out exactly what the final *fuxing* will be like, except to declare it will be a good thing.

Liu's book called for a world-class military to project China's global leadership. "China's grand goal in the 21st century is to become the world's No. 1 power," Liu declared.[30] "The competition between China and the United States," he predicted, "will not be like a 'shooting duel' or a 'boxing match' but more like a 'track and field' competition. It will be like a protracted 'Marathon.'" At the end of the Marathon, Liu contended, the ruler finally will be the most virtuous power on the planet—the Chinese.[31]

When asked in 2010 by an ABC News reporter about his provocative work, Liu held firm on the book's central positions, but stressed that China's competition and ultimate victory over the West would be peaceful. But for those of us able to read his book in the original Mandarin, that is not the tone he adopts there. The colonel alludes to the importance of studying American weaknesses, and preparing to hit the Americans once the West becomes wise to China's true game plan.[32] Liu also hints at the existence of an official Marathon strategy among the Chinese leadership, praising Mao Zedong because "he dared to craft a grand plan to surpass America, stating that beating the United States would be China's greatest contribution to humanity."[33] As the *Wall Street Journal* revealed in 2013, *The China Dream* is featured in the "recommended reading" section of all state-controlled bookstores.[34]

Liu, in fact, was a latecomer to the "Marathon" notion; the concept had been discussed in notes and articles even earlier. For example, Zhao Tingyang's *The Under-Heaven System: The Philosophy of the World Institution* was published in 2005 and is gaining increasing currency in mainline Chinese thought today. Zhao's "system" redesigns global structures based on traditional Chinese ideals. That new world is called *tianxia*,[35] which in Mandarin can be translated as "under-heaven," "empire," and "China." The China scholar William A. Callahan translates *tianxia* as a unified global system with China's "superior" civilization at the top.[36] Other civilizations, such as the United States, are part of the "barbarian wilderness." As the center of the civilized world, China would have the responsibility to "improve" all the nations and peoples of the world by "harmonizing" them—spreading Chinese values, language, and culture so they can better fit into under-heaven. This empire "values order over freedom, ethics over law, and elite governance over democracy and human rights."[37]

I met Zhao Tingyang in Beijing in July 2012, after he had achieved international acclaim. I asked him how the *tianxia* system would handle disobedience, in case any nations refused to follow the Chinese script. "Easy question," he replied. "The *Rites of Zhou* prescribed a four-to-one military superiority to enable the emperor to enforce the All-Under-Heaven system." In other words, after China wins the economic Marathon and develops an economy twice as large as America's, China's new status may have to be protected through military force. The world's largest economy will need a force more powerful than any other—one that would eventually render American military might obsolete. America itself had done this between 1860 and 1940. China hawks not only studied American strategy, but also drew lessons from China's ancient past, reaching back many centuries. The warnings the Soviet diplomats at the United Nations had provided in 1969 about Beijing's deceptive tactics and long-term global ambition were now coming true.

2

WARRING STATES

"It is too soon to ask the weight of the Emperor's cauldrons."
—*Spring and Autumn Annals*

In Chinese history, there is no 1492 or 1776. China's rich history dates back more than three millennia. China cherishes no founding myth like the story of a promised land given to Abraham or a precise moment of creation like the adoption of the Declaration of Independence. Instead, China's history is one of war and rivalries within fixed geographic boundaries—vast oceans to the east, forbidding deserts to the north, towering mountains to the west. Dynasties and rulers have come and gone, and in the Chinese way of thinking they will come and go for millennia to come. As Henry Kissinger has noted, "China's sense of time beats to a different rhythm from America's. When an American is asked to date a historical event, he refers to a specific day on the calendar; when a Chinese describes an event, he places it within a dynasty. And of the fourteen imperial dynasties, ten have each lasted longer than the entire history of the United States."[1] The Chinese *ying pai* hawks do not get lost in their long, complex history; instead, they have sought specific lessons from historical successes and failures that they can use to win the Marathon.

The hawks write books about a key era of history out of which China was forged, known as the Spring Autumn and Warring States periods[2]— five centuries of largely political struggles. The final two-and-a-half-century stretch began around 475 BC and ended with the unification of seven feuding states under the Qin dynasty. (The word *China* comes from Qin.) Both periods were plagued by power politics, intrigue, deception, and open warfare among China's warlords. It was a brutal, Darwinian world of competition, where warlords formed coalitions to oust one another, all with the goal of becoming the *ba*, roughly equivalent to the English word *hegemon*. Five *ba* rose and fell in the Spring Autumn period, then two coalitions competed in the Warring States. The hawks draw lessons for the Marathon from both.

The *ying pai* strategists in Beijing have long drawn key lessons from the Warring States period, lessons that in large measure define China's approach to strategy today. However, the China policy community in the United States has only recently come to grips with this fact—and even today this view is not widely accepted across the U.S. government. Our decades-long ignorance of China's strategic thinking has been costly; our lack of understanding has led us to make concessions to the Chinese that seem outright senseless in hindsight.

Undoubtedly, America's ignorance—and that of the West more broadly—can be at least partly attributed to two key factors. First, from the seventeenth century to the modern era, Sinologists, missionaries, and researchers who visited and studied China were essentially led to accept a fabricated account of Chinese history. Chinese sources played up the Confucian, pacifist nature of Chinese culture and played down—and in many cases completely omitted any reference to—the bloody Warring States period.[3] Additionally, Mao's campaign to "Destroy the Four Olds and Cultivate the Four News," whereby the Communist Party set out to destroy and erase the memory of long-standing Chinese customs, culture, ideas, and habits in support of the Cultural Revolution, led many in the West to conclude that China had decided to make a complete break with its pre-Communist past.

As U.S. policymakers have increasingly begun to recognize that Chinese strategy is, at its core, a product of lessons derived from the Warring States period, so too have the Chinese recently become more public about this. At first, only the hawks mentioned these ancient lessons. References to the period first appeared in internal Chinese publications in the 1990s, and the Chinese have referred to events and maxims from the Warring States period in communiqués intercepted by American intelligence and in discussions of military doctrine. In 1991, China's leaders secretly used a Warring States proverb, *tao guang, yang hui*. When the document containing this phrase leaked, Beijing translated it as the cryptic and generic "bide your time, build your capabilities."[4] But in its proper context, the proverb actually alludes to overturning the old hegemon and exacting revenge, but only once the rising power has developed the ability to do so. Many experts in America did not at first believe these references because they conflicted with their preconception that evidence of China's aggressive strategic intentions must be discarded if it emanates only from the mouths and pens of the nationalist *ying pai* hawks in China, who were widely assumed to be fringe elements.

Most scholars of China have asserted in a general way that China's ancient past influences its present, but that it does so only metaphorically.[5] However, those scholars lacked access to internal Chinese government planning documents showing how the Chinese explicitly use the ancient axioms. Nor have these scholars had access to Chinese defectors who previously held high positions inside the Chinese government. My forty years of contact with the Chinese military and Chinese security officials may have biased me in the opposite direction of my fellow China experts: I now see the hawks as mainstream. The moderates sometimes seem to defer quietly to the hawks, as if they were under Party discipline not to reveal any details about the hawks' growing influence.

Based on tips from these defectors, I began reading restricted essays by China's top generals and strategists illustrating how the Warring States lessons can and should be applied today to bring about a China-led world. I learned that the Warring States mind-set has long been dominant among China's leaders. As an official U.S. government visitor to Beijing, making annual visits starting in 1995, I was given access to China's restricted government-run bookstores, after which I would interview the authors of some of the books on sale. These books and articles explicitly distilled ideas from the hundreds of years of successes and failures of rising powers during the Warring States era.

One clear trend beginning in the mid-1990s was an increase in the number of Chinese authors who began to draw lessons from the Warring

States period. Major General Li Binyan was among the first. Thirty Chinese generals hosted a conference every few years about applying a Warring States classic, Sun Tzu's *The Art of War*, and I was invited to present a paper at three of the sessions as a scholar from the Pentagon. The hawks treated me as a fellow hawk, from the U.S. Department of Defense, which they presumed—wrongly, it turned out—knew all about the lessons of the Warring States. These conferences continue to this day. I visited one military bookstore in October 2013 and was surprised to see two things. First, there were clearly more lessons from ancient Chinese history than ever before. And when I asked one officer if there were more books of lessons from Chinese history in the newly designated part of the bookstore where the sign said "Chinese military officers only," he joked, "Yes, those books are not for foreigners to see because their lessons are too specific."

I noticed that the authors who started this movement two decades ago have formed associations and research units. The first was created in 1996, and the most recent was set up in 2012. Many colonels who launched these studies have been promoted to leadership posts as generals and admirals, and a new generation of younger authors is carrying on the work.

Stratagems of the Warring States, highly popular and closely studied in China, is a collection of fables that has never been translated into English. Were it translated, more Americans might better understand Chinese leaders and their intentions when they speak in ways inspired by lessons from that turbulent period in China's history.

Students are taught lessons of the Warring States period, most of which derive from the *Stratagems*, which is considered a manual for statecraft. China's modern military scholars and political philosophers hark back to this time in Chinese history more than any other. A committee of twenty-one Chinese generals has sponsored the publication of a nine-book series titled *Strategic Lessons from China's Ancient Past*, which draws on the Warring States period. Many proverbs used today in internal Chinese government documents come from the struggles between the Warring States.

The Marathon strategy that China's leaders are pursuing today—and have been pursuing for decades—is largely the product of lessons derived from the Warring States period by the hawks. The nine principal elements of Chinese strategy, which form the basis of the Hundred-Year Marathon, include the following:

1. *Induce complacency to avoid alerting your opponent.* Chinese strategy holds that a powerful adversary, such as the United States today, should never be provoked prematurely. Instead, one's true intentions should be completely guarded until the ideal moment to strike arrives.

2. *Manipulate your opponent's advisers.* Chinese strategy emphasizes turning the opponent's house in on itself by winning over influential advisers surrounding the opponent's leadership apparatus. Such efforts have long been a hallmark of China's relations with the United States.

3. *Be patient—for decades, or longer—to achieve victory.* During the Warring States period, decisive victories were never achieved quickly. Victory was sometimes achieved only after many decades of careful, calculated waiting. Today, China's leaders are more than happy to play the waiting game.

4. *Steal your opponent's ideas and technology for strategic purposes.* Hardly hindered by Western-style legal prohibitions and constitutional principles, China clearly endorses theft for strategic gain. Such theft provides a relatively easy, cost-effective means by which a weaker state can usurp power from a more powerful one.

5. *Military might is not the critical factor for winning a long-term competition.* This partly explains why China has not devoted more resources to developing larger, more powerful military forces. Rather than relying on a brute accumulation of strength, Chinese strategy advocates targeting an enemy's weak points and biding one's time.

6. *Recognize that the hegemon will take extreme, even reckless action to retain its dominant position.* The rise and fall of hegemons was perhaps the defining feature of the Warring States period. Chinese

strategy holds that a hegemon—the United States, in today's context—will not go quietly into the night as its power declines relative to others. Further, Chinese strategy holds that a hegemon will inevitably seek to eliminate all actual and potential challengers.

7. *Never lose sight of* shi. The concept of *shi* will be discussed in greater detail below. For now, suffice it to say that two elements of *shi* are critical components of Chinese strategy: deceiving others into doing your bidding for you, and waiting for the point of maximum opportunity to strike.

8. *Establish and employ metrics for measuring your status relative to other potential challengers.* Chinese strategy places a high premium on assessing China's relative power, during peacetime and in the event of war, across a plethora of dimensions beyond just military considerations. The United States, by contrast, has never attempted to do this.

9. *Always be vigilant to avoid being encircled or deceived by others.* In what could be characterized as a deeply ingrained sense of paranoia, China's leaders believe that because all other potential rivals are out to deceive them, China must respond with its own duplicity. In the brutal Warring States period, the naïve, trusting leader was not just unsuccessful in battle; he was utterly destroyed. Perhaps the greatest Chinese strategic fear is that of being encircled. In the ancient Chinese board game of *wei qi*, it is imperative to avoid being encircled by your opponent—something that can be accomplished only by simultaneously deceiving your opponent and avoiding being deceived by him. Today, China's leaders operate on the belief that rival states are fundamentally out to encircle one another, the same objective as in *wei qi*.

Many of the most significant elements of China's Marathon strategy were developed by members of the military, especially the *ying pai* hawks. Owing to pre-Communist Chinese civil-military traditions dating to about 1920, high-ranking Chinese military personnel are expected to play a significant role in civilian strategic planning. To get a sense of just how different this is from the American system, imagine that issues that are generally considered to properly fall under the purview of U.S. civilian leaders, such as family planning, taxation, and economic policy, were instead transferred to generals and admirals in the Pentagon. Imagine further that the United States lacked both a supreme court and an independent judiciary, and you get some sense of this tremendous disparity between the relatively narrow influence of our military leaders and the broader advisory role played by China's top military leaders since 1949.

Modern China's first foreign minister was a general. We now know, from Henry Kissinger's memoirs, that the decision to pursue an opening with the United States came not from China's civilian leaders, but instead from a committee of four Chinese generals.[6] In 1979, a Chinese weapons designer developed China's one-child policy. In 1980, metrics for measuring China's progress in pursuing its Marathon strategy were developed by a military writer from the Academy of Military Sciences, the premier research institute of the People's Liberation Army. One of the best-known books in China about grand strategy, fittingly titled *On Grand Strategy*, was written by an author from the Academy of Military Sciences.[7] A Chinese general developed China's strategy for managing its energy resources. China's long-term military science and technology plan was developed in 1986 by a team of nationalist hawkish Chinese nuclear weapons scientists.[8]

In June 1970, I, like other China experts in the U.S. government, knew none of this. That month, I was selected from a list of American PhD candidates for Mandarin-language training at Taiwan National University, which was to become my first foray into experiencing Chinese culture and history. The two-year course focused on Chinese cultural immersion. I lived in Taiwan with a Chinese family and attended classes all day in a small cubicle with one of four teachers who rotated throughout the day. The courses centered on a set of textbooks, which Chinese students still use today, of the best classical writing in Chinese history. The proverbs and stories I read in these language textbooks formed the basis of how most Chinese perceive the world, and provided me a window into Chinese thinking, history, and worldviews. These were lessons I came to appreciate fully only over the course of many subsequent decades. The teachers separated Chinese tradition into two opposite patterns: the Confucian world of benevolence and sincerity, and the ruthless world of the hegemons of the Warring States. We memorized a well-known proverb intended to sum up Chinese history: *wai ru, nei fa* (on the outside, be benevolent; on the inside, be ruthless).

The *ying pai* hawks today speak of an allegory about America and China. One of the most famous stories from the Warring States period begins with a tale of two neighboring kingdoms, one rising, one falling in relative power: Chu and Zhou. As the leader of Chu reviewed his troops with a member of the declining Zhou dynasty along their mutual border, he couldn't resist asking the size and weight of the cauldrons in the Zhou royal palace. The purpose of the meeting was for the rising leader of Chu to pledge fealty and forswear any imperial designs, but when Chu asked the weight of the emperor's cauldrons, the perceptive Zhou representative chided him. "Each time a dynasty loses the mandate of heaven, the cauldrons are moved," was the reply. "The king of Zhou has the cauldrons. His ancestor hoped to rule for thirty generations, or seven hundred years, with the mandate of heaven. Although the virtue of Zhou has declined, heaven's mandate has not yet changed. It is too soon to ask about the weight of the cauldrons."[9] By asking about the cauldrons, Chu had inadvertently revealed his intent to challenge Zhou.

The lesson is famous in China: "Never ask the weight of the emperor's cauldrons." In other words, don't let the enemy know you're a rival, until it is too late for him to stop you. On the international level, if you are a rising power, you must manipulate the perceptions of the dominant world power to not be destroyed by it. To ask the size and weight of the cauldrons was a strategic blunder by the king of Chu.

During the Warring States period, rising challengers overthrew many great powers. In each case, the successful rising power induced complacency in the old emperor by concealing any ambition to replace him. The worst thing a rising leader could do was to provoke confrontation with his more powerful rival before the point of maximum opportunity. Only in the final phase of a power bid, when the emperor was too weak to resist and had been abandoned by his former allies, did the rising challenger reveal his true aims.

As chronicled in *Stratagems of the Warring States*, some of the wisest rising challengers even persuaded the old emperor to unwittingly assist in the challenger's ascendance. In those cases, the challenger often persuaded the emperor to punish advisers who were skeptical of the challenger's intentions ("hawks") and to promote advisers whom the challenger could manipulate into complacency and cooperation ("doves").

The natural world order, the *Stratagems* explains, is hierarchical; systems without a ruler at the top are merely transitional. That world order is, of course, inconsistent with the official line from Beijing today. China's leaders claim to want a multipolar world in which the United States will be first among equals. Put differently, they do not want to ask the weight of the emperor's cauldrons.

In truth, however, they see a multipolar world as merely a strategic waypoint en route to a new global hierarchy in which China is alone at the top. The Chinese term for this new order is *da tong*, often mistranslated by Western scholars as "commonwealth" or "an era of harmony." However, *da tong* is better translated as "an era of unipolar dominance." Since 2005, Chinese leaders have spoken at the United Nations and other public forums of their supposed vision of this kind of harmonious world.

An important element of China's grand strategy is derived from what is known in the West as mercantilist trade behavior—a system of high tariffs, gaining direct control of natural resources, and protection of domestic manufacturing, all designed to build up a nation's monetary reserves. The Chinese invented mercantilism (*zhong-shang*), and the country's leaders reject the West's contention that mercantilism has been rendered obsolete by the success of free markets and free trade.[10]

Because it embraces mercantilism, China is wary that trade and markets will always provide sufficient access to needed resources. China's leaders have an almost paranoid fear of a coming crisis leading to regional or global resource scarcity. As a result, they are determined to obtain ownership or direct control of valuable natural resources overseas—just as Europe's mercantilist monarchs attempted to do by colonizing the New

World in the sixteenth and seventeenth centuries. This is one of the many lessons in the *Stratagems*.

Another lesson from the Warring States period is that success requires extreme patience. American businesses live by quarterly reports, U.S. politicians operate on short election cycles, and successful stock market strategies may be based on trading conducted in a single day. Yet the stories of the Warring States period's rising challengers teach that victory is never achieved in a single day, week, or year—or even in a decade. Only long-term plans spanning hundreds of years led to victory. Consequently, it's not uncommon for today's Chinese leaders, who automatically serve two ten-year terms, to make plans that span generations and to set goals that will not be achieved for a half century or more.

Warring States literature and other folklore stories of Chinese cultural heroes have also stressed the importance of stealing ideas and technology from the opponent. Today, Chinese intelligence services routinely steal technology and competitive information, which they provide directly to Chinese corporate leaders.[11] Many American officials assume that China's predatory economic behavior in recent years—such as conducting industrial espionage or violating intellectual property rights—is part of a passing phase. To the contrary, it is one part of a much larger strategy inspired by stratagems distilled from the Warring States period.

The contrast with the American model for national intelligence services is stark. In the United States, it is considered unethical and even illegal for the government to provide American corporations with intelligence to increase the nation's economic growth. In my forty years in the U.S. government, I have never heard of a case in which the U.S. intelligence community was tasked to attempt to increase America's GDP in such a way. It is true that U.S. ambassadors can and do assist American corporations in winning lucrative contracts in foreign countries, but that's a far cry from government spies providing stolen technologies and proprietary information directly to American corporations.

Consider also the contrast between American and Chinese views about the optimum size of military forces. Many of America's greatest military triumphs were achieved through large armies. Grant overwhelmed Lee with more men and more guns. On June 6, 1944, Dwight Eisenhower sent the largest armada in history to Normandy. Even in recent times, the so-called Powell Doctrine has advocated the necessity of a force far larger than the enemy's.

In contrast, the Warring States period did not involve great military outlays. Nonviolent competition for several decades constituted the main form of struggle. A famous strategy was to deplete an adversary's financial resources by tricking it into spending too much on its military. Two thousand years later, when the Soviet Union collapsed, the Chinese interpretation was that the Americans had intentionally bankrupted Moscow by tricking it into spending excessively on defense.

As of 2011, while the United States spent nearly 5 percent of its GDP on its military, the Chinese spent only 2.5 percent of theirs.[12] The Chinese strategy has been to forswear development of global power projection forces and to maintain a curiously small arsenal of nuclear warheads, perhaps numbering fewer than three hundred. Instead of trying to match America plane for plane and ship for ship, China has invested heavily in asymmetric systems designed to get the biggest bang for the buck. The Chinese have pioneered antisatellite technology, developed the means to counter stealth bombers, invested heavily in cyber intrusion, and built missiles costing a few million dollars that can sink a $4 billion American aircraft carrier.[13] The missile price was so low—and the capability so high— because the missile may have been based on stolen American technology.

Many Western analysts wonder why China hasn't built more powerful military forces to protect itself and its sea-lanes. The answer is found in the lessons of the Warring States period: China doesn't want to "ask the weight of the emperor's cauldrons." Chinese leaders believe that building a bigger military would be a potentially catastrophic provocation of the United States. (After all, having lived under a total U.S. embargo from 1949 through 1963, China already has a sense of just how painful arousing America's wrath can be.)[14] They think China instead needs a force level large enough to support economic growth but small enough to avoid prematurely provoking the American hegemon. However, applying the axioms of the Warring States, China could decide to cast aside its self-imposed constraints on military spending in the final phases of a multi-decade competition—once it's too late for America to stop them. Chinese writings on the revolution in military affairs have hinted for two decades about the ideal time to break out, which is still many years ahead.[15]

If the contrast between the Warring States mind-set and a traditional American view of the world can be distilled into a single, fundamental difference, it is this: Americans tend to believe that relations with other countries ebb and flow between periods of competition and cooperation; Beijing's assumption is that the U.S. government has a long-standing policy of hostility and deception toward the Chinese government. If this difference were merely a matter of Chinese misunderstanding due to ignorance, then it would be possible and indeed prudent for the United States to eliminate, or at least reduce, this misperception. Unfortunately, that's not the case. Chinese leaders' distrust of the United States is largely based on deeply held cultural axioms that underlie nearly all Chinese strategic decisions. Their distrust of the United States is therefore unlikely to change.[16]

At the heart of Chinese strategy is *shi*, which is a difficult concept to explain to a Western audience. It cannot be directly translated into English, but Chinese linguists describe it as "the alignment of forces" or "propensity of things to happen," which only a skilled strategist can exploit to ensure victory over a superior force. Similarly, only a sophisticated adversary can recognize how he is vulnerable to the exploitation of *shi*.[17] It is exactly the lack of recognition of the potential exploitation of *shi* that is dooming American strategy toward China.

A close approximation to *shi* in American popular culture is "the force" from George Lucas's *Star Wars*, which draws heavily on Eastern philosophy. Though not a perfect analogy, *shi* suggests that mystical forces allow the alert leader to identify and harness opportunities to turn events to his will. The most able can even use these opportunities to get others to act in ways that work to their advantage. As Sun Tzu described it in his chapter on *shi* in *The Art of War*, "those skilled at making the enemy move do so by creating a situation to which he must conform."[18] A simple way to think of *shi* is to recall how Tom Sawyer tricked his friends into painting the fence for him. He studied their psychologies, realized what motivated them, and then manipulated them into doing his work for him. A significant component or feature of *shi* is called *wu wei*, which means to get other nations to do your work for you.

The very idea of *shi* gets to the heart of a distinctly Chinese view of the world, because it conveys an almost mystical fatalism about the role of human actors in the universe. Humans and nations can interact with each other and change events, but those events have an independent momentum all their own. *Shi* appears in compound vocabulary terms that mean "to shape a situation," "to build up military posture," "to assess the overall strategic political situation," or "to seek a balance of power." It is the duty of "the sage"—the rough equivalent of a modern-day statesman or intelligence professional—to perceive *shi* before the opponent does.

Only recently have Western scholars come to appreciate the concept of *shi*. It first appeared in 1983, when Roger Ames, a professor of philosophy at the University of Hawaii, defined it as part of his translation of an almost unknown Chinese book on political administration from the Warring States period called *The Art of Rulership*. After the publication of *The Art of Rulership* in English,[19] a French scholar named François Jullien picked up where Ames left off. Jullien popularized *shi* in seven books that characterized it as a uniquely Chinese concept.[20] His assertion prompted left-wing critics to claim that he was "othering"—that is, treating Chinese culture as alien and therefore somehow inferior. The critics claimed *shi* was nothing unique.[21]

Jullien was not without his defenders, most notably within the Chinese military. People's Liberation Army authors asserted that *shi* and many others aspects of Chinese strategic philosophy were indeed unique to China.

When I first saw the concept of *shi* in internal Chinese government writings in the late 1990s, I did not know its exact meaning and connotation, but I immediately discerned that it was critical to Chinese leaders' strategic thinking. I met with Ames and Jullien, and their discoveries and insights into the concept helped me to decipher the meaning of Chinese military and intelligence reports that repeatedly refer to *shi*.

They told me that the concept of *shi* is heavily influenced by Taoism, a religion and philosophy whose adherents desire to live in harmony with the driving force—the Tao—behind everything in the universe. Just as Taoists believe the universe is in a constant state of reinventing itself—a belief embodied by the yin-yang symbol—both *shi*'s strength and its polarity can be suddenly reversed. Chinese military authors frequently refer to how *shi* can tip in one direction or another, or even reverse itself instantly. This puts a premium on the early detection of shifts, and the need for monitoring indicators that would show when such a change is under way.

Ames and Jullien said that *shi* has dozens of translations, such as "shaping" the situation, or "eventuating." Other translators call *shi* the creation of opportunity, or creation of momentum. "Unfolding" or "nudging" are also English words approximating the concept. *Shi* has many applications. It is used to measure the quality of Chinese calligraphy, assess the appeal of Chinese literary works, and evaluate the aesthetics of Chinese poetry. Jullien and Ames also told me that *shi* is an example of what philosophers call "incommensurability." A set of concepts may be too different to understand when considered outside the context of its own language.

Mao was fond of citing *shi*. His classic essay on Chinese strategy, which invokes *shi*, is still required reading in both military and civilian Party schools. Chinese writings after 1978 demonstrate that some strategists believe Chinese leaders failed to read *shi* correctly during the 1950s and '60s vis-à-vis China's relations with the Soviet Union. Because the Soviets discovered that China sought to usurp the USSR's leadership of the Communist world, China failed to extract further foreign investment, trade opportunities, military technology, or political support from the Soviet Union. Stung by their failure to master *shi* in their relations with the Soviets, the Chinese after 1978 vowed not to repeat the mistake as they developed their new strategy toward the United States.

Instead, China would find a way to coax the United States into providing American technology, foreign investment, political support, and access to America's domestic market for Chinese products—without tipping off the Americans to China's larger ambitions. Beijing found ways to encourage the U.S. intelligence community to help strengthen China, rather than sound the alarm—as the KGB had done with regard to China's intentions toward the Soviet Union. Beijing even encouraged American conservatives to see China as a partner against the Soviet Union, a fellow opponent of détente, and a nation that was not really even Communist.[22]

Shi—and Chinese grand strategy—partly entail encircling an enemy by building up one's own coalition while simultaneously undermining the opponent's coalition to prevent him from encircling you. The unique Chinese word for strategist, which comes from the Warring States period, means a "horizontal-vertical expert"—a reference to the two main alliances during the Warring States era. The "horizontal" alliance of states, which consisted of states laid out east to west on a map, decided to join with the dominant power, Qin, to reap the benefits of protection and association. The opposing "vertical" alliance, consisting of the many states running from north to south, joined together to oppose the rising Qin state. These two coalitions struggled for decades to erode each other by winning over allies with carrots and sticks. Finally, the horizontal alliance soothed its rivals by denying any ambition to replace them and appealing to their short-term interests. Deception successfully broke apart the opposing coalition, and Qin, its strongest member, conquered the vertical alliance. Today, Chinese authors frequently refer to the need to discreetly counter America's global alliance system in a way that will not alert the Americans that an alternative alliance is being created.

One of China's most iconic board games, *wei qi*, harks back to the Warring States period of horizontal and vertical alliances. The purpose of the game is not outright annihilation of the opponent, as in checkers. Instead, the two adversaries take turns placing stones on the board, hoping to encircle the other player's pieces. Translated literally, *wei qi* means "encirclement board." A key to victory is to deceive your opponent into complacency, whereby he expends his energy in a way that helps you even as you move to encircle him.

A second key to winning in *wei qi* is to deceive the opponent about one's real direction and intentions. To win, you must entice the opponent by opening up new positions while deceptively encircling him, hoping the opponent will not notice your true strategy. The player who designs multiple positions of encirclement and counterencirclement so that the degree of the encirclement is not apparent to the other wins, and the score is based on who has encircled more of the opponent's space.

If you can imagine playing this game without knowing that deception is critical to your opponent's strategy, you'll have some sense of how America is being played by China. Americans know nothing of the game's rules. Most of us have never heard of *shi*. We don't know we are losing the game. In fact, we don't even know that the game has begun. For this, we can blame China's superior strategy, and the illusions held so long by people like me and my colleagues.

In his book *On China*, Henry Kissinger gives five examples of how China uses *shi*, all of which deal with its approach to war and crises. Learning about the importance of *shi* has clearly influenced his views on China. In contrast to his four earlier books that recount his meetings with Chinese leaders without mentioning *shi*,[23] his new approach cites *shi* repeatedly. Kissinger highlights an important aspect of *shi* by warning that China characterizes its relationship with the United States as one of combative coexistence: "Americans to this day often treat the opening to China as ushering in a static condition of friendship. But the Chinese leaders were brought up on the concept of *shi*—the art of understanding *matters in flux.* . . . In Chinese writings, the hallowed words of the American vocabulary of a legal international order are rarely to be found. What was sought, rather, was a world in which China could find security and progress through a kind of *combative coexistence*, in which readiness to fight was given equal pride of place to the concept of coexistence" (italics mine).[24]

The Chinese attack on Vietnam in 1979, Kissinger explains, resulted from the *shi* concept: "In a broader sense, the war resulted from Beijing's analysis of Sun Tzu's concept of *shi*—the trend and 'potential energy' of the strategic landscape. Deng aimed to arrest and, if possible, reverse what he saw as an unacceptable momentum of Soviet strategy. China achieved this objective in part by its military daring, in part by drawing the United States into unprecedentedly close cooperation."[25]

Shi is crucial to understanding how Chinese strategists assess the balance of power in a given situation and then act in accordance with how the *shi* is flowing. An important part of their assessment relies on the kinds of quantitative metrics planners pioneered during the period of the Warring States. One of the striking features of Chinese assessments of *shi* is that the term is used both as a concept of measurement that analysts must examine and also as something that can be created and manipulated by the actions of the commander or national leaders.

There is a misleading popular image of ancient Chinese culture that focuses on the sayings of Confucius, poetry, calligraphy, and Chinese art. The impression given is that the ancients were more creative and philosophical than they were analytical and mathematical. Yet the RAND Corporation scholar Herbert Goldhammer has pointed out that during the Warring States period, some strategists could supposedly convince their opponents to concede just by showing them quantitative calculations dooming the opponents to defeat.[26] Quantitative measurements played a vital role in ancient Chinese politics, and they continue to do so today.

Chinese military and intelligence services use quantitative measurements to determine how China compares with its geopolitical competitors, and how long it will be before China can overtake them. When I read these quantitative measurements in a difficult-to-obtain book written by Chinese military analysts,[27] I was surprised to see how precisely China measures global strength and national progress. The most startling revelation was that military strength comprised less than 10 percent of the ranking. After the collapse of the Soviet Union—which had the world's second-mightiest military—the Chinese changed their assessment system to put more emphasis on the importance of economics, foreign investment, technological innovation, and the ownership of natural resources. These Chinese assessments of national power unambiguously predict that a multipolar world will return to a unipolar order as economic growth trends continue. The Chinese leadership believes that China will then be the world's leading power.

Key to attaining that goal is China's concept of *shi*. Beijing applies the concept in almost every aspect of its relations with the United States, and just as Tom Sawyer's friends had no idea that Tom was manipulating them into painting his fence, America's policymakers have no idea they are being used.

One of the most frequently cited examples of *shi* in Chinese military writing centers on the Battle of Red Cliff, which occurred in AD 208.[28] Also referred to by its Chinese name, the Battle of Chibi, it perfectly displays this alternative Chinese view of righteous and praiseworthy strategy emerging from deception, and of taking advantage of an enemy's miscalculations. Like the Battles of Thermopylae, Cannae, Agincourt, or Waterloo in the West, Red Cliff serves as a seminal moment in China's military history and tradition. To this day, the battle and a series of deceptions related to it are studied by Chinese military leaders and discussed in textbooks and novels.[29]

In the Battle of Red Cliff, a less powerful kingdom in the south plots against a stronger and more powerful one in the north, as both contend for total control of China. As the campaign begins, the northern commander, Cao Cao, has more than one million troops arrayed along a river, vastly outnumbering the southern forces commanded by Zhuge Liang positioned on the other side. However, many of the northern soldiers were unused to riverine warfare, and so the north lost an initial battle that gave the south control of the waterway. Next came a series of deceptions by each side. Each deceptive maneuver has been embodied in a popular proverb, and each is recounted in China's most popular novel, *The Romance of the Three Kingdoms*.

In one deception, Cao Cao, the hegemon, looks for a way to overcome his previous battle losses, so he sends one of his soldiers—a former childhood friend and fellow student of Zhuge Liang's ally Zhou Yu—to visit the southern commander and find a way to convince him to surrender. Upon arriving at the southern camp, the northern envoy pretends that he came solely to catch up with his old friend; however, Zhou Yu, a master of deception himself, discerns his friend's ulterior motive. Playing along with the deception, he invites this envoy to a banquet, at which Zhou Yu pretends to drink heavily. That night, still feigning intoxication, he allows his former friend to share his tent, expecting him to search the premises. A fake letter from two northern naval officers commanding a nearby training camp is planted on the desk; the letter tells of a spy working under the northern commander, Cao Cao. As anticipated, the envoy finds the letter, steals it, and quickly returns to the northern camp. Upon reading the false letter, Cao Cao goes into a violent rage and has his two best officers executed, thereby weakening the north relative to the south. Zhou Yu, and thus Zhuge Liang, vastly improved his position and helped shape new momentum or *shi*.

In another deception, Zhuge Liang asks the strategist Pang Tong for

his counsel on how to defeat the north. The plan is to send a false defector to disable the enemy's most formidable forces, his wooden fleet, by
persuading the opponent to lash his ships together so they will be vulnerable to attack. The plot begins when Pang Tong publicly pretends to
defect from the southern commander. Hearing that Pang Tong wishes
to defect from the southern forces, a northern agent offers to help him
escape into the service of Cao Cao. A deliberate leak is part of the plot.
Pang Tong, pretending to be drunk, lets slip how vulnerable the northern fleet may be due to seasickness that seems to be affecting the northern sailors. Always deceive by telling the opponent what he already fears.
Because Cao Cao has been worried about this sailors' seasickness, he
foolishly asks for Pang Tong's advice on how to prevent it. The "solution"
Pang Tong offers is to stabilize the boats by linking them together with
iron hoops into groups of thirty to fifty ships, and to then lay wide
planks between each boat so that the soldiers could keep their balance
and easily cross from ship to ship. Cao Cao believed the deception and
foolishly accepted this advice. If just one of his ships is set ablaze, the
whole fleet will be lost. The overall lesson is that a more powerful opponent sometimes can be cleverly persuaded to not use his most powerful
advantage against you.

Now comes the actual Battle of Red Cliff. As a strategy lesson, the
key will be how the southern leaders would assess *shi*. Zhuge Liang pays
close attention to the weather, forecasting that an easterly wind will
arise. When the sage detects the arrival of the moment of *shi*, decisive
action must be immediate. Zhuge Liang orders the assault to begin that
night. Because of the wind and the iron hoops linking the boats, the northern fleet is quickly engulfed in flames. The hegemon had been humili-
ated.[30]

Temples all over China today celebrate the God of War. His moment
came on the same day as the battle of Red Cliff. With his mighty fleet
gone, the defeated northern commander Cao Cao flees through the for-
est. He stops to rest a number of times, still cockily laughing at Zhuge
Liang's supposed incompetence for allowing his escape. Remembering
the ancient proverb from *The Art of War* that advises appearing strong
where one is weak, Cao Cao concludes that the enemy forces must be

arrayed along the main road and that fires were set to deter him from taking that trail. He has been deceived again.

In the final deception, the two greatest deception masters in Chinese history conclude their struggle. Zhuge Liang had anticipated Cao Cao's thought process, and therefore had placed his troops not on the main road, but on the trail under the smoke. The many ambushes along the now arduous trail leave the northern commander with only three hundred men, but he still manages another escape. He believes he is safe, and once again laughs at Zhuge Liang's supposed stupidity. However, once again he marches into an ambush, resulting in his final defeat.

The long series of deceptions destroy Cao Cao, who had commanded the largest military force in China. He is bested by the machinations and deceptions of a smarter, almost superhuman sage—one who detects windows of opportunity and disguises his intentions.

"A single deception can cause a vast defeat." This belief is echoed in much of the commentary on the Battle of Red Cliff authored by China's nationalist military hawks today.

Numerous authors comment that the techniques employed by Zhuge Liang in the Battle of Red Cliff were combined in a brilliant sequence: assessing propensity, practicing deception, employing special forces for decisive attack, manipulating high-level dissent, and forming a strategic coalition while isolating the opponent.[31] Conversely, Cao Cao failed to apply the lessons, causing him to lose the conflict he had begun. Two prominent Chinese military authors emphasize that the victors at Red Cliff applied the strategy of "wait and see" until propensity was favorable.[32] Another adds that espionage helps define propensity—the moment when the enemy destroys itself by internal friction and begins to decline, thereby providing the ideal opportunity to attack.[33]

For Americans today, one of the lessons of the Warring States should be that we are perceived by the Chinese to have the strategy of a Warring State, too. Chinese strategic thinking does not argue that the Warring States stratagems are relevant only to China. Our long-held view that the hawks in China are powerless, fringe fanatics handicaps our understanding. A dangerous implication of this emerges when China expects the

United States to behave like an aggressive hegemon eager to retain its dominant position; when the Americans instead promote détente, the UN Charter, and democracy and human rights for all, China gets suspicious. What are the Americans really up to? Perhaps some among China's moderates and reformists understand America's good intentions. The hawks, however, see only American deception.

3

ONLY CHINA COULD GO TO NIXON

"Ally with Wu in the east to oppose Wei in the north."
—*The Romance of the Three Kingdoms*, AD 200
Quoted in Memo to Chairman Mao, 1969

One of the great lessons of history Americans have been taught over the years is that President Richard Nixon's opening of U.S. relations with the People's Republic of China in 1971 was an act of sheer brilliance. The ever-strategic Nixon, along with his national security adviser, Henry Kissinger, believed that such an alliance would bolster America's position against the country it saw as the far greater threat to U.S. interests: the Soviet Union. History has presented Americans with the image of Nixon the chess player, seeing many moves into the future while playing nations off against other nations.

There was, to be sure, an element of brilliance in America's opening to China. And there were legitimate reasons to broker such an alliance at the height of the Cold War. But many have forgotten—if they ever even knew—that the opening was not actually initiated by Nixon or by Kissinger. During their first months in office, their focus was on improving relations with the Soviet Union. They had no desire to provoke the Soviets' ire by dallying with China. Indeed, in many ways, it was not Nixon who went to China, but China that went to Nixon.

In the case of each American president, Beijing's strategy seems to have been a product of brilliant improvisation—constant tactical shifts combined with shrewd assessments of the internal differences among the main players in Washington debates. In their assessment of *shi* vis-à-vis the United States, China's leaders benefited from something considered to be of critical importance during the Warring States period: a well-placed spy in the enemy's ranks.

A forty-year employee of the CIA, Larry Wu-Tai Chin, was accused in 1985 of engaging in decades of espionage on behalf of China. Chin was accused of providing countless classified U.S. documents regarding China to the Chinese government, charges to which Chin pled guilty in 1986. While confessing to a judge, Chin declared that he acted as he did to promote reconciliation between the United States and China. Shortly thereafter, he was found by a guard asphyxiated in his prison cell. Larry Chin seemed to admit to the judge he revealed our planning and weaknesses to the Chinese government so Beijing could have been highly effective in getting all it wanted.[1]

America, in contrast, has not had similarly placed informants to provide direct insight into Chinese strategic thinking. Because we also lack access to internal Chinese policy documents, this chapter attempts to unearth the motivations of China's leaders during the time of renewed relations with the United States through the end of the Reagan administration by examining U.S. accounts of what appeared to be driving China, as well as other open-source information that has emerged since.

Unlike the United States, China has not released, nor is it likely to ever release, official internal records showing how Chinese leaders were able to obtain essentially all of the major economic, military, and diplomatic-political assistance it sought from the last eight U.S. presidents, from Richard Nixon through Barack Obama. However, there do appear to be consistent strategic approaches followed by Beijing that have been acknowledged in general terms in interviews of and articles by Chinese scholars. The nine elements of Chinese strategy (introduced in chapter 2) help us to better make sense of China's past and prospective actions. The use of deception, *shi*, patience, and avoiding encirclement by the Soviet Union are all apparent. In particular, the nine key elements of Chinese strategy have guided China throughout its decades-long campaign to obtain support from the United States to increase China's strength.

There is wide agreement that in the late 1960s, with their outsize ambitions exposed to the Soviets, with whom they were on the brink of military confrontation, China sought out a new benefactor. For ideas about how to make America a friend—or, to be more precise, a temporary ally—Mao turned to the military rather than to his diplomats.

Many Americans discounted the influence of China's hawks. They were surprised to learn that the military secretly designed China's opening to America. In the spring of 1969, Mao summoned four hawkish army marshals who wanted to end China's decade of passivity and instead to stand up to the threat of the Soviet Union—Chen Yi, Nie Rongzhen, Xu Xiangqian, and Ye Jianying.[2] These marshals summed up the American strategy toward the Soviet Union and China in a Chinese proverb of "sitting on top of the mountain to watch a fight between two tigers."[3] In other words, they believed America was waiting for one Communist country to devour the other, and they thought in terms of ancient lessons from the Warring States period.

In May 1969, Mao asked them for further recommendations. According to Kissinger, the marshals' private secretary recorded that the group discussed "whether, from a strategic perspective, China should play the American card in case of a large-scale Soviet attack on China."[4] Marshal Chen Yi suggested that the group study the example of Stalin's nonaggression pact with Hitler in 1939.

Another marshal, Ye Jianying, cited the "Red Cliff strategy" pursued by Zhuge Liang, the southern commandeer who outwitted Cao Cao: "We can consult the example of Zhuge Liang's strategic guiding principle, when the three states of Wei, Shu, and Wu confronted each other: 'Ally with Wu in the east to oppose Wei in the north.'"[5]

In the marshals' view, America feared a Soviet conquest of China: "The last thing the U.S. imperialists are willing to see is a victory by the Soviet revisionists in a Sino-Soviet war, as this would [allow the Soviets] to build up a big empire more powerful than the American empire in resources and manpower."[6]

Chen Yi pointed out that the new president, Richard Nixon, seemed eager "to win over China." He proposed what he called "wild ideas" to elevate the United States–China dialogue to the ministerial level, or even higher.[7] Most revolutionary, according to Kissinger, was Chen Yi's proposal that the People's Republic drop its long-held precondition that Taiwan be returned to mainland China.[8] Chen Yi argued:

> First, when the meetings in Warsaw [the ambassadorial talks] are resumed, we may take the initiative in proposing to hold Sino-American talks at the ministerial or even higher levels, so that basic and related problems in Sino-American relations can be solved. . . .
>
> Second, a Sino-American meeting at higher levels holds strategic significance. We should not raise any prerequisite. . . . The Taiwan question can be gradually solved by talks at higher levels. Furthermore, we may discuss with the Americans other questions of strategic significance.[9]

China still called the United States its enemy, describing a possible visit by Nixon as an instance of China "utilizing contradictions, dividing up enemies, and enhancing ourselves."[10] In other words, the United States was merely a useful tool for China, not a long-term ally. Operating on this principle, Beijing sent a secret message to Nixon and Kissinger: since President Nixon had already visited Belgrade and Bucharest—capitals of other Communist countries—he would also be welcome in Beijing.[11] The message contained no hint of trust or future cooperation.

China has not released internal documents to substantiate the reasons for the decision to reach out to America, but several Chinese generals have told me that Mao's subtle approach to the Nixon administration was a striking example of identifying and harnessing *shi*, with some telling me that there was one moment that caused Mao to redouble his efforts: a major battle at the border of Xinjiang in northwestern China on August 28, 1969. Beijing mobilized Chinese military units along China's borders. By then, Kissinger concludes, resuming contact with the United States had become a "strategic necessity." At the United Nations in New York, I heard the Soviet version of their attack and quickly passed it to Peter and Agent Smith to inform the contentious NSC debate about the risks of reaching out to China.

In 1969, Mao was able to assess correctly the *shi* that was driving China out of the Soviet orbit and toward a new alliance with the West. Mao had taken two actions to accelerate this shift. The first was his invitation of Nixon to Beijing. The second was to test two massive hydrogen bombs without warning within days of each other near the Soviet border. The act served both as a show of force and as a signal to America that China sought to move away from the Soviet orbit.

Realizing the Americans still weren't quite getting the message, Mao did something on October 1, 1970, quite unusual for the committed and anti-Western Communist: he invited the well-known American journalist and author Edgar Snow to stand with him on the Tiananmen reviewing stage, and arranged for a photograph of both of them to be taken for all of China to see. Mao gave his guest a message: President Nixon was welcome to visit China. This was an astonishing invitation—the latest of several overtures by the Chinese government. Kissinger admits that Washington still did not get the message, or at the very least did not appreciate its sincerity. The U.S. government was too preoccupied with its own interests and strategies to care about China's. Thus the history of normalized Sino-American relations started off with a myth. Nixon did not first reach out to China; instead, China, in the person of Mao, first reached out to Nixon. The Americans just didn't realize it. Nor did Washington yet know that Chinese documents called America the enemy and likened it to Hitler.

As Nixon and Kissinger considered their grand strategic approach to China, I was playing a much smaller role in this drama. In the autumn of 1969, my interlocutors within the intelligence agencies, Peter and Agent Smith, requested that I brief Kissinger's staff about the information I had gathered while working as an intelligence asset at the United Nations. In my meetings with Kissinger's top advisers, I detected a sharp split on China. Two National Security Council staffers, John Holdridge and Helmut Sonnenfeldt, wrote memos that seemed to favor an overture, with neither fearing a Soviet overreaction.[12] But two others, Roger Morris and Bill Hyland, were opposed.[13] Morris and Hyland feared that any U.S.-China alliance would needlessly provoke Moscow and severely damage the administration's emerging policy of détente with the Soviet Union. Four senior American ambassadors had already met in person with Nixon to warn him that Moscow would respond to any U.S. opening to China by halting movement toward détente and arms control. These clashing memos help to explain why Nixon and Kissinger delayed the opening to China by two years. They had to be prodded by China, and by my own reports from the Soviets at the United Nations that Moscow would not call off détente and actually expected America to accept China's deceptive offers of an alignment. Shevchenko and Kutovoy had said exactly this to me.

My evidence seemed to play a modest role in breaking this deadlock. I relayed what I had gathered so far: that the Sino-Soviet split was in fact genuine and that the Soviets expected us to open relations with the Chinese. I reported, and others verified, that senior diplomats such as Arkady Shevchenko already assumed that Nixon would improve relations with China to some degree. Their fear was only that he would go "too far" and establish military ties—something that was not then on the table. I was a strong—and, I hoped, persuasive—advocate for a Sino-American alliance. Kissinger even sent me a thank-you note later.

But there were additional factors at work that persuaded Kissinger and ultimately President Nixon to move toward Beijing. While Kissinger was still attempting to discern Chinese intentions, Senator Ted Kennedy was seeking to visit China. The Chinese even mentioned this possibility to Kissinger during his secret trip to Beijing in July 1971, consistent with Warring States concepts about manipulating hawks and doves. Nixon reacted as anticipated and instructed Kissinger to ask the Chinese to invite no other U.S. political figure to visit China before Nixon. Nixon believed, with good reason, that Kennedy was attempting to steal his thunder and become the first American politician to travel to Beijing.[14] Raising the possibility in public speeches of renewed relations with Communist China, Kennedy was putting together what looked to be a foreign policy platform for the 1972 presidential election.[15]

Another factor was China's involvement in the Vietnam War. Beginning in the 1950s, China had been supplying North Vietnam with weapons, supplies, and military advice. China had recently reduced military aid to North Vietnam and had even drastically reduced Soviet

shipments through China, which further persuaded the Nixon administration to side with the pro-China camp. The Americans would receive
reassurance on this front during Nixon's visit to Beijing when Mao told
the president that he was eager to remove any threat from China to the
United States:

> At the present time, the question of aggression from the United States
> or aggression from China is relatively small; that is, it could be said that
> this is not a major issue, because the present situation is one in which a
> state of war does not exist between our two countries. You want to with-
> draw some of your troops back on your soil; ours do not go abroad.[16]

Kissinger asserts that this sentence indicating that Chinese troops would
not go abroad reduced the U.S. concern that China would intervene in
Vietnam, as it had done in Korea in 1950.[17] Mao correctly recognized
that this fear featured prominently in American thinking and wanted
to induce complacency.

In July 1971, Kissinger made his historic secret visit to China, the first tangible realization of Mao's long-held plans. The Chinese were coy about the
Soviet threat that had driven them to reach out to the Americans. Foreign
Minister Zhou Enlai referred only obliquely to "our northern neighbor"
and "the other superpower." Nor did the Chinese side initiate any further
discussion on the issue of the Soviet threat.[18] Were they really so terrified
of an attack?

During Kissinger's subsequent trip to Beijing, in October, Zhou placed
the Soviet Union on a list of six key issues on the substantive agenda,
although he listed it last. After the Chinese declared that they were not
opposed to improvements in American-Soviet relations, Kissinger concluded that they were displaying bravado and concealing their fear of the
Soviet threat.[19] Kissinger warned Zhou of Moscow's "desire to free itself
in Europe so it can concentrate on other areas."[20] "Other areas" meant
the People's Republic of China.

But there were glimpses even then that the Chinese saw the United

States not as an ally but as an obstacle. Referring to the United States, Zhou offered a hint of how the Chinese really felt about their new prospective friend.

"America is the *ba*," Zhou told Kissinger's interpreter, Ambassador Ji Zhaozhu of China's Foreign Ministry, repeating a term that would be frequently used by Chairman Mao and his successor, Deng Xiaoping.

U.S. government officials who understand Mandarin—a small but growing group—have long known that many Chinese and English terms cannot be fully translated between the two languages. Choices must often be made by the interpreters about what each side really means. Kissinger's translator told Kissinger that Zhou's statement meant, "America is the leader." This seemed to be an innocuous remark, and when taken in the context of the Cold War even a compliment. But that is not what the word *ba* means in Mandarin—at least that is not its full context.

Ba has a specific historical meaning from China's Warring States period, where the *ba* provided military order to the known world and used force to wipe out its rivals, until the *ba* itself was brought down by force. The *ba* is more accurately translated as "tyrant." In the Warring States period, there were at least five different *ba*. They rose and fell, as each new national challenger outfoxed the old *ba* in a contest of wits lasting decades or even a hundred years. One wonders how U.S. policy toward China might have shifted had Kissinger been told that day that the Chinese saw Americans not as leaders, but as wrongdoers and tyrants. To this day we still have to sort out and live with the consequences of that key mistranslation.

Some years later, I had the privilege of talking to Ambassador Ji Chaozhu. He omitted any discussion of how he translated the concept of *ba* to Kissinger in his otherwise chatty memoir *The Man on Mao's Right*, which provides a rare insider's account of how China's Foreign Ministry viewed the opening to the United States. I asked if the word "leader" he used in English had originally been the Chinese word *ba*.

"Did you tell Dr. Kissinger what a *ba* was?" I asked.

"No," he replied.

"Why?"

"It would have upset him."

If Kissinger had realized what Zhou meant by *ba*—if he had realized how China really viewed the United States—the Nixon administration might not have been so generous with China. Instead, the administration soon made numerous offers of covert military assistance to China[21]—all based on the false assumption that it was building a permanent, cooperative relationship with China, rather than being united for only a few years by the flux of *shi*. Perhaps if U.S. analysts had gained access to views of the anti-American hawks, China's perception of America as a tyrannical *ba* would have alerted Washington. A RAND study in 1977 warned of evidence since 1968 that there was a strong anti-American group within the Chinese leadership that used proverbs such as America can "never put down a butcher's knife and turn into a Buddha."[22]

Two months after Zhou's conversation with Kissinger, with Nixon's visit just around the corner, Kissinger made the first of many covert offers to the Chinese. Unbeknownst to a public that would have been shocked to see the United States aiding and abetting the People's Liberation Army, Kissinger gave China detailed classified information about Indian troop movements against Pakistan,[23] as well as America's "approval of Chinese support for Pakistan, including diversionary troop movements."[24] In return, Kissinger asked for Chinese troop movements on the Indian border to distract India from its efforts to invade and then dismember eastern Pakistan. China's troops did not move, but that did not dampen American expectations.

In January 1972, Nixon authorized Kissinger's deputy Alexander Haig to make another covert offer to China. Heading an advance team to China just a month before Nixon's historic visit, Haig promised substantial cooperation with China against the Soviet Union. Haig told Zhou that during the crisis between India and Pakistan, the United States would attempt to "neutralize" Soviet threats along China's borders and "deter threats against [China]." As far as covert deals go, these first two offers by Kissinger and Haig were tactical. But they represented a sharp turn after two decades of a complete American embargo on China. And, most significantly, they were a sign of larger offers to come.

China played its role to perfection once Mao sat face-to-face with Nixon in February 1972. Mao assumed the same role with the Americans that he had early on with the Soviets—portraying China as a harmless, vulnerable supplicant desperate for aid and protection. "They are concerned about me?" Mao once asked, referring to the Americans. "That is like the cat weeping over the dead mouse!"[25] Mao even put the Americans on the defensive by claiming that they were standing on China's shoulders to get at Moscow.

Years later, Kissinger reflected on the palpable uncertainty he perceived when coordinating with Chinese officials:

> Was America's commitment to "anti-hegemony" a ruse, and once China let its guard down, would Washington and Moscow collude in Beijing's destruction? Was the West deceiving China, or was the West deceiving itself? In either case, the practical consequence could be to push the "ill waters of the Soviet Union" eastward toward China.[26]

To counter these possible perceptions, Nixon promised Mao that the United States would oppose any Soviet "aggressive action" against China.[27] He stated that if China "took measures to protect its security," his administration would "oppose any effort of others to interfere with the PRC."[28]

On the same day Nixon met other leaders in Beijing, Kissinger briefed Marshal Ye Jianying, the vice chairman of the military commission, and Qiao Guanhua, the vice minister of foreign affairs, about the deployment of Soviet forces along the Sino-Soviet border. As Yale Professor Paul Bracken first pointed out in a 2012 book, *The Second Nuclear Age*, China was given nuclear targeting information in the briefing, which Marshal Ye considered "an indication of your wish to improve our relationship."[29] Discussion during the briefing included details about Soviet ground forces, aircraft, missiles, and nuclear forces.[30] Winston Lord, Kissinger's key aide on China, knew that the White House assumed that the Soviets might well "get to hear of" this exchange of information.[31] Indeed, Moscow soon did.[32]

Mao asserted that the United States and China should cooperate in dealing with the Soviet "bastard" and urged that Washington should work more closely with its allies, particularly to maintain NATO unity.[33]

Mao also urged the United States to create an anti-Soviet axis that would include Europe, Turkey, Iran, Pakistan, and Japan.[34] A counterencirclement of the Soviet hegemon was a classic Warring States approach. What the Americans missed was that it was not a permanent Chinese policy preference, but only expedient cooperation among two Warring States. Mao's calculations in 1972 were not clarified until the Chinese released a memoir two decades later.[35]

This played well with Kissinger, who told Nixon "with the exception of the UK, the PRC might well be the closest to us in its global perceptions."[36] There seemed to be little suspicion of China's strategy.

Yet the Chinese remained suspicious of the United States. They did not share Kissinger's view that the Shanghai Communiqué, the document of understanding that was signed at the end of the summit, suggested that "a tacit alliance to block Soviet expansionism in Asia was coming into being."[37] The communiqué stated:

> Neither [the United States nor China] should seek hegemony in the Asia-Pacific region, and each is opposed to efforts by any other country or group of countries to establish such hegemony; and neither is prepared to negotiate on behalf of any third party or to enter into agreements or understandings with the other directed at other states.

If the Nixon administration wanted a quasi alliance with China, China's message seemed to be that the Americans needed to offer more. Thus the Nixon administration's next covert offer of support came in a February 1973 meeting in Beijing. It also included an explicit security promise, based on finding a way that the United States and China could cooperate that would at best deter Moscow and at least get the Soviets' attention. Kissinger told the Chinese that Nixon wanted "enough of a relationship with [China] so that it is plausible that an attack on [China] involves a substantial American interest."[38] This is the concept of a symbolic trip wire, as used in U.S. troop deployments in South Korea and previously in West Germany to demonstrate that the United States has a "substantial national interest" in a given contingency. Kissinger was not promising a permanent deployment of U.S. troops to China's northern border, but he wanted something that would make a splash. This is what Mao's generals had proposed he seek from Nixon in 1969: a conspicuous gesture to Moscow.

Kissinger even provided a timeline for this strategy. "The period of greatest danger" for China, he told Huang Hua, China's ambassador to the United Nations, would be in the period from 1974 to 1976, when the Soviet Union would have completed the "pacification" of the West through détente and disarmament, the shifting of its military forces, and the development of its offensive nuclear capabilities. Kissinger wanted the trip wire in place by then.

The next covert offer—the fourth since Nixon's first meeting with Mao and the sixth since Kissinger's first trip to China—promised to offer China any deal America offered to the Soviet Union. In the run-up to the summit meeting between Nixon and Soviet leader Leonid Brezhnev in June 1973, Kissinger reaffirmed that "anything we are prepared to do with the Soviet Union, we are prepared to do with the People's Republic."[39] In fact, the United States was willing to offer China deals even better than those made with the Soviets: "We may be prepared," said Kissinger, "to do things with the People's Republic that we are not prepared to do with the Soviet Union."[40]

At about this time, Nixon sent a note stating "in no case will the United States participate in a joint move together with the Soviet Union under [the Prevention of Nuclear War] agreement with respect to conflicts . . . where the PRC is a party."[41] At the same time, he decided to circumvent U.S. law and regulations by providing technology to China through the British.[42]

The seventh covert offer was the most sensitive one, and would not be revealed for three decades, even to the CIA. It grew out of an internal debate I witnessed in October 1973 about whether to back up America's vague promises to Beijing and do something tangible to strengthen China, or to stay at the level of mere words and gestures. The United States could establish a "more concrete security understanding" with the Chinese, or instead merely promise significant progress in the diplomatic normalization of bilateral relations.[43] There was a strong case for each option.

That year, I was working at the RAND Corporation, where as a China expert I had been given top-secret access to Kissinger's conversations with Chinese leaders by Richard Moorsteen, a RAND colleague close to

Kissinger. Andy Marshall and Fred Iklé had hired me at RAND, the latter of whom soon left RAND after Nixon appointed him director of the Arms Control and Disarmament Agency. Iklé invited me to see him at his agency's offices several times in 1973 to discuss my analysis of China, and to draft a proposal to Kissinger of secret cooperation of intelligence and warning technology.

I shared Iklé's support for tangible U.S. covert cooperation with China. Though Iklé told Kissinger that a "formal relationship" (that is, a formal alliance) was not desirable, Washington could unilaterally provide help of a "technical nature." The United States could set up a "hotline" arrangement that would provide a cover for Washington to give Beijing secret early-warning information about Soviet military actions directed against China. "Given that a large portion of the Chinese strategic forces will continue to consist of bombers, hours of advance warning could be used by them to reduce the vulnerability of their forces significantly," Iklé and I wrote in one memo. "The fact that the hotline might enable us to transmit warning of a possible Soviet attack could be a powerful argument." We also advocated Washington's selling to Beijing hardware and technology to alert the Chinese if the Soviets were about to attack, and we supported providing America's superior high-resolution satellite images to heighten the accuracy of Chinese targeting of Soviet sites.[44]

Kissinger agreed with our proposal. Only a few knew that he proposed tangible U.S. covert cooperation with China. On a trip to Beijing in November 1973, Kissinger told the Chinese that in the event of a Soviet attack the United States could supply "equipment and other services." America, Kissinger said, could help improve communications between Beijing and the various Chinese bomber bases "under some guise." He also offered to provide the technology for "certain kinds of radars" that the Chinese could build.[45] In other words, Kissinger secretly offered aid to the People's Liberation Army. He was proposing the beginnings of a military supply relationship, both in peacetime and in the event of a Soviet attack.

To my surprise, the Chinese initially balked at the seventh offer, asking for time to study the proposals before responding further.[46] They said that American cooperation with early warning would be "intelligence of great assistance," but this had to be done in a manner "so that no one feels we are allies." With a mentality straight out of the Warring States era of ruthlessness and shifting alliances, China's leaders were suspicious that Kissinger's offer was an attempt to embroil China in a war with Moscow.

The Chinese perhaps did not recognize the risk Nixon and Kissinger had taken to make this offer. Kissinger's closet adviser on China, Winston Lord, had argued strongly against this step in a memo to Kissinger, saying that it would potentially be unconstitutional (not to mention widely opposed) and would inflame the Russians. Kissinger had overruled Lord's objections, though Lord himself was a strong supporter of improving relations with China.

Sino-American relations went through their biggest improvement in the late 1970s, as Deng Xiaoping took on increasing power and became the public face for China's PR offensive with the United States. To Westerners, Deng was the ideal Chinese leader: a moderate, reform-minded man with a tranquil, grandfatherly demeanor. He was, in short, the kind of figure Westerners wanted to see.

But Deng was no docile grandfather. In private meetings within the Politburo, he raged at aides and advisers over China's lack of progress against the West. He believed that under Mao and his questionable "reform" practices, China had lost thirty years in its campaign to surpass the American *ba*.

Deng was enthusiastic about a partnership with the Americans, but for a key reason not meant for public consumption. He had rightly deduced that by following the Soviet economic model, China had backed the wrong horse and was now paying the price. Internal Chinese documents, which came into the hands of U.S. intelligence officials long after the fact, showed that Chinese leaders concluded that they had failed to extract all they could from their now-faltering Soviet alliance. Deng would not make the same mistake with the Americans. He saw that the real way for China to make progress in the Marathon was to obtain knowledge and skills from the United States. In other words, China would come from behind and win the Marathon by stealthily drawing most of its energy from the complacent American front-runner.

Within the Politburo, Deng was known for referencing a favorite admonition from the Warring States, *tao guang yang hui* (hide your ambitions and build your capability). Deng, too, sent opponents messages through seemingly oblique and harmless stories. During his first meeting with President Gerald Ford in December 1975, he referred to a story from the classic Chinese book *The Romance of the Three Kingdoms* to make what in retrospect was an important point, one completely lost on Ford. The story again involves Cao Cao, discussed in the previous chapter, considered in Chinese literature to be one of history's greatest tyrants. Cao Cao, in fact, probably best exemplifies the concept of a *ba* in ancient Chinese literature.

In the particular vignette Deng told Ford, Cao Cao defeats Liu Bei, a rival challenger, and remains the *ba*. After their war, the challenger offers to work for Cao Cao, but Cao Cao remains suspicious of Liu Bei's loyalty. Deng cited to President Ford Cao Cao's famous quote "Liu Bei is like an eagle, which when it is hungry will work for you, but when it is well fed, will fly away." Ostensibly, the "eagle" in Deng's story was the Soviet Union. American attempts to accommodate the Soviets, Deng warned, would fail. Once they had what they wanted, the Soviets, like Liu Bei, would pursue their own interests. What the Americans missed from that anecdote was that the same strategic sentiment held true for China. Once America built China into an equal, China would not remain an ally but would "fly away."

However, Deng tactfully decided not to tell the most famous story about Cao Cao and Liu Bei—for if he had done so, he would have divulged China's true aims in dealing with the Americans. Chinese hawks had not yet begun to write openly about the allegory contained in these ancient stories. We would need this key to decode Chinese strategic allusions. There was no sign that either Ford or Kissinger had any idea what Deng was talking about.

The emphasis Chinese strategy places on concealing one's true intention to replace the hegemon is embodied in the story of asking the weight of the emperor's cauldrons. However, a different, related story from the

Three Kingdoms period both embodies and informs China's efforts to go beyond mere passive concealment, by actively deceiving the enemy to mask one's true ambitions.

A few years before the Battle of Red Cliff, the secretive challenger Liu Bei was summoned to meet with Cao Cao. Liu Bei, who was conspiring to overthrow Cao Cao, "had to keep his secret agenda from the attentive and intelligent Cao Cao." Upon Liu Bei's arrival, Cao Cao led him to a table beneath one of his plum trees, where the two men sat to enjoy some warmed wine. While they drank, the weather began to change as clouds gathered and a storm seemed imminent. One of Cao Cao's servants pointed to a cloud formation that resembled a dragon. All eyes turned to the dragonlike formation, and Cao Cao asked his guest if he understood the evolution of dragons.

"Not in detail," Liu Bei replied.

"A dragon can assume any size, can rise in glory, or hide from sight," Cao Cao said. "This is the midspring season, and the dragon chooses this moment for its transformations like a person realizing his own desires and overrunning the world. The dragon among animals compares with the hero among people. You, General, have traveled all lakes and rivers. You must know who are the heroes of the present day, and I wish you would say who they are."

Liu Bei feigned puzzlement. "I am just a common dullard. How can I know such things?"

"You may not have looked upon their faces, but you must have heard their names," Cao Cao responded.

"Yuan Shu of the South of River Huai, with his strong army and abundant resources: Is he one?" Liu Bei asked.

Cao Cao laughed. "A rotting skeleton in a graveyard. I shall put him out of the way shortly."

"Well, Yuan Shao then," Liu Bei offered.

"A bully, but a coward."

"There is Liu Biao of Jingzhou."

"He is a mere semblance, a man of vain reputation," Cao Cao answered. "No, not he."

"Sun Ce is a sturdy sort, the chief of all in the South Land. Is he a hero?" Liu Bei inquired.

"He has profited by the reputation of his father, Sun Jian. Sun Ce is not a real hero."

"What of Liu Zhang of Yizhou?"

"Though he is of the reigning family, he is nothing more than a watchdog."

Finally Liu Bei asked, "What about Zhang Xiu, Zhang Lu, Han Sui, and all those leaders?"

"Paltry people like them are not worth mentioning," retorted Cao Cao.

"With these exceptions I really know none," Liu Bei said at last.

"Now, heroes are the ones who cherish lofty designs in their bosoms and have plans to achieve them. They have all-embracing schemes, and the whole world is at their mercy."

"Who is such a person?" asked Liu Bei.

Cao Cao pointed his finger at Liu Bei and then at himself, and said, "The only heroes in the world are *you and I*" (italics mine).

Liu Bei gasped, dropping his chopsticks to the floor. Just then, loud thunder roared from the clouds. Liu Bei, bending over to retrieve his chopsticks, exclaimed, "What a shock! And it [referring to the thunder] was quite close."

Surprised, Cao Cao said, "What! Are you afraid of thunder?" After all, what hero is afraid of mere *thunder*? Liu Bei had succeeded in concealing his true ambitions to challenge the *ba*.

A short time later, Liu Bei recounted his experience to two close allies, noting that his goal "was to convince Cao Cao of my perfect simplicity and the absence of any ambition. But when he suddenly pointed to me as one of the heroes, I was startled, for I thought he had some suspicions. Happily the thunder at that moment supplied the excuse I wanted."

"Really you are very clever," they said.

The rest—quite literally—is history. Liu Bei soon gained his independence from Cao Cao and spent the rest of his long life fighting against him for dominance.[47]

Entranced as they were by their new relationship with the Chinese, the Nixon and Ford administrations willingly satisfied many of China's immediate political objectives. All these gifts—and more to come—were kept secret from the American public for at least thirty years. The United States not only cut off the CIA's clandestine assistance program to the Dalai Lama—Public Enemy Number One to Communist China—but also canceled the U.S. Navy's routine patrols through the Taiwan Strait, which had symbolized America's commitment to Taiwan.[48] American policy became a series of initiatives to strengthen China against its adversaries.

In 1975, while still at RAND, I wrote an article for *Foreign Policy* magazine advocating military ties between the United States and China, to create a wedge against the Soviets. Richard Holbrooke, the once and future diplomat, was then serving as the magazine's editor. He was a strong proponent of the article, labeling my idea a "blockbuster." He shared my thoughts with other editors, leading to a long story in *Newsweek*, "Guns for Peking?" Other media outlets picked up the proposal, while the Soviet press attacked both the arguments I made in the proposal and me personally.[49] Chinese military officers at the United Nations had suggested the idea to me. So in 1973 I began four decades of conversations with China's military hawks, hearing about lessons from Warring States to deal with the hegemon, which I then assumed would always mean the Soviet Union.

In early 1976, Ronald Reagan, running against President Ford for the Republican presidential nomination, read the article. (I had sent it to Reagan at Holbrooke's behest.) In a handwritten note, the former California governor said he agreed with the idea of closer ties with the Chinese as a wedge against the Soviets. But he also cautioned me about the Chinese, and worried in particular about abandoning America's democratic allies in Taiwan. After I met with Governor Reagan at his Pacific Palisades home—where he joked about being "sixty-four years old and unemployed"—he encouraged me to keep sending him material about China that he might use in speeches.

In 1978, relations with the United States moved toward normalization— that is, official American recognition of Communist China as the legitimate government of the Chinese people. That year, Deng focused immediately on what was at the top of his American wish list: science and technology. This was an example of the Warring States concept known as *wu wei*—or, having others do your work.[50] As he formulated a strategy in 1978, Deng understood, as he put it, that "technology is the number one productive force" for economic growth.[51] The only way China could pass the United States as an economic power, Deng believed, was through massive scientific and technological development. An essential shortcut would be to take what the Americans already had. Deng found a willing partner in that effort in a new American president, Jimmy Carter, who was eager to achieve the diplomatic coup of a formal Sino-American partnership.

In July 1978, President Carter sent to China the highest-level delegation of U.S. scientists ever to visit another country. Frank Press, Carter's science adviser and a former MIT professor specializing in earthquake science, led the delegation. Press had been chairman of the U.S. Committee on Scholarly Communication with the People's Republic of China from 1975 to 1977, and therefore took particular interest in scholarly exchanges with China. The Press delegation received great attention from the Chinese. The *People's Daily* rarely published speeches by foreigners, but in this case it printed Press's banquet speech, which stressed the advantages of globalization. And Michel Oksenberg, a National Security Council official for China policy who would sit in on some fourteen meetings with Deng, said he never saw Deng more intellectually curious and more involved in articulating his vision about China's future than on this trip. Again playing the role of vulnerable supplicant, Deng spoke to Press's delegation about China's all but hopeless backwardness in science and technology and expressed his concerns about American constraints on high-tech exports to his country.

In the past, Beijing kept tight control over the country's scientists going to the United States, limiting their numbers in fear that the scientists might defect. Press expected that they would likewise be cautious about expanding scientific exchanges with the West. So he was surprised when Deng proposed that the United States immediately accept seven hundred Chinese science students, with the larger goal of accepting tens of thousands more over the next few years. Deng was so intent on receiving a prompt answer that Press, considering this one of the most important breakthroughs in his career, telephoned President Carter, waking him at 3:00 a.m. Like his adviser, Carter gave little thought to the implications of China's sudden intense interest in scientific exchanges, viewing it as merely a welcome sign of improved relations.

In January 1979, Deng made his first and only visit to the United States, and he was a hit. President Carter feted him at a state dinner and, in a sign of the bipartisan flavor of U.S.-China policy, even invited the disgraced Richard Nixon to attend, the first time the former president had visited the White House since his resignation in August 1974. Deng spent thirteen days in the United States, touring Coca-Cola's headquarters, the Johnson Space Center in Houston, and even Disney World. In a sign of acceptance by the American popular media, *Time* magazine put Deng on its cover, twice.

At the National Museum in Beijing, one can see displayed a photograph of Deng smiling beneath a ten-gallon hat he received in Texas, which became the symbol of his 1979 visit. It signaled to the U.S. public that he was good-humored, less like one of "those Communists" and more like "us." But it also proved a turning point for the Chinese and the Marathon. Deng obtained far more than had Mao.

On January 31, 1979, during his visit to the United States, Deng and Fang Yi, director of the State Science and Technology Commission, signed agreements with the U.S. government to speed up scientific exchanges. That year, the first fifty Chinese students flew to America. In the first five years of exchanges, some nineteen thousand Chinese students would study at American universities, mainly in the physical sciences, health sciences, and engineering, and their numbers would continue to increase.[52] Carter and Deng also signed agreements on consular offices, trade, science, and technology—with the United States providing all sorts of scientific and technical knowledge to Chinese scientists in what would amount to the greatest outpouring of American scientific and technological expertise in history.

The Chinese reached out to the U.S. National Academy of Sciences to send a series of delegations to China to initiate U.S.-China scientific exchanges in several fields China had selected. The Chinese strategy was to get the Americans to ensure their admission to all international organizations dealing with physics, atomic energy, astronautics, and other fields. The Americans agreed, thus making an eighth offer to China.

The Americans also agreed to engage in more covert military cooperation. President Carter provided China with intelligence support to aid China's war in Vietnam, to a degree that shocked even Henry Kissinger, as he described in his 2011 book *On China*. In tones suggesting that perhaps he'd created a monster by opening the door to ties with Beijing, Kissinger denounced Carter's "informal collusion" with what was "tantamount to overt military aggression" by Beijing—aid that "had the practical effect of indirectly assisting the remnants of the Khmer Rouge."[53] A visit to China by Secretary of Defense Harold Brown, Kissinger fumed, "marked a further step toward Sino-American cooperation unimaginable only a few years earlier."

The ninth offer, Presidential Directive 43, signed in 1978, established numerous programs to transfer American scientific and technological developments to China in the fields of education, energy, agriculture, space, geosciences, commerce, and public health.[54] The following year, the Carter administration granted China most-favored-nation status as a U.S. trading partner.

President Carter also authorized the establishment of signals intelligence collection sites in northwestern China in about 1979, as the CIA operative and future U.S. ambassador to China James Lilley described in his memoir, *China Hands*. "Part of the reason I was awarded a medal from the CIA was my work setting up the first CIA unit in Beijing," Lilley wrote. "Another contributing fact was my role in developing intelligence sharing with China. . . . It sounded like a far-fetched idea—the United States and China, who had been fighting each other through surrogates just a few years earlier in Vietnam, working together to collect strategic technical intelligence on the Soviet Union."[55]

In 1978, I was serving as a professional staff member on the U.S. Senate Budget Committee, and I also worked as a consultant to the Defense Department, where I continued to read classified analyses on China and produced reports and analyses of my own. As Ronald Reagan mounted a second bid for the White House in 1980, I was appointed as one of his advisers, and I helped draft his first campaign speech on foreign policy. I expressed a view, common among his advisers, that the United States ought to help China to stave off the far greater Soviet threat. After Reagan won the election, I was named to the presidential transition team. I then advocated still more cooperation. An early ally in my efforts was Alexander Haig, who knew all about the earlier efforts with China under the Carter administration, and now as secretary of state visited Beijing and publicly offered to sell weapons to China, the next logical step.

National Security Decision Directive (NSDD) 11, signed by President Reagan in 1981, permitted the Pentagon to sell advanced air, ground, naval, and missile technology to the Chinese to transform the People's Liberation Army into a world-class fighting force. The following year, Reagan's NSDD 12 inaugurated nuclear cooperation and development between the United States and China, to expand China's military and civilian nuclear programs.

Reagan was deeply skeptical of his predecessor's policies toward China—a stance that led to a serious policy disagreement within the administration. Reagan saw China's underlying nature better than I did and better than most of the China experts who would populate his administration. On the surface, Reagan followed the Nixon-Ford-Carter line of building up China—"to help China modernize, on the grounds that a strong, secure, and stable China can be an increasing force for peace, both in Asia and in the world," in the words of Reagan's NSDD 140, issued in 1984. (Significantly, the NSC staff severely limited access to NSDD 140—only fifteen copies were produced—probably at least in part because it outlined the Reagan administration's controversial goal of strengthening China.)[56]

Reagan signed these secret directives to help build a strong China and even offered to sell arms to the Chinese and to reduce arms sales to Taiwan. But unlike his predecessors, Reagan added a caveat that should have been crucial. His directives stated that U.S. assistance to China was conditioned on China staying independent of the Soviet Union and liberalizing its authoritarian system. Unfortunately, his advisers largely ignored these preconditions, and for whatever reason so did he.

Additionally, the Reagan administration provided funding and training to newly established Chinese government-run institutes specializing in genetic engineering, automation, biotechnology, lasers, space technology, manned spaceflight, intelligent robotics, and more. Reagan even approved a Chinese military delegation visit to one of the crown jewels of national security, the Defense Advanced Research Projects Agency, the research agency that invented the Internet, cyber operations, and dozens of other high-tech programs.

During the Reagan presidency, America's covert military cooperation with China expanded to previously inconceivable levels. The United States secretly worked with China to provide military supplies to the anti-Soviet Afghan rebels, the Khmer Rouge, and the anti-Cuban forces in Angola. Our cooperation against the Vietnamese occupation of Cambodia— including the arming of fifty thousand anti-Vietnam guerrillas—was discussed in interviews by four of the CIA officers who revealed the details of this program in the book *The Cambodian Wars*.[57] There was a much larger secret that other CIA officers revealed in George Crile's book *Charlie Wilson's War*, the story of America's purchase of $2 billion in weapons from China for the anti-Soviet Afghan rebels.[58] Kissinger's memoirs reveal that there was covert cooperation in Angola as well.[59]

Why did China seek to cooperate with the United States on these large-scale covert actions? We will definitively find out only when Beijing opens its archives or a very high-level defector arrives. One thing we know now is that Beijing wanted to use American power and technology to strengthen China for the long term. The key point seems to have been the perceived need to play strategic *wei qi*, to head off encirclement by the Soviet Union. No one saw this as an effort to make broader progress in the Marathon. China made itself seem weak and defensive to us, in need of protection.

In the tenth offer, U.S.-Chinese intelligence gathering along China's border with the Soviet Union—code-named the Chestnut program—was approved, according to the *New York Times* reporter Patrick Tyler. Later, during an August 1979 trip to China by Carter's vice president, Walter Mondale, the Pentagon and the CIA airlifted to China the Chestnut monitoring stations via military transport. Tellingly, Tyler reported, the Chinese asked the U.S. Air Force C-141 Starlifter at the Beijing airport to park beside a Soviet passenger jet so the Soviets would see the cooperation.[60]

According to Tyler, these monitoring stations could collect information about air traffic, radar signals from Soviet air defenses, and KGB communications, and they could also detect any change in the alert status of Soviet nuclear forces.[61] Thus China would have an increase in its warning time in the event of a Soviet attack. This was a huge advance in Chinese security in the months before the attempted encirclement that would begin with the Soviet-backed Vietnamese invasion of Cambodia and the Soviet invasion of Afghanistan in December 1979. Through their patience, the Chinese were getting more than what Kissinger, Iklé, and I had proposed six years earlier.

According to the requirements of *shi*, Beijing must have thought it needed America's help to break up the two "pincers" of the Soviet encirclement of China—in Afghanistan and Vietnam. The circumstances justified going farther than Mao had; Deng would accept significant aid from the hegemon.[62]

From 1982 through 1989, the Sino-American Cambodian program was run out of Bangkok, with the support of the Chinese, the Royal Thai Army, Singapore, and Malaysia. This constituted the eleventh offer of U.S. assistance to China. The covert cooperation was effectively masked for two decades because it was partly overt. USAID provided funds named for the program advocates, Representative Bill McCollum, a Republican from Florida, and Representative Stephen Solarz, a Democrat from New York, for nonlethal humanitarian assistance in Cambodia. Behind these two overt programs, Reagan ordered the CIA to provide covert assistance initially in 1982 for $2 million a year, and that was raised as of 1986 to $12 million, as Kenneth Conboy notes.[63] The program was commingled under a project the Thais called Project 328. China, Malaysia, Singapore, and Thailand also contributed weapons and funds. Singapore's prime minister Lee Kuan Yew even visited Bangkok to travel to the secret camp. I visited in 1985 and 1986, to be briefed by the CIA station chief, who had transferred to Bangkok after serving as head of the Far East Division at CIA headquarters. He considered the project "the only game in town," referring to the Cold War, with China joining up against the Soviets.[64]

Starting in the summer of 1984, two years after the program in Cambodia began, Chinese covert cooperation to drive the Soviets out of Afghanistan would become fifty times larger than its effort in Cambodia.

We did not understand *shi* and counterencirclement at that time, and therefore no one thought the Chinese government would risk Soviet wrath by becoming a major arms supplier to America's efforts to aid the Afghan rebels. The discovery was made by a brilliant, Mandarin-speaking CIA friend, Joe DeTrani.[65] This Chinese connection was a tightly held secret, and no more than ten people in the entire CIA were aware of the program, according to Tyler. The Chinese still do not acknowledge that they provided such arms. In his book *Charlie Wilson's War*, George Crile reports that the first order was for AK-47 assault rifles, machine guns, rocket-propelled antitank grenades, and land mines.[66]

In 1984, Representative Charlie Wilson had drummed up $50 million to increase support for the rebels in Afghanistan. Crile reports that the CIA decided to spend $38 million of it to buy weapons from the Chinese government. The *Washington Post* in 1990 quoted anonymous sources that said that the total value of weapons provided by China exceeded $2 billion during the six years of Sino-American covert cooperation.

U.S.-Chinese clandestine cooperation reached its peak during the Reagan administration. Presidents Nixon and Ford had offered China intelligence about the Soviets. President Carter established the Chestnut eavesdropping project. But it was Reagan who treated China as a full strategic partner—albeit in secret.

The three main projects were clandestine aid to the anti-Soviet rebels in Afghanistan, Cambodia, and Angola. By now, I had been promoted to the civilian equivalent of a three-star general and made head of policy planning and covert action in the Pentagon, reporting to the official in charge of policy, Fred Iklé. Iklé and I were among the few who knew about Kissinger's 1973 offer to aid China and President Carter's Chestnut program. He and I were ready to test whether China was really willing to become a U.S. ally. The affirmative results would prejudice many senior U.S. officials to favor China for years to come.

My duty was to visit the leaders of the Afghan, Cambodian, and Angolan rebel groups in Islamabad, Bangkok, and southern Angola, respectively, to ascertain their plans and needs. I was also sent to obtain China's advice, approval, and support. We recommended that President Reagan sign National Security Decision Directive (NSDD) 166, which reflected that there was a chance that escalation in Afghanistan could provoke retaliation by the Soviets.[67] We needed China's assessment of the situation and, ideally, its support.

Two decades later, the journalist Steve Coll alleged that "the Chinese communists cleared huge profit margins on weapons they sold in deals negotiated by the CIA."[68] If the assertion is accurate that $2 billion was spent on Chinese weapons for the anti-Soviet rebel groups, then China's purchase of more than $500 million in American military equipment for itself seems relatively small.

The Chinese not only sold the weapons to us to give to the rebels, but also advised us how to conduct these covert operations. From their advice emerged a few lessons about Chinese strategy toward a declining hegemon, in this case the Soviet Union. First, the Chinese emphasized that we had to identify key Soviet vulnerabilities to exploit. One tactic, they explained, was to raise the cost of empire. When I first proposed the option of supplying Stinger antiaircraft missiles to the Afghan and Angolan rebels, the Chinese were delighted at the high costs that these weapons would impose, in the form of destroyed Soviet helicopters and jet fighters.

The second idea was to persuade others to do the fighting. This was of course a manifestation of the Warring States–era notion of *wu wei*.

The third concept was to attack the allies of the declining hegemon. The Cambodian rebels worked against the Soviets' Vietnamese puppets. The Angolan rebels expelled the Cubans, who had been flown to Angola in Soviet aircraft that might also have been shot down with Stingers, if they had been made available then. The United States, in cooperation with China, did all this, and more.

I asked the Chinese whether they thought it would be excessively provocative to take two additional steps: Should we supply and encourage Afghan rebels to conduct commando sabotage raids inside the Soviet Union (which had never been done during the Cold War)? And should we agree to the request to provide the Afghans with long-range sniper rifles, night-vision goggles, and maps with the locations of high-ranking Soviet officials serving in Afghanistan in support of what amounted to a targeted assassination program? My colleagues had been certain that the Chinese would draw the line at such actions. I had read enough Chinese history to guess that they would agree, but even I was taken aback at the ruthlessness of Beijing's ambition to bring down the Soviets when they answered affirmatively to the two questions.

Steve Coll wrote in his Pulitzer Prize–winning book *Ghost Wars* that it was the American side that declined these requests. He writes of "alarms" among the CIA's lawyers that it was almost "outright assassination" and so the local CIA station chief "might end up in handcuffs."[69] So the sniper rifles could be approved but not the maps and night-vision goggles. The commando raids inside Soviet territory, favored by the Chinese as a way to bring down the Russian hegemon, were soon curtailed as well, in spite of the Chinese recommendation to us that this would have a useful psychological shock effect on the declining hegemon.[70]

In 1985, the aid to the Chinese Marathon expanded to include American weapons, as the Reagan administration arranged for the sale of six major weapons systems to China for more than $1 billion. This program aimed to strengthen China's army, navy, and air force and even to help China expand its marine corps.[71] And in March 1986 the Reagan administration assisted China's development of eight national research centers focused on genetic engineering, intelligent robotics, artificial intelligence, automation, biotechnology, lasers, supercomputers, space technology, and manned spaceflight.[72] Before long, the Chinese had made significant progress on more than ten thousand projects, all heavily dependent on Western assistance and all crucial to China's Marathon strategy. The Reagan administration hoped it was countering Soviet power by giving a boost to the Chinese, and everyone—from Reagan on down—wanted to believe Beijing's claims that China was moving toward greater liberalization.

China's strategy to break the Soviet encirclement with help from its fellow Warring State was succeeding. In 1989, the Soviets announced they would leave Afghanistan, and Vietnam soon withdrew from Cambodia. Now, would Washington and Beijing build on this foundation of trust and therefore become true allies forever? I thought so. But according to the Warring States' axioms, now would be the time for China to get back to dealing with the real hegemon, the United States.

A critical component of *shi* involves countering the enemy's attempts at encirclement. In one of the most candid discussions of the encirclement theory of *shi*, Deng Xiaoping looked back on the successes of the 1980s when he revealed to President George H. W. Bush in Beijing in February 1989 that the Soviet encirclement of China had been a mortal threat. But now the *wei qi* game had moved toward the Chinese encirclement of the much weakened Soviets. No one foresaw how China would assess *shi* as the mighty American hegemon continued to strengthen, while Moscow began to decline.

4

MR. WHITE AND MS. GREEN

"Loot a burning house."
—*The Thirty-Six Stratagems*

In April 1989, I made my thirteenth visit to Beijing. I then held two positions in the U.S. government: I worked as an investigator for the U.S. Senate and I also drafted reports on China for the Pentagon's Office of Net Assessment, which reported directly to Secretary of Defense Dick Cheney. I had a certain authority by now, and had even had a long meeting with Deng Xiaoping in 1983. To the surprise of the U.S. ambassador at the time, Arthur Hummel, I asked Deng in Mandarin for a souvenir photo of the two of us shaking hands to use for promotion of a book of Chinese military articles I translated for the Pentagon.[1]

On this 1989 visit, I wanted to check out the reports of student demonstrations in Tiananmen Square. The protesters claimed that they were trying to accelerate the reform process that we believed was well under way in Beijing, a prodemocratic and procapitalistic tilt that those of us following China in the United States believed was all but irreversible.

On April 22, I received permission from the acting U.S. ambassador, Peter Tomsen, to drive to the square to visit with some of the students.[2] I had been a student demonstrator myself in the 1960s, and so I thought it would be instructive to see how the prodemocracy demonstrations were faring in China. Before I headed out, Peter showed me the classified farewell cable of his predecessor, Ambassador Winston Lord, to the incoming president, George H. W. Bush.

As a former envoy to China himself—during the Ford administration—Bush had more than a passing interest in building a productive relationship. In fact, he had high hopes for China. On his first overseas trip as president, Bush had visited Beijing in February 1989, two months before my arrival. Bush had come away optimistic, stating before a joint session of Congress that "the winds of democracy are creating new hope and the power of free markets is unleashing a new force."[3]

Lord's cable extolled the positive state of U.S.-Chinese relations, based on "solid" intelligence sources in Beijing. It repeated the usual canard that democratic elections had begun in Chinese villages and would soon spread; that the foundation for building a true free-market economy and ending state-owned enterprises existed in China; and that there would be no reconciliation in relations between Beijing and Moscow. The Chinese leadership was no threat to American interests, Ambassador Lord noted, nor were the students in Tiananmen seeking democratic governance.

In Lord's defense, this was the prevailing view among those of us who studied China. My report to the Pentagon reflected this. Even though the student demonstrators were already in the square, I believed that the protests were relatively unimportant and that the students would all just go home when school let out in June. Only one member of the embassy staff, Colonel Larry Wortzel, seemed to think that the students' demonstration was significant. Ultimately, he went out on a limb in predicting that the Chinese army would be used to clear the square. Wortzel, like me, had had many contacts with the hawks for years. He paid attention to them. He later told me that the hawks were the source of his insight that force would be used, a rare example that showed that the hawks sometimes knew the minds of the leaders better than did the moderates.

Many of us worried that the students might embarrass the real reformers inside the Communist Party. Most everyone thought, as many still stubbornly do today, that China was on the inevitable path to reform. True, we had been told that a few heroes at the top of the Chinese government were pushing too fast for major reforms. But it was inconceivable to us that within a year they would all be imprisoned or placed under house arrest, or would defect or be exiled. We knew there was a debate within the Politburo over reforms, but we lacked any details as to who wanted what, or how strong the enemies of reform might be.

Few facts challenged this complacent attitude, though they were there if we chose to see them. One small surprise had come only weeks earlier, when fifty thousand students marched in a Beijing memorial service for Hu Yaobang, the former head of the Communist Party, deposed by Deng Xiaoping for what the press was told was Hu's "mercurial" personality.[4] Over the next seven weeks, the students were joined in the square by approximately a million protesters demanding free speech, a free press, less corruption, and more government accountability. They held up copies of the Declaration of Independence and built a "Goddess of Democracy" that was three stories tall. They asked for a dialogue with Communist officials and went on a hunger strike on the eve of a state visit by the Soviet leader Mikhail Gorbachev. By the time Gorbachev returned to Moscow, the protests in Tiananmen Square had become worldwide news—and a major, potentially destabilizing embarrassment to the Chinese Politburo.

Americans viewed Deng as the true reformer in China, so it seemed strange that the Chinese students were instead honoring Hu in these unauthorized demonstrations of growing strength. It never occurred to most of us that maybe we had Hu—and Deng—pegged wrong all along.

Somewhere in the back of my mind, perhaps, I harbored some questions, which was why I wanted to see the protesters myself. Peter Tomsen and I drove to the square in a black Cadillac with an American flag flying on its hood. No one obstructed our way as we walked up to a cluster of several hundred students sporting T-shirts and long hair. The students we talked to did not reveal any plans for hunger strikes or open defiance of the ruling Communist Party. Flashing back to 1968, during my days on the Columbia University "strike committee" against the Vietnam War, I exchanged war demonstration stories with a young Chinese professor, who was wearing aviator glasses and chain smoking. His name was Liu Xiaobo, of Beijing Normal University. Liu had just flown back from New York a day earlier to be with the students in the square.[5] Liu had been a visiting scholar at Columbia and wanted to be part of history. He would not really enter history until he was arrested for signing the Charter 08 twenty years later, when he was sentenced to yet another prison term. He subsequently received the Nobel Peace Prize in 2010. His recent writings include direct attacks on hypernationalism and military hawks, which he seems to take seriously. At that time in 1989, the mainstream view in China and the West was that the hawks would not prevail and that force would never be used against the students.

In May, Deng Xiaoping declared martial law and rushed 250,000 troops into the Chinese capital. When the protesters refused to disperse, Deng sent in his tanks and soldiers. Hundreds, and perhaps thousands, of unarmed Chinese students died in the streets, many killed by bullets designed to expand upon impact. Whole buildings surrounding the square were raked with gunfire. Soldiers kicked and clubbed protesters and tank treads rolled over their legs and backs. A lone man stood in the path of a row of tanks in an iconic image of the massacre. He was pulled away by a group of people—never to be heard from again.

After Tiananmen, many of China's reformers were condemned to spend the rest of their lives under house arrest, while some senior intellectuals from Party think tanks managed to flee to the West. Government censorship increased—with a particular emphasis on purging all references to the protest from Chinese news and history books. Within a year of the massacre, the Chinese government "had closed 12 percent of all newspapers, 13 percent of social science periodicals, and 76 percent of China's 534 publishing companies," according to the political scientist Minxin Pei.[6] It also seized 32 million books, banned 150 films, and punished 80,000 people for media-related activities.[7]

Despite these horrific events, changes to existing U.S. policy toward China came slowly. President Bush worked hard to undermine congressional efforts to recall Tomsen's successor, Ambassador James Lilley, or to alter the U.S.-China relationship in any meaningful way.[8] Instead he followed the advice of his old boss Richard Nixon, who counseled, as Bush noted in his diary, "Don't disrupt the relationship. What's happened has been handled badly and is deplorable, but take a look at the long haul." According to Bush, Nixon didn't "think we should stop our trade [or do] something symbolic, because we must have a good relationship in the long run."[9] At one point, Bush described the students gathering at Tiananmen as "just a handful of all those demonstrators."[10]

The Chinese, as usual, saw the situation differently. For Deng Xiaoping, the burgeoning student movement in China seemed to fulfill the warnings of prominent Chinese nationalists who wrote of the damage being done within the country by the United States, as well as the danger of the growing pro-American sentiment among the Chinese people. Deng had, of course, allowed expression of this popular sentiment to gain concessions from the West. Now it had gone too far.

Extreme Chinese nationalists—the *ying pai*—had been developing an intellectual school of thought since at least the early 1980s that viewed America's way of life and culture as "spiritual pollution" that would destroy China. They believed that the United States sought to create a global culture of consumption and to dominate the world. The chief propagandists of this ideological school, Deng Liqun and Hu Qiaomu, had gained followers among members of the People's Liberation Army and the Politburo.[11]

Deng Xiaoping was by no means a charter member of this radical anti-American group, but he was clearly more sympathetic to them than we had believed. The student protests in Beijing and other major cities startled Deng and other leaders, who believed that the Communist Party maintained unquestioned legitimacy across the country. In an effort to explain what had happened, internal Party memoranda depicted the protests as purely the result of a U.S.-orchestrated psychological operation intended to overthrow the Party. The ever-paranoid Deng came to believe this false claim, writing that the United States had "started running all the propaganda machines to agitate, to encourage, and to enable China's so-called democrats, the so-called dissidents who are, in fact, scum of the nation."[12] Deng became convinced that the United States had tried to bring down the Chinese Communist Party.

No one could know yet that the Tiananmen incident led to the collapse of the liberalizing trends of Chinese governance, as Deng aligned with the conservatives and named one of them prime minister. Yet in the aftermath of the incident, Deng began utilizing anti-U.S. rhetoric taken directly from the "spiritual pollution" nationalist ideologues.[13] He strengthened the role of hard-liners such as Li Peng, Hu Qiaomu, and Deng Liqun, and began a systematic purge of reform-minded members of the People's Liberation Army and Politburo. To the shock of many Americans, Zhao Ziyang, China's reform-minded party leader, was placed under house arrest for the rest of his life. Twenty years would pass before Andrew Nathan of Columbia University mysteriously acquired and published *The Tiananmen Papers*, which showed how Zhao had struggled in vain for real reform against the hawks, facing overwhelming odds that were unknown to us at the time.[14]

China supporters in the Bush administration put the best possible spin on events. I was among those involved in perpetuating the delusion that the arrest of China's party leader was a temporary setback; that China was still on the road to democracy; that this purge was an overreaction; and that we had to protect the "moderate" faction, led by Deng, who would right the ship and keep our relationship sailing smoothly. We knew something had changed. We just hoped it had not changed forever.

Looking back, it is painful that I was so gullible. Any good analyst hedges his bets, or at least predicts a slight chance that things could go wrong—that a lethal showdown was coming between the reformers and their opponents; that the real Chinese reformers would soon be in jail, under house arrest, or in exile; and that our military sales to China would be canceled. Everyone who had access to top-secret reporting had been taught about the classic intelligence failures of the Cold War. The first National Intelligence Estimate in CIA history asserted that the Chinese would not intervene in the Korean War, largely because Beijing said it would not, but within days they did. In 1962, the CIA predicted that the Soviet Union would not deploy its missiles or nuclear weapons to Cuba, because the analysts had believed many Soviet officials who deceived us and said they would not do so. In 1979, the CIA's highest-ranking analyst, Robert Bowie, testified to Congress that the shah of Iran would remain in power, that the Ayatollah Khomeini had no chance to take over, and that Iran was stable.[15] Many sources had told this to CIA informants, but the intelligence was wrong.

No one I worked with at the CIA or the Pentagon in the 1980s raised the idea that China could deceive the United States or be the cause of a major intelligence failure. Instead, all the sources and defectors were essentially saying the same thing: China was en route to a free-market economy, elections, and ever greater cooperation. But after Tiananmen,

Chinese defectors came to the United States in increasing numbers, warning of what was to come and sounding a different, more ominous tone about their homeland's future. Yet even then we refused to listen.

One defector stood out in particular, at least in my mind. For a high-level defector, his demands were unusually modest—political asylum; a new name; a house; a decent-paying job; and, of course, a cover story that would convince Chinese intelligence that he was dead. Defectors always make demands, usually for significant sums of money. They also routinely claim they know more important secrets than others do. But this man, plump and twitchy, was different—not only because he asked for relatively little, but also because what he told us ran completely counter to our conventional wisdom and challenged many long-standing U.S. policies.

The man—let's call him Mr. White—came up for discussion in the early 1990s in the FBI's national security conference room, on the eighth floor of the Pennsylvania Avenue headquarters building. The meeting was unusual because China experts from across the government had been called in to evaluate secret information from several of these defectors. With coffee breaks but no food, the scheduled one-hour discussion stretched to three.

Mr. White was one of the primary subjects for discussion. Though his eyes darted and his fingers fidgeted as he divulged details, he otherwise seemed credible. He told us secrets that we could independently verify: the identities of a few Chinese spies in the United States, and the layout of the meeting rooms and details of the classified telephone system used by the Chinese leaders. He identified a number of Chinese secret documents that we already had obtained, sorting out fakes from real ones with a breezy confidence. He passed a polygraph examination. The only problem we had with him was the new intelligence he offered. We didn't believe it.

Mr. White revealed that for three years, from 1986 to 1989, there had been a power struggle in the Politburo over China's strategy for the future. Claiming to have read from notes of secret high-level meetings and debates, he told us of the power of the hawks, and their sweeping effort to crush pro-American sentiment in the country; that the Tianan-men Square crisis had rocked China's internal stability; and that Deng Xiaoping was now siding with these hard-liners. He knew the roles of specific hawks and how they overwhelmed the moderates. Yet he thought that we should somehow help the real reformers. I was heartened by how much he presumed we knew about internal Chinese politics, and his hope that we could save the reformers.

Deng, the defector revealed, had even more audacious plans for spreading the hawks' views of Chinese nationalism. Mr. White had attended secret meetings focusing on how to revive Confucius as a national hero, after decades of Communist Party attacks on Confucian culture and anything hinting at religion more generally.

Of course, it was nothing new for China's leaders to order, in Orwellian terms, that the country's history be rewritten. After the Communist Party seized power in 1949, teams of Chinese historians recast China's history to emphasize that all progress had come from peasant rebellions, what the historian James Harrison had termed "the most massive attempt at ideological reeducation in human history."[16] But this latest change, as Mr. White was characterizing it, was so sweeping that it defied credulity. The Communist Party, which for all of its existence had claimed to have been a break from China's past, would now embrace it? Communist ideology was being quietly discarded in favor of a hypernationalism as a means for the government's survival? Red China, in effect, was no longer quite so red? It all seemed—quite literally—unbelievable.

Complicating Mr. White's efforts was the fact that the information he offered competed with information being provided at the same time by a long-valued FBI clandestine asset, a woman whom I will call Ms. Green. Her financial demands were much higher—$2 million—but so was her purported access. She knew secrets not just of the Politburo, but also of Deng's successor as general secretary of the Communist Party, Jiang Zemin, whom she claimed to know closely. She argued that Deng remained staunchly pro-American and that Jiang was even more so. Jiang supposedly enjoyed singing Elvis Presley songs in English. She said that the Chinese wanted to cooperate more closely with the United States after the Tiananmen massacre, and she scoffed at the idea that Confucius would ever be praised or that Marxist teaching would be dropped from the national education curriculum. She asserted that the hawks were fringe thinkers, out of the mainstream, quite elderly, and rapidly losing what little influence they still had.

If we had wanted to verify Ms. Green's credibility, we easily could have done so. Unlike Mr. White, she did not, or could not, reveal the names or locations of any Chinese spies inside the United States, nor could she identify any known Chinese spies in photos. She claimed to possess no knowledge of the miles of secret underground tunnels below Beijing that senior Party officials use to commute under the city. Nor could she correctly identify classified Chinese documents.

But, unlike the brooding Mr. White, whose attempted English was largely incomprehensible, Ms. Green spoke English fluently. She was deeply optimistic about future U.S. cooperation with China in most policy areas. Unlike Mr. White, who seemed fearful, even terrified, about ever coming across his fellow Chinese again, Ms. Green said she was willing to risk her life and fly back to China once or twice a year to obtain fresh intelligence.

I argued that we could afford to keep both of these defectors on the government's retainer. My colleagues disagreed. The U.S. intelligence community thrives on consensus, and this split in views about Sino-American relations was embarrassing. Ms. Green solved the problem. We sided with her and provided the money she requested.

I arranged to see Mr. White shortly after that meeting. It wasn't that I necessarily believed what he was saying, but it did stoke my curiosity. We spoke in Mandarin. If this seemingly absurd idea of dropping Marxism from the national ideology and national school curriculum contained an ounce of truth, I wondered, how would it be carried out?

Mr. White replied that he had heard of plans to set up an innocuous-sounding "patriotic education" curriculum. There would be one hundred "patriotic education" bases across the country, new historical monuments, and new museums for national tourism. China's leaders planned to fund TV and radio programs and films chronicling the "century of national humiliation" that China had suffered at the hands of foreigners, such as Japan and the United States. They would claim that the United States was out to contain China and that it sought to block China's return to its former glory.

"Our youth and intellectuals fell in love with America in Tiananmen

Square," he said. "That must never happen again. So our leaders will smear you, and seek rejuvenation—an end to humiliation at the hands of the West."

He concluded by saying, "Two birds with one stone." It is a Chinese as well as a Western proverb.

"What are the two birds?" I asked him.

"There is no more Soviet threat," he replied. "They collapsed, so Beijing doesn't need America to protect us anymore." And the second bird? That, he obviously was indicating, was the United States. He used the word *ba*. Then he added, "*Shi* has shifted."

For the first time since Nixon's opening in 1972, America had a genuine opportunity to shift its stance on China and to take a moment to see the Chinese leadership in a less than rosy light. Instead, the U.S. government worked as quickly as possible to return the U.S.-China relationship to a calmer plateau. Even after the massacre, even after knowing that liberal reformers in China were being purged and that the moderate president had been arrested, President Bush clung to the old misconceptions. No one praised Zhao Ziyang, the reformist leader of the Party who had been placed under house arrest for life, or Hu Yaobang, the mercurial Party leader who had preceded Zhao. The U.S. government decided not to raise the fate of either the deceased Hu or Zhao. No one guessed that they were the true reformers. No one knew the extent of the reforms they had advocated at the top. That information came only later, from Chinese defectors who had worked for Hu and Zhao on democratic political reforms.

I still thought that Deng and now Jiang Zemin seemed to be the true reformers. I soon learned that supporting the false reformers and effectively abandoning the true reformers was a mistake that would come to haunt us.

To complete my report, I was sent to Paris to interview the many exiled Party officials who had escaped arrest and were now being sheltered by the French government. They adopted a ten-point platform, and elected a leader of what they hoped would be accepted by the West as a government in exile. It was called the Federation for a Democratic China. President Bush paid no attention to the organization, its ten points, or its newly elected leader, Yan Jiaqi. Yan's memoirs revealed more details about the issues in the struggle for political reform and efforts to adopt a U.S.-style system.[17] Yan had worked directly for Zhao Ziyang, and his account corroborated the memoir of another exile, Ruan Ming, who had worked directly for Hu Yaobang, Deng's predecessor.[18] But these stories were too little, too late. After all, Deng had hosted Presidents Ford, Carter, and Bush, and had been on *Time*'s cover twice, and Ms. Green insisted that Deng's handpicked successor even sang Elvis Presley songs.

"I am convinced that the forces of democracy are going to overcome these unfortunate events in Tiananmen Square," President Bush said.[19] And yet in the wake of the uprising and crackdown, Bush ordered the Pentagon to complete a promised delivery of torpedoes, radar, and other military supplies to China. Having been wed to the Nixon approach to the Chinese, Bush found it impossible to look at China in a new light. His stance was bolstered by American business leaders eager to maintain their growing relationships and business opportunities, as China almost certainly promised to be the largest emerging market in the world.

Bush's "apologist" stance toward China was sharply condemned by his successor, Bill Clinton, who had vowed in his campaign to take a more hard-nosed approach. And for a time he did. After his victory over Bush in the 1992 presidential election, Clinton took the hardest line on China of any U.S. president since Eisenhower, Kennedy, and Johnson.

Bill Clinton had never been to China, but he had visited Taiwan four times as governor of Arkansas. During the 1992 presidential campaign, he attacked President Bush for coddling "the butchers of Beijing."[20] Once Clinton was in office, his secretary of state, Warren Christopher, testified to the Senate Foreign Relations Committee that "our policy will be to facilitate a broad, peaceful evolution in China from communism to democracy by encouraging the forces of economic and political liberalization." Such efforts were joined by former ambassador Winston Lord, who was so shocked by the Tiananmen massacre and his long misreading of the Chinese leadership that he turned into one of the nation's harshest China critics. Now serving as assistant secretary of state for East Asian and Pacific Affairs, Lord promised the Senate Foreign Relations Committee tough conditions on China. If there was no progress on human rights and democratic elections, then there would be no favorable trade benefits. In 1993, Democrats Nancy Pelosi in the House and George Mitchell in the Senate led efforts to enact a dramatic set of conditions on China.[21] The wishful thinking of the 1980s about Chinese reforms seemed to be extinct.

The Clinton administration's tough stance on China reached its peak on May 28, 1993, when the president invited to the White House forty Chinese dissidents, including representatives of the Dalai Lama and a student leader of the Tiananmen Square protests. This was seen by the Chinese Politburo as an unprecedented rebuke, one that threatened the entire Sino-American relationship, which China still needed to prosper. So they went to work.

According to Mr. White, who remained in touch with his sources in China, Chinese intelligence operatives were well aware of an internal split within the Clinton administration over how to approach China, so a strategy was devised to build a winning pro-China coalition inside the American government. The Chinese identified National Security Adviser Tony Lake and his deputy Sandy Berger as holding friendlier views toward China. The Chinese also looked upon Robert Rubin, then chairman of the National Economic Council, as an ally because of his positions on globalization and free trade, which were shared by Laura Tyson, chairman of the Council of Economic Advisers, and Harvard economist Lawrence Summers, the undersecretary of the Treasury for international affairs.

Every effort was made by the Chinese to bolster these individuals, to facilitate contact between them and China's allies in the business community, and to promote China's interests in Washington. Chinese officials dangled commercial deals before influential American businessmen. Major donors to the Clinton campaign lobbied the president directly, asking him not to jeopardize the prospective sales of Boeing aircraft to the Chinese or to stand in the way of launching American commercial satellites on Chinese rockets, which would save the U.S. government hundreds of millions of dollars. In addition, new support was mobilized in Congress, based on constituents' economic interests.

By the end of 1993, in what the Chinese now refer to as "the Clinton coup," these allies persuaded the president to relax his anti-China stance. There were no new meetings with the Dalai Lama, contrary to what

Clinton had once promised. Sanctions were eased, then lifted. Many of the pro-China advocates in the Clinton administration went on to be thanked as China drew attention to their farsighted statesmanship, and to the greater access to Chinese decision makers they received by virtue of their being what Beijing has labeled "friends of China." Meanwhile, the Chinese quietly continued their crackdown against dissidents.[22]

Everything was back on track, or so it seemed. Once again, the United States viewed China as something of an ally. The American view was that the Tiananmen crackdown was an unfortunate and temporary diversion. Patience was all we needed. The Chinese side reacted very differently. They knew what the ancient hegemon always did to a challenger.

On Friday, May 7, 1999, near the end of Clinton's second term, the United States led its NATO allies in a military strike against Serbia and its proxies. Two B-2 bomber crews lifted off from Whiteman Air Force Base in Knob Noster, Missouri, bound for the Serbian capital of Belgrade. The airmen dropped five JDAM bombs on what was labeled as "Belgrade Warehouse #1." The target data, provided by the CIA, had been checked and double-checked. But the calculations proved to be woefully—and tragically—wrong. The bombs hit the southern side of the Chinese embassy in Belgrade at midnight, killing three of its employees.

This occurred almost ten years after my first encounter with Mr. White. He was not as credible as Ms. Green, but I found him entertaining and had come to like him, and I went to visit him from time to time. On the night of the Chinese embassy bombing, I reached out to ask Mr. White for his forecast of what the Chinese response would be to President Clinton's apologies.

The Belgrade bombing was of course a terrible accident. I knew it would lead to some sort of reaction from China's government. But I didn't foresee the magnitude of what was to come. Neither did most U.S. intelligence analysts, who received another warning about Chinese intentions and ignored it.

Mr. White immediately concluded that the Belgrade bombing would

offer an irresistible opportunity for the Chinese government to implement the new hypernationalism he had told us about. "There are going
to be many days of [anti-American] riots," he predicted.

Riots? I wondered. Over something that was so obviously an accident? Senior U.S. officials had apologized already.

He was unshakable in his prediction—and for good reason. He knew—
and had warned us—about the increasing power of the anti-American
forces within the Chinese government. At almost that precise moment,
James Sasser, the U.S. ambassador to China, found himself under unex-
pected siege in Beijing.

Mr. White said that China would see this as no accident, but as a probe
by the hegemon of a rival who had asked the weight of the cauldrons.
"They will see it as an American warning and test of China's resolve," he
told me.

When the riot began, Ambassador Sasser had no knowledge of Mr.
White's forecast, which was after all based on his belief that China's hawks
and Warring States allegorical thinking should be taken seriously. Nor did
Sasser yet know about the goings on three miles to the west at the secret
meeting room of the Chinese Politburo, where the American "attack" on
the Belgrade embassy proved to be an irresistible rallying cry. Within
hours of the bombing, hundreds of Chinese citizens staged a demonstration outside of the U.S. embassy's gates. Many hurled rocks, eggs, and
tomatoes, and called for "vengeance" against the United States and NATO.

Sasser had been in his office that Saturday afternoon, and it soon
became clear he could not leave the building safely. For days, as the protest
outside swelled into the tens of thousands, the highest-ranking American
in China was a virtual prisoner of these Chinese masses, unable to change
his clothes or shower. Encamped in his embassy office, he ate freeze-dried
military rations and slept on the floor without blankets.

On Sunday night, May 9, protesters threw two gasoline bombs through
the embassy's broken windows, igniting fires that marine guards put out
with extinguishers. Not far away, chunks of concrete were thrown
through the dining room window of the ambassador's residence, where
Sasser's wife and son had sought refuge. The ambassador was baffled that
he couldn't reach senior Chinese officials by telephone. As Sasser told the

New York Times, "I'm not sure they fully appreciate what's happening on the ground in front of our embassy."[23]

Contrary to the ambassador's assertions, or at least his hopes, China's leaders knew exactly what was going on. Protests in China are rarely spontaneous, which was why the Tiananmen Square demonstrations a decade earlier had been so frightening to the country's leaders. In a sign of how well the day's protests were staged by Chinese intelligence, representatives of major official religious groups arrived and marched in sequence—dozens of Buddhist monks were followed by a contingent of Tibetan monks, Taoists, and then Catholic, Protestant, and Muslim leaders.

Throughout the next day, Monday, May 10, police officers ushered marchers to within twenty-five feet of the U.S. embassy. Many chanted, "Down with American imperialism!" and sang the Chinese national anthem. Young men threw pieces of concrete over the helmeted militia soldiers into the embassy.[24] At one point, the embassy staff started to shred sensitive documents, fearing that the protesters would soon storm the building. Finally, on Monday afternoon, Tang Jiaxuan, China's foreign minister, telephoned the bewildered U.S. ambassador. He relayed four demands to "U.S.-led NATO" regarding the bombing, including a demand for "an open and official apology."[25]

In fact, as the Chinese government knew well, the United States already had apologized for the incident, repeatedly. That Monday, President Clinton himself did so again, appearing before reporters. "I apologize," he said. "I regret this. But I think it is very important to draw a clear distinction between a tragic mistake and a deliberate act of ethnic cleansing, and the United States will continue to make that distinction."[26]

Privately, within the national security community, the reaction was, like Sasser's, shock and bewilderment. Despite Mr. White's prediction of China's behavior, I shared those feelings, especially as China's official reaction to the bombing became more impassioned. The *People's Daily*, a propaganda organ of the Communist government, called the bombing of the Belgrade embassy a "barbaric crime" and referred to "NATO led by the United States" as an "arch criminal." The long, front-page article likened the United States to Nazi Germany in eight specific ways. For example, the article stated that America's "self-centeredness and ambition to seek hegemony are exactly the same. . . . If we ask which country in the world wants to be the 'lord of the earth' like Nazi Germany did in the past, there is only one answer, namely the United States, which upholds hegemonism."[27]

In contrast to the Chinese version of the Statue of Liberty erected during the prodemocracy demonstrations at Tiananmen Square ten years earlier, Chinese students now carried posters vilifying the United States, including a giant replica of Picasso's 1937 antiwar mural *Guernica*, spattered with red paint. They also made a cardboard Statue of Liberty with the face of Bill Clinton, who was holding a bloody bomb instead of a torch.[28]

Those of us in the U.S. intelligence community came to various conclusions about China's behavior. Some attributed the activities to extreme Chinese sensitivities or even paranoia. Some saw them as mostly harmless bluster to extract further American concessions on other matters. But no one, as far as I recall, saw in the Chinese reaction a more calculated plan. No one thought this required a reassessment of our own strategy toward China. To my knowledge, nobody gave greater credence to the allegations put forward by Mr. White.

In 2001, the U.S. intelligence community obtained the classified minutes of an emergency Politburo meeting held after the 1999 Belgrade bombing.[29] These minutes revealed the Chinese leadership's true view of America. Each committee member shared his view of the situation and the countermeasures they proposed. If anything, Mr. White's warning had understated the government's paranoid nationalism.

Jiang Zemin stated, "The United States wants, by means of this incident, to ascertain the strength of China's reaction to international crises and conflicts and especially to sudden incidents." Jiang presumed that the air attack could be part of an "even greater plot." Li Peng, the second-highest-ranking member in the Standing Committee of the Politburo, declared, "Comrades! The bloodstained embassy incident is not an isolated matter and is not merely an insult and challenge to the Chinese people; it is a carefully crafted plot of subversion. This incident, more than anything else, reminds us that the United States is an enemy. It is by no means a friend, as some say." Li Lanqing, the vice premier, stated, "In the future, direct confrontation between China and the United States will be unavoidable!" He put forward the idea that President Clinton ordered the bombing to "throw a stone to probe the path" to "ascertain the strength of China's reaction to international crises and conflicts; to ascertain the voice of the people, the stance of public opinion, and the government's opinion, and the measures it will take."

According to the minutes, not a single leader came to America's defense. No one stepped forward and raised the possibility that this bombing was an accident. Nor did anyone propose waiting a few hours before condemning President Clinton or asking to hear the American point of view before launching massive student demonstrations in front of the U.S. embassy. So much for the goodwill and trust our programs since 1973 should have built up in Beijing.

Yet even these revelations did little to shake our complacency and optimism about China. The Chinese hawks obviously existed, we thought, but their influence could—and would—be overcome by more rational, cooler heads. My colleagues began to call for a renewed effort to build trust and reduce misunderstandings. Soon, Jiang Zemin and "friends of China" everywhere uttered the phrase *jianshao wuhui, zengjia xinren* ("reduce misperceptions, build trust"). China's "patriotic education" sounded harmless, we concluded. After all, we thought, Americans do the same thing. The anti-Western elements within China's government were troublesome, but their sentiments were not shared by China's top leaders, we told ourselves.

Most American officials ignored the anti-American signs altogether. Some of the anti-U.S. evidence was even suppressed. On a routine visit in the 1990s to the CIA translation center in Reston, Virginia, I asked a translator why so few examples of Chinese leaders' anti-American tirades appeared in its reports.[30] Almost all U.S. officials relied on translations from the center to follow what was on the Chinese leadership's mind, because so few can actually read—and grasp the many crucial nuances of—the Chinese language.

"That's easy," she replied. "I have instructions not to translate nationalistic stuff."

I was puzzled by this. "Why?" I asked her.

"The China division at headquarters told me it would just inflame both the conservatives and left-wing human rights advocates here in Washington and hurt relations with China."

Even then my confidence in China's future was not dispelled, even if it was occasionally shaken. In spite of the information gained from Mr. White and the minutes from the Politburo meeting, I was still not a China skeptic. Many channels of intelligence seemed to prove that this was all a passing phase, a period when farsighted American statesmen needed to concentrate on China's inevitable progress toward democracy, its economic vulnerabilities, and the fact that the hard-liners were all in their late seventies or early eighties, and would be replaced by moderate reformers if only Washington would show patience. It seemed unlikely then that so many of these channels of information were being manipulated by Chinese intelligence.

And all along the way, of course, our hopes were bolstered by one of our top spies giving us inside information on China: Ms. Green. She too repeatedly assured us that Beijing posed no threat to America and that we needed the Communist leadership as a check against more radical, dangerous Chinese political elements. Her reporting and access to China's leaders continued to influence American officials until the FBI arrested her on April 9, 2003.[31] A CIA source in China had apparently exposed her. She pled guilty to failing to report the $1.7 million she had received from the FBI, and agreed to cooperate to reveal what secrets she had told China. The federal judge ruled that her right to call FBI witnesses whom she needed for her defense had been violated by restrictions placed on her FBI handler by the Justice Department, so the judge dismissed the case. She was charged again, and sentenced to three years of probation, because of her promise to cooperate.[32]

The FBI inspector general's report on the case recommended creating a system for placing red flags on the files of Chinese informants who might be providing false information. The FBI's assistant director for counterintelligence, David Szady, told a reporter that the case highlighted the FBI's need "to better control its informants, to check the information they provide."[33] The FBI has never declassified its report on Ms. Green's false reporting. Until the FBI report is released, the public cannot know which was worse—the secrets she gave China or the reassurances she gave Americans. Those who ignored the hawks' commentaries on the modern-day relevance of the Battle of Red Cliff would easily make such a mistake.

5

AMERICA, THE GREAT SATAN

> "Make something from nothing."
> —*The Thirty-Six Stratagems*

Though it was not clear to American officials at the time, June 4, 1989, was a turning point in how the leaders of the Chinese Communist Party portrayed the United States to their internal audience. While there had always been a deep-rooted sense within the Communist Party of having been wronged by the West, it had been tempered by Mao's calculation that China needed the West so China could develop into a superpower capable of rivaling the West.[1] Defectors later revealed that true democratic reforms had been considered at the highest levels of the leadership. Even James Madison's ideas on the separation of powers had been advocated. By 2001, the full story shown in official documents smuggled out of China finally revealed how the hawks had distorted what was going on to panic Deng and the elders to crack down.

One central thesis of this book depends on growing evidence that the hawks have successfully persuaded the Chinese leadership to view America as a dangerous hegemon that it must replace. This view gained authority in 1989, and as a result Beijing started systematically to demonize the U.S. government to the Chinese people. What the official Party-sanctioned media say internally contrasts starkly with how China presents itself to the American people. The hawks' cry is straightforward. They assume that the U.S. hegemon seeks to overthrow China's government, as it supposedly tried to do in the 1980s. The Chinese hawks advocate this "patriotic education" and anti-American teaching because the United States still inspires fascination among their opponents, the Chinese moderates.

Indeed, in the years immediately after Mao's invitation to Nixon, America was portrayed in a largely positive light in Chinese popular culture and state media. After Tiananmen, this was deemed a dangerous mistake by the hawks, who easily persuaded the Politburo leaders to change course. The United States could have protested, but U.S. intelligence analysts and China experts believed they were witnessing a passing phase that would blow over as soon as the more nationalist, aggressive true believers in Marxism and China's destiny as superpower died out like the dinosaurs they were.

The Tiananmen massacre dovetailed almost precisely with another major geopolitical earthquake. By 1991, twenty years after Mao's hawkish marshals advised him to ally with Wu against Wei, the Soviet Union collapsed. America's victory in the Cold War—symbolized by the fall of the Berlin Wall, the emergence of a democratic Eastern Europe, and the outright dissolution of the Soviet Union—shook Beijing. It served to underscore the Chinese leaders' anti-American paranoia, which had increased in the days since Tiananmen. In their eyes, Tiananmen was America's first great offensive in its campaign to "sow discord in the enemy camp," to borrow an axiom from the Warring States period. To the radical nationalists, the United States had almost succeeded in bringing down the Party, and was stopped only via a last-minute decision to purge reformist president Zhao Ziyang and other American "allies" from the government.

The purge of pro-American reformers in China, who had gained increasing influence throughout the 1980s, created a void in the Chinese intellectual and analyst community, which not only left few pro-American advocates remaining in positions of power, but also stanched any future advancement of these views. The ravings of China's hawks, once dismissed as "hypernationalists," became the official Party line.

The Chinese government then created, in effect, an extensive "alternate history" of Sino-American relations, which portrayed the United States as something approximating an evil twin of its actual self, continually working to undermine the Chinese people, even as, in reality, Americans worked to strengthen China. To add to the confusion and mixed messages, while Chinese leaders ordered anti-American attacks in their popular culture, they feigned surprise to American leaders about these attacks. Untold numbers of diplomats and U.S. officials heard variations of a theme I heard many times whenever a particularly undiplomatic anti-American comment made its way to the West: these were the views of a small faction of hard-line conservatives, not the "mainstream" Communist leadership.

An emerging generation of the Chinese people now believes a totally different narrative about the United States than the one most Americans know—one that holds that for 170 years America has tried to dominate China. China depicts American national heroes, including Abraham Lincoln, Woodrow Wilson, and Franklin Roosevelt, as "evil masterminds" who manipulated Chinese officials and others to weaken China. At least to some degree, this twisted view of history distorts their current vision of Sino-American "cooperation," with many seeing it as just a passing phase in America's enduring crusade to destroy China's rightful place in the world.[2]

Starting in 1990, Chinese textbooks were rewritten to depict the United States as a hegemon that, for more than 150 years, had tried to stifle China's rise and destroy the soul of Chinese civilization. This reeducation effort was placed under the innocuous label of the "National Patriotic Education Program."[3] Mr. White, the defector, had predicted that this program would bring back the distorted versions of American history that had lain dormant since the earliest days of Mao's regime—well before the overtures to the United States. One striking example was a 1951 textbook by Wang Chun titled *A History of the U.S. Aggression in China*, which was supposedly reprinted in 2012 with an online editorial comment claiming the timelessness of the book's lessons: "This book, *A History of the U.S. Aggression in China*, has been out of print for a while [and we are reprinting it]. . . . Although time has progressed, these historical facts contained in this book are still true. They do not change due to the change of the times."[4] This was posted on the website of the supposedly moderate Chinese Academy of Social Science.[5]

I saw a shocking sample of this propaganda when I visited the Chinese National Museum in the fall of 2013. China's Communist Party hawks and liberal reformers have long quarreled over the facts and presentation of their history, so it is no surprise that since Mao's rise to power the museum has spent more time closed than open. Founded in 1961 a stone's throw from Tiananmen Square, it closed at the onset of the Cultural Revolution in 1966. When Deng Xiaoping began to open up China's economy in 1979, he also reopened its museum of national history. But the museum barely made it into the new century before it was closed again, in 2001. It took ten years and a $400 million makeover before China's leaders were ready to reopen its doors in 2011. They wanted to accomplish two goals. First, they wanted to make the museum the largest in the world, bigger than the Louvre, the British Museum, and the Metropolitan Museum of Art. One floor above its grand entrance hall—which is ten stories tall and the length of almost three football fields—are three titanic cauldrons. (Unlike the unfortunate Chu leader of Chinese legend, I did *not* ask the weight of the cauldrons.)

China's second goal was for the museum to tell the story of "a great nation whose people are industrious, courageous, intelligent, and peace-loving and have made indelible contributions to the progress of human civilization." Of course, there's nothing unusual about a national history museum that paints its nation in a positive light. What surprised me about China's museum, however, is what it says—and what it doesn't say—about China's relationship with other nations, including the United States.

In a permanent exhibit called "The Road to Rejuvenation," the museum showcases the ruling party's version of modern Chinese history, from 1840 to today. That history begins with China "reduced to a semi-colonial, semi-feudal society" in a "period of large-scale expansion and plundering" by "Western Capitalist countries." These "imperial powers"—including the United States—"descended on China like a swarm of bees, looting our treasures and killing our people." In an oblique reference to the Boxer Rebellion of 1900,[6] the exhibit says "the Chinese people unflinchingly attacked the foreign invaders." Finally, in its battle against Japan in World War II, "the Chinese people won their first victory in resisting and repelling the invasion of a foreign enemy in its modern history." China then faced "the historic decision of what course to take," and it chose Mao's Chinese Communist Party—which "carried out a positive struggle for peace and democracy"—over the "autocratic rule" of the "reactionary" Chiang Kai-shek.

Through the Communist Party's leadership, the Chinese people "developed their self-reliance and overcame hardships in the course of creating an independent and relatively comprehensive industrial system and economic system, which laid a crucial material and technological foundation of material and technology for socialist modernization." Thanks to the Party, the "great nation" has built a "vibrant socialist market economy" and now enjoys a "comprehensive openness." In the future, the Chinese "shall closely unite around the CCP central leadership" and "hold high the great banner of socialism with Chinese characteristics."

Left unmentioned is that China's victory in World War II depended on the military intervention of the "Western Capitalist countries" whom the exhibit casts as villains; that American investments and the American market were indispensable to the growth of China's skyrocketing exports; and that China's technological progress depended on nearly one hundred agreements with the United States for scientific exchange programs. Instead, the only large photo I saw of any Americans showed civilians disrespecting the emperor a century ago by sitting on the Forbidden City's imperial throne during the Boxer Rebellion. There was no contextual explanation of why Americans were in China, and the visitor is left with the impression that their primary purpose was to subjugate and humiliate China. Next to the photo was a military map showing where the armies of various foreign powers, including the United States, were deployed in the aftermath of the rebellion.

At my invitation, three graduate students from China's National Foreign Affairs University toured the museum with me. They were in training to become diplomats, and they were well educated from the perspective of the Chinese Communist government. They did not, however, know much about the one hundred thousand Chinese civilians killed by the Boxer rebels, or the role of America's aid to China in World War II, or the death of twenty million Chinese in Mao's political campaign and famine from 1959 to 1962, or the death of millions more in a Cultural

Revolution that closed the nation's universities and tore China apart from 1966 to 1976. And although they had heard of the Tiananmen Square protests, they knew better than to talk about them.

The graduate students were the product of a decision made by Deng Xiaoping in the wake of the Tiananmen Square massacre—which occurred a mere two hundred yards from the museum that doesn't mention it.[7] After 1989, Deng chose to align with Li Peng and other hard-liners to solidify Party control. Never again, the leaders vowed, would China's students build Statues of Liberty, quote from the Declaration of Independence, and look to America's values as admirable alternatives to those of the Chinese Communist Party. Within a year, textbooks had been rewritten to cast America as China's archvillain, and new policies and regulations ensured that only this official view of America made it into China's classrooms and libraries.

In the latest Chinese version of history, the first American villain is President John Tyler. In the Treaty of Wangxia, signed in 1844, Tyler imposed on China what Mao called "the first unequal treaty signed as a result of U.S. aggression against China."[8] A launching pad for American manipulation of the Chinese, the treaty opened the door to U.S. "illegal actions to exploit China," according to the textbooks assigned to Chinese students. Tyler and the Americans chose to "wait at leisure while the enemy labors" (in the words of a Warring States stratagem); they didn't yet have the power to dominate China, but the United States was willing to bide its time. To Chinese hawks, John Tyler—the accidental and forgettable president most famous in real life as the second half of America's first famous campaign catchphrase, "Tippecanoe and Tyler Too"—was an evil genius, laying the groundwork for America's plan to assert complete hegemony over Chinese civilization.[9]

Following Tyler's opening salvo, the next American leader to make his mark was that supposedly anti-Chinese mastermind Abraham Lincoln. In the United States, of course, Lincoln is remembered as the honest rail-splitter who held the Union together, freed the slaves, and paid for his principles with his life. But in China, he's just another brutal, thuggish American imperialist. A professor at Renmin University named Shi Yinhong has argued that Lincoln wanted "China to be dominated, or even exploited, within the international community."[10] According to this version of history, that's why Lincoln sent the diplomat Anson Burlingame across the Pacific to normalize relations between China and the Western world. According to Mei Renyi at the Center for American Studies at Beijing's Foreign Languages University, the Burlingame Treaty of 1868 forced China "to follow Western cultural norms."[11] It broke down native rituals and China's system of etiquette in favor of Western diplomatic traditions and made possible Lincoln's dream of American control of the Pacific.

At the turn of the twentieth century, the United States showed its true colors even more. In the Boxer Rebellion of 1900, America joined an eight-nation expeditionary force that defeated the patriotic rebels who were fighting to free China from Western dominance. The foreign army raped and pillaged its way across China, and then the victors imposed $61 billion in reparations (in today's dollars) on the Chinese people. The United States was willing to "loot a burning house" and, by tricking other nations into attacking China, "kill with a borrowed sword."[12]

After the Boxer Rebellion, China may have been down but it was certainly not out. The Chinese assisted the Allies in World War I, and things were looking up for China when the victorious president Woodrow Wilson promised to negotiate at Versailles for human rights and self-determination. In the Chinese version of events, Wilson's dream of liberty and global military cooperation to secure peace was a clever ruse to fool the world into sanctioning America's hegemonic aggression. According to Deng Shusheng's seminal textbook *American History and the Americans*, Wilson wanted to "make all of China a sphere of interest of the United States."[13] He therefore ensured that the captured German colony of Shandong was transferred to Japan, rather than to the Chinese government, which was lawfully entitled to it. Like a duplicitous hegemon from the Warring States period, Wilson was clandestinely subverting a weakened Warring State. Tragically, in 1919, the news of this "betrayal" immediately caused the so-called May 4 Movement, which catalyzed modern Chinese nationalism and helped to found the Chinese Communist Party in 1921.

According to Chinese analysts' telling of World War II, the Japanese invasion of Manchuria in 1931 and the invasion of China proper in 1937 were part of the U.S. strategy to pit the two Asian nations against each other in an endless war that would prevent either from rising to threaten

American hegemony in the western Pacific. The Jinan University historian Tang Qing has explained how President Franklin Roosevelt "caused the Chinese people to pay a greater sacrifice in the War of Resistance," because it was "good for the United States to keep the Chinese fighting the Japanese, make China a base against Japan, [and] promote wartime cooperation between China and the United States, so that the U.S. could someday completely dominate China and the entire world."[14] Deng Shusheng argues that Roosevelt had "the biggest responsibility for feeding the Japanese aggressors" in China. In the style of a Warring States hegemon, Roosevelt "sat atop the mountain and watched the tigers fight," waiting until both were too decimated to resist American control.[15] He "watched the fires burning from across the river" and then "obtained a safe passage to conquer."[16]

Reaching new heights of audacity, China's leaders have now recast Richard Nixon's opening to China—an opening Beijing instigated and welcomed—as another step in a sinister American plan to dominate China. By pitting the Chinese against the Soviets, the new story line goes, Nixon hoped to provoke a nuclear war between the two Communist countries. Nixon, like Roosevelt before him, watched the tigers fight from atop a mountain so that the United States could later emerge as the global savior and the only remaining superpower. In this telling, the sage Mao saw through this strategy, and he let Nixon visit China only because Beijing needed an ally against the Soviets, even one who would eventually try to betray China. Referring to the ancient state of Shu's victory over an enemy to the north, one of Mao's top generals provided the advice Mao followed: "Ally with Wu in the east to oppose Wei in the north."[17]

In China's version of modern history, the United States used trade, economic cooperation, technology transfers, diplomacy, cultural and educational exchanges, and pressure for democratic reforms to weaken the Soviet Union from within. In the parlance of the Warring States period, it trapped the Soviet youth and idealists with a "beautiful honey pot" and then used them as "spies to sow discord in the enemy camp."

To Chinese strategists, this was a masterful display of statecraft and deception that exploited Soviet mistakes, and the Chinese have vowed to not be similarly duped as the United States employs the same strategy against China. And in 2013 the People's Liberation Army's National Defense University—the Chinese equivalent of West Point—produced a ninety-minute movie called *Silent Contest*, describing, over ominous-sounding music, efforts by the United States to infiltrate Chinese society, "disorganize China," and "brainwash politicians" in another American attempt to topple a Communist power.[18] The chief American culprits include the Fulbright Fellowship, the Ford Foundation, the Carter Center, joint military exercises, and other mechanisms for exposing American and Chinese elites to each other. Only if the Chinese "take careful precaution and look out for the smallest detail, and build a strong political and ideological line of defense" can China fend off the "so-called democratic forces" that brought down the Soviet Union and that America is grooming to bring down China.

The Chinese have also rewritten the history of the Cold War, depicting the decades-long conflict as a U.S. plan for achieving global dominance. A Chinese television miniseries, sanctioned by Beijing and broadcast in October 2013, portrays the collapse of the Soviet empire during the Reagan era as a product of American deviousness. The Soviets did not fall because, as is commonly understood, the Communist system could no longer sustain itself. Rather, the Americans deliberately deceived the Soviet Union and caused its collapse.

This official Chinese Communist Party version of U.S.-China history is, of course, fiction. John Tyler's Wangxia Treaty was a pro-China compact that established official diplomatic relations, gave Chinese ports most-favored-nation status, and repealed a ban on Americans learning Mandarin. Abraham Lincoln hardly had two minutes to think about China, and the treaty negotiated by his emissary Anson Burlingame was advantageous to the Chinese; it recognized Chinese sovereignty rights that had been threatened by European powers, and it provided the nineteenth-century equivalent of today's conflict "hotlines" to head off aggression and misunderstandings. In the Boxer Rebellion, the United States was a leader in restraining the abuses of foreign soldiers. Woodrow Wilson made the return of Qingdao to China one of his priorities at Versailles and fought tirelessly—though unsuccessfully—for it. According to Western scholars, Wilson tried his best to return Chinese territory, even risking a Japanese walkout from the peace conference, and extracted a Japanese promise to return the territory, which Japan later violated. Far from seeking to subjugate China, Franklin Roosevelt saved it with American aid and intervention in the Pacific—and by waging war against Japan. Richard Nixon never imagined that his overture to China would spark a nuclear war, and the protests at Tiananmen Square were the product of a Chinese student movement seeking to build a better China, not an American front seeking China's ruin.

Because China's leaders, on the whole, have not been exposed to an accurate history of the U.S.-China relationship, I wasn't surprised when Chinese authors warned me in June 2012 that the purportedly secret anti-China plans of Barack Obama were well known in Beijing.

Chinese scholars and officials who are truly familiar with America's history know better than to parrot the official line. They rarely volunteer to American visitors any of these anti-U.S. views. They are not being deliberately dishonest. They are just embarrassed by the history they must teach. On a visit to Beijing in the fall of 2013, I tried asking a professor directly for some of the textbooks in his course. What he didn't know was that I already had obtained copies of his syllabus and textbooks.

"You see, I was just curious," I began. "I've read so much about Presidents Tyler, Wilson, and Lincoln in your books. More specifically, about their, well, 'evil' China policies."

The color drained from his face as he stammered, "Y-y-you see, we have recently obtained microfilmed documents from the U.S. archives . . ."

"I know," I replied. "I've reviewed the documents, too. It's just that I can't find any mention of these anti-China policies in our U.S. textbooks. In fact, it seems we were very pro-China at the time. If I recall correctly, the U.S. Founding Fathers, Ben Franklin and Thomas Jefferson in particular, had great admiration for the Chinese system."

He looked out the window, sighed, and explained his predicament. "I do not pick the text materials. The entire faculty is Party members and the Central Committee keeps files on us. Deviating from approved teaching materials would end our careers."

I smiled understandingly. "So this decision is made above your pay grade?"

"Yes," he replied.

That week, I also visited, for at least the fifteenth time, the prestigious Institute of American Studies. It is three miles from the fifteen-story concrete building known as the Chinese Academy of Social Sciences because it is too large to fit inside the main building. I arrived with a delegation from the American embassy. The facility was adorned with greenery and concrete barriers.

We were expected on the fifth floor. Unfortunately, the elevators were out of service and we needed to climb the concrete stairs, with which many older members of our delegation struggled. After our ascent, we walked single file through a concrete hallway with flickering industrial lighting. As I walked down the dusty and poorly lit corridor, I observed that there were still signs on the doors of each unit for the study of American strategy, domestic politics, and foreign policy.

When we arrived, we were met by sixteen Chinese scholars, most in their forties or fifties; all were wearing casual American-style clothing from their days as graduate students in the United States.

The director, Huang Ping, who had earned his PhD from the London School of Economics, welcomed everyone and began the session. After about twenty minutes, I posed a few questions about the Chinese portrayal of the United States.

"Colleagues, after an exhaustive effort, I couldn't find one example where the author said something positive about U.S. contributions to Chinese development. Recently, I reviewed a masterpiece of history of how Westerners contributed to China, a book by Jonathan Spence of Yale called *To Change China*. It discusses missionaries who helped China, the Rockefeller Foundation's contributions, and how the United States built the MIT of China, Tsinghua University, from the refunds of the Boxer Rebellion. Among the twenty of you who are here, is there any article that expresses any appreciation for American aid to China? Any textbooks or articles that claim the United States helped China during its century of humiliation? Does anyone write that, since 1978, our experts think that one half of China's growth rate has been due to the United States endorsing China as a place of investment? What about articles or books on how America has lowered tariffs and provided guidance in banking, science, and maritime development? I've never seen this acknowledged in a single Chinese textbook. Clearly I must have overlooked something. Can anyone give me just one example?"

An uncomfortable silence ensued, with awkward glances exchanged among my Chinese colleagues.

One of the scholars meekly answered, "We learned these stories as students in American schools about how you helped us, but they are not included in our authorized syllabi."

Outside of the large group meetings, I was given books and articles outlining plans by Presidents George W. Bush and Barack Obama to encircle and blockade China; plunder its maritime resources; choke off its sea-lanes; dismember its territory; aid rebels inside China; foment riots, civil war, and terrorism; and strike China from aircraft carriers. As is the case with Chinese leaders' version of the past, the frightening thing about their vision of the future isn't that they spout lies about the United States; the frightening thing is that they actually believe their own propaganda.

At first, it seemed impossible to me that any thinking person in China would believe that American presidents from John Tyler to Barack Obama had all somehow learned the statecraft axioms of the Warring States period and decided to apply these little-known concepts to control China. But then I realized that many in China think of these axioms as universal truths. They know America is the most powerful nation in the world, and they assume America will act as selfishly, cynically, and ruthlessly as did every hegemon in the era of the Warring States. As the U.S.-China Economic and Security Review Commission wrote in 2002, "China's leaders consistently characterize the United States as a 'hegemon,' connoting a powerful protagonist and overbearing bully that is China's major competitor."[19]

According to that same commission,

China has traditionally characterized as hegemons only foreign powers with which it has highly antagonistic relationships. . . . [Its] leaders believe that the fundamental drive of the United States is to maintain global hegemony by engaging in the shameless pursuit of "power politics," often disguised as a quest for democratization.... [Its] strategic assessments and public portrayals of U.S. power are shaped by the view that U.S.-style democratic liberalism and the U.S. presence and position of power in the Asian periphery threaten the Communist Party's monopoly on political power.[20]

As evidence, China points to almost every U.S. intervention abroad, no matter how altruistic. As the commission observes, "Beijing has compared the United States to Nazi Germany for the bombing of the Chinese embassy in Belgrade; it has labeled U.S. involvement in Bosnia and Kosovo as an attempt to maintain U.S. dominance in Europe; it has characterized the enlargement of NATO as an effort to contain and encircle China; and it has criticized U.S. development of ballistic missile defenses as contributing to the proliferation of weapons of mass destruction."[21]

In short, Chinese leaders believe the United States has been trying to dominate China for more than 150 years, and China's plan is to do everything possible to dominate us instead. Chinese leaders view the global environment as fundamentally zero-sum, and they plan to show the same lack of mercy toward America that they believe the long line of China-hating American imperialists—dating back to John Tyler—have showed toward them.

China's view of America would be less troubling if Chinese leaders weren't prepared to act on their misconceptions. While China doesn't at first glance seem to be preparing to take on the United States, the hard truth is that China's leaders see America as an enemy in a global struggle they plan on winning. That vision of our relationship explains why, time after time, China aids America's enemies in an effort to chip away at American power, especially in America's war against terrorism. For example, in the aftermath of the September 11 attacks, China's government produced a video called *The Pentagon in Action*, which depicts Saddam Hussein as a wise voice of reason and "painstakingly portrays the U.S. government as a wounded bully whose hegemonic power and ego have been challenged and which is obsessed with irresponsible military retaliations," as the U.S.-China Economic and Security Review Commission put it.[22]

The China hawks' recommendation to Deng Xiaoping that he launch a defamation campaign against America has largely succeeded. He tapped into deeply held, popular Chinese attitudes about ancient hegemony.

Deng assessed *shi* both domestically and internationally. He cast aside two decades of rapprochement with the United States, from 1969 to 1989. Yet he did not do so in a manner that alerted or alarmed the U.S. government. He no longer needed a counterbalance to the threat of a million Soviet troops on his border. On the American side, few intelligence officials gave credence to the idea that the Chinese leadership really believed what they were saying about the United States. Nobody in Washington took these anti-American harangues seriously at all. Few Western leaders ever mentioned it in public; most simply didn't notice. So these claims of a devious America were never rebutted. The few who raised the issue have been told these views are held by only a few fringe hawks in China.

For decades, China's leaders have attempted to control political discussions of China, both domestically and internationally. To further this objective, China's leaders established a system to create messages to influence perceptions of China and its government, largely to trick its American rival to help China rise and eventually surpass it. Since 1995, Chinese leaders knew that victory in the Hundred-Year Marathon would depend on a powerful propaganda system to shape perceptions of China in foreign media. It would be expensive, but a great deal was at stake.

China's leadership not only distrusts the United States; it also distrusts the U.S. media. Toward the end of 2013, China prepared plans to drive approximately two dozen American journalists out of China.[23] Many of the journalists have done nothing to offend the Chinese regime, but they are being punished for the supposed sins of their employers, the *New York Times* and Bloomberg News. In June 2012, Bloomberg published an article about the wealth accumulated by relatives of President Xi Jinping.[24] Then, in October of that year, the *Times* reported on the wealth amassed by the sitting prime minister, Wen Jiabao, and it followed it up in a *Times*-owned online Chinese-written lifestyle magazine with a similar story about secret consulting fees paid by J. P. Morgan to

Wen's daughter.[25] In response, China blocked its Internet users from accessing websites run by Bloomberg and the *Times*.[26] The Chinese government likely sees American journalists as just the latest in a long line of Americans out to sow discord among the Chinese people and block China's legitimate rise.

Today, this kind of thinking, standard in China's elite circles, is taken to bizarre extremes. Colonel Dai Xu, an influential military strategist and a professor at China's National Defense University, routinely makes headlines in China with allegations about U.S.-led conspiracies. This would not be possible were it not at least tacitly sanctioned by the Chinese government. In 2013, for example, he accused America of waging "biopsychological" warfare by planting an outbreak of the H7N9 bird flu virus in Shanghai. He has frequently warned that America seeks to reduce the world population by 20 percent, secretly controls China's industries, and wants to break up China into different states.[27]

All the while, the U.S. government doesn't realize that China views America, today and throughout history, as a villain. The U.S.-China Economic and Security Review Commission contracted a major study by the University of Maryland in 2004 "to provide empirical evidence on the messages and tone of Chinese reporting on the United States over time."[28] The commission found that the "U.S. Government has dedicated insufficient resources to collect, translate, and analyze Chinese writings and statements. Consequently, it has a limited understanding of the perceptions of the United States held by Chinese leaders and the Chinese people."[29]

China's influential hawks have probably never seen the American movie *The Usual Suspects*, in which an evil genius, played by Kevin Spacey, outsmarts everyone by pretending to be a soft-spoken, physically handicapped simpleton. They would like the iconic line from that master of deception, which was, "The greatest trick the Devil ever pulled was convincing the world he didn't exist."[30] He meant that the best deception conceals its very existence. China's hawks attempt to conceal China's concerted defamation campaign. China wants the benefits of American investment, trade, and education, and Washington's benign tolerance of China's rise. So they need China to present a friendly face.

Yet another strategic goal of China's hawks seems to be demonizing the American government in a way designed to undermine any appeal of American models of government in the eyes of the next generation of Chinese civilians, military officers, and political leaders. The hawks fear the spread of the supposedly subversive American model of free-market economics and elections. Yet it is okay to study science, business management, and other politically safe subjects by going to school in the United States—as 240,000 Chinese students do today.

China's hawks believe they have found a way to undercut the appeal inside China of U.S.-style political models: just ask the Chinese moderates to deny the existence of any defamation program, and then hope the United States never makes an issue of it.

CHINA'S MESSAGE POLICE

"Deck the tree with false blossoms."
—*The Thirty-Six Stratagems*

China's Marathon strategy depends heavily on goodwill from other countries, especially the United States. That goodwill translates into massive foreign investment, the acceptance of Chinese exports, indulgences when the government or state-affiliated organizations are caught stealing technology or violating WTO rules, and looking the other way on human rights abuses. Western countries offer such concessions primarily because their leaders are convinced that overall China is moving in the "right" direction toward freer markets, productive international cooperation, and political liberalization.

That perception—or, more accurately, misperception—about China is not the result of happenstance or naïveté, though there is an element of the latter involved. Over the past several years I and other experts have learned from Chinese defectors and dissidents that Beijing has a sophisticated system in place to mislead foreigners about what is going on in their country and reconfirm Western biases and wishful thinking. At the top, the person who runs the system is the number three leader of China.[1]

The dissident artist Ai Weiwei went to prison after revealing one component of this secret operation, the crackdown on Chinese bloggers who have proven essential to revealing the truth about China to Western reporters.[2] As the organization Reporters Without Borders detailed, Ai

Weiwei "made a mockery of the surveillance arrangements [he was under by Chinese authorities] by installing four webcams in his office and bedroom which filmed him around the clock. His web feed was shut down after a few hours."[3] Ai Weiwei knows what others do—that the Chinese government, at its highest levels, uses a false reality to cultivate the goodwill of foreign governments, policymakers, academics, reporters, business leaders, and analysts. This is more than an elaborate PR operation. It is an essential component of the Marathon to induce complacency in the hegemon, to hide in plain sight. And the Chinese are succeeding brilliantly. Indeed, they have been successful with this secret, largely undetected operation for decades.

Since the 1960s, U.S. policymakers have been led to believe that China is a backward nation, not militarily active, and certainly not focused on the United States as a military threat. This was the message that Beijing's leaders conveyed to Westerners to great effect. In 1999, Patrick Tyler, the Beijing bureau chief for the *New York Times*, reported the following: "Today the evidence suggests that while China is working to master state-of-the-art technologies in its laboratories, it has little expertise and few resources to build the industrial base necessary to become a modern military power."[4]

The first sense that this might not be wholly accurate came that very year, when Westerners became familiar with a book published in Mandarin and released throughout China called *Unrestricted Warfare*.[5] The book had caused a splash in the Chinese military community for the bluntness with which it discussed America's vulnerabilities. Instead of direct military action, the authors proposed nonmilitary ways to defeat a stronger nation such as the United States through lawfare (that is, using international laws, bodies, and courts to restrict America's freedom of movement and policy choices), economic warfare, biological and chemical warfare, cyberattacks, and even terrorism. The work raised eyebrows further because it was written by two colonels serving in the People's Liberation Army—Qiao Liang and Wang Xiangsui.

Once news of the study made its way to the West, Beijing quickly withdrew all copies from its bookstores.[6] The Chinese government disavowed the book as unrepresentative of its thinking,[7] though it was published by the People's Liberation Army press and both authors were promoted after the book's publication. After the September 11, 2001, attacks on the United States, Qiao Liang was quoted on Chinese websites, labeling the American casualties "the sacrificial victims of the United States government's policies."[8] In 2004, he teamed up with others to publish a best seller on how today's international politics resembles the Warring States period.[9]

A chorus of pro-China academics and business leaders in America quickly came to Beijing's defense—with the standard line that the colonels were on the "fringe" of Chinese thought and that their ideas should be dismissed. Indeed, the official translation service of the U.S. government refused to translate the book until my office in the Pentagon sent a formal request. Moreover, U.S. officials invited the authors of the book to visit Washington in 2005 (and again in 2013), perhaps under the theory that once they saw what America was really like, they would disavow the views put forward in their book. Instead, Wang Xiangsui went on to produce another volume on lessons from the Warring States for our era. China's *ying pai* hawks do not mind being called "fringe," Wang told me, because "we have a lot of influence."

China's government operates differently. Its leaders don't roll out the red carpet for academics, journalists, and scholars who are critical of their government. As is now well known, Beijing is ruthlessly efficient in how it promotes messages that are helpful to its cause and long-term strategy and censors those that are not. As it did after Tiananmen, the government revises official Chinese history and punishes those who do not toe the favored line. Imagine what might happen to U.S.-Chinese relations if U.S. policymakers, or the general public, actually had an unfettered view of the anti-Americanism rife within senior levels of the Chinese government. In Beijing's view, that cannot be allowed to happen. Indeed, a carefully managed, secret, and audacious PR and opinion-shaping operation, supervised by top leaders in Beijing, is still under way. It is an operation that intelligence officials have known about for many years.

I first heard about such efforts in 2003 from a Chinese defector—I will call her Ms. Lee. Meeting with a group of American officials, she shared a historical vignette from the Warring States period to make a larger point. Between 490 and 470 BC, the story goes, the heads of two warring states were like America and China—Fuchai was the old hegemon, and Goujian was the rising challenger who aspires to become ruler of the world. Fuchai takes Goujian prisoner. The hegemon's "hawkish" adviser, Wu Zixu, urges him to kill Goujian. Always suspicious of possible threats and eager to preempt them, Wu Zixu warns that Goujian will eventually escape and potentially topple the old hegemon. Other advisers, working secretly with the captured Goujian, systematically defame and undermine Wu Zixu to the point that Fuchai decides that it is Wu Zixu who deserves to die. Eventually, after a long series of manipulations, Fuchai sends his now-disgraced adviser a sword to commit suicide. The popular movie of his story includes this scene because Wu uttered a famous proverb when he demanded that his eyeballs be plucked out after his death and hung on the city gate of the hegemon's capital so that he could "see" the rising challenger's troops enter the city in conquest. The now furious hegemon denied his adviser this last request.

Goujian meanwhile convinces the king to let him serve as his personal servant for three years in exchange for his freedom, after which Goujian promises to be a strategic partner of the hegemon. When the king gets sick for an unknown reason, Goujian boldly demonstrates his extreme loyalty by tasting the king's excrement to diagnose his illness.

Once he is released, however, Goujian violates his promises. Just as Wu Zixu had predicted, Goujian vows revenge for the humiliation he has suffered. He sells poisoned grain that will not germinate when planted, thus causing a famine. Then he invades the kingdom and captures Fuchai. In captivity and disgraced, the king commits suicide, leaving Goujian to become the new hegemon.

Ms. Lee told us that this vignette guides China's strategy for dealing with the West today. America, she said, is playing the role of Fuchai, a ruling king being persuaded by duplicitous or foolish advisers to ignore warnings about its rival's true intentions. In her telling, the Communist leadership is the modern-day version of Goujian—a subservient leader promising partnership and loyalty to the West until the time is right.[10] Beijing, like Goujian, operates with stealth and secrecy, making false promises and concealing its motivations.[11] All the while Chinese leaders, using the stratagem of *shi*, seek an optimal moment to avenge their grievances, much as Goujian did at the point where Fuchai's power had so badly deteriorated that the kingdom was ripe for conquest.[12]

I asked various scholars about this allegory when I made my next trip to China in 2004. They knew it well, held it up as valuable guidance, and even pointed me to several books and articles that addressed the story. An author of one of these works commented, "If you want to control the whole world, you better not appear as being ambitious. Show no aspiration for greatness. If you appear as having an agenda you will be revealed . . . the success of [Goujian] is a good example."[13] One People's Liberation Army author commented on the principle that Goujian followed: "Delay action and create a more favorable strategic condition."[14] This, Ms. Lee maintained, was exactly what China is doing with the West.

Ms. Lee detailed a secret unit at the top of the Chinese leadership that controlled the media carefully to ensure that only the "right" messages got out about China. The key, she said, was to shape messages to foreign nations, and especially the United States, by first disseminating them in domestic channels. She had heard an American marketing analogy that it is not the quality of the beer that determines successful sales, but the quantity of the distribution channels. She provided three pieces of evidence to support her assertion, although none definitively proved her claim. Her main point seemed inconceivable: China's leaders devoted tremendous time and energy to controlling the message *inside* China in a way that would directly influence *foreign* perceptions of China. The U.S. government uses diplomacy and strategic communications to put its best foot forward. But imagine trying to control every U.S. media outlet—every local newspaper, every TV station, every blogger—all in a way designed to influence foreign perceptions of America. It would be immoral and—at least in the American context—illegal and impossible. The White House staff and pollsters who advise the president cannot just order the *New York Times* and the Associated Press what to print.

She told us how China's government routinely monitors—and attempts to muffle—prominent critics of Chinese government policies. She said the hard-line *ying pai* hawks often fought with the moderates about devising the specific messages. This was consistent with the information provided by Mr. White, who had revealed that in the 1980s the hard-liners were in control of the Chinese Communist Party's propaganda office and had fought with moderates over how much to demonize America to internal audiences. They receive feedback from their embassies abroad, and even the Chinese intelligence agencies, so that the message can be readjusted in a kind of feedback loop.

She revealed that the operation had a $12 billion annual budget and was run by the Politburo's Standing Committee, which met weekly in a secret room in Beijing, spending much of its time creating messages to be promoted by a propaganda system that controlled Chinese newspapers, television programs, and magazines published overseas, as well as the Chinese Internet. The other component of this operation was a secret unit across the street from the Party leadership's compound that had more than one thousand employees in its headquarters. It is called the United Front Work Department and has its own intelligence collection and analysis capability. I had visited the department in 1999, but its director told me that the organization's focus was "domestic" issues. We did not understand the double meaning. Working together, these groups, directly controlled by the Chinese leadership, seek to ensure that only the right messages get out first domestically, and especially to foreign audiences. This may explain why so much Chinese foreign propaganda has a strange ring to it with its proverbs and slogans that make sense only to Chinese, not foreign audiences.

Ms. Lee's first example of the impact of this program was how it supposedly influenced a U.S. congressional vote in 2000 on trade normalization between China and the United States as well as China's full membership within the World Trade Organization, both of which would be windfalls for China's economy. The strategy of the program in this instance was to suppress information both inside China and overseas about China's absolute opposition to relinquishing its socialist economy, and to imply instead that China's moderate reformers wanted to move to a free market and were likely to succeed in doing so. This line would be needed to win over a generally skeptical U.S. Congress.

Her second example was how messages were devised to neutralize President Bill Clinton's effort to pressure China to negotiate the return of the Dalai Lama to Tibet. The goal was to demonize the Dalai Lama by exaggerating his political demands and calling him a politician, not a religious leader, using the term "a jackal in Buddhist monk's robes," and promoting other Tibetan leaders instead.[15]

Her third case provided details about how Beijing had undermined

American support of Chinese human rights advocates, and particularly the Chinese exiles who were former senior Party officials. Of the program's three efforts she told us about, she said that she thought the attempt to influence the vote on China's accession to the WTO was the most successful.

Though Ms. Lee's allegations caught many of us by surprise, others in and out of the U.S. government had suspected that China tried to influence Congress and the White House. A 1996 Senate inquiry, led by Senators Fred Thompson and John Glenn, had uncovered an attempt by the Chinese to directly influence the U.S. political process. Under what was known as "the Plan," Chinese cash was intended to make its way directly to the campaigns of friendly members of Congress, in contravention of U.S. campaign finance laws.[16] In March 2000, an unclassified report by the FBI and the CIA to Congress noted Beijing's "monitoring as well as influencing . . . worldwide perceptions of China." Among China's goals, the report noted, were efforts to gather "information about key players and developments in countries that might affect China's interests. Penetrating the U.S. intelligence community is a key objective of the Chinese."[17] Ms. Lee said that by 2000 China had ceased its efforts to provide direct campaign contributions to American politicians because of the Senate inquiry, which had brought the activities to light. But China hadn't given up its attempts to influence the American political process. It instead found a legal means to achieve the same results by focusing on passing messages from Chinese media and think tanks to its allies in Washington, and suppressing unpleasant ideas at their source by controlling the domestic media on subjects that would alert the old hegemon. Ms. Lee's details revealed that China was far more effective than we had thought.

Ms. Lee explained that the Chinese have for years divided foreign countries' policymakers into various categories according to the degree to which the Chinese believe they will promote Beijing's preferred messaging. Major Chinese embassies formed "friendship committees" to track these individuals, evaluating key politicians, business leaders, and media figures in each national capital and situating them on a spectrum ranging from friendly to hostile. The Chinese refer to those considered sympathetic as China's "dear friends." In the United States, the list includes a plethora of academics and current and former government officials, including a large number of American national security policy advisers from both political parties.

William C. Triplett II, a former professional counsel to the Senate Foreign Relations Committee and the coauthor of two books on China, coined the term "Red Team" to describe American experts seen as pro-Beijing—a play on the fact that most of them either fail to recognize the Communist nature of the People's Liberation Army or go to great lengths to ignore it. The opposing group of China specialists is what Triplett calls the "Blue Team"—analysts who consider themselves locked in an ideological struggle with the pro-China experts. Obviously, those labeled the Red Team resent the label and deny being dupes of China. They assert that the Chinese government does not lie to them, or to anyone else.

Official Chinese government guidance to members of the Chinese media stresses that China must support "Red Team" members—or, as the Chinese government describes them, Americans who are "familiar with China" and can be "good assistants in China's public relations."[18] In that regard, Beijing has found no lack of "good assistants" in the United States.[19] The "dear friends" are invited to China; given access to various leaders and scholars; praised in the media; and, in some cases, given government contracts or opportunities for investment. Their Chinese interlocutors talk in glowing terms about Adam Smith and Thomas Jefferson, and warn about Chinese instability if the country is pushed too hard or criticized too much by outside governments or from internal dissidents. The key theme is simple: China is not a threat. America should help China to peacefully emerge as a global power.

Officials in Beijing prize certain China specialists in the United States as important outlets for expressing Beijing's views. I know because I used to be one of the Red Team, long before the term was invented. We all tend to know one another, and together we would barely fill an average-size auditorium. Thus China has a relatively easy time monitoring our discussions and writings to determine who is with them and who is not. Chinese leaders understand that if they can influence enough of these scholars, their views will disseminate to other writers, analysts, policymakers, and reporters looking for the expert take on Beijing's activities.

China has many ways to reach into American centers of thought and opinion. As the Harvard historian Ross Terrill describes the process, "A symbiosis occurs between Americans who benefit from business or other success with China and American institutions. Money may appear from a businessman with excellent connections in China and it is hard for a think tank, needing funds for its research on China, to decline it."[20] Chinese companies have begun to make substantial donations to think tanks and universities to fund U.S. policy studies of China that support Beijing's views. It is the orchestration of the messages back in Beijing by the Politburo that makes the difference in winning the Marathon.

To cultivate more allies, the Chinese government in 2004 launched one of its cleverest operations—the establishment of Confucius Institutes across the world. In a sign of how important the Confucius Institutes are to the government in Beijing, the organization is headed by Liu Yandong, a vice premier and the first woman to obtain membership on the Politburo. Confucius is of course a perfect symbol to convey the image of a kindly, complacent China. In the West, the name conjures notions of a wise, peaceful philosopher known for clever sayings.

Officially, the Confucius Institutes offer Chinese language and cultural instruction to interested foreigners, often in partnership with local universities. But what they also do is whitewash China's history, portraying China to foreigners as a pacifistic, happy nation that considers Confucius the sole guide to understanding Chinese culture. The institutes encourage a reinterpretation of Sun Tzu's *Art of War* as a nonviolent treatise. Students are regaled with stories of happy Confucian families and cultural heroes who implement sincere and honorable courses of action. Pacifism and sincerity are highlighted as China's main cultural values. As the Chinese government's website bills them, the institutes offer "a bridge reinforcing friendship and cooperation between China and the rest of the world and are much welcomed across the globe."[21]

In the past decade, the institutes have been welcomed on some 350 college campuses across the world, including Stanford, Columbia, and the University of Pennsylvania.[22] Indicating their importance to China's approach to the United States, one fifth of all the Confucius Institutes worldwide are in America.[23] That is four times the number in any other country.[24]

"For cash-strapped university administrators, the institutes can seem like a godsend," the *New York Times* reported in 2012, "bringing not just Beijing-trained and -financed language teachers and textbooks but also money for a director's salary and a program of public events."[25] Schools also received hundreds of thousands of dollars, with the opportunity for more money for various special programs. The money all comes from the Hanban, which one publication described as "an arm of the Chinese government that's chaired by the minister of education."[26] The Hanban, chaired by Liu Yandong, is governed by senior party officials from twelve state ministries and commissions. "Simply put, Hanban is an instrument of the party state operating as an international pedagogical organization," wrote the *Nation* in a lengthy exposé.[27]

In 2011, the government's English-language newspaper *China Daily* placed a two-page ad in the *New York Times* touting the institute's benefits and claiming it goes "all out in meeting the demands of foreign learners and contributing to the development of multiculturalism." The institute, the advertisement read, "focuses its programming on culture and communication and avoids ideological content."[28] This is untrue.

As Jonathan Lipman, a professor of Chinese literature at Mount Holyoke College, warns, "By peddling a product we want, namely Chinese language study, the Confucius Institutes bring the Chinese government into the American academy in powerful ways."[29] Similarly, a professor at the University of Miami noted that China's generosity comes with strings. "You're told not to discuss the Dalai Lama—or to invite the Dalai Lama to campus. Tibet, Taiwan, China's military buildup, factional fights inside the Chinese leadership—these are all off limits." [30] As Bloomberg News reported, "When a Beijing organization with close ties to China's government offered Stanford University $4 million to host a Confucius Institute on Chinese language and culture and endow a professorship, it attached one caveat: The professor couldn't discuss delicate issues like Tibet."[31] Sydney University, one of Australia's most exclusive educational institutions, received withering criticism for canceling a planned visit by the Dalai Lama over the university's fear it would damage its ties to China and funding for its Confucius Institute.[32]

I visited a Confucius Institute in Washington, DC, and was surprised to see that the "unpleasant" fifth of the five "Confucian Classics" had been included in the curriculum—it is the *Spring and Autumn Annals,* which includes the rise and fall of all five *ba* of the Warring States period. Canadian professor Terry Russell, whose university refused to accept Chinese money to establish an institute on campus, said, "They're nothing more than a propaganda and public relations exercise within the legitimizing framework of a university."[33]

It is difficult to know exactly what the Confucius Institutes demand from universities, since much of the negotiations take place in secret. A reporter for the *Nation* claimed to have gotten hold of the language in one such agreement. It read as follows: "The two parties to the agreement will regard this agreement as a secret document, and without written approval from the other party, no party shall ever publicize, reveal, or make public, or allow other persons to publicize, reveal, or make public materials or information obtained or learned concerning the other party, except if publicizing, revealing, or making it public is necessary for one party to the agreement to carry out its duties under the agreement."[34]

Critics warn that in addition to academic censorship, the Confucius Institutes may provide a cover for "industrial and military espionage, surveillance of Chinese abroad and undermining Taiwanese influence."[35] In Sweden, several staff members at Stockholm University demanded that the university sever ties with the Nordic Confucius Institute on claims that "the Chinese Embassy in Stockholm was using the Confucius Institute to carry out political surveillance, covert propaganda and inhibit research on sensitive areas such as the Falungong."[36] A professor at Canada's University of Manitoba expressed his concern that the institutes employed Chinese faculty who would "monitor the activities of Chinese international students studying there."[37]

The spread of the institutes are a point of pride within the Chinese government, and touted as an example of China's growing parity with the United States. As *People's Daily* boasted in 2011, "Why is China receiving so much attention now? It is because of its ever-increasing power. . . . Today we have a different relationship with the world and the West: we are no longer left to their tender mercies. Instead we have slowly risen and are becoming their equal."[38] As Chinese leaders often do when confronted by Western criticism, they dismissed the critics of Confucius Institutes as warmongers or harmful anachronisms. "Some people are not comfortable to see the rapid growth of Confucius Institutes," the Chinese ambassador to the United Kingdom said in 2012. "They cling to the outdated 'cold war' mentality."[39]

Building on their successes on university campuses, the Confucius Institutes are now moving into high schools and elementary schools worldwide—with a similar modus operandi. In Australia, the Chinese offered local schools more than $200,000 to promote Chinese "language and culture." The money came with one proviso: that "it would be best" if students were not allowed to discuss subjects such as the Tiananmen Square massacre or human rights.[40] In effect, students instead would focus only on a view of China that was sanctioned: a peaceful nation that seeks harmony with all.

PUNISHING CHINA CRITICS

At the other extreme are the bad guys—Westerners seen as skeptical of or even openly hostile toward China. This list currently includes many members of Congress, various pundits on the left and right, human rights organizations, labor unions, and others. On the left are human rights advocates such as Richard Gere and members of Congress who take a hard line on China, such as Nancy Pelosi. On the right are U.S. defense hawks, as well as trade protectionists such as Donald Trump. These are the people who are to be "frozen out" by the Chinese government and marginalized wherever possible. Some are denied visas into China. Others are denied access to information and to Chinese officials. Articles and blogs are encouraged, and in some cases created, in both Chinese and English, to undermine their scholarship or points of view. Chinese experts on the U.S. political system have frequently told me that this "grand coalition" of China skeptics from the left and right in the United States was initially their nightmare scenario, before they learned that these various groups seemed to dislike each other more than they cared about China's long-term strategy.

It has long been known among China scholars that the people most trusted to report on China are those academics, journalists, and writers who have been denied visas into the country. The rest routinely make compromises, consciously or subconsciously, to maintain their access. They may avoid praising the Dalai Lama or making reference to disputes over Taiwan in a way that may anger Beijing. "Because China never explains its refusals or spells out what kind of scholarship is disqualifying," the *Washington Post* reported in 2013, "the result is a kind of self-censorship and narrowing of research topics that is damaging even if impossible to quantify."[41]

One of the most respected China scholars in the United States, Perry Link, has been denied access to China for eighteen years because of his refusal to echo what Beijing would prefer he writes. "The costs to the American public," Link says, "are serious and not well appreciated.... It is deeply systematic and accepted as normal among China scholars to sidestep Beijing's demands by using codes and indirections. One does not use the term 'Taiwan independence,' for example. It is 'cross-strait relations.' One does not mention Liu Xiaobo, the Nobel Peace Prize winner who sits in prison.... Even the word 'liberation' to refer to 1949 is accepted as normal."[42] Academics understand the code, he adds, "but when scholars write and speak to the public in this code, the public gets the impression that 1949 really was a liberation, that Taiwan independence really isn't much of an issue, that a Nobel Prize winner in prison really is not worth mentioning."[43]

I learned about the carrot-and-stick approach to academics firsthand. During the 1980s and 1990s, when I was a prominent advocate for military sales to China and considered a strong promoter of U.S.-China relations, I was warmly welcomed in China. I was given access to Chinese think tanks, scholars, military officials, government workers, and more. I was allowed into the country under a visa reserved for academics and scholars. In September 2006, that changed. My increasing skepticism about China within U.S. government circles led to my becoming the subject of a profile in the *Wall Street Journal*. The article's tone was set from its opening lines: "Michael Pillsbury, influential Pentagon adviser and former China lover, believes most Americans have China all wrong. They think of the place as an inherently gentle country intent on economic prosperity. In that camp he lumps the lower ranks of the State Department, the Central Intelligence Agency, most U.S. investors and the majority of American China scholars, whom he chides as 'panda huggers.' Mr. Pillsbury says his mission is to assure that the Defense Department doesn't fall into the same trap."[44]

"Beijing sees the U.S. as an inevitable foe, and is planning accordingly," I stated in the article. "We'd be remiss not to take that into account." Elsewhere I said that "we must start with the acknowledgment, at least, that we are unprepared to understand Chinese thinking. And then we must acknowledge that we are facing in China what may become the largest challenge in our nation's history."[45] This, needless to say, was not the line favored by those in Beijing.

Almost immediately, I fell into Beijing's disfavor. My access to Chinese generals and academics vanished. I later learned that China supporters in the United States—the "panda huggers" I had referred to in the *Journal* article—went to their Chinese interlocutors and urged them to cut off my access. My visiting scholar visa requests, once routine, were now denied. To gain entry to China in the future, I needed official diplomatic notes from the U.S. government. My interactions were more carefully monitored than before. Some of my "friends" in the Middle Kingdom no longer spoke to me. In the United States, there were various efforts to debunk my scholarship and warnings about Chinese intentions.

Such was my status for several years. Then, in 2013, something unusual happened. Once again I applied for entry to China under a scholar's visa, never expecting to have it granted. For the first time in six years, however, the Chinese approved it. What's more, I was even invited to lunches and dinners by various People's Liberation Army generals. I was asked to co-chair a panel in Beijing on "win-win" scenarios in the South China Sea. While at a conference, many Chinese officials I hadn't seen in years made a point to come over to me and say hello. Two People's Liberation Army generals told me I had "made a big contribution"—*da gongxian*—to China in the 1970s and 1980s, and they hoped I would do so again.

"I'm amazed," I told one of my Chinese defector friends back in the United States. "What do you think is the cause of this?"

"Let me ask you something," he replied. "Have you ever discussed your book [referring to this book] on e-mail?"

"Yes," I replied, as a light turned on in my head.

"That explains it," he said.

In the Chinese propaganda operation, no American is considered entirely unwinnable or irredeemable. The bad guys, with enough pressure and inducements, might become good guys again. The Chinese apparently had gambled that if they were nice to me, and granted me more access, then maybe this book would be a little softer on them.

The Chinese leadership has demonstrated no reluctance in deploying far more aggressive methods to control its image. Buddhist monks are one of the last remaining sources of information about Chinese aggression in Tibet, and they are now under routine surveillance by Chinese officials, their monasteries threatened with raids.[46] A similarly extensive program is under way with members of the foreign press. Some analysts estimate that there are more than seven hundred Chinese journalists working in the United States today. Many of them are considered "propagandists" for spreading China's favored views or actual Chinese intelligence agents who monitor those considered anti-China within the United States.[47]

A recent study by the Center for International Media Assistance finds that "China's media restrictions have begun to seriously affect the reportage and operations of international organizations."[48] Specifically, the report highlighted four main strategies that the Chinese utilize to influence or manipulate the Western media. As reported by the *Business Insider* on November 5, 2013, they include:

- **Direct action** by Chinese diplomats, local officials, security forces, and regulators, both inside and outside China. These measures obstruct news gathering, prevent the publication of undesirable content, and punish overseas media outlets that fail to heed restrictions.

- **Employing economic carrots and sticks** to induce self-censorship among media owners and their outlets located outside mainland China.

- **Applying indirect pressure** via proxies—including advertisers, satellite firms, and foreign governments—who take action to prevent or punish the publication of content critical of Beijing.

- **Conducting cyberattacks and physical assaults** that are not conclusively traceable to the central Chinese authorities but serve the Party's aims.[49]

Many foreign journalists in China assume that everything they say and write, their phone calls, and their e-mails are monitored by Chinese authorities. The *New York Times* has been targeted for cyberattacks by the Chinese government, as have the *Wall Street Journal* and CNN, after each reported stories that displeased the Chinese government. In February 2013, Twitter announced that the accounts of approximately 250,000 of its subscribers were the victims of attacks from China similar to those carried out against the *New York Times*.[50]

In 2013, 10 percent of foreign correspondents in China reported difficulty obtaining press accreditation because of their reporting or the reporting of their predecessors.[51] The Chinese have denied a visa to the *Washington Post*'s Beijing bureau chief Andrew Higgins since 2009. Higgins had been deported from the country in 1991 after his acclaimed reporting on Chinese dissidents and has never been reaccredited to report from the country.[52] The *Christian Science Monitor* has reported on the crackdown on coverage of riots in 2011 during the so-called Jasmine Revolution:

> The Chinese government contacted foreign journalists to tell them not to cover the riots. In some cases, police actually went to the homes of journalists to issue the warning. If journalists did cover the riots, their visas would be denied outright. [The journalist Paul] Mooney says that was the only time he decided not to cover a story because of its potential effect on his status in the country.[53]

Paul Mooney, a journalist who has covered China for eighteen years, has similarly been denied entry into the country. Mooney's reporting was certain to infuriate Chinese officials since he focused on issues such as corruption, pollution, and China's cancer and AIDS villages.[54] Mooney became one of several other foreign correspondents, including Andrew Higgins and Melissa Chan, who were forced to leave China or forbidden from entering because the Chinese government deemed their reporting unfavorable.[55] The deportation of Chan, a journalist for Al Jazeera English, was China's first expulsion of a foreign journalist in fourteen years. As the *Washington Post* noted, many other journalists "have been threatened with expulsion and others have had long delays getting visas approved."[56]

Bloomberg News reporters have accused their bosses of withholding pieces on China out of fear of similar repercussions.[57] Bloomberg journalists compared the situation to "Nazi-era Germany, where news organizations had censored themselves to maintain access to the country."[58] The crackdown on the Internet in China is both well known and extensive. In a sense, as the news agency Agence France-Presse noted, "the Chinese Communist Party runs one of the world's biggest digital empires."[59] Its networks, comprised of China Telecom, China Unicom, and China Mobile, are all controlled by the state. The government's efforts to install tools to police the Internet are collectively known as the "Great Firewall of China."[60] Chinese authorities are able to block Chinese citizens' communications as well as any efforts at encryption. "Monitoring is also built into social networks, chat services, and VoIP."[61] Offending bloggers are routinely harassed and in some cases arrested by Chinese authorities, thus depriving them of opportunities to send information and messages to reporters in the West.

The Chinese also strong-arm Western corporations to assist in their censorship activities. In 2006, the Quality Brands Protection Committee, which represents more than two hundred multinational companies operating in China such as Toyota, Apple, and Nokia, sent an e-mail to its members informing them of the Chinese authorities' concerns about efforts by their employees in China to bypass the Great Firewall and communicate with other corporate branches outside the country, and warning them they may be visited by police.[62]

Apple acquiesced to a Chinese government request to remove applications connecting users to a television station and overseas bookstore featuring anti-China content. Apple has been trying for years to reach an agreement to sell its iPhones on China Mobile. Eutelstat, a French satellite provider, worked with the anti-China TV station NTDTV until 2005, when the provider sought to win state-affiliated Chinese clients.[63] The NASDAQ also has acquiesced to Chinese pressure. As one report revealed:

> [I]n January 2007, the company's representative in China, a U.S. citizen, was summoned and interrogated by the State Security Bureau about NTDTV staff reporting from its New York offices. He was released the same day but under pressure, "may have pledged to Chinese authorities that NASDAQ would no longer allow" NTDTV to report from the exchange headquarters.
>
> Starting in February 2007, NTDTV's correspondent was suddenly barred from the building, after reporting from there on a daily basis for more than a year. The station suspected Chinese pressure behind the unexpected change of heart but did not know what had happened until the leaked cable was discovered in 2012. Soon after NTDTV's exclusion, NASDAQ received Chinese regulatory approval to open its first representative office in China.[64]

"Recent troubles in China for Apple Inc. and Volkswagen AG represent a growing risk for global companies, as their dependence on the booming Chinese economy leaves them exposed to Beijing's shifting winds," the *Wall Street Journal* reported in 2013. "In some cases, foreign companies are coming under withering attacks from state-run media. In others, they are running afoul of Chinese regulators or government policies, such as an anticorruption campaign that limits ostentatious gifts."[65]

"Any big companies in the United States won't want to be involved with [us]; even foundations have offices in Beijing," says Meicun Weng, the founder of a Chinese news site called Boxun, which regularly reports on human rights abuses and is supported by the European Union. "China does track down who gives money [to disfavored overseas outlets]. They will get a phone call."[66]

All of these tactics—manipulating opinion, rewarding those who advance helpful messages, and punishing those voices who are discordant—are based on precedents from the Warring States. The proverbs and the succinct advice on strategy that advisers offered their rulers during the decades-long process of bringing down the old hegemon usually includes assessments of how to deal with the hawks and doves in the rival states. Of course, there is no universally applicable, one-size-fits-all approach. The goal is always to disrupt the plans of your rival. To prevent him from seeing the true geopolitical situation. If he sees the shape of *shi* before you do, you cannot place your pieces well on the *wei qi* board.[67]

7

THE ASSASSIN'S MACE

"Let your plans be dark and impenetrable as night,
and when you move, fall like a thunderbolt."

—Sun Tzu, *The Art of War*

"Mr. Secretary," said the sailor, "it is your move." The sailor was dressed in his white Class A uniform and standing above a massive floor map of the Asia-Pacific region. The map was broken into hexagons and occupied the entirety of the black-and-white tile floor. All eyes were focused on one particular spot on the map—the coast of a nation invaded by China, with a long shoreline and a history of frustrating the best-laid plans of the America military: Vietnam.

"The secretary of defense is ordering four carrier battle groups to sail at full speed toward the South China Sea," said a U.S. Navy officer. "We'll at least be able to hold Hawaii with that."

The fictional year was 2030, and the officer who spoke for the secretary of defense was on a team playing a war game at the Naval War College in Newport, Rhode Island. For more than seven decades, many similar strategy games had been conducted in this room. Some concerned peacetime competitions testing diplomatic prowess. Others simulated military invasions, naval blockades, and war on a global scale. It was in this room, now adorned with ornate stone tiles and World War II memorabilia, that the Japanese attack on Pearl Harbor was first foretold—and then ignored. Being there was like visiting Delphi, where oracles had once advised the great Athenian lawgiver Solon on creating one of the world's first constitutions and told Alexander the Great that he was "unbeatable."

On this day, not only was I present for the war game, I was a participant. My "Red Team" represented China. I'd been invited to think like a Chinese military leader, to be creative, and to channel the Chinese asymmetric approaches I'd been investigating. I was to deploy them against the most powerful armada in the history of naval warfare.

It was three hours before the war game ended, but when the final move was made, the map on the floor was like a chessboard showing checkmate, with the American king trapped and defenseless. For the first time in the history of Pentagon-sanctioned military simulations, the United States had lost a war game. To win, I had employed tactics derived from my evolving understanding of Chinese strategy. The weapons and military strategy that guided my tactics had their roots in ancient Chinese warfare, and their modern incarnations are being developed by the People's Liberation Army each day. They are called the "Assassin's Mace"[1]—a weapon in ancient Chinese folklore that ensures victory over a more powerful opponent.

Twenty similar war games were conducted by the Pentagon over the next few years. Whenever the China team used conventional tactics and strategies, America won—decisively. However, in every case where China employed Assassin's Mace methods, China was the victor.[2] The lessons acquired from these simulations were a driving factor behind the Obama administration's strategic "Asia pivot."[3]

Many American officials—myself included—were slow to realize that China's strategy is largely designed in response to Chinese fears, which we have consistently been slow to understand. What's worse is that we have often held a flawed perception of the basis for China's fears. The accumulation of significant evidence—particularly the information provided by Ms. Lee—helped some but hardly all of us to open our eyes to just how wrong we were.

While Chinese leaders harbor deep, even paranoid, insecurities about the United States and Western-led efforts to "encircle" their country, there is little evidence that China seeks to intentionally incite a war with America. Indeed, military confrontation in the near term could be one of the greatest threats to the Marathon strategy, unraveling years of patient, assiduous efforts to build China into an economic and geopolitical hegemon. Chinese leaders know that building, in the near future, a military capable of parity with the conventional capabilities of the U.S. military—with all the ships, aircraft, tanks, and soldiers (although the People's Liberation Army, with 2.3 million soldiers, dwarfs the U.S. Army) that would entail—would cause alarm in Western capitals and potentially provoke an arms race. Chinese leaders are playing a long game, aiming to build up their deterrent capability quietly and to improve their conventional forces gradually.

In ancient Chinese folklore, there is a legend of a hero confronted by a more powerful enemy. Stronger than a giant and armed with the most expensive and technologically advanced weapons of the day, the adversary was feared by all. But the hero did not shrink from challenging this mighty enemy in a fight to the death, because the hero had a secret weapon. Hidden in his wide shirtsleeve was a short, lightweight, spiked club capable of splitting a sword—or a skull. On its own, the club—or mace, as it was called—did not appear dangerous, but in the hands of the hero, it could be used to knock out an enemy with a single blow. He had been trained in its use for years, and the combination of the peculiar weapon, the element of surprise, and the hero's knowledge of his enemy's weakest point spelled doom for his seemingly superior adversary.

The legend is similar to the biblical story of David and Goliath, but instead of the underdog being saved by God the Chinese hero is saved by a secret weapon called *shashoujian*. The term is formed by three Chinese characters meaning "kill," "hand," and "mace." Roughly translated into English, it means "Assassin's Mace."

The Assassin's Mace is the trump card that ensures victory over a powerful opponent. The term can be traced at least as far back as the Warring States period, and is used in ancient statecraft texts, martial-arts novels, and China's daily military newspaper. The Chinese refer to the Assassin's Mace in a variety of contexts. In the context of dating, a man with an Assassin's Mace has a subtle appeal that makes him irresistible, even to the hardest-to-get woman. When running a business, an executive with an Assassin's Mace has a particular skill that allows him to surpass larger competitors. When playing soccer, the team with an Assassin's Mace has a goal scorer who cannot be stopped.

China is investing a disproportionate amount of its resources on asymmetric capabilities in the hopes of building an Assassin's Mace. Defectors in the late 1990s and early 2000s referred to new military technologies that the People's Liberation Army was developing that could be used "beyond Taiwan," meaning that the scenario planned for and gamed out by U.S. strategists wasn't necessarily the most likely eventuality. One defector in particular referred excitedly to *shashoujian* to describe these breakthrough weapons programs. The most discussed scenarios have centered on Taiwan, including China's development of antiaccess strategies to ensure success if the United States attempts to defend the island in the event of an invasion from the Chinese mainland.[4]

Assassin's Mace technologies fall under a military doctrine dubbed in Chinese military circles "the Inferior Defeats the Superior." For this doctrine to be successful, China assumes it can initially lull the opponent into complacency, or deceive him to act in ways that will help China win. Superior intelligence information about the opponent is also vital, particularly to anticipate the opponent's actions, to be able to deceive him, to disrupt his coalition, to stealthily build a countercoalition, and to strike at just the right moment to disrupt the *shi* and move events in China's favor. These assessments are akin to identifying acupuncture points that, if struck at the right time, will paralyze the more powerful opponent.

I first came across the term "Assassin's Mace" in 1995 when reading an article titled "The Military Revolution in Naval Warfare," written by three of China's preeminent military strategists. The authors listed new technologies that would contribute to the defeat of the United States. They linked military supremacy in outer space to success in naval operations. "The mastery of outer space will be a prerequisite for naval victory with outer space becoming the new commanding heights for naval combat. . . . The side with electromagnetic combat superiority will make full use of that Assassin's Mace weapon to win naval victory." They called for China to pioneer in "Assassin's Mace weapons" such as tactical laser weapons, which "will be used first in antiship missile defense systems," and stealth technology for both naval ships and cruise missiles. "Lightning attacks and powerful first strikes will be more widely used," they noted.[5]

In addition, the authors listed a host of tactics that would be essential against a superpower like the United States, such as assaulting radar and radio stations with smart weapons; jamming enemy communication facilities via electronic warfare; attacking communication centers, facilities, and command ships; destroying electronic systems with electromagnetic pulse weapons; wiping out computer software with computer viruses; and developing directed-energy weapons.

After further investigation, I realized that in the military context the Assassin's Mace refers to a set of asymmetric weapons that allow an inferior power to defeat a seemingly superior adversary by striking at an enemy's weakest point. My first reaction upon seeing the term appear repeatedly was that these were merely aspirational technologies and goals. There was also enough ambiguity in the term to leave open the possibility that *shashoujian* was simply a way of describing a weapon as "advanced" or "futuristic." But as I explored further and asked U.S. intelligence analysts to scour documents, *shashoujian* appeared frequently.

America saw conflict only through the lens of military means, instead of the broader strategic picture encouraged by ancient Chinese thinkers such as Sun Tzu, which emphasized intelligence, economics, and law. "Clearly, it is precisely the diversity of the means employed that has enlarged the concept of warfare," Qiao and Wang wrote in their controversial 1999 book *Unrestricted Warfare*. "The battlefield is next to you and the enemy is on the network. Only there is no smell of gunpowder or the odor of blood. . . . Obviously, warfare is in the process of transcending the domains of soldiers, military units, and military affairs, and is increasingly becoming a matter for politicians, scientists, and even bankers." Two days after the September 11 attacks, the two colonels were interviewed by a Chinese Communist Party newspaper and said of the attacks that they could be "favorable to China" and were proof that America was vulnerable to attack through nontraditional methods.[6]

In 2000, I wrote a study on the Assassin's Mace program for the CIA. A year later, I received a call from Langley. Vice President Dick Cheney and his chief of staff had seen mentions of the Assassin's Mace in the president's daily brief, the update given by CIA analysts to the president and to members of the National Security Council. The vice president wanted background on *shashoujian* and a review of what the term signified. His aide was surprised by my reports. I forecasted a decline in China's exports of dangerous weapons and thought the Assassin's Mace concept was only an aspiration—not something they were actively pursuing or capable of doing at the time. Cheney authorized the further collection of intelligence to learn whether China really had an antisatellite program, a counterstealth program, or aircraft carrier–killer missiles. We got our answer soon.

I know now that the Assassin's Mace is a key component to China's military strategy in the Hundred-Year Marathon. Building such technologies is not merely an aspirational or quaint notion that Chinese military leaders hope they'll one day have the resources to execute. They are doing so now, investing billions of dollars to make a generational leap in military capabilities that can trump the conventional forces of major Western powers. The idea is to keep it small in scale so as not to alarm the West.

Chinese leaders' ambitions to enhance China's relative power through the acquisition of high technology extend beyond the pursuit of high-tech weapons systems. Initiated in March 1986, China's National High-Technology Program (also known as the 863 Program) was a major effort by China to overcome shortcomings in its national security through the use of science and technology. The ongoing 863 Program encompasses development of dual-use technologies, with both civilian and military applications, including biotechnology, laser technology, and advanced materials. The program has also laid the foundations for China's "indigenous innovation" strategy, which is embedded in the 2006 National Medium- and Long-Term Plan (MLP) for the Development of Science and Technology (2005–2020). China's indigenous innovation strategy encompasses the country's efforts to identify, understand, reinvent, and employ certain technological capabilities—for both military and civilian uses—through foreign R & D investment, technology transfers, and the training of Chinese engineers and scientists at corporations and research institutes overseas.

In recent years, China's leaders have significantly increased the 863 Program's funding and scope. Indeed, the 2006 MLP is the country's most ambitious national science and technology program ever. Sixteen "national megaprojects" within the MLP, deemed "priorities of priorities," related to telecommunications, aerospace, and other sectors, have been announced, although three of the sixteen areas are classified. The dual-use character of development under both the 2006 MLP and the 863 Program reflects the fact that China's longer-term military programs are increasingly embedded in China's civilian science and technology base.[7]

Many so-called China hawks in the United States have hyped the threat of the Chinese military buildup, consisting of a growing blue-water navy, new stealth fighters, a ballistic missile buildup, and so forth. War with China, in their thinking, is just around the corner and will be waged in the skies and on the open ocean.[8] Yet China's actions have frequently belied these hawks' assertions. Their expectation that China will strive to create a large military oriented toward the offensive projection of force to dominate its neighbors and beyond—à la Hitler or Stalin—has been shown to be unfounded.

The elements of the U.S. power projection system include forward-deployed intercontinental ballistic missiles (ICBMs) and military bases; aerial refueling capabilities; nuclear-armed bombers; and long-distance troop transport capabilities. Rather than attempting to replicate the U.S.-style system of power projection, as the Soviets did, China has elected not to do so because it would be a violation of the rules of the Warring States–era lessons for China to provoke the hegemon, or *ba*, prematurely. Chinese leaders have studied how the United States had become alarmed at the Soviet Union's military buildup, and how this buildup supposedly provoked the Americans to end wartime cooperation with Stalin and initiate the Cold War and a massive U.S. trade and investment embargo on the Soviet Union. Beijing has vowed not to follow Moscow's example in this regard. To do so would spell the end of the Marathon.

Rather than enhancing its power projection capabilities to compete with the United States, China has made little or no investment in various means of power projection, such as long-range bombers, massive ground forces, and nuclear-armed ICBMs. Indeed, China has actually made significant reductions across its power-projection capabilities. Chinese military spending on advanced weapons has increased dramatically over the past decade. In 2002, the Defense Department's annual report on Chinese military spending made a bold assertion, one that registered in

Beijing: China's defense budget was double what the Chinese government claimed it was.

Why would China misrepresent its actual level of military spending
to such a extent? Undoubtedly, Chinese leaders engage in this misrepre-
sentation for strategic purposes, and draw their inspiration for doing so
from ancient Chinese history. Chinese leaders know that to maintain the
image of China's "peaceful rise," it must keep its military spending and
investment in new advanced capabilities quiet, lest it alarm others in the
region and nations in the West—particularly the American *ba*—and
provoke an arms race.

From now through 2030, the Chinese will have more than $1 trillion
available to spend on new weapons for their navy and air force, according
to a study conducted for the Pentagon by the RAND Corporation.[9] This,
combined with U.S. trends, which are headed in the other direction (for
example, the U.S. Navy will have fewer than two hundred ships by 2050,
most of them small vessels for littoral combat; and the U.S. Air Force still
relies on many technologies developed in the 1970s), paints a picture of
near parity, if not outright Chinese military superiority, by midcentury.
The future military balance of power is slowly shifting, from a ten-to-
one U.S. superiority, toward equality, and then eventually to Chinese
superiority. Congressional testimony in December 2013 revealed that
the U.S. Navy's shipbuilding budget may be as low as $15 billion annu-
ally for the next thirty years, while the price of each new navy ship will
escalate.[10] Our only chance to remain dominant will be to develop superior technology and countermeasures for the Assassin's Mace program,
such as the Defense Department's new doctrine of AirSea Battle, which
combines naval and air assets to defend against adversaries intent on
denying freedom of navigation.[11]

Much of what China has done to advance its Assassin's Mace program
has come from espionage rings operating in the United States. In 2005,
nine days before an FBI suspect named Tai Wang Mak and his wife were
to board a Cathay Pacific flight from Los Angeles to Hong Kong, FBI
agents taped Tai making a phone call to a known intelligence agent in
China and saying that he was "with Red Flower of North America," a
code name in keeping with Chinese intelligence protocol. The FBI found
torn-up documents in Tai's brother's trash. Tai's brother, Chi Mak, turned

out to be Red Flower. Red Flower had been assigned to gather information on the U.S. Navy's most advanced technologies, such as submarine silent propulsion systems, shipboard communications systems, and advanced destroyer capabilities.[12] If Chi had succeeded, it would have greatly aided the Assassin's Mace program.

America has also been a willing partner in developing Chinese military capabilities. The arms sales and technology transfers I urged Washington to green-light in the 1980s arguably made sense in a Cold War world, but many of them continue to this day.

Beyond seeking to avoid arousing the American *ba* by inducing complacency, China's strategy is largely intended to respond to the types of threats Chinese leaders believe the United States poses to China. Many U.S. officials—myself included—were late to recognize just how seriously Chinese leaders considered the U.S. "threat" to be; the accumulation of evidence to this effect convinced many, although not all, of us to look at Chinese perceptions differently. China was far less interested in conventional force projection than it was concerned with countering the American threat. The Assassin's Mace is a key component of this approach.

I was tasked by the Pentagon to study Chinese threat perceptions. Many of my findings were greeted, then and now, with disbelief. Yet these Chinese threat perceptions, which I refer to as China's "Seven Fears," reflect the underlying attitudes of Chinese military and political leaders, particularly because those who wrote about these fears did not intend for their writings to shape popular opinion. The Seven Fears are derived solely from internal Chinese military sources; this was no propaganda effort designed to influence public opinion more broadly.

As China's leaders see it, America has sought to dominate China since at least the time of Abraham Lincoln. I asked my Chinese contacts for evidence of this purported grand American scheme. Several Chinese military and civilian authors handed over a set of books and articles. From these materials, as well as interviews I conducted during six trips to China from 2001 to 2012, I concluded that China's leaders believe the United States behaves like an ancient Chinese hegemon from the Warring States era. At first, it seemed to me to be illogical, even bizarre, for

Chinese leaders to assert that American presidents from John Tyler to Bill Clinton had somehow learned the statecraft axioms of the Warring States and then decided to apply these esoteric concepts to contain China's growth. This is a radical departure from the reality; in truth, the United States has labored to support China's sovereignty, to promote Chinese economic development, and to give China a strong place in the global community.[13]

I was astonished that my own report confirmed a revelation that I and others had previously dismissed as implausible even though it came from one of the highest-ranking Chinese defectors. Chen Youwei, a defector from the Chinese Foreign Ministry, identified several pathologies in Beijing's decision making: reading the worst intentions into an adversary's actions, ideological ossification, and disconnection from reality.[14] Strangely, the Chinese had presumed that China was at the center of American war planning.

China's Seven Fears are as follows:

America's war plan is to blockade China. The behavior of most strategic actors is influenced by their psychological peculiarities: factors such as emotions, culture, and fears. China seems to fear blockades of its long coastline, and the string of islands off most of its coast makes the leadership feel even more vulnerable.[15] Many in the Chinese military fear that China could be easily blockaded by a foreign power because of the maritime geography of the first island chain stretching from Japan to the Philippines that is perceived to be vulnerable to fortification.[16] The islands are seen as a natural geographical obstacle blocking China's access to the open ocean.[17] Indeed, a former Japanese naval chief of staff has boasted that Chinese submarines would be unable to slip into the deep waters of the Pacific through the Ryukyu island chain, north or south of Taiwan, or through the Bashi (Luzon) Strait without being detected by U.S. and Japanese antisubmarine forces.[18] Chinese military authors frequently discuss the need for training exercises and a military campaign plan to break out of an island blockade.[19] One operations-research analysis describes seven lines of enemy capabilities that Chinese submarines would have to overcome to break a blockade.[20] The United States, in their estimation, has supposedly built a blockade system of antisubmarine nets, hydroacoustic systems, under-water mines, surface warships, antisubmarine aircraft, submarines, and reconnaissance satellites.[21]

America supports plundering China's maritime resources. Chinese authors claim that valuable resources within China's maritime terri-torial boundaries are being plundered by foreign powers because of China's naval weakness, thereby threatening the country's future devel-opment. Various proposals have been advocated to improve the situa-tion. Zhang Wenmu, a former researcher at a Ministry of State Security think tank, goes so far as to say, "The navy is concerned with China's sea power, and sea power is concerned with China's future develop-ment. As I see it, if a nation lacks sea power, its development has no future."[22] A 2005 article in the Chinese military journal *Military Eco-nomic Research* states that China's external-facing economy, foreign trade, and overseas markets all require having a powerful military force as a guarantee.[23]

America may choke off China's sea lines of communication. Many Chi-nese writings touch on the vulnerability of China's sea lines of commu-nication, especially the petroleum lifeline in the Strait of Malacca. Advocates of a blue-water navy cite the insecurity of China's energy imports.[24] According to one Chinese observer, the U.S., Japanese, and Indian fleets together "constitute overwhelming pressure on China's oil supply,"[25] though another study concludes that "only the U.S. has the power and the nerve to blockade China's oil transport routes."[26] Simi-larly, *Campaign Theory Study Guide*, a 2002 textbook written by schol-ars at China's National Defense University, raises several potential scenarios for the interdiction and defense of sea lines of communica-tion.[27] *The Science of Campaigns*, an important text also published by that university, discusses the defense of sea lines of communication in its 2006 edition.[28] Some authors express urgency: "Regarding the problems . . . of sea embargo or oil lanes being cut off . . . China must . . . 'repair the house before it rains.'"[29] These advocates seem to want to shift priorities from a submarinecentric navy to one with aircraft carri-ers as the centerpieces.

America seeks China's territorial dismemberment. China has outlined campaign plans against various invasion scenarios in a training manual intended only for internal military consumption.[30] An influential 2005 study conducted by researchers from China's National Defense University, the Academy of Military Science, and other top strategy think tanks assessed the vulnerabilities of each of China's seven military regions, examining the various routes that an invading force could take.[31] They used the military geography of each region and the frequency of historical invasion by foreign forces to forecast future vulnerabilities to land attack, even identifying neighbors as potential invaders. Recent changes to the structure of the People's Liberation Army appear to be directed at improving the country's resistance to land invasion.[32]

America may assist rebels inside China. The three military regions along the northern border with Russia, including the Beijing military region, are said to be vulnerable to armored attacks and to airborne landings, as expressed in the 2005 study *China's Theater Military Geography.*[33] The "Northern Sword" exercise in Inner Mongolia in 2005 involved elements of two armored divisions: more than twenty-eight hundred tanks and other vehicles performed China's largest field maneuver involving armored troops and an airlift over two thousand kilometers that simulated an attack on terrorists who were receiving foreign military support. Chinese spokesmen claimed the exercise scenario was foreign support of domestic terrorists but did not mention America explicitly.[34]

America may foment riots, civil war, or terrorism inside China. Constant Chinese proclamations against foreign support for "splittists" in Taiwan, Tibet, and Xinjiang have become accepted as part of ordinary Chinese rhetoric, but these statements reflect a deep concern about China's territorial integrity.[35] A researcher with the Central Party International Liaison Department placed internal threats from splittists and the Falun Gong religious movement on the same level as the threat posed by U.S. hegemony.[36]

America threatens aircraft carrier strikes. For at least a decade, Chinese military authors have assessed the threats from U.S. aircraft carriers and analyzed how best to counteract them.[37] Operations-research analysis has suggested how Chinese forces should be employed to deal with the vulnerabilities of U.S. aircraft carriers,[38] while other research cites specific weapons systems that China should develop.[39] The Chinese anticarrier missile is one of the responses to this fear of carrier strikes.

Another key difference I discovered when reviewing People's Liberation Army materials and documents was that China is prepared to use what it calls a "warning strike" that would increase *shi* and tilt the flow of events in China's favor. *Da ji zeng shi*, a term that appears in Chinese military texts and is discussed among military insiders, means "strike with force to increase *shi*." While China has historically not used force for territorial conquest, it has instead done so for political motives of a different sort: to achieve psychological shock, reverse a crisis situation, or establish a fait accompli.[40] As in the surprise intervention against U.S. and UN forces in Korea in 1950[41] and in surprise offensives against its neighbors India (in 1962), the Soviet Union (in 1969), and Vietnam (in 1979), Chinese military leaders believe that the preemptive surprise attack can mean the difference in determining the outcome of a military confrontation and can set the terms for a broader political debate (such as a territorial dispute). There was nothing particularly rational about China's intervention in 1950 when the United States had an enormous military advantage—a nuclear monopoly, possibly a hundred thousand troops who could march north across the Yalu River, and aircraft carriers within striking distance. For Chinese leaders in 1950, the calculation did not come down to the traditional military balance. Today, the greatest likelihood of military confrontation between the United States and China may come through a similar misunderstanding, and a calculation by Chinese leaders that a shock strike will not lead to a broader escalation.

Though it is rarely uttered publicly, there is a consensus among most U.S. policymakers and defense experts who deal with China that the deep-seated suspicion among Chinese leaders could lead to a war that neither side wants. Susan Shirk, who served as deputy assistant secretary of state for East Asian and Pacific affairs from 1997 through 2000, has warned that "we face the very real possibility of unavoidable conflict with rising China," given that "the more developed and prosperous the country becomes, the more insecure and threatened they feel."[42] The way America approaches China's rise, she argues, "can either reinforce its responsible personality or inflame its emotional one."[43] Other China experts have echoed this view. Robert Suettinger, a longtime CIA analyst, calls China's senior political decision-making system "opaque, noncommunicative, distrustful, rigidly bureaucratic, inclined to deliver what they think the leaders want to hear, and strategically dogmatic."[44]

To execute a warning strike, the People's Liberation Army needs the *shashoujian*. Chinese officials are highly reluctant to talk with Americans about their military's exploration of Assassin's Maces. When I asked a senior Chinese military strategist about it, he told me that the term absolutely could not be discussed. However, after seeing references to Assassin's Mace weaponry in three military books and more than twenty articles by modern military strategists in China, I was able to piece together a portrait of the arsenal the Chinese are discussing—and building.

The Assassin's Mace weapons are far less expensive than the weapons they destroy. They are developed in as much secrecy as possible. They are to be used at a decisive moment in a war, before the enemy has had time to prepare. Their effect on an adversary is confusion, shock, awe, and a feeling of being overwhelmed. As the Department of Defense wrote in its 2002 report to Congress on China's military capabilities, China's strategy emphasizes "operations that will paralyze the high-tech enemy's ability to conduct its campaign, including operations to disrupt and delay the enemy campaign at its inception and operations that are highly focused on identifying the types and locations of enemy high-tech weapons that pose the greatest threat."[45]

Even though the original Assassin's Mace of legend was a single weapon, today's Assassin's Mace is a whole arsenal of asymmetric weapons. "To build an Assassin's Mace," writes Yang Zhibo, a senior colonel in China's air force, "China must first complete a development program. It is a difficult, systematic process and not just one or two advanced weapons. It is something that all the services will use. It is an all-army, all-location, composite land, sea, and air system."[46]

Former Chinese president Jiang Zemin was a strong advocate of the Assassin's Mace, and it was at his direction in the 1990s that China began the program. In 1999 he told the army leadership, "It is necessary to master, as quickly as possible, a new shashoujian needed to safeguard state sovereignty and security."[47] Later that year, he repeated that China should "master several new Assassin's Maces for safeguarding our national sovereignty and security as quickly as possible."[48] In 2000 he said, "As a big nation, China should have procured some Assassin's Mace weapons in the struggle against global hegemony."[49] And when discussing a possible conflict over Taiwan that same year, he said that "it is necessary to vigorously develop some Assassin's Mace weapons and equipment."[50] The next year, he again demanded, "New Assassin's Maces [are] needed to safeguard our national sovereignty and security."[51] One American expert has concluded that there is a formal program office in Beijing tasked with doing this.

The question then arises: Against whom did Jiang believe China needed to safeguard its sovereignty? The answer, as suggested by his reference to "the struggle against global hegemony," is the United States. In the modern military context, the whole concept of the Assassin's Mace revolves around finding ways to exploit perceived American weaknesses and neutralize American strengths. That's why Major General Li Zhiyun, the director of foreign military studies at China's National Defense University, published a book of articles by sixty-four army authors detailing a long list of American military weaknesses.[52] The book's theme was that the United States could be defeated with an Assassin's Mace strategy.

One perceived U.S. weakness is America's reliance on high-tech information systems. No nation in the world has been as active as China in exploring the defenses and vulnerabilities of computer systems involving key U.S. military, economic, intelligence, and infrastructure interests. According to Larry Wortzel, who served as a commissioner on the U.S.-China Economic and Security Review Commission, "strong evidence has emerged that the Chinese government is directing and executing a large-scale cyber espionage campaign against the United States."[53] Although China routinely denies such attacks, the People's Liberation Army has sixteen spy units that "focus on cyber penetrations, cyber espionage, and electronic warfare."[54]

The first years of the twenty-first century demonstrated that those spy units—and other Chinese cyber warriors—have tremendous capabilities. Major General William Lord of the U.S. Air Force has characterized Chinese actions as "a nation-state threat" and has observed that "China has downloaded 10 to 20 terabytes of data" from a Pentagon computer network.[55] The *Washington Post* reported in 2013 that a classified study by the Defense Science Board revealed that cyber intruders had accessed more than twenty-four American weapons system designs, including "the Patriot missile system, the Aegis missile defense system, the F/A-18 fighter, the V-22 Osprey multirole combat aircraft, and the Littoral Combat Ship."[56] The *Post* added that "senior military and industry officials with knowledge of the breaches said the vast majority were part of a widening Chinese campaign of espionage against U.S. defense contractors and government agencies."[57]

One of the more audacious series of cyberattacks occurred between 2003 and 2005, against U.S. military, government, and government contractor websites. The intrusions, collectively dubbed "Titan Rain," struck hundreds of government computers. *Time* magazine reported that the incursions originated on a local network that connected to three routers in Guangdong Province in southern China, though U.S. officials still offer only generic comments about this and other published reports about the attack.[58]

In the years since Titan Rain, a single unit of the People's Liberation Army—Unit 61398—"has penetrated the networks of at least 141 organizations, including companies, international organizations, and foreign governments," according to Wortzel.[59] In addition, a group of China-based hackers called the Hidden Lynx has been linked to several of the most infamous cyberattacks coming out of China. The Hidden Lynx hackers have attacked tech companies such as Google and Adobe, financial service providers, defense contractors, and government agencies.[60] An American cyber security firm says that the hackers "have the tenacity and patience of an intelligent hunter" and are "pioneers of the 'watering hole' technique" of "infecting computers at a supplier of an intended target and then waiting for the infected computers to be installed and call home."[61] In a related development, according to Paul Strassmann, a former senior U.S. information security official, more than 730,000 American computers are infested by Chinese "zombies"—malicious software packages that infect computers and allow hackers to turn them into "slave" computers for use in cyberattacks that can bring down a network or website with an overwhelming data dump.[62]

Major General Sun Bailin of China's Academy of Military Science has written that the United States depends too much on "information super-highways" that are vulnerable to attack by "electrical incapacitation systems" that could disrupt or destroy electrical power systems, civilian aviation systems, transportation networks, seaports, television broadcast stations, telecommunications systems, computer centers, factories, and businesses.[63] In *Weapons of the 21st Century*, Chang Mengxiong, the former senior engineer of the Beijing Institute of System Engineering, wrote that "attacking and protecting space satellites, airborne early-warning and electronic warfare aircraft and ground command sites will become important forms of combat."[64]

China's development of Assassin's Maces begins with weapons that can disable surveillance systems, land-based electronic infrastructure, or U.S. aircraft carriers. They include electromagnetic pulse (EMP) weapons, which knock out all electronics over a wide area by replicating the electromagnetic effects of a nuclear explosion. In recent years, China has tested EMP weapons on mice, rats, rabbits, dogs, and monkeys. It is also researching high-power microwave weapons that Chang Mengxiong says are designed to "destroy the opponent's electronic equipment."[65] Imagine trying to fight World War III after computer viruses and weapons that emit EMPs and microwaves have incapacitated America's computers, cell phones, and air traffic control centers on the home front, and the command-and-control mechanisms for fighters and smart bombs on the battlefield.

Consider this assertion from an official People's Liberation Army newspaper:

> Some people might think that things similar to the "Pearl Harbor Incident" are unlikely to take place during the information age. Yet it could be regarded as the "Pearl Harbor Incident" of the 21st century if a surprise attack is conducted against the enemy's crucial information systems of command, control, and communications by such means as . . .

electromagnetic pulse weapons. . . . Even a superpower like the United States, which possesses nuclear missiles and powerful armed forces, cannot guarantee its immunity. . . . In their own words, a highly computerized open society like the United States is extremely vulnerable to electronic attacks from all sides. This is because the U.S. economy, from banks to telephone systems and from power plants to iron and steel works, relies entirely on computer networks. . . . When a country grows increasingly powerful economically and technologically . . . it will become increasingly dependent on modern information systems. . . . The United States is more vulnerable to attacks than any other country in the world.[66]

The Chinese believe that another acute American weakness is America's reliance on space satellites. Satellites gather intelligence in part by photographing enemy positions and monitoring radio and phone calls. They are also used to guide unmanned drones, cruise missiles, and other guided ordnance. They are the reason why the U.S. Central Command, which is responsible for U.S. military actions in the Middle East, can be based in Tampa, Florida, and they're the reason why the U.S. Pacific Command in Honolulu can communicate with fleets and other forces across an area of 105 million square miles. In 2004, the United States sent seven of its twelve carrier groups into the waters around China in a show of tremendous force, but without the communications and intelligence satellites flying high above them in space, each battle group would have been incapable of communicating.

For two decades, China has been building a number of Assassin's Mace weapons to destroy or incapacitate those satellites, including a land-based laser that would either blind American satellites or blow them up. It has also begun to build "parasitic microsatellites." As their name suggests, these small devices would cling to an American satellite and either disable it or hijack the information it gathers. Other Chinese microsatellites could neutralize an American satellite through electronic jamming, EMP generation, or pushing the satellite out of orbit.[67]

China has additionally explored ground-based antisatellite missiles that simply blast satellites out of the sky. In a successful test in 2007, China used such a weapon to destroy a defunct Chinese weather satellite. A Pentagon report said, "The test raised concern among many nations, and the resulting debris cloud put at risk the assets of all spacefaring nations, and posed a danger to human space flight."[68] Joan Johnson-Freese of the U.S. Naval War College has observed that China's test left "over 3,000 pieces of debris irresponsibly created by the kinetic impact that will dangerously linger in and travel through highly populated low earth orbits for decades."[69]

Among the more troubling things about China's antisatellite test was its lack of transparency. "China has not explained the intent of this weapons test," said a National Security Council spokesman after the test, "nor has it stated whether or not it plans future tests." He added that China had offered no explanation of how its test was "compatible with its public stance against the militarization of space."[70]

Perhaps the most disturbing thing about this test was the U.S. intelligence community's failure to anticipate it. In the Pentagon's three previous annual reports to Congress about the People's Liberation Army, the secretary of defense told Congress that China could destroy a satellite "only" with a "nuclear weapon."[71] The *Washington Times* reported that the test "raised alarm bells" by exposing "a key strategic vulnerability," and some American defense officials "said that there are major gaps in U.S. intelligence about which other space weapons and capabilities China has or is developing that could cripple or disable U.S. satellites, which handle about 90 percent of all military communications, as well as intelligence and missile guidance."[72]

China has followed up the 2007 test with subsequent ones, including a test in 2013 of a ground-launched antisatellite missile that U.S. officials said was disguised as a rocket for space exploration.[73] Later that year, China's army launched three satellites capable of attacking U.S. satellites, which a U.S. official called "part of a Chinese 'Star Wars' program" that is "a real concern for U.S. national defense."[74] The People's Liberation Army has also developed a collection of other weapons and jammers to upset or eliminate communication from satellites, possibly including lasers, microwave weapons, particle beam weapons, and EMP weapons.[75]

In addition to depending on satellites, another weakness of the U.S.

military is relying on long supply lines for ammunition, fuel, and other resources essential to waging war. In the First Gulf War, the U.S. Navy used nineteen million gallons of oil a day and twenty times more ammunition than in the Korean War. None of that would have been possible without open sea-lanes, which are vulnerable to asymmetric attacks from submarines, sea mines, torpedoes, and carrier-killer missiles, all of which are already in China's arsenal. Partly because of the threat it is able to pose to American sea lines, the submarine is believed by China's Navy Research Institute to be the most important ship in the twenty-first century.

China is also developing an Assassin's Mace to neutralize America's air superiority. The AGM-88 High Speed Anti-Radiation Missile (HARM) is attached to American military planes and protects them by homing in on the radar emissions of incoming surface-to-air missiles before shooting them out of the sky. American air superiority depends largely on the HARM, but the Chinese have already created black boxes with thousands of microtransmitters that broadcast 10,000 signals on the frequency HARM uses to detect a surface-to-air missile. China likely hasn't yet perfected the technology but, if it can, the box would give HARM the impression of 10,001 incoming missiles to set its target on—the 10,000 decoy signals and the one, almost impossible to find, real missile.

Assassin's Maces would play an important role in any naval conflict over Taiwan, because they are China's best means for challenging America's far larger and more technologically advanced navy. To defeat America's fleets, China has built shore-based missiles and aircraft, which are, according to an article in the *Naval War College Review*, "regarded as a means by which technologically limited developing countries can overcome by asymmetric means their qualitative inferiority in conventional combat platforms." China's DF 21s/CSS-5 ballistic missiles can hit aircraft carriers more than 1,500 miles away from shore, and China's supersonic, precision-guided cruise missiles can hit targets more than 180 miles away. "They can be armed with conventional, antiradiation, thermobaric, or electromagnetic pulse warheads, or even nuclear warheads," the *Naval War College Review* reports, and the United States' Aegis missile defense system is "ineffective against these supersonic cruise missiles."[76] The Pentagon reports that China "has greatly expanded its arsenal of increasingly accurate and lethal ballistic missiles and long-range strike aircraft," and it already currently has enough missiles to wipe out every one of the U.S. Navy's carrier battle groups.[77]

Other weapons in China's Assassin's Mace arsenal include rocket-propelled sea mines designed to destroy aircraft carriers, as well as thousands of outdated fighter jets that can be converted into unmanned, remote-controlled kamikaze-style bombs, complete with extra fuel tanks and high explosives. Beijing is also developing what it calls "magic weapons," such as tactical laser weapons, that can disable antiship missile defense systems, and it is arming its growing fleet of submarines with Shkval rocket torpedoes. Shkvals, which have a range of 7,500 yards and travel at the lightning speed of 230 miles per hour, can sink battle groups. The United States has "no known defense" against these torpedoes.[78] A 2001 article in *Junshi Wenzhai*, a Chinese military journal, discussed how "sea mine emplacement, timely jamming, and electronic confusion, submarine ambush, focused surprise attack with guided missiles, and [other] raids which take the enemy by surprise" could destroy an American fleet.[79]

In short, whether it involves fighting an enemy army, navy, or air force, China's "operational theory," as the Pentagon has reported, calls for "destroying the enemy command system; crippling the enemy information systems; destroying the enemy's most advanced weapons systems; crippling the enemy support (logistics) systems; and denying the enemy the synergies that accrue from its technological superiority."[80] To use a metaphor the Chinese use, Beijing's strategy is to be like the boxer who uses his knowledge of vital body points to knock out a bigger opponent. Americans are more familiar with Greek mythology's similar story of a powerful warrior with a weak spot. For two decades, the Chinese have been building arrows designed to find a singular target—the Achilles' heel of the United States.

Some hawks told me in Beijing in 2013 that they could not gauge clearly how serious America may be about President Obama's so-called "rebalance" and "pivot" to Asia.[81] They seemed worried whether China might have miscalculated, and whether America would overreact to the

Assassin's Mace program by building stronger forces aimed at China. If America continues its current plan to reduce defense spending by $1 trillion over the next decade, the Chinese said, there will be no money to fund any "rebalance." I replied by telling the truth: it is hard to predict if U.S. defense spending will be increased to deal with China.

8

THE CAPITALIST CHARADE

"Take the opportunity to pilfer a goat."
—*The Thirty-Six Stratagems*

In 2005, a Chinese defector I will call Ms. Tang confirmed for us the economic component of China's Marathon strategy—to compete with and surpass the United States as the world's leading economic power. Senior Chinese Communist Party officials, from at least the vice-ministerial level up, were studying strategy at a secret program at the Party's Central Committee School, on a campus in downtown Beijing. The cohort included future military generals, and completing the program was mandatory for promotion. The curriculum included studies of ancient history lessons. More important, the defector confided that the faculty used translations of at least six books on how America had become the largest economy in the world through a two-century-long strategy, and how China could follow America's example, but on a faster pace.[1]

She said the key lessons were from Charles Darwin, and concerned the ways the U.S. government had supported corporations to help surpass both Germany and Great Britain during the period from 1840 to World War I. This, the courses taught, was a significant part of how America became the hegemon—and it was what China needed to do if it sought to surpass the United States. She said the course examined roughly twenty case studies that discussed how Chinese leaders had learned and applied lessons from the history of many American companies in different industries, with a focus on the strategic role played by the U.S. government.

The U.S. strategies examined included protection of the domestic market, financial subsidies of domestic companies, and export promotion. The course examined America's practice of enforcing antitrust measures to intensify competition, another American example China has followed. The American system of securities regulation attracted more capital from investors and made the United States the home of the largest and most efficient market in the world. She added that the overarching lesson was that government-fostered industry expanded the overall size of the American market. During the nineteenth and early twentieth centuries, the United States promoted big business firms to increase their markets, in part via subsidies. Chinese Party officials were taught that the Americans stole the technology for the automatic, gradual reduction mills in which carloads of wheat and oats were processed into flour and cereals. The first firm to use this stolen European technology was the Pillsbury Company, for flour, she said with a laugh, looking squarely at me.[2] The U.S. government supposedly helped brewers such as Anheuser-Busch, soft drink makers such as Coca-Cola, and others to build factories abroad. I knew some of this was true.

The United States overtook Germany's leadership in the paper industry with new technology following mergers fostered by the U.S. government in 1900, the course taught. Similarly, in the steel industry, America's government somehow aided Andrew Carnegie to become the steel industry's first hegemonic leader, in 1879. Next, the Americans decided to dominate the production of copper and aluminum by acquiring European technology. The Americans then came to dominate the rubber and oil industries in the 1880s.[3] B. F. Goodrich became the world leader with U.S. government help.

Before World War I, the Americans had nearly completed their strategic goal of usurping world leadership from Europe. Part of this story was the formation of General Electric in the mid-1890s, also supposedly fostered by the U.S. government to outperform the German companies Siemens and AEG. General Electric supposedly stole from Siemens and AEG the idea to form a credit company to take payment in stock from the many utility companies it equipped.

The second phase of the story, or "second wave," as she called it, was the period from 1914 to 1950, when the Americans came to dominate the new automobile, electronics, and pharmaceutical industries. The U.S. government was supposedly particularly close to General Motors, and helped it to develop diesel locomotives, which made the steam locomotives used in Europe obsolete. She also said the American government supported the five American oil firms in their efforts to outmaneuver British Petroleum and Royal Dutch Shell in access to foreign oil reserves. She said the Chinese Communist Party leaders were taught how the Americans had exploited the patents of German pharmaceutical technologies that produced aspirin, antibiotics, and Novocain.

After World War II, the "third wave" of American government support to its massive corporations was supposedly focused on dominating the aerospace and petrochemical industries. DuPont acquired, possibly through coercion, the patent from the British Imperial Chemical Industries for polymers.[4] She also discussed the role of the U.S. government in fostering new pharmaceutical products, such as in 1942, when Merck marketed the first industrially manufactured penicillin.

I asked if the word "marathon" was ever used in the course. Yes, she told me, and said that I needed to find a translated book in the Central Party School bookstore called *Innovation Marathon: Lessons from High-Technology Firms.* It was there—written by Marianne Glimek and Claudia Bird Schoonover and published by Oxford University Press in 1990. Another book that discussed the marathon concept, she said, was called *Computer Wars: How the West Can Win in a Post-IBM World,* written by Charles R. Morris and Charles H. Ferguson.[5]

So, I asked, did the United States provide the model for saving the Soviet-style state-run companies? Oh, no, she said. America does not have such companies, except for the Tennessee Valley Authority. All those ideas for China's strategy came from the World Bank, she said. Our brief conversation had extended to over an hour. My notebook was full. It was time to visit the economists at the World Bank's office tower in Beijing.

Chinese leaders over the past two decades have persuaded the world that the nation is on the path toward economic freedom, replete with private property rights and a free market. Covers of *Time* and *Newsweek* boast of China taking "the capitalist road," with Western-style democracy following behind. China's vigorous pursuit of modernization since 1978, assisted by the World Bank and other Western institutions, has achieved remarkable success. China has enjoyed a nearly constant economic boom for more than thirty years. Despite minor fluctuations over this period, its economy has grown at a rate roughly three times the global average. Since 2001, China's annual rate of growth has averaged 10.1 percent. In 1980, China's nominal GDP was about $70 billion. By 2011 it had risen to more than $7 trillion.[6] An economic backwater in 1980, China now boasts the world's second-largest economy, behind only the United States. Some ninety-five Chinese corporations appear on the 2014 Fortune Global 500 list.[7] Five of these are in the top fifty.[8] In 2000, there had been none. China is now the world's largest producer of automobiles, the largest energy user, and the largest emitter of carbon dioxide.[9] It remains the world's most populous country, with a population of 1.35 billion, despite significant efforts to limit population growth.[10]

This is nothing short of an economic miracle, and the West—including the United States—is largely responsible for it. Media and political commentators hailed the movement of China toward a capitalist, free market economy—although China was doing anything but. By 2014, roughly half of China's economy would still be in the government's hands, decades after the myth that capitalism had arrived.

According to most Western experts, that is attributable to modest reforms and a willingness to keep the currency artificially low, which allows for cheap labor, cheap manufacturing, and the undercutting of Western prices.[11] Yet what has accelerated Chinese growth more than anything is not reform at all, but a commitment to subsidizing state-owned enterprises (SOEs), which still comprise 40 percent of China's GDP.[12] These SOEs, or "national champions," as they are known inside the halls of government in Beijing, are a vital component of the Hundred-Year Marathon. Despite their inefficiencies, they have successfully undercut Western competitors to help fuel the nation's economic rise.[13] This commitment to a ruthless brand of mercantilism traces back to China's earliest days, when competing governments in the Warring States era used state-controlled economics as an extension of warfare.

China's economy remains misunderstood. The world's leading economists plead some ignorance about how China's economic juggernaut really works, which is one reason why China has been able to claim that they are making steps toward economic liberalization, without much scrutiny or pushback. Ronald Coase, a Nobel laureate in economics, and Ning Wang warned in 2013, "There is still much we don't know about China's market transformation. Moreover, many of the reported facts on the subject are actually not true."[14] They cite surprising examples of China's leaders concealing their strategy and telling foreign leaders they have pursued more private, free market approaches than is actually the case.[15] Other scholars have noted a consistent spin about how China explains its strategy of "going capitalist" in a way that feeds wishful thinking.

In other meetings, China played down its growth prospects after learning from internal estimates in the early 1990s that its GDP would surpass that of the United States by 2020 or so. Why would China conceal strategic elements of its successful thirty years of economic growth? Why exaggerate the degree of movement toward a free market? The answer is simple: Beijing's leaders, drawing on the most basic lessons of ancient Chinese statecraft, have sought to induce complacency by promoting soothing messages and concealing alarming information that could give rise to suspicions about China's hostility. If China's internal estimate about surpassing America by 2020 had been made as a loud, boastful announcement, it might have alarmed the hegemon and provoked an attempt at containment. So, instead, the approach was to tell foreigners how many obstacles China faced and to downplay its prospects.

In recent years, a few Western analysts have challenged this conventional wisdom advanced by China's leaders.[16] They see China pursuing a nakedly mercantilist strategy of subsidizing key industries and government-guided efforts to acquire ownership of foreign natural resources and energy reserves born of an almost paranoid view that oil and gas are reaching a global peak of production. In their thinking, wars over natural resources are inevitable in the decades ahead, and therefore China must buy resources overseas and stockpile them at home, while denying scarce resources to others.[17]

Many Chinese strategists adhere to the "peak oil" theory: the idea that energy supplies will soon dwindle and prices will consequently skyrocket.

According to this perspective, the world is a giant *wei qi* game board, where resources such as copper, oil, and lithium must be obtained and denied to competitors. Echoing a concern prevalent in much analysis of China's geostrategic challenges, one analyst at the Chinese Academy of Social Science writes, "Facing the challenge of global energy supply shortages, in the future China and the U.S. cannot avoid disagreement and conflict (especially on the issue of oil)."[18] Wang Xianglin writes, "Expert analysis indicates, China will face peak oil in 2015: oil production will peak and from there begin to decline. After crossing peak oil, China will face a huge problem: shortages of oil and gas will intensify; oil consumption will increasingly rely on imports."[19]

Outsiders have yet to blow the whistle on China for conveying these misleading messages. Instead, China's false narrative has largely been accepted. Many believed that Mao Zedong's old command system that killed all the sparrows had now been used to order the embrace of free enterprise and a trade policy of abiding by international rules. Chinese leaders knew that they had alienated and alarmed the Soviet Union with their boasting, which had led Moscow to cut off all aid to China. They would avoid similarly offending the West, for they had learned to never again attempt a "kill the sparrows campaign." They would instead persuade Western leaders that China now wanted to be like the West. This charade was not as hard to pull off as you might think.

Along with rats, flies, and mosquitoes, sparrows were one of four "pests" that, in Mao's thinking, posed a threat to hygiene—and economic progress—in China. "The Great Sparrow Campaign" of 1958, part of the Great Leap Forward, was born of a burning desire to move China's agrarian economy into the twentieth century. Mao and his top advisers reasoned that the sparrows consumed thousands of tons of grain that could be used to feed the Chinese people and fuel the communes and mass industrialization that were the centerpieces of China's competitive drive to bring its economy on a par with those of the West. Farmers fanned out across the countryside, tearing down nests, breaking eggs, and chasing flocks of sparrows with pots and pans. The campaign was devastatingly effective. By 1959, sparrows were nearly exterminated in China.

What the Chinese authorities hadn't realized was that, in addition to grains, insects constituted a large component of the sparrows' diet. In the following years, without sparrows as predators, locusts ravaged harvests—and this was compounded by severe droughts. Between 1958 and 1961, more than thirty million Chinese perished due to famine. Communist China's first major experiment to make itself economically competitive relative to the West had failed.

When Deng Xiaoping became China's "paramount leader" in 1978 and contemplated his nation's economic backwardness under Mao, he vowed to pursue a different economic course.[20] Deng saw that without a vibrant private sector, China could never be a highly competitive global power. He began pushing major reforms, thereby shifting away from traditional Marxism-Leninism by degrees. Summarized as the "Four Modernizations," these reforms focused on agriculture, industry, technology, and the military. Among the most important were those that integrated national planning with market forces in the service of "socialism with Chinese characteristics."

Today most outsiders believe that Mao's command system has given way to an embrace of free enterprise and a trade policy of abiding by international rules. Because of a largely credulous community of international bankers, academics, and think tank experts, China has gotten away with this message that it aspires to be more and more like the West. But a closer look at China's economy reveals something entirely different.

In October 2001, the Pentagon allowed me to hold a second job, and I joined the newly created U.S.-China Congressional Commission as its first "senior research adviser." The commission had been created as part of an effort to get more votes in the U.S. Senate for legislation allowing China to join the World Trade Organization. Our mission was set out in the law that established our group: we sought to determine the effect of Chinese economic policy on U.S. national security. Democrats were especially suspicious of China's intentions as it sought WTO membership and the claim frequently made by free market voices that trade would inevitably bring democracy to China.

The commission's chairman and I received CIA briefings that emphasized two points, both later proved wrong: the first was that China was moving toward a free market economy and would sell off all of its massive government-run corporations, and the second was that there was no chance China would surpass the United States economically, and even if it did—by, say, the year 2100—China would be a free-market, peace-loving democracy by then anyway—at least according to the "Golden Arches Theory of Conflict Prevention" popularized by the *New York Times* columnist Thomas Friedman and in vogue at the time. According to Friedman's book *The Lexus and the Olive Tree*, the theory states that "no two countries that both had McDonald's had fought a war against each other since each got its McDonald's." [21]

We then flew to interview Chinese officials in Beijing.

The Boeing 747 airliner we flew in was nearly empty. The flight attendants were visibly nervous—it was less than a month after the 9/11 terrorist attacks. Americans were right to be worried, but their concerns were misplaced. They should have been more concerned about the country we were flying toward.

China had been one of the poorest countries in the world in the 1950s. Its per capita GDP then was lower than that of Europe and the United States back in the 1820s, when they were in the initial phases of industrialization. Even in 1975, China's per capita income was among the lowest in the world.[22] Within a few decades, however, China's economic condition improved dramatically. China's growth soon soared to five times that of the United States.

In 2001, it was widely believed that China's economic double-digit growth rate could not be sustained. The assessments we had received in classified CIA briefings reflected what most economists assessed as well. Almost all U.S. forecasts of the Chinese economy were pessimistic. China had a poor, uneducated workforce, it was said. China had few indigenous natural resources relative to its population size. It was still in thrall to an anachronistic, bankrupt Marxist-Leninist ideology. For decades, there had been few entrepreneurs in Communist China. Political bureaucrats with no knowledge of contemporary business practices or sound economic management were in charge. It was widely believed that growth rates of 10 percent or more were unsustainable for decades on end. No major country in the West had ever approached such high growth rates, not even the United States during the heyday of industrialization. Much slower annual growth rates were believed to be inevitable.

As one CIA economist later told me apologetically, "Our model was wrong."

Today, the assumptions about China's rise have been reversed. No serious financial institution believes China's economy will remain smaller than America's for long. According to the standard accounts in many books, China's growth was achieved by "groping stones to cross the river," a proverb that Deng Xiaoping cited often to foreign visitors.[23] The proverb connotes that China lacked an overarching strategic plan, and that it instead just experimented before luckily stumbling upon one that worked. China's leaders often used the proverb to explain China's seemingly miraculous economic rise.[24]

However, this improvisation narrative was only part of the truth. In fact, it was cleverly designed to defuse criticism and protect the secrecy of the true origins—and aims—of China's development strategy.

When it came to attaining global economic hegemony, Deng drew on the ancient Taoist principle of *wu wei*—literally translated as "without doing" or "without effort," and operationally defined in this case as achieving a great deal by drawing on the strengths of others. Deng was pragmatic enough to realize that in the post–World War II global economic order drawn up at Bretton Woods in 1944, it wasn't enough to rely on the tenets of Marxism-Leninism. To catch up to the United States and other highly developed countries, China would need to join the WTO and obtain loans from the International Monetary Fund and the World Bank—all of which were aggressively pushed by political, government, and business elites in Western capitals.

The supposed willingness of China, a Communist country, to meet the conditions for WTO membership was still justifiably viewed skeptically by many in the U.S. government; as a result, China's entry into the WTO took fifteen years and was the subject of the most detailed agreement ever made with any new member of the WTO—contrasting strongly, for example, with the far less demanding terms applied to India a few years earlier. China knew that it would benefit enormously by joining the WTO. But would the Americans let them in? When China joined the WTO in 2001, it agreed to accept the organization's provisions that member governments not influence, directly or indirectly, the commercial decisions of their state-owned enterprises.[25] However, China has not kept this commitment. All Chinese SOEs operate to serve state objectives rather than respond to market forces, and the Communist Party isn't shy about directing SOE investments. If a Chinese mining company is directed to exploit a mine in Afghanistan or Angola to expand China's political footprint, it will do so, even if it must do so at a loss.[26]

The Chinese defector who I named Ms. Lee provided detailed examples gleaned from her access to secret meetings, documenting how China had made false claims from 1995 to 2000 to persuade Congress to grant China permanent normal trade relations and pave its way into the WTO. Ms. Lee revealed that China's leaders' strategy was to leave nothing to chance by aiding those who favored the vote, and suppressing information about their mercantilist economic strategy. They reasoned that if Congress knew that a free market was off the table for the foreseeable future—if not forever—the vote would not pass. They launched a program of propaganda and espionage that was more sophisticated than anyone in the U.S. intelligence community suspected. She explained in detail how China had studied American political fault lines to exploit divisions within the U.S. foreign policy community, using as a guide an old essay by Mao Zedong from the 1930s about how to analyze political differences.[27] Among the key messages China sent then were that the SOEs would be phased out, free market policies would be forthcoming, China's currency would not be manipulated, China would not accumulate large trade surpluses, and America's innovations and intellectual property would, of course, be respected. WTO membership requires all this. Also, during the debate over China's admission to the WTO, the China Initiative failed to persuade President Clinton to insert conditions into the trade deal to influence the fates of two thousand to three thousand Chinese political prisoners.

The House of Representatives approved trade normalization on May 24, 2000, by a vote of 237 to 197.[28] The Senate followed suit, giving its approval on September 19 by a vote of 83 to 15.[29]

In a classic example of *wu wei* and studying *shi* by turning the energy and momentum of others to your advantage, China would borrow the best techniques from the West to develop stock and debt capital markets, a mutual funds industry, pension funds, sovereign wealth funds, currency markets, foreign participation, an internationalist central bank, home loans and credit cards, and a burgeoning car industry—all with the active tutoring from institutions such as the World Bank and private firms such as Goldman Sachs. Meanwhile, the Communist government, when it wasn't looking the other way, openly sanctioned and encouraged audacious covert programs to steal technology and Western intellectual property. Counterfeiting became the basis for as much as 8 percent of China's GDP.[30]

Justin Lin, a top Chinese economic adviser who in 2008 would become the World Bank's chief economist, was one of the best sources about the origins of China's economic strategy, through his writing and speeches, many of which were in English.[31] His credibility was beyond reproach. I remembered his name from my two years at National Taiwan University in 1971, when he was elected student body president. Ten years later, he defected to mainland China and earned a master's degree in political economy at Peking University before obtaining a doctorate in economics from the University of Chicago. Dr. Lin returned to advise China on how to restructure its Soviet-style SOEs.[32]

Lin's description of China's economic rise was astounding: Deng Xiaoping had long been publicly oversimplifying the nature of China's deliberate strategy, that market economics are central to its plan for competitiveness. Lin wrote three remarkably candid books about China's economic strategy, which he asserted came from two main sources: China's ancient history and the World Bank.[33] These points were confirmed by at least one other defector, who added more details about the role of the World Bank and how America's free market advocates had paradoxically provided lessons that China used to consolidate its mercantilist approach to the world. Lin's views (that China does indeed have a grand strategy) ran counter to those of China's most authoritative expert on the United States, Wang Jisi, an Oxford-educated head of a prestigious research institute in Beijing. Wang, like Deng Xiaoping, frequently argues that China has no grand strategy and has just been muddling through the past three decades. Wang wrote in "China's Search for a Grand Strategy," a 2011 essay in *Foreign Affairs*, that anyone who asserts that China has a strategy is mistaken, likely a product of their anti-China ulterior motives.[34] Similarly, Deng had told visitors until his death in 1997 that China had no overarching economic strategy.[35]

In 1983, A. W. Clausen, the president of the World Bank, visited China to meet Deng. They secretly agreed that a team of World Bank economists would study China's economy and, looking ahead two decades, recommend how China could catch up with the United States economically. During that period, the World Bank released a few vague reports to the public about the need for China to move toward a free-market economy.[36] In private, the World Bank's economists recommended something different: they explained how China could overtake the United States. Apparently the bank did not suggest concealing the whole idea, and instead pretending that China was going capitalist. Rather, that was a Chinese decision based on the Warring States–era principle of inducing complacency in the old hegemon.

In 1985, the World Bank team confidentially noted that China could catch up to the developed world by 2050. Doing so would require a remarkably high and sustained annual growth rate of at least 5.5 percent. Only Japan had caught up with the United States and other developed nations from a level of economic backwardness comparable to China's. The bank advised that it might be possible for China to catch up if a certain kind of strategy could be followed. No other nation had tried it, but others had experimented with it in part.[37]

The World Bank pointed out that China's savings rate was remarkably high, and that if China could obtain productivity growth—especially via the use of science and technology—coupled with restrained population growth, the ambitious goal was achievable. The bank made six recommendations in private, not revealing them to the outside world because the bank had made the politically sensitive decision to endorse China's socialist approach and made no genuine effort to advocate for a true market economy. The first recommendation, for the two decades after 1985, was that China needed to change the composition of its exports to increasingly emphasize manufactured goods, particularly high-tech products. Second, the bank warned Chinese leaders not to slide into excessive borrowing from foreign sources. Third, the bank economists warned China to encourage foreign direct investment only for advanced technology and modern management techniques. The fourth recommendation was to spread foreign investment and joint ventures out from the special economic zones to a wide range of locales. The fifth recommendation was to phase out its foreign trade companies and let each SOE establish its own foreign trade arrangements. And, finally, the bank recommended that a long-term framework for the whole Chinese economy should be worked out regularly.[38]

By 1990 the largest World Bank staff mission was in Beijing. Without revealing the bank's behind-the-scenes role, China's leadership followed almost all of the international organization's advice. Peter Harrold became the bank's principal economist and was assisted by E. C. Hwa, who had been deeply involved in the 1984 study. One Chinese vice minister told me years later that Hwa was one of the economic founding fathers of China, even though he had virtually no recognition outside of Chinese economic circles. No one I knew had ever heard of Hwa.

In the years following the collapse of the Soviet Union, Chinese economists debated whether to follow the example of the Russians and Eastern Europe, whose SOEs had quickly been privatized with prices set freely. Though American officials did not know it at the time, some reform-minded Chinese politicians wanted to follow Russia's model of privatization. China stood at yet another crossroads. America's China experts had missed the debate in the years before Tiananmen, standing by as two Communist leaders were deposed for being true reformers. Then the United States decided not to support the Chinese exiles in Paris. President Clinton apparently did not even know about this debate over whether China should move toward a free market and private property, or create a slew of government-controlled corporations that would engage in technology theft, counterfeiting, and intelligence collecting to outcompete the United States.

Had we known, it would have been wise to support those seeking a truly liberalizing path, but more hard-line voices, such as that of Zhou Xiaochuan, the future head of China's central bank, won out. Zhou formed an early alliance with the World Bank, greatly aiding China's Marathon strategy. We learned later that, after the Soviet collapse in 1991, some influential Chinese politicians wanted to follow Russia's reform model. We could have backed those advocates and opposed those like Zhou. But we did not know about the secret debate.

Zhou rejected privatization and political reform. Instead, he and his allies among the World Bank economists recommended preserving

Party control of its strategy of improving the profitability of the SOEs. Zhou produced a confidential paper for the World Bank to detail his plan to reject Western, market-oriented economics and lessons from the positive experiences of Russian and East European reform. Instead, Zhou and the bank's Chinese department head, Peter Harrold, designed the new strategy to transform China's inefficient, poorly structured, and poorly run SOEs. They were running large losses, covered by direct credits from the government-controlled banking system.[39] The idea was to save the dinosaurs and turn them into national champions, something that had never been done before.

After detailed studies, the Chinese team and the World Bank economists decided against privatization and political reform. Together, they determined that the most stable path of economic growth was to preserve the socialist economic policies and the political monopoly of the Chinese Communist Party. They rejected privatization partly on the grounds that they estimated China's industrial SOEs were valued at 2 trillion Chinese yuan, and the population was estimated to have only 1 trillion Chinese yuan in total savings, so it simply would not be possible for China's citizens to invest and become owners in state companies. China would thus not take the road of privatizing its Soviet-style enterprises. There would be no private property in the countryside, either. Even in 2014, six hundred million Chinese farmers still do not own their land. Zhou produced a confidential paper for the World Bank to detail his plan to reject Western, market-oriented economics and lessons from the positive experiences of Russian and Eastern European reform.

Some of this debate was revealed by Mao Yushi in 2013, when he was awarded the 2012 Milton Friedman Prize for Advancing Liberty by the Cato Institute.[40] If American officials had known about this conflict between moderate free-market advocates and the *ying pai* hawks, perhaps different decisions could have been made in Washington.

In the early 1990s, those Westerners involved in finance might have been able to name Tsingtao Brewery Co. as the only well-known Chinese company. Today, some of the world's leading companies are Chinese—and state-owned: Sinopec, Bank of China, China Telecom, China Mobile, and

Huawei. While many countries have SOEs, they are usually designed to mobilize economic resources for industries believed to be crucial to the country's economic welfare, in the belief that the free market cannot be trusted to ensure the adequate provision of each.

China has taken the concept several steps farther, building on the model of the South Korean *chaebol* and Japanese conglomerates. In the Chinese SOE model, the Communist Party creates the SOE and defines its strategic purposes. These purposes must advance the interests of the state, typically via advancing one or more of the Four Modernizations. The Central Committee of the Chinese Communist Party selects all key SOE managers, many of whom come from the country's intelligence or military services, and those ties continue as the SOE moves forward. Chinese state banks favor SOEs over private sector firms. With large capital injections, these national champions are encouraged to acquire foreign technology and secure raw materials from abroad. All of these government subsidies, while inefficient and corruption-fostering, give Chinese corporations a huge competitive edge against the West.[41] Almost all of the nearly one hundred Chinese corporations on the Fortune Global 500 list are SOEs.

In a remarkable reversal, the normally private sector–oriented World Bank and International Monetary Fund acknowledged that the Chinese regulations required the SOEs to safeguard the interests of the Chinese government. This was a violation of China's original commitments. Indeed, the World Bank went so far as to warn in a confidential paper in 1993 that China's other reforms would fail if the SOEs could not be improved and ultimately made profitable.[42] The concept was to "corporatize" them, which meant a relaxation of state control to push some of the enterprises to go bankrupt or be dissolved, while others would be consolidated from many small, loss-making ones into a few large, profit-making ones. This is the beginning of what became known a decade later as the "national champions" system.

The World Bank advised China to go much farther—and so China did. The bank recommended creating portfolio holding companies, much like mutual funds in free-market economies. The most shocking proposal of all was that stock exchanges should be established to sell shares in the SOEs. (Stock markets are for private companies, not government agencies.) This arrangement was euphemistically termed partial privatization. Once again, China followed the World Bank blueprint—behind the scenes. Although the United States, Europe, and Japan placed sanctions on China in the aftermath of Tiananmen, the World Bank was quietly assisting the Chinese. Again following the bank's advice, China also established the equivalent of the U.S. Federal Reserve system.[43]

Starting in 2003, Chinese officials began talking about creating national champions, which referred to a secret plan to subsidize fifty Chinese firms so they would earn a place on the Fortune Global 500 list by 2010. They achieved this goal. The national champions in strategic industries such as armaments, power generation, energy, information technology, civil aviation, and shipping receive the support of the Communist Party in the form of land and energy subsidies, favorable tax policies, and below-market interest rate loans from state banks (with little or no expectation of repayment).[44]

Today the state-owned and -controlled portion of the Chinese economy is huge. Available data suggest that SOEs and entities directly controlled by SOEs account for more than 40 percent of China's nonagricultural GDP. If the contributions of indirectly controlled entities, urban collectives, and public town and village enterprises (TVEs) are considered, the share of China's GDP that is publicly owned and controlled is roughly 50 percent, or more, of the entire economy. This is an inconvenient truth if you want to convince the old hegemon that you are going capitalist and that your middle class will soon demand democracy.

China's five largest banks hold 50 percent of all Chinese deposits. In a country of 1.35 billion people, there are just twenty-nine banks owned by the central and local governments, thirty-four banks in Special Administrative Regions, and two privately owned banks.[45] These sixty-five Chinese banks contrast with the approximately nine thousand privately owned banks in the United States.[46] By the end of 2013, China's central bank had accumulated approximately $3.66 trillion in foreign exchange reserves.[47] This enormous sum is roughly 40 percent of China's entire GDP.[48]

Evidence of the long-term performance of SOEs is mixed.[49] Most economists agree that SOEs tend to respond to political imperatives, not market demands. They have trouble adjusting to changing demands for products and services, and tend to be inefficient relative to private sector competitors. They often fall victim to cronyism. Their systems of corporate governance are seldom transparent.

Interference by the state creates inefficiencies in how China's SOEs operate. Without Western help, the SOEs would have languished and would have eventually been outcompeted by China's private entrepreneurs.[50] The SOEs nonetheless thrive because Westerners have saved them. Western companies such as Goldman Sachs and Morgan Stanley have restructured the SOEs and have taught their executives how to comply with international financial and accounting requirements.[51] As a result, the SOEs were able to go public through initial public offerings on global stock exchanges from London to New York, with secondary listings in Shanghai, Shenzhen, and Hong Kong.

Some of China's most prominent SOEs were created by Western investment bankers. China Mobile, for example, grew out of an effort to patch together several mismanaged provincial telecom entities and sell them to international fund managers. A dual listing in 1997 raised more than $4.5 billion[52] for what is today the world's largest cellular phone company. The company is so big that on the day Apple announced it would sell the iPhone through China Mobile, Apple's stock rose by nearly 4 percent.[53]

Westerners have also been crucial to the education of Chinese entrepreneurs and investors. For example, China has lured away American and European business school leaders to help them develop their own MBA programs. The former heads of the London Business School and the Rotterdam School of Management now work at the China Europe International Business School, and business schools such as Duke's and Harvard's are educating business leaders in China.[54] Chinese citizens with Stanford and Wharton MBAs often spend time at U.S. venture capital and private equity firms, where they are quickly deployed to China to identify investment opportunities.

While aware of this economic critique from the West, Chinese leaders seem likely to continue to rely on SOEs, at least for the foreseeable future, for several reasons. First, SOEs have been economically successful so far; China has risen from a basket case to an economic giant in just a generation. Second, China's SOEs provide a continuing role for, and justification of, the continued political dominance of the Chinese Communist Party; "socialism with Chinese characteristics" is a banner under which the Party can rally the masses. Third, Chinese leaders believe that major industries important to China's economic and national security will move in the right direction only if they remain wholly or largely under government control; the state must remain the major player through majority ownership. Fourth, SOEs are a major mechanism for maintaining Party control over the country, as they provide patronage and legitimacy. Fifth, SOEs encourage indigenous innovation in China, thereby reducing reliance on foreign technologies, another national objective. And finally, Chinese leaders may wish to move slowly to avoid the worst of the Russian experience in the post-Soviet era—the selling of state industries to political cronies for pennies on the dollar, resulting in a small number of incredibly rich oligarchs running sclerotic companies unable to compete internationally.

China's latest five-year plan includes a national champions strategy for important strategic, and cutting-edge, nascent industries.[55] China has begun to enter international markets by selling sophisticated, Chinese-designed technologies. This has stirred apprehensions that go beyond the SOEs' economic prowess. For example, Huawei Technologies, one of the world's largest telecommunications companies, may maintain a close association with Chinese intelligence services.[56] Over the long term, many worldwide telecommunications links, including those connecting U.S. corporations, government agencies, and military services, will likely employ Huawei networks. The possible threats in an increasingly globalized world are obvious. Could Chinese spy services monitor or reroute certain lines of telecommunications? Could they use these networks to steal information? Could they create "kill buttons" during a future emergency, blocking crucial international network traffic?[57] For these reasons, the U.S. and British governments, among others, have blocked sales of Huawei equipment in their countries.

China has also deployed its capital abroad to expand its SOEs. The Chinese have even fashioned a phrase to describe the internationalization of their business interests: the "going out" (*zou chu qu*) strategy. China has advocated the internationalization of the renminbi to replace the U.S. dollar as the global reserve currency of choice.[58] As part of China's "going out," Chinese enterprises have embarked on so-called overseas bottom-fishing (*haiwai chaodi*), which allows them to buy up foreign companies at discounted prices.[59] With plenty of capital from state banks, and little need for a return on investment, the SOEs have ample opportunity to acquire their competitors.

At the heart of Chinese economic policy is a superagency called the National Development and Reform Commission (NDRC). It determines state policy for strategic industries and approves major investments, as well as mergers and acquisitions of SOEs. The NDRC has sweeping powers to impose prices for all consumer goods, from bottles of whiskey to gasoline. The NDRC also appears to be the nerve center of Chinese economic strategy.[60]

As China expands even farther into international markets, there's one thing China's competitors can count on: China won't play by the rules. According to a recent U.S. government report, China continues to raise many nontariff barriers to protect its industries from foreign competition. These barriers include "state trading, excessive domestic subsidies and stockpiling of commodities, discriminatory taxes, uncalled-for antidumping duties, and slow approvals of biotechnology applications for U.S. crops."[61] All of these violate WTO strictures.

Not playing by the rules pays off. According to one study, a dramatic example of how quickly China has expanded its global market share has been by increasing subsidies and offering tax breaks, cheap land, and technology in four key industries: steel, auto parts, glassmaking, and paper production—all fields where China has no major comparative advantage, including in labor.[62] According to classical free-market economics, this should be considered distorting, inefficient, and costly. But the results proved the opposite. China in a decade overtook the United States to become the world's largest producer of paper. China achieved more than 30 percent of global glass production, and exports exceeded domestic production. China shifted from a net importer of steel in 2000 to the world's largest producer and exporter, with 40 percent of the global market. After 2001 China became one of the world's largest producers and exporters of auto parts. This was not due to cheap labor, which amounts to less than 10 percent of costs in all these sectors, nor to a deliberately undervalued currency. Needless to say, China did not draw attention to these impressive conquests of market share, nor explain them publicly.

China also engages in counterfeiting of non-Chinese products on a large scale. This includes the unauthorized production, distribution, or use of products and their design or key technologies via unauthorized means, without permission. In 2002, ABC News estimated that foreign firms' losses due to counterfeiting in China stood at $20 billion annually.[63] Others believe the total is far higher.[64] In a recent speech to the National Association of Manufacturers, Thomas Boam, a former minister counselor at the U.S. embassy in Beijing, asserted that 10 to 30 percent of China's GDP is founded on pirated and counterfeited products.[65] By some other estimates, pirated and counterfeit goods based on Western products now account for 15 to 20 percent of retail sales in China. In some local markets, the share approaches 90 percent.

A recent U.S. government report from the Office of the National Counterintelligence Executive describes China as "the world's most active and persistent perpetrator of economic espionage."[66] China collects sensitive economic information (including trade secrets, patented processes, business plans, cutting-edge technologies, and export-controlled commodities) to support its domestic industries. It does so by using both traditional and cyber-based methods of collection. China's use of the latter may be the most robust in the world.

The use and sophistication of these methods have grown dramatically since 2000 because of the rapidly growing importance of cyberspace. The Chinese are sophisticated exploiters of cybertechnologies in support of domestic industries, using cyberspace to steal sensitive economic information from businesses, governments, academic institutions, research organizations, and other targeted organizations. To evade detection, they use rapidly evolving tools such as malicious software, cybertool sharing, hacker proxies, routing of cyberoperations through third or fourth countries, and more.

American businesses and cybersecurity specialists have reported an onslaught of network intrusions originating in China. Unfortunately, the U.S. intelligence community has in many cases been unable to confirm who is responsible.[67] Estimates of losses from these attacks are usually unreliable, but it is possible to get some grasp of the scale of a cyber-based loss. Dongfan Chung, an engineer who worked with U.S. corporations on the B-1 bomber, space shuttle, and other projects, was sentenced in 2010 for economic espionage in support of the Chinese aviation industry. When he was arrested, his home contained approximately 250,000 pages of sensitive documentation. The total amount of information he passed to Chinese officials between 1979 and 2006 is unknown. But all the data contained in the 250,000 pages could be stored on a single compact disc costing less than a dollar.[68]

In 2005, two defectors revealed the origins of the economic component of China's Marathon strategy. Unlike Mr. White and Ms. Green, their accounts agreed completely. Much of China's strategy was a hybrid, not a free-market or capitalist strategy at all, but a combination designed by the World Bank staff in Beijing and a distorted view of American economic history. These planners were allied with anti-free-market Chinese leaders, who defeated advocates of market-oriented economic policy reforms. They instead designed the hybrid, mercantilist strategy and essentially covered it up for three decades. The *ying pai* hawks had won again. We had no real chance to influence the debate because, once again, we did not know who was who.

9

A CHINA WORLD ORDER IN 2049

> "The guest becomes the owner."
> —*The Thirty-Six Stratagems*

For more than two decades, the United States has been the world's only superpower. America's military is without equal, as is its economy—for now. The world watches America's movies, sings America's pop songs, drinks America's soda, eats at America's chain restaurants, studies at America's universities, and tracks America's presidential elections. Most of the globe's seven-billion-plus people cannot imagine a world in which the culture, military, and economy of the United States do not affect countless aspects of their everyday lives. Likewise, most Americans have no idea what the world would look like if their country weren't the leading world power.

It is time to start imagining that world. By 2050, China's economy will be much larger than America's—perhaps three times larger, according to some projections[1]—and the world could then be a unipolar one, with China as the global leader. Other scenarios project China and the United States as dual superpowers,[2] and still others predict a tripolar world of China, India, and the United States.[3]

A factor common to all of these scenarios is that China will be the most economically dominant nation. The U.S. dollar will no longer be the leading currency, but will yield to a multicurrency monetary system consisting of the dollar, the euro, and the Chinese renminbi.[4] China will be able to outspend America militarily. It will be able to exert over its neighbors and allies the robust influence that America has enjoyed for decades. And, at least to some degree, China will be able to shape the world in its image.

What will that world look like? Will it be easier or harder for the oppressed to throw off autocracies? Will the air we breathe be cleaner or more toxic? Will the institutions that protect trade and foster freedom be stronger or weaker?

Some of these questions are, of course, unanswerable. Yet one thing is certain: if China's government retains its current priorities, continues its same strategies, and clings to the values it has held dear since Mao Zedong's rise to power, a world shaped in China's image will be very different from the world we know today.

A China-led world in 2049 will be worse if the *ying pai* hawks decide China's policies. If the moderates and real reformers take over, with Western help, then a dominant China would not be as menacing. How much we can influence China's choices between the hawks and the moderates will be addressed in the final chapter. What is at stake if we fail to bolster the real reformers is the world described below.

CHINESE VALUES WILL REPLACE AMERICAN VALUES

American society is highly individualistic. Our nation was founded by individualists such as Thomas Jefferson and Benjamin Franklin, and a collection of rebels who rejected being a part of the British Empire. We celebrate them. Our Bill of Rights protects the right of all Americans to speak as they so please, to pray as they wish, and to live in homes safe from unreasonable searches by law enforcement. The right of all Americans to chart the course of their own destiny is sacrosanct.

For China, however, personal rights in the American sense do not exist. The literary scholar Lydia Liu points out that an American missionary named Martin, while translating in the 1860s the first text on international law into Chinese, realized the Chinese language did not have a term for rights, so he had to invent a new word, *chuan li*, still used today, by combining "power" with "benefits."[5] The society the Chinese Communist Party has helped to shape is collectivist, a cultural fact that predates 1949. "In China," say two international business strategists who have studied the country extensively, "to be human is to be an appendage of a larger humanity."[6] Although there are numerous references to free speech, free association, and religious freedom in China's constitution, these rights are hardly safeguarded in practice.[7]

For decades, China's government has denied individual rights to its own people. As the nation has grown stronger, it has even begun to interfere with the rights of Chinese citizens beyond its borders. After Wen Yunchao, a Chinese human rights activist in New York, gave a speech at the United Nations, his cell phone, e-mail, and Twitter accounts were hacked in what appeared to be coordinated attacks by the Chinese government.[8] At a U.S. congressional hearing, when Senator Sherrod Brown asked Wen why he was not in prison with the rest of China's protesters, he replied that it was because he was not in China.[9] Additionally, China in 2009 launched a project with a $6.58 billion budget called *waixuan gongzuo*, which means "overseas propaganda."[10] Its goal was—and is—to create a network of overseas bureaus to portray China in a favorable light to countries.

Attacks on foreign human rights groups are common.[11] As Louisa Greve, vice president of the National Endowment for Democracy, has testified, China routinely hacks into the computer systems of human rights organizations and NGOs.[12] The aim of these attacks is to "undermine trust among dissidents . . . raise costs, and induce fear."[13] They are, Greve concluded, "a remarkable extraterritorial extension of the tactics of repression practiced by authoritarian states."[14]

The question is whether these repressive tactics will remain relatively isolated, or whether an emboldened China will increasingly make them the norm. Once China is strong enough economically and militarily to defy the United States and its allies, Chinese officials could use cyberattacks to harass anyone whose speech they disapprove of; many people outside of China, from Asia to North America, would consequently have to watch what they say and wonder whether they'll be punished.

CHINA WILL "HARMONIZE" DISSENT ON THE INTERNET

One of China's weapons in its war on free speech is censorship of the Internet. There are more than one million Chinese employed in the online censorship business.[15] Most of the world's Internet users are Chinese, but because Chinese government officials monitor and block access to the websites of human rights organizations, foreign newspapers, and numerous other political and cultural groups, Chinese citizens don't have access to the same Internet that free people do. To be "harmonized" is a euphemism for being censored.[16]

China makes enormous efforts to erase the memory of the Tiananmen Square massacre. In June 2012, on the twenty-third anniversary of the military crackdown, Chinese censors blocked any reference to it on the Internet in China. When three activists applied for a permit to hold a memorial march, they were subsequently incarcerated.[17] When Internet users tried to get around censors by inserting a big yellow duck in the iconic photograph of a student standing in front of a column of tanks, the Chinese government banned the phrase "big yellow ducks."[18] The Chinese censorship army is so widespread that June 4 (the anniversary of the Tiananmen Square protests) is sarcastically known as "Internet maintenance day."[19]

In addition to suppressing information, the Chinese government employs legions of progovernment bloggers to tout official points of view, discredit opposition activists, and disseminate false information.[20] Their misinformation makes it challenging for Internet users to distinguish between factual news and government propaganda.[21]

All sorts of repressive regimes have abused their control over information for thousands of years. A key difference between domestic censorship in the past and China's potential for global censorship by the year 2050, though, is China's growing ability to censor not only what its citizens see, but also what many other nations' citizens see. China's predatory Internet practices used to be limited to China, but these tactics are increasingly being deployed internationally. China's innovative Internet control practices have already been adopted in at least eleven other countries.[22]

Of course, China may never be able to stop the *New York Times* and the *Wall Street Journal* from reporting real news on China. But the number of nations who work with the Chinese to prevent their people from being able to view such websites is likely to increase as does China's influence and power. For example, two enormous Chinese companies—Huawei and ZTE—are the leading suppliers of Internet and telecommunications hardware to a number of countries in Central and Southeast Asia, Eastern Europe, and Africa.[23] Those states and customers—including Kazakhstan, Vietnam, Belarus, Ethiopia, and Zambia—may well see China's tight political and technological control as a model for how the Internet can be controlled—and may purchase the technology from China.[24]

CHINA WILL CONTINUE TO OPPOSE DEMOCRATIZATION

Chinese officials prefer a world with more autocracies and fewer democracies. Since 1955, Beijing has proclaimed its Five Principles, which prohibit interference in countries' internal affairs. As China's power continues to grow, its ability to protect dictatorial, pro-China governments and to undermine representative governments will likely grow dramatically as well. Like many of China's efforts to further its Marathon strategy, such efforts have begun with the manipulation of news and information. Part of its $6.58 billion "overseas propaganda" project expressly advocates autocratic forms of government.[25] Beijing has officially and repeatedly endorsed President Robert Mugabe of Zimbabwe and has not been shy about publicly supporting President Omar al-Bashir of Sudan, an indicted war criminal who fears traveling internationally because he could be extradited to The Hague to stand trial.

Another Chinese tactic for propping up autocracies is strategic lending and investment.[26] In 2009 and 2010, China provided more loans to firms and governments in developing countries than did the World Bank.[27] China uses this economic clout to advance its political agenda around the world. It is currently spending $2 trillion of sovereign wealth reserves to advance an anti-Western agenda through unconditional lending assistance in Africa.[28] According to Freedom House, "This unconditional assistance— devoid of human rights riders and financial safeguards . . . is tilting the scales toward less accountable and more corrupt governance across a wide swath of the developing world."[29]

Zimbabwe is "among the most vivid and best-known African examples" of the China effect in the words of Stefan Halper of the University of Cambridge.[30] China has been instrumental to the maintenance of Mugabe's iron grip over his devastated country, first by supplying arms and later by sending Internet surveillance hardware and other technology crucial to his efforts to control the Zimbabwean people. China has also vetoed UN sanctions against Mugabe.[31]

One of China's strategies is to form "mutually beneficial arrangements" with African governments based on the principle of noninterference. The Chinese government ignores abuses that Chinese business partners inflict on the people of Africa, with a policy of "just business with no political conditions," in the words of former president Hu Jintao.[32] By ignoring international standards,[33] China may further weaken democracy and strengthen autocracy in Africa.

China has applied the Zimbabwe model in Asia, Africa, and South America. It has supported dictatorships in Syria, Uzbekistan, Angola, the Central African Republic, Cambodia, Sudan, Myanmar, Venezuela, and Iran.[34] When China's economy is triple the size of America's, China's actions to stifle efforts to resolve conflicts and promote sound governance will be far more influential.[35]

Of course, there's a chance that between now and 2049, China will turn away from tyranny and embrace democracy at home and abroad. But there is little reason to be optimistic. For decades, many Western scholars have predicted that China was on the long road toward something approximating liberal democracy; many of these scholars have been embarrassed by their rosy forecasts, although a few continue to hold out hope—however unfounded—that democracy is coming to China. After all, wishful thinking, by its very nature, is often difficult to rebut.

CHINA WILL FORM ALLIANCES WITH AMERICA'S ADVERSARIES

The hard truth is that China's leaders see America as a rival in a global struggle—one that they plan on winning. That vision of our relationship explains why, time after time, China aids America's enemies in an effort to chip away at American power, especially in America's war on terrorism. In 2001, U.S. intelligence discovered that the People's Republic of China was aiding the Taliban, which was harboring terrorists from Osama bin Laden's network. Specifically, two major Chinese telecommunications companies were helping the Taliban build a major telephone system in Kabul, an effort that continued after the September 11 attacks.[36]

When pressed about reports of the Afghanistan telephone contract,

China did what virtually every other abettor of autocracy does when confronted: it feigned ignorance about the activities of the supposedly private companies implicated in the reports. But the companies were far from private, and Beijing was far from ignorant. One of the companies had been founded by at least one official of the People's Liberation Army and had helped build communications networks for the Chinese military.[37]

China's ties to the Taliban extended beyond building a phone system. In 1998, the Taliban received additional assistance from the Chinese government, perhaps because the Taliban secretly provided Beijing with unexploded Tomahawk cruise missiles launched in the Clinton administration's attempt to destroy al Qaeda terrorist camps in Afghanistan—an intelligence windfall for China. Three years later, on the day of the September 11 terrorist attacks, a group of Chinese officials in Kabul concluded another agreement with the Taliban covering economic and technical assistance. These were just two of many agreements the Chinese reached with the Taliban.

China's cooperation with the al Qaeda terrorist network was not entirely indirect. Intelligence reports obtained by the Pentagon in December 2001 revealed that China had supplied arms to al Qaeda after the September 11 attacks. The Taliban and the al Qaeda fighters embedded among them took delivery of a shipment of Chinese-made surface-to-air missiles just a week after the attacks, and U.S. Special Forces discovered thirty of these missiles in May 2002. It's no wonder that one Taliban commander publicly praised China for its assistance, telling an Urdu-language newspaper in Pakistan that "China is . . . extending support and cooperation to the Taliban government."[38]

China also extended support to the regime of Saddam Hussein in Iraq. One of the same Chinese telecommunications companies that worked for the Taliban was involved in violating UN sanctions against Iraq. In May 1999, working through the United Nations oil-for-food program, it asked the United Nations for permission to sell Iraq a fiber-optic communications system. After the United Nations denied the Chinese request—twice—the company ignored the world body and transferred the equipment anyway.[39]

When I was working at the Pentagon during the Second Iraq War, a senior U.S. defense official confirmed to me that the Chinese had been helping Iraq "construct a fiber-optic connection network to better integrate the air-defense system of Iraq. These are largely buried fiber-optic cables that would protect them from a variety of things like weather—or coalition air attacks."[40] When reports of this military assistance got out, President George W. Bush admitted that the reports were disturbing. "We're concerned about the Chinese presence in Iraq, and my administration is sending the appropriate response to the Chinese," he told reporters. "Yes, it's troubling that they'd be involved in helping Iraq develop a system that will endanger our pilots."[41]

In response, China again denied the allegations. "This is a rumor, an excuse for the U.S. and British bombing of Iraq," said Shen Guofang, China's deputy representative to the United Nations. "China does not have any military or civilians working in Iraq."[42] In fact, the Chinese company had maintained an office in Iraq, and Iraqi officials visited its offices in southern China. The Iraqis placed orders from 2000 to 2001, and confirmation of the illegal relationship came in 2002 when Iraq submitted to the United Nations a twelve-thousand-page dossier regarding its banned arms programs. Three Chinese firms had supplied the fiber optics and communications-switching equipment for the Iraqi air-defense network.

In late 2003, a former air-defense unit commander in the Iraqi army admitted that not only Chinese telecommunications specialists but also Chinese military officials had played a substantial role in supporting Iraqi military forces in the months leading up to the American-led invasion in March of that year. "They arrived in the spring of 2002," he said. "They were personally greeted by Saddam. A couple of them grew mustaches and wore keffiyehs [Arab-style scarves] around their heads so that they would look more like us." According to the former Iraqi officer, the Chinese developed a high-technology decoy device that diverted guided bombs dropped by U.S. and Allied warplanes, frequently causing them to miss their targets. "The Chinese devices only cost $25, but were very successful," he said.[43]

Another notorious Chinese friend of rogue states is a state-run weapons manufacturer called the China North Industries Corporation, or NORINCO. In 2002, the company was caught selling specialized steel to Iran for its missile programs, and the following year it was slapped with economic sanctions. Paula DeSutter, an assistant secretary of state for verification, compliance, and implementation, testified before the China Joint Security Review Commission that "the Chinese government has taken no action to halt NORINCO's proliferating behavior." While "the Chinese government has claimed that it opposes missile proliferation and that it forbids Chinese firms and entities from engaging in transfers that violate its commitments to the United States," she continued, the unfortunate "reality has been quite different." She went on to list China's promises not to export missiles and dangerous goods to nations such as Pakistan, showing how in each case the U.S. government proved that the Chinese were being deceptive.[44]

DeSutter also testified about China's irresponsible sales of technology to build weapons of mass destruction. Even though China has signed a number of nuclear nonproliferation agreements, she said, "it's clear that China continues to contribute to the nuclear programs of both Pakistan and Iran." In addition, China has contributed to the poison gas and chemical weapons programs of a number of rogue states, including Iran. And, according to DeSutter, "despite being a member of the Biological Weapons Convention, China maintains a [biological weapons] program in violation of those obligations." Like so much of what China tells the world about its government's programs, China's claims that it has never researched, produced, or possessed biological weapons "are simply not true."[45]

CHINA WILL EXPORT THE AIRPOCALYPSE

In January 2013, a "fetid smog" engulfed Beijing. Dubbed the "Airpocalypse," it lasted for several weeks, during which time residents and visitors "could smell, taste, and choke on" the pollution.[46] China's rise today is like the Industrial Revolution on steroids, although this time around the Chinese have the ability to destroy much of the planet. In fact, they have already begun to do so.

China is not only projected to soon possess a GDP twice the size of America's; it is also projected to emit twice the level of dangerous emissions as the United States by 2015.[47] According to a study by the *Economist*, "Between 1990 and 2050 [China's] cumulative emissions from energy will amount to some 500 billion tons—roughly the same as those of the whole world from the beginning of the Industrial Revolution to 1970."[48]

The results of that pollution will be fatal for thousands of people every year. The Organization for Economic Cooperation and Development predicts, "With growing transport and industrial air emissions, the global number of premature deaths linked to [air pollution] is projected to more than double to 3.6 million a year, with most deaths occurring in China and India."[49] Smog and soot pollution from China have blanketed portions of Japan for days on end. Pollution even crosses the Pacific Ocean and accounts for 29 percent of particulate pollution in California.[50] And, of course, global warming respects no national boundaries.

A major cause of emissions is China's reliance on coal, one of the world's worst air pollutants. The U.S. Energy Information Administration reports that China burns nearly as much coal as do all other countries combined.[51] Even though China has announced steps to improve its environmental footprint, its record suggests that the problem will continue to worsen. China is still one of the few countries that subsidize coal consumption. Fossil fuels account for 75 percent of China's total commercial primary energy consumption, and it will remain the country's main fuel for the foreseeable future.[52] China's coal consumption grew by more than 9 percent in 2011, which accounted for 87 percent of the total global rise in coal use.[53]

As China continues to grow, the pollution problem will only worsen. To slow its emissions rates, China would have to seriously compromise its growth rates, which are sacrosanct to all other policy objectives. That condemns the world in 2049 to—quite literally—"smell, taste, and choke" on Chinese success.

CHINA'S GROWTH STRATEGY ENTAILS SIGNIFICANT POLLUTION AND CONTAMINATION

To stay in power, China's leadership knows it needs rapid growth. If we project the current impasse forward three decades, the effects are alarming. Since the 1980s, China has built ten thousand petrochemical plants along the Yangtze River and four thousand plants along the Yellow River.[54] As a result of these factories and China's choice to prioritize development over environmental considerations, 40 percent of the country's rivers are seriously polluted, and in 20 percent of its rivers the water quality is too toxic to touch safely, let alone drink.[55] At least 55 percent of the ground-water in China—and there is not that much groundwater in China—is unfit for drinking. In fact, the wastewater that Chinese factories dump into rivers causes about sixty thousand premature deaths annually.[56] Of course, because of the state's control of information and its vast network of censors, many Chinese do not even know that their drinking water may kill them.[57]

China's neighbors are already feeling the spillover effects of its reckless approach to development. Due to water contamination in China, much of the country's fishing industry has moved into the contested waters of the East China Sea, the South China Sea, and the Pacific Ocean.[58] In 2011 alone, the South Korean Coast Guard sent back 470 Chinese fishing boats for illegally entering South Korean waters.[59] There are regular disputes like these between China and Vietnam, the Philippines, and Japan. They have the real potential to lead to armed conflict.

China's neighbors also have reason to be concerned about China's spree of dam building. The country plans to triple its hydropower capacity by 2020, which will cause many Chinese rivers to simply turn into a trickle. Because China does not recognize shared water rights and does not share information concerning its water use, China's neighbors will have to either accept a depletion of their water resources or push back against China in a manner that could be highly risky and destabilizing.[60]

China's management of its water resources will have implications not only for Asia, but also for the entire world. By 2050, scientists predict that the world's population will increase to more than nine billion people, and nearly 70 percent of the world's population will live in urban areas. This will have serious consequences for the management of waste and water.[61] This sounds like a purely internal affair for China, although it is not. It will become a global concern when China is three times stronger than the United States. Today, many call for a greater environmental protection movement inside China. It has not happened.

CANCER VILLAGES

The human cost of China's air and water pollution can be seen first-hand in the number of "cancer villages" that have appeared near Chinese factories. Those factories dump waste, toxic chemicals, and other questionable materials into rivers, killing wildlife, ruining the water, causing birth defects, and even leading to death. Largely because the country's standards remain woefully behind those of industrialized nations—only 40 percent of Chinese regulation is in line with international norms[62]— China has produced more cancer clusters in a few decades than has the rest of the world combined.[63]

The damage is not limited to villages alongside China's rivers. Cancer is now the leading cause of death in Beijing, and high pollution is one of the main reasons.[64] China's cancer rates are still below those of the United States, but if China continues along its current path it won't stay that way for long.

China regularly points out that developed nations had their share of pollution problems while they industrialized. But at least two things make China different. First, China's industrial revolution is larger, and so the amount of actual and potential damage is unprecedented. China will soon have the largest economy in the world, and with it the largest appetite for fossil fuels, toxic chemicals, and other pollutants.

Second, China lacks a robust and productive civil society that represents the interests of the people exposed to carcinogens and the other poisons produced by China's rapid development. One woman who lives in a cancer village and lost her husband and son to cancer stated, "All I want is to breathe clean air, drink safe water, and use uncontaminated soil . . . but I guess it is just too much to ask."[65] As Senator Sherrod Brown has explained, "there is no free press to help bring problems to public light," and even when the truth is exposed, "there is no free civil society to sustain long-term advocacy."[66]

As China's international trade has grown, its farming and food processing practices have also had a greater negative impact internationally. China's more odious practices include the use of dangerous or banned pesticides to increase yields, unsafe antibiotics and hormones to improve livestock and fish growth, and illegal preservatives to increase marketability of semi-processed products.[67] These practices have led to bans of Chinese food products throughout East Asia, the European Union, Japan, and the United States.[68]

CHEATERS WIN—CHINA WILL UNLEASH THE NATIONAL CHAMPIONS

When it comes to trade and growth, America is losing to China, and the reason is simple: China cheats. It steals technology, promotes Chinese monopolies, and unfairly insulates its state-owned companies from foreign competition. For decades, it has broken the rules according to which modern nations trade across national boundaries and treat foreign investment within them. China has played by its own rules, and as its power grows an increasing number of countries will be forced to play by those rules as well.

A core component of China's successful growth strategy is acquiring, often through illegal means, foreign science and technology. China has set up counterfeiting factories employing ten thousand to fifteen thousand people.[69] China's national industrial policy goals have the effect of encouraging intellectual property theft, and a massive number of Chinese business and government entities engage in this behavior.[70] So dramatic is intellectual property (IP) piracy in China that a software company sold a single program in China and then received thirty million requests for an update.

China is at the forefront of IP theft, and regularly hacks into foreign commercial entities and turns over their IP to Chinese businesses, making China the world's largest perpetrator of IP theft.[71] This allows the Chinese to cheat their way up the technology ladder.[72] Such IP theft represents an estimated loss of $107 billion in additional annual sales[73] and costs 2.1 million jobs in the United States alone.[74] In the future, when China's economy is even bigger, and when its alliances are more extensive, it will be harder to incentivize innovators to invest in the creation of IP whose value is so easily depressed by widespread theft.

In addition to forced technology transfers, China tilts the playing field toward Chinese state-owned enterprises.[75] They control numerous economic sectors, and are major players in seven strategically important sectors: defense, power generation, oil and gas, telecommunications, coal, aviation, and shipping.[76]

China's leaders can direct the SOEs with subsidies from massive foreign exchange reserves, so targeting foreign markets will be far more common. From 1985 to 2005, China spent $300 billion to support the largest publicly owned companies.[77] Their access to cheap capital and underpriced inputs is notoriously unavailable to their international rivals,[78] and they are aggressively increasing their outward investment. They are on a hunt to enlarge their markets, exploit natural resources, and create more advanced technology.[79]

China has prevailed in creating asymmetry in its market access.[80] The Organization for Economic Cooperation and Development has determined that China's foreign investment laws are the most restrictive among the world's twenty largest national economies.[81] China's antitrust policy is a prime example. China enacted an anti-monopoly law in 2007, but its SOEs are exempt from its terms.[82] Rather, the law is primarily directed at foreign companies trying to acquire native Chinese businesses.[83] Furthermore, China employs a number of questionable tactics during the course of its "investigations" under the antitrust law, including warning companies not to seek lawyers, and pressuring them into confessing to engaging in anticompetitive practices in violation of antitrust legislation.

Another tool that the Chinese government uses to deny companies market access is its new National Security Review on Foreign Investment. Unlike its American counterpart, the Committee on Foreign Investment in the United States, China's law added "economic security" and "social stability" to the list of security concerns and reasons for blocking foreign investors in the market.[84] Foreign companies in China face outright bans, caps on foreign ownership, restrictions on hiring, duplicative testing, and long government approval processes for permits.[85] As a result, China freezes out foreign companies from what will soon become the world's largest economy, even while China continues to enjoy most-favored-nation status with all WTO members.

CHINA WILL INCREASINGLY UNDERMINE THE UNITED NATIONS AND THE WORLD TRADE ORGANIZATION

The United Nations is far from perfect, but it is the only political institution in the world with essentially universal membership. It is also the only forum in the world where any nation can come to all other nations to discuss and cooperate on issues such as health, labor, telecommunications, finance, security, and trade. This cooperative web supports our international political order, but its chief virtue—universal membership—may not survive in a world dominated by China.

In 2001, China and several other Asian countries developed an organization that they viewed as a potential counter to NATO—the Shanghai Cooperation Organization (SCO). The SCO's members are China, Kazakhstan, Kyrgyzstan, Russia, Tajikistan, and Uzbekistan.[86] Both the SCO and NATO have signed charters, named a permanent secretary-general, set up issue-based centers in regional capitals, and held annual summits. The SCO, however, goes beyond NATO's simple security cooperation and includes mechanisms for collaboration on trade, finance, and legal matters.

The biggest difference between the SCO and NATO is the nature of the governments of its members. NATO is an alliance of twenty-eight democracies. The SCO is essentially a coalition of autocracies. Although it is possible that the SCO's observers—such as democratic India—may one day become full members and bring democratic values to the SCO, an alternative future dominated by China seems more likely, due to China's status as the country with the largest economy and military.

Beijing is already expanding its role in the SCO. For example, to assist with financing, China granted billions of dollars' worth of loan credits for members through the SCO Business Council and Development Fund.[87] The SCO also created an International Bank Association and a forum of academic advisers to examine issues such as education, health, culture, and judicial and legislative issues. China's Foreign Ministry has described the SCO as a "successful example of Beijing's 'new security concept.'"[88] SCO members regularly conduct a number of joint military exercises, which are often highlighted in China's official news outlets.

The SCO will by 2050 include three of the largest economies in the world, if India expands from observer status to full membership. Its members will have the economic influence to undermine any global institution simply by not participating in it or by not abiding by its decisions. In that case, a United Nations without the SCO's members would be like the League of Nations without the United States, because China and its SCO allies account for a growing share of world GDP. Some experts have even recommended that the group create a trading system that uses the currencies of the SCO member nations only.[89]

Like the United Nations, the World Trade Organization (WTO) faces the threat of becoming decreasingly relevant. What began as a rule-making body to promote free trade and freer markets has become stuck in a web of emerging markets. China's record of dragging its feet on some of the WTO accession promises it made and holding out on enhancing market access undermines the WTO. Despite these tactics, China still demands more concessions from the developed nations in trade talks.

In a few decades, the United States and other Western powers will no longer have the advantage of being the largest economies, a circumstance that allows them to drive standards and free trade principles. Unless the West persuades China to accept these principles soon, this power shift will be a huge step back from open markets and free trade, and it will handicap the WTO and similar efforts to foster multilateral trading.

If China succeeds in weakening the United Nations and the WTO, it will be in keeping with its goal of creating a new world order by first delegitimizing the old one. As China's Warring States period shows, the challenger often accused the old hegemon of not showing respect for the royal dynasty. The idea was to appeal to other states to abandon the old hegemon and to support the challenger because the hegemon had demonstrated, by its supposed disrespect of the royal dynasty, that he lacked the legitimacy to rule. This was a slow, multidecade process. Today, a rising challenger must delegitimize the hegemon's global authority to succeed. This means that China must delegitimize the institutions created by the West, such as the United Nations and the WTO. By creating an image of the current order being in terminal decline, the challenger can change the system to fit its revisionist model.[90]

CHINA WILL PROLIFERATE WEAPONS FOR PROFIT

For many years, China has sold missile technology to rogue states that develop weapons of mass destruction, act aggressively toward their neighbors, arm terrorists, and oppress their own people. Their clients have included Iran, Libya, and Syria. The Missile Technology Control Regime (MTCR) is an international export-control agreement designed to prevent states such as these from acquiring missile-related exports.

In 1998, the United States prepared to offer China a secret deal I was sure it would take. (I was as naïve as the rest of my colleagues then.) In exchange for effective missile export controls, the United States would "expand commercial and scientific space cooperation with China," issue a "blanket presidential waiver of Tiananmen Square sanctions to cover all future commercial satellite launches,"[91] and increase the number of U.S. satellites that could be launched on Chinese boosters.[92]

The U.S. proposal wisely included a number additional carrots, as well as several sticks. Through membership in the MTCR, China would gain "political prestige, the ability to shape future MTCR decisions, substantial protection from future U.S. missile sanctions, and [membership] would expedite somewhat the consideration of MTCR-controlled U.S. exports to China," according to a leaked NSC memo written by Gary Samore. As for the stick, the same memo noted that the United States would "make clear to the Chinese that, as a practical matter, a lack of progress on the missile issue would prevent us from increasing launch quotas and could even endanger the existing [satellite launch] quota."[93]

China's reaction to the offer is highly revealing about its priorities and intentions: it turned America down flat. China was much less interested in technological cooperation and political prestige than in exporting weapons to rogue states.

China's response also tells us much about what a China-led world will look like. Rather than slowing the proliferation of WMD, an increasingly powerful China will accelerate it. Rather than isolating rogue states, China will empower them. And rather than cooperating with the United States and its allies, China will undermine and weaken them at every opportunity, especially when it comes to its own national security.

Even if China were to join the MTCR, there is reason to doubt whether it would abide by the regime's rules. In a devastating report on Chinese arms duplicity, Senator Jesse Helms stated, "During the past twenty years, the People's Republic of China (PRC) has made fifteen formal nonproliferation pledges—seven related to the proliferation of nuclear technology, six regarding the transfer of missile technology, and two commitments undertaken at the time the PRC joined the Biological Weapons Convention in 1997." He added, "None of these pledges has been honored." Helms's staff produced a chart showing the timeline of Chinese broken promises and violations that had undermined U.S. national security. These violations included selling nuclear weapons components to Pakistan and Iran as well as ballistic missile transfers to Pakistan, Iraq, Syria, Iran, Libya, and North Korea.[94]

In November 2003 came perhaps the most compelling evidence of China's links to a much broader proliferation network, when the Libyan government supplied Western officials with a trove of documents, including a detailed instructional manual, printed in Chinese, for making a thousand-pound bomb with conventional explosives wrapped around fissile material to create a nuclear blast. Media reports claim that these documents showed that Chinese nuclear weapons experts were still collaborating with Pakistani nuclear scientists for years after initially supplying the design information to Pakistan and Libya.[95]

Why hasn't Beijing ceased its weapons and missile exports to rogue regimes? Assistant Secretary of State Paula DeSutter suggested in 2006 that the failure reflects either the Chinese government's "inability" to fight proliferation or its simple "unwillingness"[96] to do so. The latter is surely more accurate. China's goal is partly to decrease the influence of world powers such as the United States by proliferating weapons to autocratic and often anti-Western governments.

No manifesto of the Chinese world order exists to date, but in the past decade two successive Chinese presidents have hinted at Chinese intentions. In September 2005, President Hu Jintao delivered a major speech at the UN General Assembly—titled "Build Toward a Harmonious World of Lasting Peace and Common Prosperity"[97]—in which he discussed the idea of a "harmonious world."[98] In the speech, Hu vaguely said, "Let us join hands and work together to build a harmonious world with lasting peace and prosperity."[99] Eight years later, his successor, Xi Jinping, provided a major clue to the world's future in just five words of his keynote speech—"development is of overriding importance," adding later that "we must constantly tamp the material and cultural foundations for the realization of the Chinese dream."[100] Xi was laying out the goal of harmonizing the world according to Chinese values.

Without the proper context, the words of Hu and Xi seem innocuous. But, as explained in chapter 1, China's notion of "harmony" in the field of geopolitics means unipolar dominance, and as explained in chapter 2, the "Chinese dream" is for China to be the world's only superpower—unrivaled economically, militarily, and culturally.

In sum, if the China dream becomes a reality in 2049, the Sinocentric world will nurture autocracies; many websites will be filled with rewritten history defaming the West and praising China; and pollution will contaminate the air in more countries, as developing nations adopt the Chinese model of "grow now, and deal with the environment later" in a race to the bottom in food safety and environmental standards. As environmental degradation expands, species could disappear, ocean levels will rise, and cancer will spread. Some international organizations will not be able to step in as effectively as they can today because they will be marginalized. Chinese state-owned monopolies and Chinese-controlled economic alliances will dominate the global marketplace, and one of the world's mightiest military alliances may be controlled by Beijing, which will be able to easily outspend the United States on military research, troop levels, and weapons systems.

This is hardly a future worth looking forward to. Yet, in effect, many who have not made the effort to understand the long-term consequences of Chinese strategy are doing just that. Pressuring China to change has become less and less feasible. Unfortunately, our leverage has declined even as a few have begun to wake up. These many potential "nightmares" we could see from the hegemony of an unreformed China by midcentury have all been postulated without a word about the future balance of military power. In the tales of the Warring States era, a military buildup by a rising power that threatens the old hegemon comes at the very end of the story. To go beyond a few Assassin's Mace programs or to launch a real global challenge to American military power must be postponed if

China continues to follow the ancient model. To build a blue-water navy, set up overseas bases, deploy a strong air force, any of this done too soon would be to ask the weight of the emperor's cauldrons. This was the lethal mistake the former Soviet Union made. Even taxi drivers in Beijing know this story.

10

WARNING SHOTS

"Better to see once than to hear a hundred times."

—Chinese folk proverb

At the beginning of the 2013 film *Gravity*, the astronauts portrayed by Sandra Bullock and George Clooney receive a troubling message from Mission Control in Houston. The Russians have fired a missile into one of their defunct satellites, and the explosion has created a chain reaction of potentially deadly debris heading toward the Americans on their space walk. A routine mission to repair the Hubbell Space Telescope becomes a fight for survival. In the end, Bullock's character returns triumphantly to Earth with the assistance of an unoccupied Chinese space station that houses a pod she can pilot home.

Amid the glowing reviews, there were a few complaints about the film's more unrealistic elements. Because of surface tension, it was said, Bullock's tears would not have floated off her face, as they do in the film. Her journey from the Hubbell Space Telescope to the Chinese space station, with a pit stop at the International Space Station, would have been impossible because the three systems are in different orbits. And Bullock would in reality have been wearing a diaper, not form-fitting underwear—the factual discrepancy most commented upon.

But there are other issues with the movie, ones to give us pause. They have less to do with dramatic license than with the Hundred-Year Marathon.

First, Sandra Bullock's character would never have been allowed to enter—let alone operate—the Chinese space station. When Chinese engineers designed their system, they may have deliberately built it so that it could not interface with its American counterparts.[1] They wanted no cooperation between the United States and China in space.

Second, the Russians have never sent a missile into one of their own satellites, as the movie depicts. But the Chinese did exactly that in 2007. Using a ground-based antisatellite weapon (one that they could someday use against American satellites), the Chinese blasted a defunct weather satellite out of orbit. According to a Pentagon report, China's test "raised concern among many nations, and the resulting debris cloud put at risk the assets of all spacefaring nations, and posed a danger to human space flight."[2] U.S. intelligence officials were given no warning by the Chinese about their missile launch and in fact had been repeatedly assured that the Chinese government did not have an antisatellite program. The Chinese recklessly created by far the largest, most dangerous space debris field in history, but the Russians get the blame in the movie.

The effect of these misrepresentations is that the Chinese look like heroes in *Gravity*, while the Russians look like villains. The writers of *Gravity* went out of their way to distort the history of what has happened in space, and the reality of what could happen there. But then it shouldn't be all that surprising: China's massive population offers a huge potential audience for American films—and profit for Hollywood studios—provided the Chinese are portrayed in the proper light. Otherwise the movie would be banned from China altogether.[3]

Once again, due to either shortsightedness or self-interest, Western elites and opinion shapers provide the public with rose-colored glasses when it comes to looking at China. That, of course, is just as the Chinese have planned it.

China's destruction of its weather satellite in 2007 was the first in a series of warning shots—intentional provocations and hostilities seemingly designed to test the resolve of the United States and allied nations and the boundaries of what is deemed acceptable by international norms—that most of the world has overlooked, ignored, or explained away. The incidents have become steadily more brazen in the years since 2007. Tensions in East Asia, as a result, are at the highest point they have been since World War II.

On the heels of the Chinese antisatellite test came a marked shift in tone toward America and its new president, Barack Obama. In December 2009, President Obama traveled to Copenhagen, where representatives from 192 countries had gathered to ratify new global policies on climate change. This summit was marked by a significant change in the public tone of Chinese officials. They demonstrated uncharacteristic rudeness, interrupting Western diplomats on several occasions and providing little constructive input to the discussions.[4] Premier Wen Jiabao had already snubbed the other heads of government by refusing to attend most of the negotiations. China surprised observers by making a side agreement with other developing nations that blocked the hoped-for commitments from being included in the climate change draft agreement, which effectively torpedoed the goals of the conference.[5] According to a senior U.S. government official, the Chinese defiantly organized a meeting without President Obama at the end of the conference to block U.S. initiatives; their scheme was revealed when President Obama and Secretary of State Hillary Clinton intruded into the meeting unannounced.[6]

Taiwan has long been a source of contention between the United States and China, but the new assertiveness with which the People's Republic protested long-standing arms sales to the island in late January 2010—when the Obama administration approved a $6.4 billion arms deal to Taiwan—caused a wholesale rethinking of U.S.-Taiwan relations and cast doubt on future arms sales. China called the deal "a gross intervention into China's internal affairs," a far more combative response than Beijing's past practice. China then temporarily suspended military-to-military contacts with the United States and imposed sanctions against some of the U.S. companies that had sold the matériel to Taiwan.[7] Bowing to this pressure, the administration decided not to make the next proposed U.S. arms sale of advanced F-16 aircraft to Taiwan, prompting criticism from members of Congress, who accused the administration of not standing up to China.[8] Subsequently, the Obama administration has expanded military engagement between the United States and China.[9]

China's increased assertiveness is a product of Chinese leaders' recognition that *shi* has shifted decisively in China's favor and America's relative decline has accelerated faster than they had anticipated. This recognition is partly a product of China's use of wide-ranging metrics to assess comprehensive national power.[10] The 2008 and 2009 global financial crisis, which had originated on Wall Street, was seen in Beijing as a harbinger of things to come. Chinese commentators believed that the U.S. economy would recover but would never be the same. In the coming era, global economic leadership would eventually be more diffuse and less reliant on the U.S. dollar.[11] That China has waited until *shi* has shifted in its favor before acting more aggressively abroad also reflects China's adherence to the strategic element of having patience, even if that meant having to wait decades.

One clue supporting this Chinese recalculation came in 2010. It was a four-page secret briefing given to Chinese officials by a foreign affairs expert of the Central Committee. The briefing sought to answer the question "What is the most important foreign policy challenge our nation faces in the next decade?" According to the notes obtained by the U.S. government, the expert's answer was, "How to manage the decline of the United States" (*guanli meiguo shuailo*). He discussed several tactics that could be used to achieve this goal. If accurate, his account implied that China's surpassing America's economy would occur within a decade.

Another piece of evidence about America's decline came in 2012: the implications of the Chinese reaction to a U.S. government study claiming that the military balance had tilted toward China, as expressed in an authoritative 2011 U.S. National Defense University book, *The Paradox of Power: Sino-American Strategic Restraint in an Age of Vulnerability*, by David C. Gompert and Phillip C. Saunders. The Chinese translated and circulated the book, telling foreign visitors that they would not accept its policy proposals for restraint but admired its frank admission of relative American military decline and growing Chinese power in nuclear forces, cyberattack, and space weapons.[12] Chinese officials told me that its conclusions were a revelation. They said the book indicated that the U.S. government had acknowledged China's success in changing the regional military balance of power in a manner more favorable to its interests. Indeed, many Chinese political and military figures were surprised by American assessments of how powerful China had already become. Based on comments I heard in Beijing in 2012 and 2013, I concluded that this study inadvertently provided evidence for the Chinese officers who had been debating whether the time had come to exploit the new tilt in the military balance.

I was told that many in China's government and military did not believe the book's assertion that "there is little stomach in the United States for trying to frustrate China's rise, encircle it with alliances and forces, or start a Sino-American cold war."[13] Their view was that this was too good to be true and was more likely an intentional effort to deceive China into becoming complacent. Yet they appreciated the authors' assessment of a shift toward China in the military balance. They were also puzzled why the U.S. government would release evidence of American decline and what amounted to a pessimistic assessment of *shi*, from the U.S. perspective. They dismissed my assertions that the two authors were merely speaking for themselves.

Chinese military officers and scholars in several meetings even ridiculed my attempts to downplay the book as amounting to just two authors' private proposals, and not a statement of official U.S. government policy. They laughed and said they knew that one author was a close friend of and coauthor of articles with Evan Medeiros, President Obama's lead China staffer on the National Security Council. The other author was no less authoritative in China's eyes; he was the deputy to the U.S. director of national intelligence, Dennis Blair, who had once been commander of the U.S. Pacific Command. They were sure this was a message, a signal that the balance of power had tilted toward China and that a shift in *shi* had taken place. And they agreed with the book's finding that any U.S. threat of nuclear escalation to deter a Chinese attack on Taiwan is "already slight and will decline" as China improves its nuclear retaliatory capabilities.[14] But they also wondered why the United States would reveal such a negative finding to the public.

It is understandable that America and China could disagree about how to interpret the balance of power. After all, the two countries operate within different strategic environments and do not face the same set of threats; thus they are unlikely to emphasize identical factors in assessing national power.[15] Writing in 1982 about the differing Soviet and American assessments of the strategic balance between the superpowers,

Andrew Marshall, the director of the Pentagon's Office of Net Assessment, observed,

> A major component of any assessment of the adequacy of the strategic balance should be our best approximation of a Soviet-style assessment of the strategic balance. But this must not be the standard U.S. calculations done with slightly different assumptions. . . . [R]ather it should be, to the extent possible, an assessment structured as the Soviet would structure it, using those scenarios they see as most likely and their criteria and ways of measuring outcomes. . . . [T]he Soviet calculations are likely to make different assumptions about scenarios and objectives, focus attention upon different variables . . . perform different calculations, use different measures of effectiveness, and perhaps use different assessment processes and methods. The result is that Soviet assessments may substantially differ from American assessments.[16]

Second, beyond being largely the product of subjective interpretation, the relative position of the different states in a balance of power relationship may be fully perceived by those states only in hindsight. As the great English statesman Lord Bolingbroke once remarked,

> A precise point at which the scales of power turn . . . is imperceptible to common observation . . . . [T]hey who are in the rising scale do not immediately feel their strength, nor assume that confidence in it which successful experience gives them afterwards. They who are the most concerned to watch the variations of this balance, misjudge often in the same manner and from the same prejudices. They continue to dread a power no longer able to hurt them, or they continue to have no apprehensions of a power that grows daily more formidable.[17]

Reflecting the subjective nature of balance of power assessments, some American scholars reject the notion that the balance has tilted, or is likely to tilt, toward China in the future. Michael Beckley of Tufts University argued in 2011 that "the United States has not declined; in fact it is now wealthier, more innovative, and more militarily powerful compared to China than it was in 1991"[18] before asserting that "China is rising, but it is not catching up."[19] Of course, both of these considerations are relevant for Chinese and American assessments of their own and each other's power.[20]

Furthermore, because different states assess the balance of power differently, Beijing may begin to believe it is pulling ahead long before the United States agrees. In the final decades of the Marathon, this could create mutual misperceptions, which very well could lead to war.[21]

With the Marathon on the verge of success, the Chinese now see room to be more belligerent than ever before, while still keeping their greater aspirations in check. Their more urgent priorities are close to home. Tensions have flared in the seas surrounding China, both to the south with neighboring Vietnam, the Philippines, Malaysia, and Brunei, and to the east with Japan.

Since 2010, China has dusted off centuries-old maps seeking to prove China's historical linkage to islands in the East and South China Seas to justify asserting expansive territorial claims. The South China Sea became a flash point when, at a summit meeting in May 2010 with the United States, China asserted its claim to the Spratly Islands, adding tens of thousands of square miles of ocean with rich energy and fishing resources to its exclusive economic zone and extending its territorial waters nearly to the coasts of Vietnam and the Philippines.[22]

Secretary of State Hillary Clinton drew angry reactions from China when she expressed America's desire to mediate the dispute between China and its southern neighbors. What followed were months of harassment of Vietnamese and Philippine vessels.[23] The president of the Philippines, Benigno S. Aquino III, likened the situation to that faced by Czechoslovakia in 1938: "At what point do you say, 'Enough is enough'? Well, the world has to say it—remember that the Sudetenland was given in an attempt to appease Hitler to prevent World War II."[24] China called Aquino's comments "outrageous."[25]

But it is with Japan that tensions are highest. Some Chinese authors regard the Japanese as a "mongrel race" and as a proxy for the United States in Asia. Resentments remain as well from Japan's brutal occupation of China during World War II. In the East China Sea, a series of rocks stretching westward from Japan's archipelago have become the site for skirmishes that could devolve into a full-scale naval battle.

On September 7, 2010, a Chinese fishing boat collided with Japanese patrol vessels near the disputed islands known to the Chinese as Diaoyu and to the Japanese as Senkaku. The Chinese boat's captain and his crew were detained by the Japanese coast guard and taken to Japan, over the Chinese government's strenuous objections.[26] In response, China blocked a number of rare earth exports to Japan, and arrested four Japanese nationals for allegedly trespassing in restricted Chinese military areas.[27]

I was surprised two years later when six Chinese maritime surveillance vessels in two fleets sailed into the Senkaku/Diaoyu Islands region, overwhelming any Japanese efforts to pursue them.[28] The patrol followed the Chinese announcement of an expansion of its territorial waters to encompass the islands.[29] I was surprised because this event marked the beginning of several months of increased Chinese patrols around the islands, with Chinese ships sometimes operating in the region for weeks at a time, often coming within fourteen miles of the islands.[30] At the same time, anti-Japanese protests erupted across China following the purchase of several privately owned islands in the Senkaku/Diaoyu area by the Japanese government.[31] Thousands of protesters surrounded the Japanese embassy in Beijing, while other groups held protests in dozens of Chinese cities.[32] The Chinese government sought to encourage the protests by broadcasting announcements such as "Japan has violated China's rights and it is only natural to express your views."[33]

We needed to do something on November 23, 2013, when China's Ministry of National Defense announced the establishment of an air defense identification zone (ADIZ) in the East China Sea. While other countries, including Japan and the United States, had declared their own ADIZs in the past, China's stood out for its unusually strict requirements, requiring aircraft in the zone not only to identify themselves and provide their flight plan, but also to maintain radio contact with the Chinese ADIZ administration.[34] Shortly after Beijing's declaration, I was delighted that U.S. Secretary of Defense Chuck Hagel authorized two B-52s to overfly the ADIZ to assert America's nonrecognition of Beijing's requirements. I advised him China would not react.

In response to Japan's protests, the Chinese Foreign Ministry stated,

"The Japanese side is not entitled to make irresponsible remarks and malicious accusations against China" and "We call on the Japanese side to stop all actions that undermine China's territorial sovereignty."[35] Prime Minister Shinzo Abe of Japan caused a controversy at the World Economic Forum in Davos, Switzerland, in January 2014 when he likened the tensions between China and Japan over the East China Sea islands to pre–World War I relations between Germany and Britain. It was lost on no one that those two nations had gone to war in 1914 despite having robust economic ties with one another—as China and Japan do today.[36]

A major test of the effectiveness of China's Marathon strategy will be how Japan responds to the growing aggressiveness in its western waters. For at least the past two decades, Beijing has pursued the Warring States–era axiom of undermining the hawks in a rival state—in this case, Japan. China has launched an anti-Japan demonization program across Asia, including focusing on Japan's domestic audience. The message has not changed: Japan's hawks are covertly trying to restore Japan's 1930s-style militarism, and as such they must be identified and rendered politically impotent.

To demonize Japan, China has sent the message that it regards Japan's wealth, and its position as America's main ally in Asia, as products of ill-gotten gains from World War II. Professor Arne Westad of the London School of Economics calls this phenomenon a "virulent new form of state-sanctioned anti-Japanese nationalism."[37] Nations in the "Confucian zone" of civilization are supposed to accept China's natural leadership, not attempt to resurrect old empires or align with a foreign hegemon such as the United States.[38] An August 2013 survey of Chinese and Japanese citizens' views of each other's countries helps shed light on these issues.[39] This survey, which was commissioned by *China Daily* and the Japanese think tank Genron NPO, asked 1,805 Japanese citizens and 1,540 Chinese citizens about their views of the other country. The survey found that more than 90 percent of Chinese respondents hold unfavorable views of Japan, a startling rise from 62 percent the year before. Similarly, 90 percent of respondents in Japan had an unfavorable or relatively unfavorable view of China, compared with 84.3 percent the previous year. Hostility has peaked at the highest level since the previous nine annual surveys. When asked why overall Sino-Japanese hostility had increased so significantly, many of the respondents said that the Senkaku/Diaoyou Islands issue was the reason: 77.6 percent of the Chinese respondents and 53.2 percent of the Japanese surveyed identified the islands dispute as a key source of their animosity.

The next most common reason was historical grievances: 63.8 percent of Chinese cited "Japan's lack of a proper apology and remorse over the history of invasion of China" as one of the reasons they hold negative views of Japan. Perhaps the most ominous finding was that 52.7 percent of Chinese respondents and 23.7 percent of their Japanese counterparts said that they believed there will be a military conflict between China and Japan at some point in the future.

It is possible that China's growing assertiveness toward Japan is actually counterproductive to China's long-term goal to prevail in the Marathon— and, in any event, it is unlikely that the cautious and strategic-minded Chinese leadership would provoke America's closest ally in the region if it still feared the American hegemon. In some ways China's battle against Japan may serve as a proxy fight in the secret struggle against the United States—if it can weaken Japan, it will further weaken a declining hegemon.

In 2013, partly in response to China's increased regional bullying, the United States and Japan agreed to broaden their security alliance, in an effort to demonstrate America's determination to remain a key player in the region. The agreement will result in U.S. Navy reconnaissance planes being sent to Japan, which are expected to patrol the waters in the region, including those around the Senkakus and the entire disputed island chain. The U.S. secretaries of state and defense, John Kerry and Chuck Hagel, personally traveled to Tokyo to sign the agreement. While the United States has refused to take sides in the dispute, Hagel reiterated the Obama administration's assurances that the U.S.-Japan security treaty, which obligates the United States to help Japan defend itself if attacked, covers the islands.

Japanese leaders have talked openly about amending Japan's pacifist constitution, which forbids the use of force to settle international disputes and allows only the minimum force necessary to defend the nation. Usually circumspect, the Japanese speak bluntly about strategic competition with China and the perils of continued Chinese assertiveness in the region. China has reacted sharply to the prospects of a Japanese military buildup and the possibility of a reprise of the pre–World War I naval buildup between Great Britain and Germany. It's worth noting as well that the Chinese have not always been so negative in their view of Japan's military development. Indeed, in the 1970s, China encouraged Japan to increase its defense expenditures from 1 percent of its GNP to 3 percent. In 1978, Deng Xiaoping told a Japanese delegation that he was "in favor of Japan's Self-Defense Force buildup."[40] China was recruiting a new ally against the Soviets.[41] However, ten years later, China's assessment of *shi* had changed, and in 1988 Huan Xiang, Deng's national security adviser, made strong criticisms of Japan.[42]

Suspicion about the stability of Japanese democracy is deep-rooted in China. Many Chinese scholars believe that today, many on the Japanese right "want to amend Japan's constitution to restore the old imperial system." Chinese analysts frequently comment on visits by Japanese politicians to the Yasukuni Shrine, a Japanese Shinto shrine to Japan's war dead from 1867 through 1951, including a number of World War II–era Japanese war criminals. These analysts write that the visits are used for "spiritual mobilization for further aggressive expansion in China."[43] Many Chinese strategists believe that the growth of Japan's military strength is bound to become "uncontrollable."[44]

The prospects of future Japanese militarism worry China. He Xin, perhaps China's best-known hypernationalist author and an adviser to Premier Li Peng, predicted in 1988 that Japan's predatory need for resources would cause it to try to "colonize" China. "Since the nineteenth century," he added, "Japan has never abandoned its long-established global strategic goals. . . . At the same time, in the overall strategic arrangement, Japan will completely carve up and isolate China."[45]

Then, in November 1995, China called for the closing of American bases on Okinawa and called into question the need for a U.S.-Japan mutual security treaty in the post–Cold War environment.[46] Lu Guangye, a fellow at the Chinese National Defense Strategic Institute, went so far as to warn, "The NATO bloc and the Japanese-U.S. military alliance have become the two black hands helping the tyrant to do evil."[47]

Lu Zhongwei, the vice president of the China Institutes of Contemporary International Relations, a long-standing Party think tank, points out, "In Asia's diplomatic history, there has never been such a precedent as the coexistence of a strong China and a strong Japan."[48] Gao Heng of the Chinese Academy of Social Sciences also believes that the American occupation did not eradicate militarism in Japan. Moreover, he argues, because the United States wanted to use Japan to counter the Soviet Union, North Korea, and China during the occupation, "it preserved Japan's entire national machinery and war machinery (although the names were changed)."[49] Chinese scholars have noted that Japan is "constraining China's territorial policy and interfering in China's sovereignty over the Nansha [or Spratly] Islands and the Diaoyutai [or Senkaku] Islands."[50] The so-called Miyazawa doctrine to form a regional forum to discuss Asian security issues modeled on the Conference on Security and Cooperation in Europe was criticized by Chinese authors as a thinly veiled effort to contain China. The *New York Times* reported in 1993 that a Chinese official revealed that the Chinese military has asked for additional defense spending in the five-year plan to deal with Japanese military capabilities.[51]

An immediate concern for China is the Japanese development of an antiballistic missile defense system in cooperation with the United States. Detailed Chinese commentary has also emphasized Japan's goal of acquiring nuclear weapons and aircraft carriers.[52] Also, Chinese analysts claim that Japan already has transport ships that "have the functions of an aircraft carrier."[53] Even on the issue of nuclear weapons, some Chinese analysts predict that in the future Japan, like India, will become a nuclear power. "There is no doubt that Japan has the capacity to produce a nuclear bomb. . . . Japan has measures to avoid international supervision and undertake secret research on nuclear weapons," wrote Ding Bangquan in *World Military Trends*, a journal published by China's Academy of Military Science.[54]

In 2009, my colleagues and I were still making the mistake of assuming that the Chinese think the way Americans do. We misunderstood the evidence of a new Chinese aggressiveness toward the United States and toward its neighbors because it did not fit our existing assumptions and because our Chinese contacts had assured us that a series of episodes that seemed to indicate greater Chinese assertiveness were not part of any overarching plan. I was not alone in giving China the benefit of the doubt. After all, my understanding of the Marathon strategy was that there was no real urgency in making it to the finish line—at least not anytime soon. A series of seemingly random episodes of China's increasing assertiveness became the subject of American debate. China's message was that there was no overarching pattern—or *strategy*—linking these separate episodes. This fit with earlier messages that China had no grand strategy. Indeed, China's leading expert on America, Wang Jisi, had written an essay to this effect in the journal *Foreign Affairs*.[55]

My colleagues and I took for granted that China would avoid provoking the American hegemon at all costs and that it would take at least two decades for Chinese economic and military power to overawe America. All this meant that the last thing that China would attempt would be a self-defeating posture of aggressiveness toward its neighbors and America. And yet by 2014, U.S. government officials were telling Congress there was just such a new pattern of assertiveness. Why had it taken so long to figure this out?

One reason the U.S. intelligence community and I missed the signs of China's greater assertiveness was a total misreading of China's apparent moderation in its stance toward Taiwan. Starting with Hu Jintao's administration in the 2000s, China has avoided threatening Taiwan with force, instead placing greater emphasis on softer and more indirect methods, largely involving economic means, of influencing the island's government.[56] In this way, China has made significant inroads among Taiwan's ruling and opposition parties, corporate leaders, media, and populace. Hu reportedly confided to his closest advisers that it is easier and cheaper to "buy" Taiwan than to conquer it.[57] China and Taiwan signed an Economic Cooperation Framework Agreement in 2009 to normalize economic relations between the two countries, and there are now nearly seven hundred cross-strait flights weekly, with 2.8 million Chinese visiting Taiwan in 2013. Moreover, Beijing has made direct efforts to co-opt Taiwan's business elite, many of whom have become strong advocates of cross-strait rapprochement. Pro-China Taiwanese merchants have purchased major Taiwanese newspapers and television stations, thereby enabling Beijing to influence these media outlets, as well as others that have received Chinese funding.[58]

It wasn't until a trip to Beijing in the fall of 2013 that I realized how wrong we had been and how quickly China has mobilized to take advantage of America's decline, as perceived by Beijing. Beijing's weather was clear and cool, but morning traffic was worse than usual. More than a million residents were headed out of town because of the arrival of the nice weather after a week of rain. I did not want to be late to meet five Chinese generals and sixty security experts at the two-day conference to be held at the Presidential Hotel, seven miles west of the U.S. embassy. I started an hour early and chose to drive by Tiananmen Square, past the Politburo's secret meeting center. Big mistake. An unmoving line of cars stretched at least a mile ahead, along Heavenly Peace Avenue. The driver sighed, and I asked him to turn right along the red walls of the Forbidden City, then left to take the shortcut to the north.

I looked over the notes for my debate, to be conducted in Mandarin, about the current military balance of power. My debating opponent was one of China's most famous military hawks, Major General Zhu Chenghu, who had made worldwide headlines in 2005 when he revealed China's nuclear war scenarios for retaliation against a U.S. attack.[59] Fittingly, one subject for the conference was the future nuclear balance, and the prospects for arms control. Another hawk, Major General Peng Guangqian, the author of China's classic textbook *Science of Strategy*, would be speaking about how to assess the balance of power. Chinese law professors would outline Beijing's claims to the South China Sea.

My driver made it in time, and I distributed copies of my speech for the conference in both English and Chinese with its newly stamped seal, which read, "Cleared for Public Release by Office of the Secretary of Defense." The speech was designed to provoke reactions during the two-day conference, a tactic I had followed at three earlier Chinese military conferences. The proverb for the tactic is "toss a brick to get back jade." This conference was a rare opportunity to obtain authoritative Chinese views about how the Marathon would be played out during the next thirty-five years. A Chinese defector had previously told me an allegory about the Hundred-Year Marathon, namely that victory in the Warring States system was like a long-term, multiphase *wei qi* game. It took seven generations of kings to win ultimate hegemony.[60] An average *wei qi* game consists of about three hundred moves, divided into the opening, the middle game, and the end game. The defector said that Beijing's leaders in 2014 believe they are still in the middle game, the period when China pulls ahead of the United States in GDP but not in comprehensive national power.

My visit to Beijing had been ordered by Washington because I had been assigned a task to understand what preparations, if any, the U.S. government should make to counter a Chinese Marathon strategy to surpass America. How did Chinese experts in the military and government research institutes envision the Marathon playing out? Many of my conversations over the next two days examined these questions.

I had mistakenly projected the "bide our time, keep a low profile" approach all the way out to 2049. I had reasoned that only then would China assume world leadership, administer the final blow, and roll out its plans for global governance. I had not anticipated that there would be a phased approach as the balance of power tilted more and more against the declining United States. Thus I realized that a new scenario was emerging: China would become more assertive with each improvement in the balance of power relative to the United States, according to Beijing's calculations.

Another reason why I had been slow to see the acceleration is because I believed China's claims that its grand strategy was fixed and designed to lull others into complacency. Chinese scholars and officials stressed that their intention was to exercise strategic patience for at least the next two decades, I thought. Many American scholars returned from Beijing and told me that China did not think the balance of power would tilt their way for many decades. China has actively fostered this perception. Starting in mid-2009, think tanks at the Chinese Communist Party School and the China Institute of International Relations held a series of internal conferences to debate the implications to China of America's relative decline. As Harvard University's Alastair Iain Johnston wrote of these conferences, "More moderate voices—those who believed there had been no major shift in power . . . were not obviously on the defensive in these debates. In other words, the question about whether and how much the United States was in relative decline has not been answered" at this time. "Moreover," he continued, "there is no evidence that the core decision making group on foreign policy in this period . . . accepted the claim that a major shift in the distribution of power had occurred or had given China new opportunities to push its interests."[61]

But some Chinese leaders have concluded that China was ahead of schedule in the Hundred-Year Marathon. Scholars and intelligence officials began to speak of China's being at least ten years or possibly even twenty years ahead of schedule.[62] China's leaders debated whether to make a tactical shift in pursuing the Marathon strategy, a kind of dash to the finish.

Still, China's actions have been calibrated not to exceed the limits of prudence—so as not to alert the hegemon to China's greater strategic goal. Each of these episodes constituted a foreign policy "success" for China; in each instance, aggressive Chinese actions yielded significant political benefits. And although the United States and many of China's neighbors have complained, China has paid essentially no price for its behavior from its rival.

Each of these episodes is a result of China applying one or more of the nine elements of the Hundred-Year Marathon, as outlined in chapter 2:

1. Induce complacency to avoid alerting your opponent.
2. Manipulate your opponent's advisers.
3. Be patient—for decades, or longer—to achieve victory.
4. Steal your opponent's ideas and technology for strategic purposes.
5. Military might is not the critical factor for winning a long-term competition.
6. Recognize that the hegemon will take extreme, even reckless action to retain its dominant position.
7. Never lose sight of *shi*.
8. Establish and employ metrics for measuring your status relative to other potential challengers.
9. Always be vigilant to avoid being encircled or deceived by others.

Looking forward, the United States should expect a new phase of increased Chinese assertiveness. Beijing will push diplomatic demands that seem impracticable or inconceivable today—and other nations will yield to China's pressure. China may pursue gains not through military conquest, but by creating a situation whereby its neighbors will feel that making concessions to China is prudent, given Beijing's increased capability to inflict financial punishment upon them. For example, China may demand that India shutter the Dalai Lama's exile government in Dharamsala. Beijing may also pressure—or force—India, the European Union, and the United States to cease their financial support of the Tibetan exiles— support that has been provided since 1959. Beijing may pressure Washington to halt its arms sales to Taiwan—an issue that has long touched a nerve for China, and one that an emboldened China will no longer be willing to tolerate. Another long-standing Chinese grievance has been its decades-old territorial claims on neighboring regions containing valuable natural resources.

It is possible that China will be able to compel the United States to revoke the military-related components of its security treaties with China's neighbors. Since the 1990s, Beijing has stridently condemned these agreements and the U.S. arms sales made under their auspices, labeling them "relics of the Cold War."[63] A hegemonic China is likely to do far more than merely condemn these arrangements. As China increases in strength and bellicosity, those voices opposing China's growing aggressiveness, like Shinzo Abe's and Benigno Aquino's, will likely become louder and more distressed. Unfortunately, America has shown little awareness of the challenge and, in any event, even less of an appetite to confront it.

11

AMERICA AS A WARRING STATE

> "Steal the firewood from under the cauldron."
> —*The Thirty-Six Stratagems*

It's easy to win a race when you're the only one who knows it has begun. China is thus on its way to supplanting the United States as the global hegemon, creating a different world as a result. Yet it doesn't have to end this way. The People's Republic of China may stand as the most serious and strategically brilliant challenge America has faced, but it is not the only one.

Not long ago, the United States beat back the threat posed by another major power with designs on global dominance. It won the Cold War with a collection of programs and tactics that drew bipartisan support. A similar approach could form the core of a strategy for defeating, or at least restraining, China's outsize ambitions. One idea for doing that, of course, is for policymakers to recognize the achievements of China by adapting its wisdom and strategies for themselves. While some of the lessons of ancient Chinese statecraft are best applied by a weaker state against a stronger one, there are insights in Chinese strategic culture that apply to interstate relations more broadly. You don't have to be German to apply the ideas of Clausewitz on the battlefield; in the same spirit, the United States can adapt a few Chinese concepts from the Warring States era to beat China at its own game.

STEP 1—RECOGNIZE THE PROBLEM

The China that Beijing's leaders want us to see is not the real China. America's political and opinion leaders need to distinguish between the "messages" they are sent by the Chinese versus the underlying reality. Sun Tzu and Confucius agreed on the necessity of discerning appearance from reality. Even though he was one of its biggest advocates, Sun Tzu warned against falling for deception by clever adversaries. Confucius advocated the supreme importance of calling things by their correct names, what he called *zheng ming*, as the foundation for correct strategy. Put simply, know what the opponent is trying to make you think about his nature; do not accept appearances at face value.

It has been foolish to accept stories about China's overwhelming obstacles to growth only to discover that China's economy has tripled in size between 1997 and 2007 alone,[1] just as it has been foolish to accept repeated assurances by Beijing that it will support freer trade, move to combat intellectual property theft, and end its currency manipulation practices. It has also been foolish to be told repeatedly by Chinese leaders that China seeks a partnership with America and to ignore that the government sanctions and encourages America's demonization, just as it has been foolish to be promised assistance against North Korea and Iran and to later learn that both regimes are sustained and supported by Beijing.

If America is going to compete in the Marathon, its thinking about China must change radically. This means recognizing that China is a competitor, not a welfare case. It means learning how Chinese leaders think by studying *shi*, the Warring States period, and the strategies for toppling a hegemon. It also means recognizing how the Chinese government is translating those ideas into actions. A long list of policies and strategies will need to be examined.

STEP 2—KEEP TRACK OF YOUR GIFTS

Every year, a small fortune of American tax dollars is being spent to aid China's rise. Most of this aid is kept low-profile, unnoticed by the media and the public. This is done intentionally.

Testifying before Congress in 2005, a State Department official disclosed many of the unknown ways America is aiding China. He discussed the many Labor Department experts who the U.S. government had sent to China to boost Chinese productivity. He talked about the support that the Treasury Department and the comptroller of the currency offered China to improve its banking practices. He outlined the Federal Aviation Administration's assistance to Chinese aircraft manufacturers. And he documented how other U.S. government agencies have facilitated hundreds of science assistance programs in China.

After the hearing, the diplomat took me aside. Knowing of my background in Sino-American relations as well as my position as a congressional staff member, he asked, "Can you make this annual testimony requirement go away?" I wondered why he wanted to be excused from future testimony. "The more you get this out, the better known it will become and the more likely congressional critics of China will try to eliminate it," he said. "Such cuts will set back our relations with China three decades."

There is still no available accounting of all the activities funded by the U.S. government to aid China. Not only is America funding its own chief opponent; it doesn't even keep track of how much is being spent to do it.

To compete in the Marathon, Congress should enact an annual reporting requirement of all agencies and departments of their assistance to China. If such programs were identified and publicized, three beneficial results would follow. First, Americans seeking a more skeptical, cautious approach in U.S.-China relations would be armed with information against the vast majority of academics, analysts, and government elites pushing for more aid to and support of Beijing. Second, identifying the large areas in which America is assisting China would allow policymakers to have a better sense of what leverage we have to influence Beijing's behavior. And third, Americans can use this list to counter the allegations in Chinese history textbooks (discussed in chapter 5) that claim that American presidents since John Tyler have sought to contain and hurt China.

STEP 3—MEASURE COMPETITIVENESS

Many of the Warring States stories involve carefully measuring the balance of power before strategies are chosen. It is a classic American business principle that "What you measure improves." The lesson is simple but profound: You can't improve unless you know what you need to improve. You can't come from behind in a race against your competitors unless you know the respects in which you have fallen behind. Every year, the Chinese create an annual analysis of their competitiveness relative to the United States. Why isn't America doing the same thing?

The nonprofit Council on Competitiveness, established in 1986, seeks to bolster America's global economic competitiveness. It brings together CEOs, university presidents, the heads of national labor organizations, and prominent research institutions. The council's publications detail how the United States will drop in manufacturing competitiveness through at least 2017, while China will remain number one, due to factors such as Beijing's high levels of investment in manufacturing and industry.[2]

The U.S. government should be conducting a similar—but more robust—measure of American competitiveness. The White House should provide Congress with an annual report that includes trends and forecasts about how the United States is faring relative to its chief rivals. Many departments of the U.S. government, including the intelligence community, would have to be involved. It need not cover all other nations, just the top ten—beginning with China.

STEP 4—DEVELOP A COMPETITIVENESS STRATEGY

Stratagems of the Warring States frequently describes how leaders compete by adopting "reforms" to grow their power more rapidly than their competition. The point was to be open-minded enough to recognize and act when one's strategy needed to change, and then impose new tactics to achieve one's desired result.

Kent Hughes, the director of the Woodrow Wilson Center's Program on America and the Global Economy and the former president of the Council on Competitiveness, compares the challenge posed by China's technological rise to the Soviet launch of the Sputnik satellite in 1957. He notes that while the launch was viewed as a challenge to America's technological and military dominance, it also spurred U.S. investment in its engineering and science education and private sector innovation. China's rise has yet to stimulate a similarly robust response. Hughes has put forward a number of promising policy proposals to remain competitive. These include collaboration between the U.S. private and public sectors to increase competitiveness; fiscal and monetary reform; technological innovation; the creation of a lifelong learning culture;[3] and increased U.S. civilian research and development.[4] Similarly, Ralph Gomory of New York University, a former vice president at IBM, suggests countering China's "massive government subsidies of land, energy and technology, in addition to low- or no-cost loans" by promoting a "real manufacturing renaissance in America."[5] Patrick Mulloy of the China Commission also details the need for a new national competitiveness strategy because "overall the situation poses a long-term threat to America's economic primacy and even our national security."[6]

The public policy analysts Robert Atkinson and Stephen Ezell have proposed a multiagency program to enhance American competitiveness, but they fear that it will be hampered or eliminated because of partisan political considerations. They warn conservatives that "the Right is almost hypersensitive to any perceived relative decline in America's global lead in military might, but is strangely oblivious to the deleterious impact that America's declining economic position will have on its security in general and defense capacity in particular." As for those on the left, Atkinson and Ezell caution them, "If the United States is losing the race for global innovation advantage, members of the Left need to acknowledge that their mission of advancing social justice cannot be effectively met."[7]

STEP 5—FIND COMMON GROUND AT HOME

Warring States leaders tried to keep their allies closely aligned and built ever-shifting coalitions united behind a common goal. Disunity was dangerous. There are many advocates for reforming American policy toward China—inside and outside of the U.S. government—but they are fractured into factions that often do not see each other as allies. Since at least 1995, Chinese scholars in Beijing have delighted in telling me stories of how Americans who criticize U.S. policy toward China are so divided by their political differences that they never cooperate.

It's long past time to foster cooperation among those of us seeking change in China. A grand coalition should be formed in the United States with the common mission of bringing change to China and altering a harmful and outdated U.S. approach to promoting reform in Beijing. This means that Americans who champion the Dalai Lama should ally with U.S. defense experts who promote spending for the Pentagon's AirSea Battle program. It means human rights advocates should work with American businesses demanding protection of intellectual property. It means antiabortion groups, which seek modification of the "one child policy," must make common cause with the democracy promotion organizations set up by Congress.

STEP 6—BUILD A VERTICAL COALITION OF NATIONS

There is a reason why China has been expanding its South China Sea claims, bullying Philippine fishing boats, cutting the cables of Vietnamese seismic survey ships, and recently establishing an Air Defense Identification Zone in the East China Sea. China wants to guarantee access to a wealth of natural resources in the region and is hoping to intimidate its neighbors so they are too scared of China to unite and oppose its ambitions.

Whether you play *wei qi* or not, you know that encirclement by a group of adversaries is dangerous. China's natural fear is that its neighbors will form such an alliance. That's exactly what the United States should be encouraging with nations including Mongolia, South Korea, Japan, and the Philippines. Even the threat of such a coalition—through movements in that direction—might give Beijing pause and temper its bellicosity. China knows how America and its allies contained the Soviet Union. As the United States increases aid and facilitates cooperation among China's neighbors, China's hawks will get the blame when China feels isolated and alone in the region.

STEP 7—PROTECT THE POLITICAL DISSIDENTS

Many of the soldiers on the front line of the Cold War were Soviet and Eastern European dissidents who refused to surrender to an unending future of censorship, propaganda, religious persecution, and economic enslavement. Their field marshals were men such as Václav Havel, Lech Wałesa, and Aleksandr Solzhenitsyn. And with their courage and passion and principles, they brought down the Soviet Union and the Iron Curtain. But they didn't do it alone. Presidents from Truman to Reagan championed their cause. When they were imprisoned, American presidents demanded their release. When they needed money, Americans sent them funds. When they needed a platform for the free speech their regimes denied them, Americans shared their printing presses and broadcast their battles and beliefs into millions of homes through Radio Free Europe.

Today China has increased its persecution of Buddhist Tibetans and Muslim Uighurs. In Tibet, the government has imposed curfews, arrested protesters, killed innocent civilians, and transformed the region into, in the recent words of the Dalai Lama, a "hell on earth."[8] In Xinjiang, the Internet and phones are routinely shut off, and the percentage of Han Chinese in Tibet and Xinjiang has risen dramatically due to state-sponsored migration.[9]

China also persecutes Christians. It is a common practice in China for foreigners to show their passports before being allowed to attend a church service in China. Why? Because China is ruled by the atheistic Communist Party, and its government wants to keep Chinese nationals out of non-state-run churches. Many experts estimate that there are 60 million to 100 million Christians in China and that the number is growing.[10] Bob Fu, the founder and president of China Aid, seeks to equip the Chinese people to defend their faith and freedom. The organization's purpose is to promote legal reforms, fund "house churches" in China, and assist imprisoned Christians. He highlights violence due to the one-child policy and supports other human rights activists in China. Most recently, Fu was instrumental in helping the blind activist Chen Guangcheng escape from house arrest in China and arrive safely in the United States.[11]

Yang Jianli, a Chinese dissident who survived the massacre at Tiananmen Square in 1989, has been fighting for twenty-five years to foster accountability within China's government. He founded Initiatives for China, a group that seeks to connect prodemocracy groups within China with human rights activists around the world.[12] Because of his work, he was imprisoned in China for five years, and he was released only after a unanimous vote from both houses of the U.S. Congress, a UN resolution, and work from nonprofit groups calling for his release. His release shows that outside support for dissidents can make a big difference. Just imagine how much more effective China's many other dissidents could be if the U.S. government expended as much effort supporting them as it did working for Yang's release.

Just as Representative Nancy Pelosi has unfailingly supported the Dalai Lama, President George W. Bush supported Fu's efforts to increase religious freedom in China. Regrettably, Fu says that President Obama has responded with silence to his pleas for help.[13] President Obama has not tied China's human rights achievements to issues Beijing cares about, such as trade relations. The Obama administration did not even include human rights in the Strategic and Economic Dialogue, the establishment of which was announced in April 2009 by President Obama and President Hu Jintao.

The U.S. government should not undermine the efforts of those who might be the most effective allies in countering the Hundred-Year Marathon.

STEP 8—STAND UP TO ANTI-AMERICAN COMPETITIVE CONDUCT

China is not just a source of cyber spying against the United States; it is the primary source. According to some estimates, more than 90 percent of cyber espionage incidents against America originate in China.[14] Chinese hackers regularly infiltrate American businesses and government entities. An abridged list of victims includes Google, Booz Allen Hamilton, AT&T, the U.S. Chamber of Commerce, Visa, MasterCard, and the Departments of Defense, State, Homeland Security, and Energy. Hacking is central to China's decades-long campaign to steal technologies it can't invent and intellectual property it can't create. A report by the Commission on the Theft of American Intellectual Property, led by the former director of national intelligence Dennis Blair and by the former

U.S. ambassador to China Jon Huntsman, found that the theft of U.S. intellectual property likely costs the American economy more than $300 billion per year.[15]

Representative Frank Wolf of Virginia has consistently worked to protect U.S. technological assets from China and to improve human rights there. Recognizing how China takes advantage of America's openness and willingness to share information, he helped establish a few minimal safeguards for such assets. Wolf inserted a clause in the 2011 federal budget that prohibited NASA and the White House Office of Science and Technology Policy from engaging in any joint scientific activities with China that year.[16]

However, Wolf is something of a lone wolf in seeking to rein in China's ability to access U.S. technological expertise. He has not been able to push through similar legislation since his 2011 effort. Due to the success of the "Wolf clause" in denying Chinese journalists access to the launch of the U.S. space shuttle *Endeavour* and Wolf's other work on human rights in China through the Tom Lantos Human Rights Commission, he has become a victim of Chinese cyberattacks himself.[17]

Wolf's intense concern about the theft of sensitive technology, military secrets, and intellectual property is greatly needed. But he announced his retirement from Congress in 2014. If the United States has any hope of being able to compete with China in the Hundred-Year Marathon, it will need to reinvigorate Wolf's proposals and look for ways to expand them.

STEP 9—IDENTIFY AND SHAME POLLUTERS

While the United States and Europe together are cutting their greenhouse gas emissions by sixty million tons a year, China is increasing its own by more than five hundred million tons annually. Perhaps the strongest manifestation of China's environmental problems—thus far at least—occurred during the January 2013 "Airpocalypse," when the air pollution in Beijing and other cities in China reached forty times the level that the World Health Organization deems safe. But even the Airpocalypse didn't inspire China to change its environmental tune. Beijing refuses to abide by any international agreement that might force it to prioritize environmentally responsible, long-term sustainable growth.

One of the more effective approaches to protecting the environment with regard to China occurred when Ambassador Huntsman authorized the U.S. embassy in Beijing to tweet the pollution levels in Beijing.[18] Similarly, Ma Jun, the director of the Institute of Public and Environmental Affairs, a leading environmental watchdog organization in China, has compiled online maps of China's water, air, and solid waste pollution.[19]

But is fostering greater awareness the best we can do? The United States needs to go from asking China to act in an environmentally responsible way to insisting that China do so, even if that means using far more leverage than past administrations have been willing to exert. Otherwise, China will be at a competitive economic advantage—with Washington constraining American businesses in an effort to protect the environment while China goes right on exporting its products and its pollutants at breakneck speed.

STEP 10—EXPOSE CORRUPTION AND CENSORSHIP

One of the Chinese government's greatest fears is of a free press. It knows that sunlight is a disinfectant for wrongdoing, and it is terrified of what its people would do if they knew the whole truth about Chinese leaders' corruption, brutality, and history of lying about the United States and our democratic allies. Yet it remains a mystery why the United States doesn't do more to fight China's censorship and propaganda campaigns against the Chinese people.

China's major news outlets are state-owned. The responsibility for calling out corruption frequently falls on foreign reporters in China. Western media have largely risen to the challenge—pointing out instances of embezzlement, harassment of anticorruption officials, mismanagement by state-owned enterprises, tax fraud, sex scandals, targeting of foreign companies, bribery, and so on. For instance, within a span of only a few months in 2013, the journalist Andrew Jacobs reported on the questionable detention of a Chinese journalist for "picking quarrels and making trouble"[20] and the killing of unarmed Tibetans in Sichuan Province.[21] Similarly, David Barboza, a *New York Times* correspondent in Shanghai, wrote a story in October 2012 about former prime minister Wen Jiabao's family's $2.7 billion in questionably obtained assets.[22]

But the government in Beijing uses its various tools to prohibit such information from reaching the Chinese people. In 2012 the Chinese government blocked Bloomberg News after it published a story on the family wealth of Xi Jinping.[23] The implicit deal of working in China seems to be this: you may report on China's fantastic growth, but if you start criticizing the Communist Party or its top officials you will be kicked out of the country.

Chinese leaders also pressure American technology companies to censor their websites in China. Internet service providers and social media companies seeking to operate in China face a stark reality: either cooperate with the Chinese government's censorship or be shut out of the Chinese market by the government's blocking of their websites.

For Jimmy Wales, the founder of Wikipedia, the choice was easy. Wikipedia refused to comply with Chinese government requests to restrict information.[24] What has been dubbed "the Chinese Great Firewall" has blocked Wikipedia on multiple occasions.[25] Wales says that Wikipedia stands "for the freedom for information, and for us to compromise . . . would send very much the wrong signal: that there's no one left on the planet who's willing to say: 'You know what? We're not going to give up.'"[26]

Why has the U.S. government not supported Wikipedia in its fight? It should be pressuring the Chinese government to back off its bullying of American companies such as Wikipedia, Yahoo!, Facebook, and other media. It also should redouble efforts to communicate with the Chinese people—in Mandarin—through Radio Free Asia. During the Cold War, Radio Free Europe was an oasis for anti-Communist dissidents in a desert of Soviet censorship and propaganda. There's no reason why Radio Free Asia couldn't serve a similar purpose in the Hundred-Year Marathon, but its budget needs to be increased at least threefold.

STEP 11—SUPPORT PRODEMOCRACY REFORMERS

Much of U.S. strategy in the Cold War is not relevant—at least not yet. Calls for a new Cold War play into the hands of the hawks in China who seek to exaggerate the threat from the United States. There is no global ideological struggle, no need to create an anti-China alliance akin to the NATO alliance to contain an expanding empire. But one lesson from the

Cold War that America ought to heed is reviving the support for democratic and civil society groups within China. China's concern when it
talks about a new Cold War[27] is that the Americans will revive their Cold
War–era programs that helped to subvert the Soviet Union from within
by using the power of ideas. Most Chinese hawks believe that this plan
to subvert Chinese democracy has already been put into motion, much as
it was for the Soviet Union in 1947. At least two Chinese books claim the
CIA leads it.[28]

Former secretary of defense Robert Gates has noted that the 1975 Helsinki Accords galvanized prodemocracy groups inside the Soviet Union
and played "a key role in our winning the Cold War."[29] His view seems to
be shared by the hawks of China, who write often about their fear that the
United States has mounted a program to influence impressionable future
civilian Chinese leaders to move toward democratic multiparty elections
and a free market.[30] In October 2013, China's hawks revealed another
fear—that America is seeking out a Chinese Gorbachev-like figure, a
leader who will bring one-party rule to an end. The hawks' distrust of
China's own leaders is shown in the tone of a ninety-minute video released
in October 2013 called *Silent Contest*.[31] China's hawks fear their civilian
leaders are susceptible to influence from Western leaders who want to
see multiparty rule and an evolution toward democracy.

In an online interview, Major General Luo Yuan has described a CIA
program to monitor the Chinese military press and then to single out
"hawks" whose names are brought to the attention of senior Chinese
civilian leaders who will then demote or otherwise punish these hawks.
General Luo's interview gives three examples when this was done, and
even cites me by name as someone who expresses delight at this operation. I don't mind his mentioning me, but there is no such program.[32]

The truth is that there is no such concerted effort by the United States
or the West to subvert China's Communist Party rule. The annual spending on programs to support democracy in China is less than $50 mil-
lion.[33] While the U.S. government has some underfunded civil society
programs, they are not CIA covert actions, and they are small in scale
compared to what will be needed. There are at least six such programs,
originating during the Cold War and run by various American organizations with U.S. government funds, including the AFL-CIO, the Chamber

of Commerce, and both major U.S. political parties. They provide funding for a wide range of Chinese organizations inside China as well as for exile groups.[34]

The U.S. State Department should fund more projects to promote the development of the rule of law and civil society in China, including efforts to provide legal and technical assistance, to reform criminal law, to improve legal adjudication, training for elected village officials, and to support the independence of judges.[35] More funds will also support election observation missions and technical assistance in drafting local election regulations and improving oversight of budgets and government decision making. We also need projects that increase the capacity of independent nongovernmental organizations.[36]

In tandem with prodemocracy initiatives, America must also get serious about promoting free-market reforms, instead of assuming that China will inevitably open its economy. For example, congressional funds through the National Endowment for Democracy and the Center for International Private Enterprise support the Beijing-based Unirule Institute of Economics,[37] which has advocated for bilateral investment treaties.[38] This would shrink the advantages of the state-owned enterprises, including the "national champions." Chinese abusive labor practices also have been focused on, both by Chinese NGOs and by U.S.-funded assistance efforts.[39]

The American government has not always been passive regarding or ignorant of internal Chinese debates. During the 1980s, Secretary of State George Shultz insisted that China abide by an international norm against nuclear proliferation.[40] The United States helped to build organizations and train individuals inside China to reverse Beijing's unwillingness to join the nuclear nonproliferation treaty (NPT).[41] Senator Joseph Biden described China as a nation that is "rapidly becoming a rogue elephant among the community of nations"[42] and called for withholding most-favored-nation trading status for China unless China changed its nonproliferation policies and practices. American government exchange programs joined private NGOs such as the MacArthur Foundation and the Ford Foundation[43] to launch the funding initiatives to facilitate capacity building within China's arms control community.[44] Foreign pressure and funding helped set up China's first export control system to monitor and to prevent companies from exporting forbidden technologies.[45]

More recently, however, the United States has lapsed into passivity. Xi Jinping ignited a promising debate about abiding by the Chinese Constitution when he used the term how to "put power in a cage." Seventy-two academics signed a petition drafted by law professor Zhang Qianfan. Zhang pointed out that the Chinese Constitution demands that "no organization or individual may enjoy the privilege of being above the Constitution and the law." To enforce this single sentence would severely limit the current dictatorial role of the Communist Party. The debate continued when President Xi said on the thirtieth anniversary of the Constitution that "The Constitution should be the legal weapon for people to defend their own rights."[46] Calling for separation of party and state institutions and deeper market reforms, the *New York Times* reported on February 3, 2013, that "some of Mr. Xi's recent speeches, including one in which he emphasized the need to enforce the Constitution, have ignited hope among those pushing for change."[47] This is the kind of news that Beijing's hawks dread. To this end, America should be a participant, not a bystander.

STEP 12—MONITOR AND INFLUENCE THE DEBATES
BETWEEN CHINA'S HAWKS AND REFORMERS

Today, as China pursues its own Cold War strategy against America, it monitors carefully various factions in Washington, DC—those who are supporters of Beijing and those who are skeptics, those who can be manipulated and those who have caught on to the Marathon strategy. America used to be good at this, too. During the Cold War, the United States invested time, technology, and personnel into discerning the activities among various members of the Soviet Politburo—those who advocated a more harmonious relationship with America and those who viewed the United States as a dangerous rival that must be overtaken. Yet unlike our activities against the Soviets, America is far behind when it comes to China.

It is crucial that the United States possess an understanding of the various actors in Beijing's sensitive internal debates. Though the Marathon strategy is moving apace, the Chinese government is not monolithic in its thinking. Hard-liners are certainly in the majority, but on the margins there are still sincere advocates of reform and liberalization who want a China that moves closer to an American-style model. They exist, and they must be identified and supported. The problem is that the U.S. intelligence community has not invested in the resources to determine who those true reformers are—as differentiated from the many Chinese leaders who make misleading reformist claims. This remains a massive intelligence challenge.[48]

The challenge has been persistent. In 1980, during the Carter administration, Michel Oksenberg invited me to a meeting of the National Security Council staff to discuss a classified memo he had drafted to Zbigniew Brzezinski, the national security adviser, warning that our intelligence about China was so poor that "we are vulnerable to the same massive intelligence failures we suffered on Iran,"[49] when the shah was ousted in 1979. There was some progress in the years following, but not much. In testimony to Congress in 1996, James Lilley, a former U.S. ambassador to China and a twenty-seven-year veteran of the CIA, noted the size of the challenge: "You know that the Chinese have a statement that they've had since Sun Tzu, twenty-five hundred years ago: When capable, feign incapacity. Their budgets, their Soviet acquisitions, their transfer of technology, their power projection, all of these things are kept from you. The only way you are going to get them is through clandestine collection and technical means. But again and again it's been human work that's made the essential difference."[50] As noted earlier, in August 2001, twelve years after the Tiananmen Square massacre, Lilley told a congressional commission that his greatest regret was learning a decade too late about internal Chinese documents revealing just how far China had moved toward democracy and how close the protests came to removing the Communist government. If only he had known at the time, the former ambassador said, he would have urged President George H. W. Bush to intervene firmly on the side of the real reformers, rather than being deceived by Beijing's leadership into siding with it.[51]

The hawks and the reformers in China differ sharply about America's intentions toward China's neighbors. The hawks see every American action as if it were a move on the *wei qi* board, with the goal of encircling

China and neutralizing its threat. In recent years, no move was seen as more important than President Obama's November 2012 visit to Myanmar (formerly known as Burma), and a reciprocal visit by Myanmar leaders to America the following spring. Indeed, Myanmar has become a centerpiece in the competition between America and China in Asia. As the *New York Times* noted earlier that year, "With the United States reasserting itself in Asia, and an emboldened China projecting military and economic power as never before, each side is doing whatever it can to gain the favor of economically struggling, strategically placed Myanmar."[52]

In 2013, I had occasion to visit the American embassy in Rangoon to see my friend Derek Mitchell, who had recently been appointed as the U.S. ambassador to Myanmar, the first to hold the position in more than two decades.[53] Mitchell and I had first worked together at the Department of Defense in 1996, when he drafted the first and only Pentagon "East Asia Strategy Review." More recently, Mitchell was one of the strategic planners who had created the pivot to Asia under President Obama. He had left the Pentagon and volunteered to serve as ambassador to this geopolitical hot spot, where he had taken a special interest in promoting human rights.

Meeting with the new ambassador, I gleaned his view of the divisions within the Chinese Politburo. While more hawkish elements viewed U.S.-Myanmar relations as a clear and present danger, Mitchell and I agreed that China's reformers tended to be relaxed about the American opening to Myanmar, perceiving common interests in Myanmar's economic development. China, for example, wanted a stable Myanmar for its investment in energy, specifically a series of dams on the Irrawaddy River. This was the opposite of the hawks' view of Americans playing *wei qi*—and a stance that should be appreciated and cultivated by the U.S. government.

I was curious as to how Myanmar leaders saw China's long-term strategy. Did they, like so many in the West, view China as a capitalist wannabe, intent on a peaceful rise in the community of nations?

Mitchell said that Myanmar intellectuals were reading the views of Lee Kuan Yew, the eighty-nine-year-old former prime minister of Singapore and one of Asia's most revered leaders. Lee, hailed as the father of the Singaporean miracle, has won widespread praise in the West; Richard Nixon once compared him to Churchill, Disraeli, and Gladstone,[54] and Bill Clinton and George H. W. Bush were among many hailing him as a visionary leader. Yet curiously many in the West have chosen to ignore his views on China.

A Myanmar official pointed me to a new book on Lee's views that was for sale at Rangoon's five-star Strand Hotel, a Victorian-style structure built during the British imperial era and that now stands as a relic of a declining Western empire.

"The rise of China [is] the issue about which Lee undoubtedly knows more than any other outside observer or analyst," wrote the book's editors, the Harvard professors Graham Allison and Robert Blackwill.[55] I scanned the book myself and found that Lee has clearly understood China's long-term strategy, a country he has observed closely for decades, long before most of us in the West.

"It is China's intention to be the greatest power in the world," Lee says bluntly, "and to be accepted as China, not as an honorary member of the West. . . . At the core of their mind-set is their world before colonization and the exploitation and humiliation that brought." Beijing, Lee continues, has masterfully harnessed the aspirations of the Chinese people—a far cry from their position after Tiananmen in 1989. "If you believe that there is going to be a revolution of some sort in China for democracy," he states, "you are wrong. . . . The Chinese people want a revived China." Asked by the book's interviewers how China would become number one, Lee replies, "Their great advantage is not in military influence but in their economic influence. . . . Their influence can only grow and grow beyond the capabilities of America."[56]

Lee seems to confirm essential elements of the Marathon strategy, though he believes that the period of Chinese dominance is still decades away. "The Chinese have figured out if they stay with [claims of a] 'peaceful rise' and just contest for first position economically and technologically, they cannot lose," he observes. "To [directly] challenge a stronger and technologically superior power like the United States will abort their peaceful rise. China is following an approach consistent with the Chinese television series *The Rise of the Great Powers*, produced by the Party. . . . I believe the Chinese leadership has learnt that if you compete with America in armaments, you will lose. You will bankrupt yourself. So, avoid it, keep your head down, and smile for forty or fifty years."[57]

I could not have put it better myself. At least I have one ally.

Despite the bipartisan, even global, acclaim Lee Kuan Yew has received, his sobering forecast about China has been met with resistance by China policy experts in the West. One reason for this pushback has been his critics' wishful thinking and false assumptions that China will somehow either collapse or become a Western-style democracy. A second reason has been China's vigorous efforts to act humble and downplay its growth prospects. A third reason is that there are too many false alarms about a near-term China threat. Like Lee Kuan Yew, I address how strong China will be in 2049. My focus on the longer term means that there is plenty of time to pursue the twelve steps I have laid out.

All too often, talk about China takes the form of sensationalized warnings about China's imminent global takeover and military dominance—neither of which are near-term possibilities. The Harvard political scientist Joseph Nye correctly warns, "The greatest danger we have is overestimating China and China overestimating itself. China is nowhere near close to the United States. So this magnification of China which creates fear in the U.S. and hubris in China is the biggest danger we face."[58]

An arrogant, aggressive China that provokes its neighbors and helps coalesce an alliance of like-minded countries in the region aids America in the long term. As Napoleon Bonaparte famously said, "Never stop your enemy when he is making a mistake." That is not an argument for doing nothing, however.

Competing with Beijing in the long term means being clear-eyed about China's ambitions and criticizing Chinese actions when they overstep boundaries of commonly accepted international norms. I advocate doing this by borrowing concepts from China's Warring States period, which entails respecting the quality and originality of China's strategic thinking. It is undeniable that the twelve steps outlined in this chapter will provoke friction with China. My colleagues often warn against criticizing the prickly Chinese. But that stance ignores Aristotle's admonition that "criticism is something we can avoid easily by saying nothing, doing nothing, and being nothing."

Beijing's strategy to replace the United States as the dominant geopolitical power requires America's goodwill and assistance. The United States must behave as Great Britain did during the gradual American rise and eclipse of the British Empire. That's one reason China works so hard to shape American perceptions of it. Liu Mingfu, in *The China Dream*, advocated that China try to shape American perceptions of China. He said that China must make America become "not a Satan but an Angel." His approach parallels a book by four *ying pai* hawks titled *The New Warring States Era*.[59] These and other Chinese hawks assert that the coming decades will be filled not with wars and territorial conquest but rather with struggles over economics, trade terms, currency, resources, and geopolitical alignments.

There are at least three intellectual traps we may fall into that will prevent recognition of the true nature of the problem. The first is premature fear of a China threat. China is not about to "rule the world," as Martin Jacques's 2012 book claims.[60] China has made no progress toward establishing a worldwide military base system of U.S.-style power projection capabilities. The Chinese currency is hardly poised to replace the dollar as the global reserve currency.[61] As David Shambaugh of George Washington University has argued, China is merely a "partial power." [62] The Pentagon has already initiated a major response to China in its strategic planning,[63] prompting critics to publish articles with titles like "Who Authorized Preparations for War with China?"[64]

The second trap for critics of China is to misidentify its strategy to replace America. Although the strategy is secret, we have enough evidence to know what it is not. No serious Chinese scholar advocates the approach to conquest of Hitler or Stalin or Tojo. No *ying pai* hawk author ever raises a strategy of territorial expansion or global ideological domination. Instead, China's hawks seem obsessed with books about America's rise to world power, like Ambassador Warren Zimmerman's *First Great Triumph: How Five Americans Made Their Country a World Power*.[65] As we have seen, the Communist Party School teaches that American trade and industrial policies enabled the United States to surpass both Britain and Germany, and the classic *ying pai* text *On Grand Strategy* praises American craftiness in exploiting World War II to push aside Europe and establish the current global order in 1945.[66]

Lessons from the Warring States era fit nicely with the lessons that China's hawks have learned from the rise of the United States. In addition to the many books about America's rise I described in chapter 8, the Communist Party School in Beijing uses at least three books to illustrate how the rising challenger successfully and peacefully persuaded the old hegemon to yield: Ann Orde's *The Eclipse of Great Britain*, Aaron Friedberg's *The Weary Titan*, and Lanxin Xiang's *Recasting the Imperial Far East*.[67] One nationally known Chinese scholar has even examined decisive moments in American diplomatic history from 1880 to 1914 to show how the United States soothed and reassured Great Britain in order to replace it as the leading world power. He admires how American strategy cleverly and deliberately eased an unsuspecting, war-weary Britain out of its global role.[68]

China's admiring descriptions of American strategy often use Chinese strategic concepts, such as claiming that the United States is exploiting *shi*, using *wu wei*, and borrowing the strength of others. China imputes the use of these concepts to the United States, which is also pursuing its own marathon strategy today, as China sees it.

Chinese strategy is based on both Western historical successes and careful study of how ancient Chinese empires rose and fell. China's strategy does not use rigid road maps or timetables or blueprints. It is poised to seize opportunities—suddenly if necessary.

The third intellectual trap is relevant only to U.S. government officials. The American public is unaware of the extent of the covert cooperation between Washington and Beijing over the past forty years. There is a long history of Chinese support for U.S. clandestine activities, which in turn has convinced many U.S. officials to see China as a current and prospective partner. Our history of clandestine cooperation has prejudiced many American policymakers in favor of China's hawks, who were responsible for implementing these covert programs.

The first step, recognizing that there is a Marathon, may be the most difficult to take, but it is also the most important. America may fail to recognize the problem and may refuse to face the long-term scenario of China not only surpassing us but also growing to double and then triple the size of our economy, by 2049. Then China will have won, by default.

AFTERWORD TO THE PAPERBACK EDITION

In the early summer of 2015, my wife and I hosted a book party at our home in Georgetown for a rather unlikely guest of honor: Liu Mingfu, the former People's Liberation Army colonel whose bestselling book, *The China Dream,* outlines the elements of Beijing's "marathon" against the West and the coming conflict with the United States. It was in Liu's book that I first came across the phrase "the Hundred-Year Marathon," a reference to Beijing's long-term strategic plan to vault China from third-world status to global preeminence.

The competition currently underway between the Middle Kingdom and the United States, Liu declares in the opening to his book, is "the largest game of global power in human history." The colonel would later tell *The New York Times,* "China was once called the sleeping lion in the East, but now we have been awakened, and Xi Jinping is the leading lion of the lion packs, who dare to fight anytime." He added, "There are flames around Asia, and every place could be a battlefield in the future."[1]

The colonel, a genial, energetic man whom I've known for a decade in my interactions with Chinese military and intelligence leaders, sought a forum to celebrate the book's English-language publication, and I was happy to oblige. And so, before a room filled with American journalists and defense and foreign policy experts—all of us representatives of "the world hegemon"—Colonel Liu held forth on his views of China's rise in what his book calls the "post-American era." One sample of his recommendations? He advocates that China should follow the example of the Monroe Doctrine, when America decreed that European powers must keep out of Latin America, but China should apply this concept to all foreign powers and to all of Asia.

The reason I hosted the party for Colonel Liu was simple. I wanted my guests from the CIA and the Pentagon to see one of China's "hawks" up close and to understand that his views—often dismissed in the United States as being part of the hard-line "fringe"—are in fact very much a part of mainstream Chinese thought. There was ample evidence to support this. For one, the English translation of Colonel Liu's book was published by a U.S.-based publishing house that, according to *The New York Times,* was founded by "a former employee of the Beijing municipal propaganda bureau."[2] An article in the *Times* profiling Colonel Liu in October was headlined "Chinese Colonel's Hard-Line Views Seep into the Mainstream."[3] With my permission, a Voice of America reporter who attended the party even broadcast Liu's remarks back to China, and the VOA broadcast was not jammed, as if approving his call to surpass America.

As I've noted in this book, American intelligence and national security officials have for too long succumbed to wishful thinking about China's strategy and ignored the obvious evidence of its deliberate challenge to the West. Ignoring the rise of China's hawks may be the greatest intelligence failure in our history. If our leaders would prefer not to take it from me, they can read it in the pages of *The New York Times.* Only now, after a forty-year slumber, are we finally beginning to awaken to China's detailed and deliberate strategy to surpass us by 2049. We can only hope it is not too late.

Indeed, in the months since this book was first published, the Chinese government has added evidence to prove *The Hundred-Year Marathon's* central thesis: that Beijing seeks to remake the global hierarchy, with itself as leader, and to counter and undermine the power and influence of the United States. China's actions and new publications have cast serious doubts about the repeated assertions of many U.S. scholars and policy makers that Beijing has no long-term strategy and intends merely to seek a "peaceful" rise into the pantheon of democratic, free-market nations.

EXTENDING CHINA'S GLOBAL MILITARY REACH

On November 5, 2015, a bespectacled man with a grim expression arrived aboard the USS *Theodore Roosevelt,* the flagship of a Navy strike group jutting through the South China Sea. Standing on the aircraft carrier's great steel deck—and within full view of mainland China's radars and in range of the hundreds of sophisticated anti-surface and ballistic missiles positioned along China's southern coastline—Ashton Carter, the U.S. secretary of defense, watched Navy fighter jets roar into the sun in what was a decidedly unsubtle display of U.S. military power.

Indeed, Carter made little secret of his message or its intended recipient. Citing increasing tensions in the region "perpetrated by China," Carter offered Beijing a very public display of American resolve. Standing alongside Carter was the defense minister of Malaysia, one of many neighbors unnerved by Chinese belligerence. In his remarks, Carter perhaps understated things by noting, "There's a lot of concern about Chinese behavior out here."[4] Unfortunately, within days Malaysia invited China's navy to visit its key port of Kota Kinabalu and said it was not taking sides between China and the United States. Many Asian leaders are hedging their bets and seem to be wary that America plans to continue its four-decade-long embrace of China.

In the months since *The Hundred-Year Marathon* was published, the People's Republic of China has embarked on an unprecedented campaign to militarize islands in the South China Sea and to make aggressive territorial claims by dredging new islands out of the sea itself, claiming them as Chinese soil and building airfields, harbors, and barracks on these atolls to accommodate a Chinese military presence. For many years, China's ambitions were thought to be largely centered on its economic emergence. Defense Secretary Carter's actions were just the latest demonstration that in the West, this decades-long illusion has been shattered.

The primary purpose of the islands that the People's Liberation Army is busy "reclaiming" in the South China Sea is strategic positioning against its neighbors—which include key American allies such as South Korea, Taiwan, the Philippines, and Japan. The harbors on these man-made islands will enable the Chinese Navy and Coast Guard vessels to establish a round-the-clock presence in the South China Sea without the need to return to ports on the mainland. The airfield on Fiery Cross Reef, for example, is able to accommodate almost every aircraft in China's inventory, including heavy transport and combat aircraft. As the Chinese Navy currently lacks a fully operational aircraft carrier and has limited in-flight refueling capabilities, the atolls should enable China's military to base fighter aircraft far from China's shores on a permanent basis.[5] And the installation of new radar and satellite communications systems on these islands will significantly enhance China's maritime domain awareness in the South China Sea.

This expansion shows no signs of slowing. China has prioritized its navy in its military modernization plans. In what once would have been heresy in the Chinese military, a defense white paper issued by the government entitled *China's Military Strategy* declared, "The traditional mentality that land outweighs sea must be abandoned."[6] China "plans to extend its global military reach to safeguard its economic interests, while defending its territorial claims at sea against 'provocative actions' by neighbors and 'meddling' by the United States."[7]

Patrick Cronin, an Asia policy expert at the Center for a New American Security, said the white paper amounted to "a blueprint for achieving slow-motion regional hegemony."[8]

CONQUERING SPACE

As readers of this book are aware, a Chinese program called "Assassin's Mace weapons" focuses on technology to exploit America's military weaknesses. Part of this new technology may be aimed at conquering another frontier: space. A report from the U.S. government's U.S.-China Economic and Security Review Commission claims that China is developing co-orbital antisatellite weapons. "These systems consist of a satellite armed with a weapon such as an explosive charge, fragmentation device, kinetic energy weapon, laser, radio frequency weapon, jammer, or robotic arm," the report details. A *Washington Times* analysis of the report explains further: "The co-orbital arms maneuver in space close to satellite targets and then deploy weapons to disable or destroy them. They also can crash into satellites or grab them with a robotic arm."[9]

According to the *Times*, the commission also found that China is readying two new missiles to take out other satellites:

> Two direct-ascent missiles capable of hitting satellites in both lower and higher orbits are under development, the SC-19 and the DN-2. Antisatellite missile tests were carried out as recently as last year. The high-orbit DN-2 can hit U.S. Global Positioning Satellites but appears more suited for blowing up U.S. intelligence, surveillance, and reconnaissance satellites. The DN-2 could be deployed in five to ten years.[10]

China's antisatellite technology has the potential, of course, to pose a clear and present danger to American communications systems.

CHINA'S GROWING ECONOMIC MIGHT

Despite growing and hopeful chatter in the United States that China's economy is slowing or even collapsing, it still grows at a rate three to four times as fast as ours. In 2015, the U.S. growth rate was just 2 percent, compared to nearly 7 percent in China.[11] This has led to continued speculation as to when China will surpass America—"when," not "if."

In some ways, China has already overtaken us, in exports, household savings, and the number of billionaires. As the Nobel Prize–winning economist Joseph Stiglitz wrote in *Vanity Fair*: "With savings and investment making up close to 50 percent of GDP, the Chinese worry about having too much savings, just as Americans worry about having too little."[12] In some areas, like manufacturing, they surpassed us only relatively recently. But with over 200 new Chinese billionaires established from 2014 to 2015 (as tracked by the Hurun's China Rich List report), China now boasts 596 billionaires, compared to 537 in the United States.[13]

Chinese companies have likewise swarmed the Fortune Global 500 list. In 2000, there wasn't a single Chinese company on the list. By 2015, there were 98. According to *Fortune*, "That puts China second only to the United States, which has 128."[14] And the system of "national champions" described in this book has succeeded, as the top twelve Chinese companies are all state-owned. These include some of the world's largest banks and oil companies.[15]

In October 2015, the Chinese currency—the renminbi—surpassed the Japanese yen to become the fourth most-used currency for global payments. It now trails only the U.S. dollar, the euro, and the British pound.[16] And at the end of November, the International Monetary Fund decided to add the renminbi to its prestigious basket of reserve currencies, a vote of confidence in China's long-term prospects.

In a telling contrast to Western media speculation that China's economy is doomed, China's prominent economists are bullish, just like the IMF. One of the most prominent Chinese economists, Justin Yifu Lin, posited in January 2015 that China's economy would maintain 7 to 7.5 percent GDP growth for the next ten to fifteen years.[17] Lin also forecast that by 2030, China's per capita income might be 50 percent of that of America's, and its economic size will be double that of America's.[18] Lin's forecasts deserve great weight—he is a former chief economist of the World Bank and earned a doctorate from the conservative economics department of the University of Chicago. Other recent estimates indicate that the United States will lose its position as the world's top economy—unless there is an enormous effort by America to become more competitive.[19]

According to Robert Atkinson in *The Christian Science Monitor:*

> The Chinese are investing tens of billions of dollars to build up domestic production that can substitute for U.S. imports in key industries such as semiconductors and software; [blocking access] to U.S. websites, applications, and other digital content platforms; forcing disclosure of our proprietary intellectual property, technology, and source code; using anti-monopoly laws as a club to extract concessions from U.S. companies; and even pressuring Chinese enterprises to stop using American-made hardware and software. Furthermore, China is utilizing a panoply of additional mercantilist measures that seek to provide an unfair advantage to Chinese producers—from currency and standards manipulation to special benefits for state-owned enterprises.[20]

By contrast, American competitiveness has declined. According to the Census Bureau, U.S. businesses are now failing faster than they are being created for the first time since this data began to be measured in

1980. Meanwhile, the 2014 Global Innovation Index saw the U.S. innovation ecosystem fall to sixth place, while ranking thirty-ninth in ease of starting a business.

On the other hand, the situation isn't all rosy for Chinese indigenous innovation. As Stiglitz reports, the Chinese "still trail America when it comes to the number of patents awarded, but they are closing the gap."[21] China wishes to dominate in production of advanced technology products such as airplanes, semiconductors, and pharmaceuticals, as well as in commodity manufacturing. Ultimately, Chinese policymakers are trying to independently supply Chinese markets for advanced technology products with their own production while still benefitting from unfettered access to global markets for their technology exports. These actions have earned China the number-one spot on the Global Mercantilist Index.[22]

THE OBAMA-XI SUMMIT

The challenges of playing the delicate game of diplomacy with China were on full display during the summit meeting between President Barack Obama and President Xi Jinping in Washington, DC, in September 2015. What was especially telling was the outsized influence of conservative military hawks in the Chinese government.

China's military hard-liners reportedly urged Xi to avoid discussing certain issues with the Obama administration.[23] Those who I call China's "scholar-generals"—former military officials now working in state-approved think tanks—predicted to me with pride what Xi would do during the summit.

The military hard-liners told me they did not passively surrender all the planning of the summit to the Foreign Ministry. Instead, they cleverly used Xi's weekly meetings with a roomful of generals to reshape the trip. Within the People's Liberation Army is a little-known foreign policy team known as the General Political Department, a group of hard-liners who assesses policy opportunities and often conflict with the more wooly-headed intellectuals in the Foreign Ministry, who resemble the more typical diplomatic corps you see everywhere.[24] In four or five sessions, the military, with no diplomats in the room, gamed out the military aspects of President Xi's speeches and meetings with President Obama. Their first recommendation, which Xi accepted, was that no Chinese senior general would accompany him to the United States and that discussions of American concerns about military issues must be excluded from the talks.[25] Six areas in particular were ruled out of discussions with President Obama:

1. *Chinese cyberattacks:* There could be no written cyber security agreement between America and the United States and no discussion about five PLA officers whom the U.S. Justice Department had indicted for cyber espionage in 2014.

2. *Space:* No discussions of PLA activities in space, a ban on the Chinese antisatellite program, or arms control in space.

3. *Military exchanges:* The Chinese would seek increases in the type of military exchanges that provide China with opportunities to understand U.S. operational weaknesses, while refusing access to sensitive PLA facilities.

4. *Technology:* No restrictions that would decrease China's covert acquisition of defense industrial technology.

5. *Taiwan:* No discussion of limits on the PLA's arms buildup against Taiwan.

6. *South China Sea:* China would not agree to discuss any restraints on dredging or military construction in the South China Sea.

The hard-liners further recommended that Xi should instead use the visit with Obama to volunteer harmless but warm-hearted "American-style" phrases and to make mention of American books that he admires. Following the script, Xi said during a soothing speech, "The Chinese people have always held American entrepreneurship and creativity in high regards." He added, "In my younger years, I read *The Federalist Papers,* by Alexander Hamilton, and *Common Sense,* by Thomas Paine."

The Obama administration went along with all of this, taking great pains to discuss only private sector cyber criminals and to avoid chastising China over its blatant government-sponsored cyberattacks against the U.S. government. Asked by the media before the summit about negotiating a cyber security agreement with China, Dan Kritenbrink, the senior director for Asian affairs at the National Security Council, replied, "I would be reluctant to raise expectations about an agreement along the lines of what you just described. That would be a long-term goal. We're a long ways from getting there."[26] He did not mention that no senior military leader or military cyber expert was even part of the large Chinese delegation—by design. China's hawks were probably thrilled that, while standing next to the American president at the White House, Xi boldly reiterated China's claim to the entire South China Sea.

GRAPPLING WITH THE CHINA CHALLENGE

Most scholars today have begun to accept the reality of a growing long-term U.S. competition with China. For example, Noah Feldman of Harvard University has coined the phrase "cool war" to describe our current relations with China. As we seek to maintain a strategic edge, the need for a unified policy that matches China's economic and military strategy becomes clearer if we aim to keep the "cool war" from getting colder, or worse, hot. That will be the challenge of the next president of the United States, and his or her successors. They will determine America's pace as the Hundred-Year Marathon goes on.

The real challenge is the controversy created by those who continue to cling to their wishful thinking that China has no strategy at all, or at most is just naturally rising out of historic poverty. My argument has been challenged by a strongly held view that China has neither the desire nor the strategy nor the capability to replace America. But this argument will wear thin in the years ahead. If China is haplessly growing by accident without a strategy, why then does the new defense white paper speak of the need to protect China's global interests? Why do prominent Chinese economists forecast China will be double, and then triple, the size of America's economy? Why does the Chinese government publish plans for a regional restructuring that many have called "Asia for Asians"?

And why did President Xi personally announce on April 1, 2015, a grand strategic plan called "One Belt, One Road" to unify and harmonize the foreign trade practices of half the world's economy, without even mentioning the United States?[27]

Finally, why would thirty-five Chinese military officers publish a little-noticed book entitled *Science of Strategy* that advocates a global network of Chinese military bases?

All these new proposals hardly sound like a nation without a strategy to me.

NOTES

INTRODUCTION: WISHFUL THINKING

1. See Susan Watters, "No Longer a Party Divided at Sackler Museum," *Women's Wear Daily*, December 3, 2012, available at http://www.wwd.com/eye/parties/no-longer-a-party-divided-6517532; and Miguel Benavides, "Arthur M. Sackler Gallery Celebrates 25th Anniversary," *Studio International*, November 2012, available at http://www.studiointernational.com/index.php/arthur-m-sackler-gallery-celebrates-25th-anniversary.

2. A video of the "Black Christmas Tree" display is available at http://www.youtube.com/watch?v=UeZyGnxTWKY.

3. Maura Judkis, "Sackler to Celebrate Anniversary with a Daytime Fireworks Display," *Washington Post*, November 29, 2012, available at http://www.washingtonpost.com/entertainment/museums/sackler-to-celebrate-anniversary-with-a-daytime-fireworks-display/2012/11/29/7fdf2104-3a35-11e2-8a97-363b0f9a0ab3_story.html.

4. Ibid.

5. Remarks by Secretary of State Hillary Rodham Clinton at the Art in Embassies Fiftieth Anniversary Luncheon, November 30, 2012, available at http://m.state.gov/md201314.htm.

6. "Medal of Arts Conversation," U.S. Department of State, November 30, 2012, available at http://art.state.gov/Anniversary.aspx?tab=images&tid=106996.

7. For a similar view, see Yawei Liu and Justine Zheng Ren, "An Emerging Consensus on the US Threat: The United States According to PLA Officers," *Journal of Contemporary China* 23, no. 86 (2014): 255–74. For a more skeptical view of the

role of the hawks, see Andrew Chubb, "Are China's Hawks Really the PLA Elite After All? [Revised]," *southseaconversations* blog, posted December 5, 2013, accessed on April 7, 2014, available at http://southseaconversations.wordpress .com/2013/12/05/are-chinas-hawks-actually-the-pla-elite-after-all/. As Chubb argues, "My contention, however, is that while the 'hawks' *may* often represent PLA thought, they only do so *in public* when approved." (Italics in original.)

8. William A. Callahan, "Patriotic Cosmopolitanism: China's Non-official Intellectuals Dream of the Future," *British Inter-University China Centre (BICC) Working Paper Series* 13 (October 2009): 9, available at http://www.bicc.ac.uk /files/2012/06/13-Callahan.pdf.

9. Ibid.

10. Ibid. Callahan states on pages 8–9 that this book is "a call by a pair of People's Liberation Army colonels for Beijing to use asymmetrical warfare, including terrorism, to attack the United States." See also Qiao Liang and Wang Xianghui, *Chaoxianzhan: Quanqiuhua Shidai Zhanzheng Yu Zhanfa [Unrestricted Warfare: War and Strategy in the Globalization Era]* (Beijing: Social Sciences Press, 2005 [1999]).

11. An English translation of the *The Thirty-Six Stratagems* is available at http:// wengu.tartarie.com/wg/wengu.php?l=36ji.

12. "Medal of Arts Conversation."

13. See, for example, Lydia Liu, *Translingual Practice: Literature, National Culture, and Translated Modernity-China, 1900–1937* (Stanford, CA: Stanford University Press, 1995).

14. For further discussion of the purported influence of the China hawks, see Andrew Chubb, "PLA Hawks, Part One: Good Cop, Bad Cop with China's Generals," *Asia Times Online*, July 29, 2013, available at http://www.atimes.com /atimes/China/CHIN-01-290713.html; Andrew Chubb, "PLA Hawks, Part Two: Chinese Propaganda as Policy," *Asia Times Online*, August 15, 2013, available at http://www.atimes.com/atimes/China/CHIN-01-150813.html.

15. See, for example, Jacques deLisle, *Pressing Engagement: Uneven Human Rights Progress in China, Modest Successes of American Policy, and the Absence of Better Options* (Washington, DC: Carnegie Endowment, 2008); Sharon Hom, "Has U.S. Engagement with China Produced a Significant Improvement in Human Rights?," *Framing China Policy: The Carnegie Debate*, March 5, 2007.

16. "Text of President Bush's 2002 State of the Union Address," *Washington Post*, January 29, 2002, available at http://www.washingtonpost.com/wp-srv/onpoli tics/transcripts/sou012902.htm.

17. Aaron L. Friedberg, *A Contest for Supremacy: China, America, and the Struggle for Mastery in Asia* (New York: W. W. Norton, 2011), 187–88. See also David Shambaugh, *China's Communist Party: Atrophy and Adaptation* (Washington, DC: Woodrow Wilson Center Press, 2008). Shambaugh writes that the "forces for change already exist [in China] and are only going to become more intense over time. This is as close to a 'law' of political development as exists—when a

nation makes the transition from developing country to newly industrialized country, the pressures from society on the state to effectively govern arise. The ruling party-state has essentially only two options once this process begins: Stifle or suppress the demands, *or* open channels to accommodate the demands" (Italics in original.), p. 180.

18. James Mann, *The China Fantasy: Why Capitalism Will Not Bring Democracy to China* (New York: Viking, 2007), 27. Kellee S. Tsai, *Capitalism without Democracy: The Private Sector in Contemporary China* (Ithaca, NY: Cornell University Press, 2007), notes that "Chinese entrepreneurs are not agitating for democracy. Most are working eighteen-hour days to stay in business, while others are saving for their one child's education or planning to leave the country. Many are Communist Party members. Based on years of research, hundreds of field interviews, and a sweeping nationwide survey of private entrepreneurs, *Capitalism without Democracy* explores the conventional wisdom about the relationship between economic liberalism and political freedom." (From back cover.) See also Ann Florini, Hairong Lai, and Yeling Tan, *China Experiments: From Local Innovations to National Reform* (Washington, DC: Brookings Institution Press, 2012).

19. John Fox and François Godement, *A Power Audit of EU-China Relations* (London: European Council on Foreign Relations, 2009), 1.

20. Steven Levingston, "China's Authoritarian Capitalism Undermines Western Values, Argue Three New Books," *Washington Post*, May 30, 2010, available at http://www.washingtonpost.com/wp-dyn/content/article/2010/05/28/AR2010052801859.html.

21. Andrew J. Nathan, "China's Changing of the Guard: Authoritarian Resilience," *Journal of Democracy* 14, no. 1 (January 2003): 6–17. See also Stephanie Kleine-Ahlbrandt and Andrew Small, "China's New Dictatorship Diplomacy," *Foreign Affairs* 87, no. 1 (January/February 2008).

22. Geoff A. Dyer, *The Contest of the Century: The New Era of Competition with China—and How America Can Win* (New York: Alfred A. Knopf, 2014).

23. Arthur Waldron, "The China Sickness," *Commentary*, July 2003, available at http://www.commentarymagazine.com/article/the-chinese-sickness/.

24. Gordon G. Chang, *The Coming Collapse of China* (New York: Random House, 2001).

25. Anna Yukhananov, "IMF Sees Higher Global Growth, Warns of Deflation Risks," *Reuters*, January 21, 2014, available at http://www.reuters.com/article/2014/01/21/us-imf-economy-idUSBREA0K0X620140121; *OECD Economic Outlook* 2013, no. 2 (November 2013): 6; "World Economic Situation and Prospects 2014: Global Economic Outlook" (chapter 1), United Nations Department of Economic and Social Affairs, December 18, 2013, available at http://www.un.org/en/development/desa/publications/wesp2014-firstchapter.html.

26. Chang, *Coming Collapse of China*.

27. The original report is Ruth Bunzel, "Explorations in Chinese Culture," Research

in Contemporary Cultures, Margaret Mead Papers, Division of Special Collections, Library of Congress; Ruth Bunzel, "Themes in Chinese Culture," Margaret Mead Papers, Library of Congress, March 18, 1948, G 23, vol. 8, chapter 686; Hu Hsien-chin, "The Romance of the Three Kingdoms," Margaret Mead Papers, Division of Special Collections, Library of Congress, G 21, vol. 2, chapter 33; Warner Muensterberger, "Some Notes on Chinese Stories," June 1, 1948, Margaret Mead Papers, G 23, vol. 7, chapter 348; Margaret Mead, "Minutes of the Chinese Political Character Group," Margaret Mead Papers, Division of Special Collections, Library of Congress, G63, January 16, 1951. Mead provides background on the study in Margaret Mead, "The Study of National Character," *The Policy Sciences: Recent Developments in Scope and Method*, ed. Daniel Lerner and Harold D. Lasswell (Stanford, CA: Stanford University Press, 1951), 70–85; a few findings are in Weston La Barre, "Some Observations on Character Structure in the Orient: The Chinese, Part Two," *Psychiatry* 19, no. 4 (1946): 375–95.

28. Lucian W. Pye and Nathan Leites, "Nuances in Chinese Political Culture," RAND Corporation, 1970, Document Number P-4504, available at http://www .rand.org/pubs/papers/P4504.html.

29. Dore J. Levy, *Ideal and Actual in the Story of the Stone* (New York: Columbia University Press, 1999); Andrew H. Plaks, *Archetype and Allegory in the Dream of the Red Chamber* (Princeton, NJ: Princeton University Press, 1976); Frederick W. Mote, *The Intellectual Foundations of China* (New York: Alfred A. Knopf, 1989); Peter K. Bol, *"This Culture of Ours": Intellectual Transitions in T'ang and Sung China* (Stanford, CA: Stanford University Press, 1992); Sarah Allan, *The Heir and the Sage: Dynastic Legend in Early China*, Asian Library Series, no. 24 (San Francisco: Chinese Materials Center, 1981); John B. Henderson, *Scripture, Canon, and Commentary: A Comparison of Confucian and Western Exegesis* (Princeton, NJ: Princeton University Press, 1991); Stephen Owen, *Readings in Chinese Literary Thought* (Cambridge, MA: Harvard University Press, 1996); David L. Rolston, *Chinese Fiction and Fiction Commentary: Reading and Writing Between the Lines* (Stanford, CA: Stanford University Press, 1997); and Victor H. Mair, ed., *The Columbia History of Chinese Literature* (New York: Columbia University Press, 2001).

30. I learned of the unpublished study and its sponsorship by the U.S. Air Force and the U.S. Navy from Professor Ruth Bunzel, who taught a course I attended at Columbia University in 1968.

31. Dai Bingguo, "Stick to the Path of Peaceful Development," *China Daily*, December 13, 2010, available at http://www.chinadaily.com.cn/opinion/2010-12/13 /content_11690133.htm.

32. Edward I-hsin Chen, "In the Aftermath of the U.S.-China S & E D and New Military Relations," Center for Security Studies in Taiwan, April 17, 2012, available at http://www.mcsstw.org/web/content.php?PID=5&Nid=849.

33. Throughout this book, the phrases "the West" and "Western" appear. This is meant to be taken generally and to include Western allies in Asia such as South Korea, Japan, and Taiwan.

34. John Kennedy, "Diaoyu Dispute Unites Liberals and Nationalists Online," *South China Morning Post*, August 16, 2012, available at http://www.scmp.com/com ment/blogs/article/1015948/diaoyu-dispute-unites-liberals-and-nationalists -online.

35. Michael Pillsbury, ed., *Chinese Views of Future Warfare* (Washington, DC: National Defense University Press, 2002), available at http://www.au.af.mil/au /awc/awcgate/ndu/chinview/chinacont.html.

36. Michael Pillsbury, *China Debates the Future Security Environment* (Washington, DC: National Defense University Press, 2000), available at http://www.fas.org /nuke/guide/china/doctrine/pills2/.

37. The second book was translated into Chinese by the government-controlled Xin-hua Press in 2003.

38. For example, the *Journal of Contemporary China* recently published six articles on these issues: Michael Yahuda, "China's New Assertiveness in the South China Sea," vol. 22, iss. 81 (2013): 446–59; Yawei Liu and Justine Zheng Ren, "An Emerging Consensus of the U.S. Threat: The United States According to PLA Officers," vol. 23, iss. 86 (2014): 255–74; Suisheng Zhao, "Foreign Policy Implications of Chinese Nationalism Revisited: The Strident Turn," vol. 22, iss. 82 (2013): 535–53; Jianwei Wang and Xiaojie Wang, "Media and Chinese Foreign Policy," vol. 23, iss. 86 (2014): 216–35; James Reilly, "A Wave to Worry About? Public Opinion, Foreign Policy and China's Anti-Japan Protests," vol. 23, iss. 86 (2014): 197–215; and Hongping Annie Nie, "Gaming, Nationalism, and Ideological Work in Contemporary China: Online Games Based on the War of Resistance Against Japan," vol. 22, iss. 81 (2013): 499–517.

39. World Bank, "China—Long-Term Development Issues and Options" (Washington, DC: World Bank, October 31, 1985), 13364.

CHAPTER 1: THE CHINA DREAM

1. See, for example, "Monument to People's Heroes," TravelChinaGuide.com, available at http://www.travelchinaguide.com/attraction/beijing/tiananmen-square /people-heroes-monument.htm.

2. James Reeves Pusey, *China and Charles Darwin* (Cambridge, MA: Harvard University Press, 1983), chapter 6; and Xiaosui Xiao, "China Encounters Darwinism: A Case of Intercultural Rhetoric," *Quarterly Journal of Speech* 81, no. 1 (1995).

3. Quoted in Guoqi Xu, *Olympic Dreams: China and Sports, 1895–2008* (Cambridge, MA: Harvard University Press, 2008), 19.

4. Pusey, *China and Charles Darwin*, 190–91. Pusey wrote that "China's first, and most important, 'scientific' justification of revolution . . . was based on a mistranslation of one of Darwin's most importance sentences. Just who was responsible remains unclear" (209).

5. Riazat Butt, "Darwinism, Through a Chinese Lens," *Guardian*, November 16, 2009, available at http://www.theguardian.com/commentisfree/belief/2009/nov /16/darwin-evolution-china-politics.

6. Pusey, *China and Charles Darwin*, 208.

7. Orville Schell and John Delury, *Wealth and Power: China's Long March to the Twenty-First Century* (London: Little, Brown, 2013), 131. For more on Chinese conceptions of race and race relations, see, for example, M. Dujon Johnson, *Race and Racism in the Chinas: Chinese Racial Attitudes Toward Africans and African-Americans* (Bloomington, IN: AuthorHouse, 2007); Frederick Hung, "Racial Superiority and Inferiority Complex," *China Critic*, January 9, 1930, available at http://www.chinaheritagequarterly.org/030/features/pdf/Racial%20Superiority%20and%20Inferiority%20Complex.pdf; Nicholas D. Kristof, "China's Racial Unrest Spreads to Beijing Campus," *New York Times*, January 4, 1989, available at http://www.nytimes.com/1989/01/04/world/china-s-racial-unrest-spreads-to-beijing-campus.html; Frank Dikotter, *The Discourse of Race in Modern China* (Stanford, CA: Stanford University Press; 1992); and Frank Dikotter, *Imperfect Conceptions: Medical Knowledge, Birth Defects, and Eugenics in China* (New York: Columbia University Press, 1998).

8. Pusey, *China and Charles Darwin*, 208.

9. A few selections from *The General Mirror* have been translated in Peter K. Bol, *This Culture of Ours: Intellectual Transitions in Tang and Song China* (Stanford, CA: Stanford University Press, 1992), 233–46. For example, on foreign relations with barbarians, "Although their chi is of a different sort [from humans], they are the same as human beings in choosing profit over loss and preferring life to death. If one gets the tao for controlling them, they will accord and submit. If one loses that tao, they will revolt and invade" (244).

10. Carine Defoort, *The Pheasant Cap Master (He Guan Zi): A Rhetorical Reading* (New York: State University of New York Press, 1996), 206.

11. Salisbury reports he learned this important clue to understanding Chinese strategic thinking during an interview with Chairman Mao's secretary and biographer Li Rui. See Harrison E. Salisbury, *The New Emperors: China in the Era of Mao and Deng* (New York: Harper Perennial, 1993), 480, n. 17. Salisbury reports, "A visitor dropped in to see Deng in early 1973. He found him perusing *The General Mirror for the Aid of Government*" (325). Salisbury also notes that when Mao entered Beijing in 1949 to take over China, he brought *The General Mirror for the Aid of Government* with him. "If he was to rule the empire, he must be guided by the wisdom of the past emperors" (9). Salisbury further states that "not all Mao's survivors believed that he had read so widely in the history of how princes won kingdoms and emperors lost them" (53).

12. Butt, "Darwinism, Through a Chinese Lens."

13. Xu Jianchu, Andy Wilkes, and Janet Sturgeon, "Official and Vernacular Identifications in the Making of the Modern World: Case Study in Yunnan, S.W. China," Center for Biodiversity and Indigenous Knowledge (CBIK), October 2001, 4.

14. Jeanne Vertefeuille accompanied Golitsyn. Sandra Grimes and Jeanne Vertefeuille, *Circle of Treason: A CIA Account of Traitor Aldrich Ames and the Men He Betrayed* (Annapolis, MD: Naval Institute Press, 2013), 4. See also Elaine Shan-

non, "Death of the Perfect Spy," *Time*, June 24, 2001, available at http://content
.time.com/time/magazine/article/0,9171,164863,00.html; and Tennent H. Bagley,
Spymaster: Startling Cold War Revelations of a Soviet KGB Chief (New York: Sky-
horse Publishing, 2013).

15. Robert Buchar, *And Reality Be Damned . . . Undoing America: What Media Didn't
Tell You About the End of the Cold War and the Fall of Communism in Europe*
(Durham, CT: Eloquent Books, 2010), 211, n. 9.

16. John Limond Hart, *The CIA's Russians* (Annapolis, MD: Naval Institute Press,
2003), 137.

17. For more on Ian Fleming's use of code names and the code name "007," see these
historical studies: Donald McCormick, *17F: The Life of Ian Fleming* (London:
Peter Owen Publishers, 1994); Nicholas Rankin, *Ian Fleming's Commandos: The
Story of the Legendary 30 Assault Unit* (New York: Oxford University Press, 2011);
John Pearson, *The Life of Ian Fleming* (New York: Bloomsbury, 2013); and Craig
Cabell, *Ian Fleming's Secret War* (Barnsley, UK: Pen and Sword, 2008).

18. See, for example, Hal Ford, "Soviet Thinking about the Danger of a Sino-US
Rapprochement," CIA Intelligence Report, Directorate of Intelligence, Reference
Title: ESAU LI, Feb. 1971, available at http://www.foia.cia.gov/sites/default/files
/document_conversions/14/esau-50.pdf.

19. H. R. Haldeman, *The Ends of Power* (New York: Dell, 1978), 91; Roger Morris
Memorandum for Henry Kissinger, November 18, 1969, declassified memo, Subject: NSSM 63, Sino-Soviet Rivalry—A Dissenting View, Nixon Presidential
Library; Helmut Sonnenfeldt Memorandum to Henry Kissinger, Secret, August
19, 1969, Nixon Presidential Library. For more on Kissinger's relations with Haldeman, see Robert Dallek, *Nixon and Kissinger: Partners in Power* (New York:
HarperCollins, 2007), chapter 11.

20. The project name SOLO was devised to cover the fact that it was two agents,
Morris Childs and his brother Jack, in the SOLO program that self-disclosed after
the two brothers received the Medal of Freedom from President Reagan in 1983.
See John Barron, *Operation Solo: The FBI's Man in the Kremlin* (Washington, DC:
Regnery History, 1997). Barron states one report smuggled out of Moscow in 1965
concerning Soviet views of China was termed by the CIA to be "the most significant piece of intelligence data ever supplied concerning the Soviet Union" (125).
As a result, the FBI decided "to assemble all SOLO reports pertaining to China
back to 1958." Barron reports in 1971 that SOLO revealed that Mikhail Suslov, the
second secretary of the Communist Party of the Soviet Union, had vowed that
"no matter what Nixon and China agreed to, we are going to negotiate with the
US constantly" (183). "FBI Records: The Vault - SOLO," US Federal Bureau of
Investigation (accessed March 5, 2014), available at http://vault.fbi.gov/solo.

21. Kutovoy discussed all this again in 2010 at the Diplomatic Academy in Moscow.
He said "I told you so forty-five years ago."

22. Arthur Cohen, "Soviet Thinking about the Danger of a Sino-US Rapprochement,"
CIA Directorate of Intelligence, Intelligence Report, February 1971. See also

"Signs of Life in Chinese Foreign Policy," CIA Directorate of Intelligence, April 11, 1970, no. 0501/70. Another important report was POLO 28; see "Factionalism in the Central Committee: Mao's Opposition Since 1949," (Reference Title: POLO XXVIII), September 19, 1968, RSS no. 0031/68, declassified in May 2007.

23. In an October 22 memorandum to Kissinger, Fred Iklé, director of the Arms Control and Disarmament Agency, suggested offering intelligence to China about the Soviet threat. Richard Solomon sent Iklé's memorandum to Kissinger under a November 1 covering memorandum. National Archives, RG 59, Policy Planning Staff (S/P), Director's Files (Winston Lord) 1969–1977, Entry 5027, Box 370, Secretary Kissinger's Visit to Peking, October 1973, S/PC, Mr. Lord, vol. II, National Archives, College Park, MD.

24. Central Intelligence Agency, Memorandum for Colonel T. C. Pinckney, Subject: GNP Data for the USSR, Communist China, North Korea, and North Vietnam, 1971, declassified in 1998, available at http://www.foia.cia.gov/sites/default/files /document_conversions/89801/DOC_0000307804.pdf; and U.S. Gross National Product (GNP)-10 Year Chart, ForecastChart.com, last updated on December 16, 2013, available at http://www.forecast-chart.com/chart-us-gnp.html.

25. There is an extensive literature written by the *ying pai* hawks on *The Thirty-Six Stratagems*. The short text is a popular distillation of ancient stories to which later authors have appended historical illustrations. Two Chinese books in English that amplify them are Sun Haichen, *The Wiles of War: 36 Military Strategies from Ancient China* (Beijing: Foreign Languages Press, 1991); and Chinghua Tang, *A Treasury of China's Wisdom* (Beijing: Foreign Languages Press, 1996). See also Stefan H. Verstappen, *The Thirty-Six Stratagies of Ancient China* (San Francisco: China Books & Periodicals, 1999), available at http://wengu.tartarie .com/wg/wengu.php?l=36ji&&no=3.

26. Jeremy Page, "For Xi, a 'China Dream' of Military Power," *Wall Street Journal*, March 13, 2013, available at http://online.wsj.com/news/articles/SB10001424127 887324128504578348774040546346. Page further reports that "Mr. Xi is casting himself as a strong military leader at home and embracing a more hawkish worldview long outlined by generals who think the U.S. is in decline and China will become the dominant military power in Asia by midcentury."

27. Ibid.

28. Ibid.

29. Like many China engagement supporters in the West, Kissinger refers to Colonel Liu only briefly, as a fringe nationalist, whose views are "contrary" to, for example, President Hu. Henry Kissinger, *On China* (New York: Penguin Press, 2011), 505.

30. Erich Follath, "China: Troublemaker on the World Stage?," ABC News, February 23, 2010, available at http://abcnews.go.com/International/china-troublemaker -world-stage/story?id=9918196#.UaT1goVc0SQ; and Chito Romana, "China: 'White Knight' or 'Angry Outsider'?," ABC News, April 1, 2009, available at http://abcnews.go.com/International/story?id=7229053&page=1#.UaT 1vYVc0SQ.

31. Quoted in Chito Romana, "Does China Want to Be Top Superpower?," ABC News, March 2, 2010, available at http://abcnews.go.com/International/china-replace -us-top-superpower/story?id=9986355.

32. William A. Callahan, *China Dreams: 20 Visions of the Future* (New York: Oxford University Press, 2013), 58–62.

33. William A. Callahan, "China's Harmonious World and Post-Western World Orders: Official and Citizen Intellectual Perspectives," 33, in *China Across the Divide: The Domestic and Global in Politics and Society*, ed. Rosemary Foot (New York: Oxford University Press, 2013).

34. Page, "For Xi, a 'China Dream' of Military Power."

35. Zhao Tingyang, "A Political World Philosophy in Terms of All-under-heaven (Tian-xia)," *Diogenes* 56, no. 1 (February 2009): 5–18, cited in Callahan, *China Dreams: 20 Visions of the Future*, 52.

36. William A. Callahan, "Chinese Visions of World Order: Post-hegemonic or a New Hegemony?," *International Studies Review* 10 (2008): 749–61, 757, available at http://williamacallahan.com/wp-content/uploads/2010/10/Callahan-TX-ISR -08.pdf.

37. According to William A. Callahan, Hu sees the world as tolerant of intersection among equal civilizations. Zhao's *tianxia*, however, is holistic and hierarchical with one singular global civilization harmonizing peoples of the world. Liu's China dream likewise sees China as a singular ruler after competition among civilizations. Callahan, *China Dreams*, 63.

CHAPTER 2: WARRING STATES

1. Henry Kissinger, *Does America Need a Foreign Policy?* (New York: Simon & Schuster, 2001), 137.

2. I use the term *Warring States* more broadly than some Sinologists to include the earlier period known as the Spring Autumn era. Instead of dividing in half the five centuries from 771 BC to 221 BC, I use the term *Warring States* to refer to the entire five hundred years of interstate struggles. The era began with the collapse of the power of the king of the Zhou dynasty. He was defeated and killed in 771 BC by an alliance of his own lords and non-Chinese peoples. He and his predecessors, dating back to 1000 BC, had ruled with real power. After this defeat of 771 BC, the capital city was moved and the king's descendants were virtually powerless. The world of interstate struggles began with competition and warfare enduring until a new king, calling himself the first emperor, unified these Warring States in 221 BC. Most Sinologists divide this period from 771 BC to 221 BC into two periods. In both periods, the ceremonial king was too weak to impose his will. Sometimes he at least attended interstate conferences or sent his envoy. The so-called hegemon had the most power and ruled. The hegemon system evolved into a struggle among the seven major states, who formed contending coalitions and no longer selected a single hegemon. The period from 475 BC to 221 BC is commonly called Warring States. The distinction is a bit artificial.

The names of the two periods do not seem to have been in use at the time, but were created later by historians. For more on the Warring States period, see Ralph Sawyer, *The Tao of Deception: Unorthodox Warfare in Historic and Modern China* (New York: Basic Books, 2007), especially chapter 2, "Spring and Autumn Precursors," and chapter 4, "Warring States Commanders." Sawyer states on p. 447, n. 34, that "an English language history of the Warring States remains to be written." See also Ralph Sawyer, *The Tao of Spycraft: Intelligence Theory and Practice in Traditional China* (Boulder, CO: Westview Press, 2004), chapter 3, "The Warring States Period"; James Irving Crump, *Legends of the Warring States: Persuasions, Romances, and Stories from Chan-kuo Ts'e* (Ann Arbor, MI: Center for Chinese Studies, 1998); William H. Mott and Jae Chang Kim, *The Philosophy of Chinese Military Culture: Shih vs. Li* (New York: Palgrave Macmillan, 2006); Yuri Pines, *Envisioning Eternal Empire: Chinese Political Thought of the Warring States Period* (Honolulu: University of Hawaii Press, 2009); and William A. Callahan and Elena Barabantseva, eds., *China Orders the World: Normative Soft Power and Foreign Policy* (Baltimore, MD: The Johns Hopkins University Press, 2012).

3. Lionel M. Jensen, *Manufacturing Confucianism: Chinese Traditions and Universal Civilization* (Durham, NC: Duke University Press, 1997), is an excellent guide by a Western scholar who discovered these fabrications.

4. Cited in Pillsbury, *China Debates the Future Security Environment*, prologue.

5. Salisbury, *New Emperors*, and Ross Terrill, *The New Chinese Empire: And What It Means for the United States* (New York: Basic Books, 2003).

6. Kissinger, *On China*, 211.

7. Wu Chunqiu, *On Grand Strategy* (Beijing: Current Affairs Press, 2000).

8. For additional information on the Chinese military's involvement in civilian strategic planning, see Evan A. Feigenbaum, *China's Techno-Warriors: National Security and Strategic Competition from the Nuclear to the Information Age* (Stanford: Stanford University Press, 2003).

9. Yang Bosun, *Chunqiu Zuozhuan zhu*, 2nd ed., *Zhongguo Gudian Mingzhu Yizhu Congshu* (Beijing: Zhonghua Press, 1990). There are slightly different translations in Wai-yee Li, *The Readability of the Past in Early Chinese Historiography*, Harvard East Asian Monographs, 253 and 300 (Cambridge, MA, 2007); David Schaberg, *A Patterned Past: Form and Thought in Early Chinese Historiography*, Harvard East Asian Monographs 205 (Cambridge, MA, 2001), 60; and James Legge, "The Ch'un Ts'ew with the Tso Chuen," in *The Chinese Classics*, 2nd ed. (Oxford: Clarendon, 1895), V, 293.

10. Although it's true that the size of the private sector has increased in China, the role of the private sector has slowed, and there is consensus among Chinese leaders to maintain control of all strategic economic sectors and of foreign trade policy. In particular, Chinese scholars and officials devote special attention to the control of currency, in part because each of the Warring States had its own currency and used it to conduct what amounted to economic warfare against the others.

11. Indeed, the intelligence services are ordered to make economic growth their

highest priority. William C. Hannas, James Mulvenon, and Anna B. Puglisi, *Chinese Industrial Espionage: Technology Acquisition and Military Modernisation* (New York: Routledge, 2013). For background on Chinese intelligence, see Jeffrey T. Richelson, *Foreign Intelligence Organizations* (Cambridge, MA: Ballinger, 1988), chapter 9; Patrick E. Tyler, "Cloak and Dragon: There Is No Chinese James Bond. So Far," *New York Times*, March 23, 1997, available at http://www.nytimes.com/1997/03/23/weekinreview/there-is-no-chinese-james-bond-so-far.html; Lo Ping, "Secrets About CPC Spies—Tens of Thousands of Them Scattered over 170-Odd Cities Worldwide," *Cheng Ming*, January 1, 1997 (U.S. Foreign Broadcast Information Service [FBIS] Daily Reports, CHI-97-016, January 1, 1997); Tan Po, "Spy Headquarters Behind the Shrubs—Supplement to 'Secrets About CPC Spies,'" *Cheng Ming*, March 1, 1997 (FBIS Daily Reports, CHI-97-047, March 1, 1997); Peter Mattis, "China's Misunderstood Spies," *Diplomat*, October 31, 2011, available at http://thediplomat.com/2011/10/chinas-misunderstood-spies/; and David Wise, *Tiger Trap: America's Secret Spy War with China* (Boston: Houghton Mifflin Harcourt, 2011).

12. David C. Gompert and Phillip C. Saunders, *The Paradox of Power: Sino-American Strategic Restraint in an Age of Vulnerability* (Washington, DC: National Defense University, 2012), 169.

13. For background on the cost of Chinese missiles, see Gompert and Saunders, *Paradox of Power*, 81, 106. As the *Washington Post* editorial board notes, "China strives to be a regional superpower, not a global one, at least for now. It has put an emphasis on developing advanced weapons systems that could deliver what the United States calls 'anti-access/area denial,' meaning to deter adversaries from areas that China claims—or to expel them. Thus, China is investing in weapons such as long-range cruise missiles and an antiship ballistic missile designed to hit an aircraft carrier. Such investments pose asymmetric threats to the United States and its allies. Andrew S. Erickson of the Naval War College presented estimates to the U.S.-China Economic and Security Review Commission in January that China could build some 1,227 of the antiship missiles for what it costs the United States to build a single Ford-class aircraft carrier. It might take just one missile to kill a carrier." "Beijing's Breakneck Defense Spending Poses a Challenge to the US," editorial, *Washington Post*, March 12, 2014, available at http://www.washingtonpost.com/opinions/beijings-breakneck-defense-spending-poses-a-challenge-to-the-us/2014/03/12/359fc444-a899-11e3-8d62-419db477a0e6_story.html. See also Andrew S. Erickson, Testimony before the U.S.-China Economic and Security Review Commission Hearing on China's Military Modernization and its Implications for the United States, January 30, 2014, available at http://www.uscc.gov/sites/default/files/Andrew%20Erickson_testimony1.30.14.pdf; and Henry Hendrix, *At What Cost a Carrier?* (Washington, DC: Center for a New American Security, March 2013), 8, http://www.cnas.org/files/documents/publications/CNAS%20Carrier_Hendrix_FINAL.pdf.

14. For more on the U.S. embargo of China, see Shu Guang Zhang, *Economic Cold War: America's Embargo against China and the Sino-Soviet Alliance, 1949–1963*

(Washington, DC: Woodrow Wilson Center Press; Stanford, CA: Stanford University Press, 2001).

15. Pillsbury, *China Debates the Future Security Environment*, 300.

16. As a Chinese handbook called *The Science of Military Strategy* says, "Strategic thought is always formed on the basis of certain historical and national cultural tradition, and formulation and performance of strategy by strategists are always controlled and driven by certain cultural ideology and historical cultural complex." Thomas G. Mahnken, "Secrecy & Stratagem: Understanding Chinese Strategic Culture," Lowy Institute for International Policy, February 2011, 3, available at http://www.lowyinstitute.org/files/pubfiles/Mahnken,_Secrecy_and_strata gem.pdf.

17. David Lai, "Learning from the Stones: A Go Approach to Mastering China's Strategic Concept, *Shi*," U.S. Army War College Strategic Studies Institute (May 1, 2004), available at http://www.strategicstudiesinstitute.army.mil/pubs/display .cfm?pubID=378.

18. Quoted in ibid., 2.

19. Roger T. Ames, *The Art of Rulership* (Albany: State University of New York Press, 1994).

20. François Jullien, *The Propensity of Things: Toward a History of Efficacy in China*, trans. Janet Lloyd (New York: Zone Books, 1999); François Jullien, *A Treatise on Efficacy: Between Western and Chinese Thinking*, trans. Janet Lloyd (Honolulu: University of Hawaii Press, 2004); François Jullien, *The Great Image Has No Form, or On the Nonobject through Painting*, trans. Jane Marie Todd (University of Chicago Press, 2009); François Jullien, *The Impossible Nude: Chinese Art and Western Aesthetics*, trans. Maev de la Guardia (University of Chicago Press, 2000); François Jullien, *The Silent Transformations*, trans. Krzysztof Fijalkowski and Michael Richardson (New York: Seagull Books, 2011); François Jullien, *Detour and Access: Strategies of Meaning in China and Greece*, trans. Sophie Hawkes (New York: Zone Books, 2000); and François Jullien, *In Praise of Blandness*, trans. Paula M. Varsano (New York: Zone Books, 2004).

21. As one critic has said of Jullien's work in general, "his books easily lead readers to develop a too strong notion of cultural otherness, thereby glorifying a long-gone literati culture and, rather naturally, developing a certain contempt for the Chinese present." Kai Marchal, "François Jullien and the Hazards of 'Chinese' Reality," *Warp, Weft, and Way*, September 27, 2012, available at http://warpweftandway .com/2012/09/27/francois-jullien-and-the-hazards-of-chinese-reality/.

22. For example, China invited the U.S. senator Henry Jackson to visit Beijing in 1976. For more on Senator Jackson, see Robert G. Kaufman, *Henry M. Jackson: A Life in Politics* (Seattle: University of Washington Press, 2000).

23. Henry Kissinger, *Diplomacy* (New York: Simon & Schuster, 1994); Henry Kissinger, *White House Years* (New York: Little, Brown, 1979); Henry Kissinger, *Years of Renewal* (New York: Touchstone, 1999); and Henry Kissinger, *Years of Upheaval* (London: Weidenfeld & Nicolson, 1982).

24. Kissinger, *On China*, 235.

25. Ibid., 371.

26. Pillsbury, *China Debates the Future Security Environment*, xxxvii.

27. Ibid., chapters 6 and 22.

28. Kimberly Besio and Constantine Tung, eds., *Three Kingdoms and Chinese Culture* (Albany: State University of New York Press, 2007); John J. Tkacik, "A Spirit-Visit to an Ancient Land," *Wall Street Journal*, February 28, 2014, available at http://online.wsj.com/news/articles/SB20001424052702303775504579397221926 892100.

29. According to Chinese authors, the southern commander's victory at Red Cliff was due to four factors in the southern coalition's assessment of *shi*: avoid anxiety and confusion about superficial phenomena; a coalition is needed to strike the main enemy; strike the enemy first and by surprise; and attack the enemy's weakest point. Zhang Tieniu and Gao Xiaoxing, *Zhongguo gudai haijun shi [Chinese Ancient Naval History]* (Beijing: Ba yi chubanshe, 1993), 46, 47. An Academy of Military Science author emphasizes that the victors at Red Cliff applied the strategy of "wait and see" until propensity was favorable. Yue Shuiyu and Liang Jingmin, *Sun Zi bingfa Yu Gao Jishu Ahanzheng [Sun Zi's Art of War and High Technology Warfare]* (Beijing: Guofang daxue chubanshe, 1998), 122.

30. One author summarized the northern commander's defeat as "faulty strategy," especially "failing to transform your disadvantages into advantages when dealing with a superior enemy . . . [he] was suspicious of the people who he should have trusted, and trusted the people that should have been suspect. He was arrogant." Yu Xuebin, *Shuo San Guo, Hua Ren Sheng: "Sanguo Yanyi" Fengyun Renwu Bai Yin Qianshuo [A Discussion on the Lives of the Main Characters in the Three Kingdoms: An Elementary Introduction to the Reasons the Main Characters Were Defeated in "The Romance of the Three Kingdoms"]* (Beijing: Jiefangjun chubanshe, 1996), 247–48. Other authors stress the tragedy of the battle's outcome. The northern commander "could have been one of the outstanding military strategists in our nation's history." Pu Yinghua and Hua Mingliang, *Yunchou Weiwo—Zhuge Liang Bingfa [Devise Strategies Within a Command Tent—Zhuge Liang's Art of War]* (Beijing: Wuzi chubanshe, 1996), 47.

31. "A single deception can cause a vast defeat." Central Television Station Military Department and the Navy Political Department Propaganda Department, *Sanshiliu Ji Gujin Tan [Ancient and Modern Discussions on the Thirty-Six Deceptions]* (Jinan: Huanghe chubanshe, 1995), 166. This belief is echoed in much of the PLA commentary on the Battle of Red Cliff. Several authors stress that the technique of sowing political discord is the key factor in the southern commander's victory at Red Cliff. Mao Zhenfa, Tian Xuan, Peng Xunhou, *Moulue Jia [Strategists]* (Beijing: Lantian chubanshe, 1993), 119. Several Chinese authors believe that the formation of the southern coalition was crucial to victory. Zhang Feng, *Zhongguo Lidai Canmouzhang [Chiefs of Staff in Past Chinese Dynasties]* (Beijing: Kunlun chubanshe, 1999), 180. "Red Cliff occurred one year after the strategic planning conference at Grand Central Village. That was the first step in implementing the coalition strategy which made possible the transformation of

258   NOTES

the inferior southern side to defeat the hegemon." Ren Yuan, *Zhisheng Bijian-Zhuge Liang De Chengbai Deshi* [*Getting the Upper Hand Must Be Examined: Zhuge Liang's Successes and Failures*] (Changan: Xibei daxue chubanshe, 1997), 58. Similarly, another PLA author emphasizes that without the formation of the southern coalition, there would have been no defeat of a superior power. Li Zhisun, *Zhongguo Lidai Zhanzheng Gailan* [*An Outline of Warfare in Past Chinese Dynasties*] (Beijing: Junshi kexue chubanshe, 1994), 108.

32. Yue Shuiyu and Liang Jingmin, *Sun Zi Bingfa Yu Gao Jishu Zhanzheng*, 122.

33. Central Television Station Military Department and the Navy Political Department Propaganda Department, *Sanshiliu Ji Gujin Tan*, 174–75.

CHAPTER 3: ONLY CHINA COULD GO TO NIXON

1. For more on Larry Chin and his role in providing classified U.S. intelligence to the Chinese government, see Tod Hoffman, *The Spy Within: Larry Chin and China's Penetration of the CIA* (Hanover, NH: Steerforth Press, 2008).

2. Chen Jian, *Mao's China and the Cold War* (Chapel Hill: University of North Carolina Press, 2001), 245–46.

3. Kissinger, *On China*, 210. The first book to translate the Chinese account in 1992 of the strategy proposed to Mao by the four marshals was Patrick Tyler's *A Great Wall*, published in 1999. Kissinger's account in *On China*, based on the same evidence, appeared in 2012. Tyler reported that the four marshals met twenty-three times in 1969, and that their cynical recommendations to Mao equated America to Hitler and to a ruthless hegemon determined to prevent an expansion of Soviet power. Kissinger appears to be alone in detecting a Chinese desire to cooperate with America for other than these cynical reasons. Patrick Tyler, *A Great Wall: Six Presidents and China: An Investigative History* (New York: PublicAffairs, 1999), 71–73.

4. Xiong Xianghui, "The Prelude to the Opening of Sino-American Relations," *Zhonggong Dangshi Ziliao* (*CCP History Materials*), no. 42 (June 1992): 81, as excerpted in William Burr, ed., "New Documentary Reveals Secret US, Chinese Diplomacy behind Nixon's Trip," National Security Archive Electronic Briefing Book, no. 145, December 21, 2004, available at http://www2.gwu.edu/~nsarchiv/NSAEBB/NSAEBB145/.

5. Kissinger, *On China*, 212. Although I rely on Kissinger's *On China* here, there are at least four other books based on archival evidence that strongly dispute Kissinger's account of Chinese strategy and his claim that any hope emerged in 1969–72 for long-term Sino-American cooperation. Elsewhere in this chapter, I cite these books by William Burr, Evelyn Goh, James Mann, and Patrick Tyler. Unfortunately, Kissinger has not attempted to rebut these many detailed attacks on his credibility about the opening to China. The critics offer substantial documentation that he misunderstood Chinese strategy, which was apparently not based on any trust that America would defend China against Soviet attack, or any desire for long-term cooperation with America. The critics propose an alternative theory that China's strategy successfully manipulated not only Kissinger but also

later American leaders. Kissinger's account of the opening to China set the paradigm of future Sino-American cooperation, according to James Mann: "American policy toward China was based on a series of beliefs and assumptions, many of which turned out to be tragically inaccurate." James Mann, *About Face: A History of America's Curious Relationship with China, from Nixon to Clinton* (New York: Vintage Books, 1998), 6.

6. Kissinger, *On China*, 211. I again rely heavily on Kissinger's analysis of the 1969 opening, especially his analysis of General Xiong's memoir, the sole informative document released by China so far. Patrick Tyler also quotes from General Xiong's account. Tyler, *Great Wall*, 71–73.

7. Kissinger, *On China*, 212.

8. Ibid.

9. Ibid., 212–13.

10. Ibid., 274. James Mann reports that a CIA study he obtained disputes Kissinger's version of Chinese strategy: "Recently declassified records and memoirs show, however, that Kissinger's account was at best misleading and incomplete." Mann, *About Face*, 33. According to Mann, "The secret CIA study found that the leaders in Beijing were often able to exploit or manipulate the differences in Washington, rewarding and flattering China's friends, instilling a sense of obligation, freezing out those US officials who were considered less sympathetic." Ibid., 11.

11. A 1999 book, *A Great Wall: Six Presidents and China: An Investigative History*, by the *New York Times* reporter Patrick Tyler, who lived in Beijing and then spent four years researching the opening, has influenced the Chinese view of how they brought Nixon to Beijing. In Nixon's first months in office, the Chinese were put off by Nixon's public seemingly anti-China statements. He even concluded from interviews that Nixon and Kissinger at first sided with Moscow after the border clashes—a necessity given that Nixon had already asked the Soviets to help him extricate U.S. forces from Vietnam. When the book was published, it fed paranoia in Beijing, as it contained the revelation that Kissinger, on Nixon's behalf, had asked for a classified study in July 1969 of how an American nuclear attack could be launched on China, in support of Moscow. Tyler claimed this was the first time such a study, focusing exclusively on a U.S. nuclear attack on China (and not the Soviet Union), had ever been undertaken. In his July 14 memorandum to the CIA and the Pentagon, Kissinger said, "The president has directed" preparation of a study of "a range of possible situations in which a U.S. strategic nuclear capability against China would be useful." Kissinger later denied this and wrote to Tyler, "we never considered cooperating with the Soviets to wipe out the Chinese nuclear capability." Tyler, *Great Wall*, 63.

12. Helmut Sonnenfeldt and John H. Holdridge to Henry Kissinger, October 10, 1969, Subject: State Memo to the President on Sino-Soviet Relations and the U.S.

13. Roger Morris Memorandum for Henry Kissinger, November 18, 1969, declassified memo, Subject: NSSM 63, Sino-Soviet Rivalry—A Dissenting View, Nixon Presidential Library. NSC staffers Hyland and Morris addressed how America might not want to deter a Soviet attack on China, or take China's side. In contrast,

Kissinger argues in *White House Years* that he "could not accept a Soviet military assault on China. We had held this view before there was contact of any sort." Kissinger, *White House Years*, 764. However, Patrick Tyler concludes that Kissinger's description of his desire to defend China is false: "This self-serving statement is clearly contradicted by the record of Nixon's and Kissinger's other statements over the years ... and also contradicted by the recollections of Secretary [of Defense] Laird as well as those of key Kissinger aides." Tyler, *Great Wall*, 66.

14. Jerome A. Cohen, "Ted Kennedy's Role in Restoring Diplomatic Relations with China," *Legislation and Public Policy* 14 (2011): 347–55.

15. The July 1969 accident at Chappaquiddick necessarily moved Kennedy's focus away from China and tempered his presidential ambitions, but in 1977 Kennedy made his first trip to China and met with Deng Xiaoping. The senator's March 20, 1969, speech advocating an American opening to China had attracted worldwide media attention, including front-page headlines in the *New York Times* that Yevgeny Kutovoy and Arkady Shevchenko excitedly showed me that day.

16. Memorandum of Conversation, Participants: Mao Tse-tung, Chou En-lai, Richard Nixon, Henry Kissinger, Winston Lord (notetaker), February 21, 1972, 2:50–3:55 p.m., Beijing, Document 194, in Foreign Relations of the United States, 1969–1976, vol. XVII, China, 1969–1972, available at https://history.state.gov/historicaldocuments/frus1969-76v17/d194.

17. Kissinger, *On China*, 259.

18. Memorandum of Conversation, Participants: Chou En-lai, Yeh Chien-ying, Huang Hua, Chang Wen-chin, Hsu-Chung-ching, Wang Hai-jung, Tang Wen-sheng and Chi Chao-chu (Chinese interpreters and notetakers), Henry Kissinger, John Holdridge, Winston Lord, W. Richard Smyser, Beijing, July 10, 1971, 12:10–6:00 p.m., in Foreign Relations of the United States, vol. XVII, document 140, available at http://2001-2009.state.gov/documents/organization/70142.pdf.

19. Kissinger to Nixon, "My October China Visit: Discussions of the Issues," 11 November [1971] Top Secret/Sensitive/Exclusively Eyes Only, pages 5, 7, and 29. Source: RG 59, State Department Top Secret Subject-Numeric Files, 1970–1973, POL 7 Kissinger, available in William Burr, ed., with Sharon Chamberlain and Gao Bei, "Negotiating U.S.-Chinese Rapprochement: New American and Chinese Documentation Leading Up to Nixon's 1972 Trip," National Security Archive Electronic Briefing Book, no. 70, May 22, 2002, available at http://www2.gwu.edu/~nsarchiv/NSAEBB/NSAEBB70/doc22.pdf.

20. Memorandum of Conversation, Participants: Prime Minister Chou En-lai, Chi P'eng-fei, Chang Wen-chin, Xiong Hsiang-hui, Wang Hai-jung, Tang Wen-sheng and Chi Chao-chu (Chinese interpreters and notetakes), Henry Kissinger, Winston Lord, John Holdridge, Alfred Jenkins, October 22, 1971, Great Hall of the People, Peking, 4:15–8:28 p.m., General Subjects: Korea, Japan, South Asia, Soviet Union, Arms Control, in "Foreign Relations, 1969–1976, Volume E-13, Documents on China, 1969–1972," released by the Office of the Historian of the U.S. Department of State, available at http://2001-2009.state.gov/r/pa/ho/frus/nixon/e13/72461.htm.

21. This was not made public until many years later. In 1976, James Schlesinger, former U.S. secretary of defense, said publicly that American officials discussed the possibility of giving China military assistance. *Lethbridge Herald*, April 13, 1976, 3, available at http://newspaperarchive.com/ca/alberta/lethbridge/lethbridge-herald/1976/04-13/page-3. American officials, said Schlesinger, discussed giving military assistance to China but never discussed it formally. "There was speculation on this subject but there was never a formal addressing of the issue of military assistance to China," he said. Schlesinger said that such aid would have to be considered in light of the circumstances, but he added that he "would not reject it out of hand." "Weighing of Aid to China Seen," *Victoria Advocate*, April 12, 1976, 5A, available at http://news.google.com/newspapers?nid=861&dat=19760412&id=IhZZAAAAIBAJ&sjid=XkYNAAAAIBAJ&pg=3791,2033685.

22. Thomas M. Gottlieb, "Chinese Foreign Policy Factionalism and the Origins of the Strategic Triangle," RAND Corporation, 1977, Document Number R-1902-NA, available at http://www.rand.org/pubs/reports/R1902.html.

23. Lord to Kissinger, "Your November 23 Night Meeting," November 29, 1971, enclosing memcon of Kissinger–Huang Hua Meeting, Top Secret/Sensitive/Exclusively Eyes Only, Source: RG 59, Records of the Policy Planning Staff, Director's Files (Winston Lord), 1969–1977, Box 330, China Exchanges October 20–December 21, 1971, in Burr, ed., "Negotiating U.S.-Chinese Rapprochement."

24. Evelyn Goh, *Constructing the U.S. Rapprochement with China, 1961–1974: From "Red Menace" to "Tacit Ally"* (Cambridge, UK: Cambridge University Press, 2005), 189.

25. Yang and Xia, "Vacillating Between Revolution and Détente," *Diplomatic History Journal* 34, no. 2 (April 2010): 413–14.

26. Kissinger, *On China*, 290.

27. Memorandum of Conversation, February 23, 1972, 2:00 p.m.–6:00 p.m., Location of original: National Archives, Nixon Presidential Materials Project, White House Special Files, President's Office Files, Box 87, Memoranda for the President Beginning February 20, 1972, page 21, in William Burr, ed., "Nixon's Trip to China: Records Now Completely Declassified, Including Kissinger Intelligence Briefing and Assurances on Taiwan," National Security Archive, December 11, 2003, Document 2, available at http://www2.gwu.edu/~nsarchiv/NSAEBB/NSAEBB106/.

28. Kissinger, *White House Years*, 906.

29. Memorandum of Conversation, February 23, 1972, 9:35 a.m.–12:34 p.m., Nixon Presidential Materials Project, National Security Council Files, HAK Office Files, Box 92, Dr. Kissinger's Meetings in the PRC During the Presidential Visit February 1972, page 20, in William Burr, ed., "Nixon's Trip to China: Records Now Completely Declassified, Including Kissinger Intelligence Briefing and Assurances on Taiwan," National Security Archive, December 11, 2003, Document 4, available at http://www2.gwu.edu/~nsarchiv/NSAEBB/NSAEBB106/.

30. Memorandum of Conversation, February 22, 1972, 2:10 p.m.–6:10 p.m., Location of original: National Archives, Nixon Presidential Materials Project, White

House Special Files, President's Office Files, Box 87, Memoranda for the President Beginning February 20, 1972, page 10, in William Burr, ed., "Nixon's Trip to China: Records Now Completely Declassified, Including Kissinger Intelligence Briefing and Assurances on Taiwan," National Security Archive, December 11, 2003, Document 1, available at http://www2.gwu.edu/~nsarchiv/NSAEBB /NSAEBB106/; Memorandum of Conversation, February 23, 1972, 9:35 a.m.–12:34 p.m., Nixon Presidential Materials Project, National Security Council Files, HAK Office Files, Box 92, Dr. Kissinger's Meetings in the PRC During the Presidential Visit February 1972, page 20, in William Burr, ed., "Nixon's Trip to China: Records Now Completely Declassified, Including Kissinger Intelligence Briefing and Assurances on Taiwan," National Security Archive, December 11, 2003, Document 4, available at http://www2.gwu.edu/~nsarchiv/NSAEBB/NSAEBB106/.

31. According to Professor Evelyn Goh, Anatoly Dobrynin, the Soviet ambassador in Washington, told Kissinger in March that Moscow had concluded, based on Chinese sources, that Kissinger had given the Chinese "a complete rundown of the 'dislocation' of Soviet forces on the Chinese border, as well as of the location of Soviet missile installations." See Goh, *Constructing the U.S. Rapprochement with China*, 174–75. Kissinger denied it. See Memorandum of Conversation, March 9, 1972, Box 493, National Security Files, Nixon Presidential Materials Project, page 3, Nixon Presidential Library.

32. For an excellent Western retrospective on the Sino-Soviet split, see Harold P. Ford, "The CIA and Double Demonology: Calling the Sino-Soviet Split," *Studies in Intelligence* (Winter 1998–99): 57–61, available at https://www.cia.gov/library /center-for-the-study-of-intelligence/kent-csi/vol42no5/pdf/v42i5a05p.pdf.

33. See, for example, Zhou-Ye Jianying–Kissinger Memcon, June 20, 1972, 15–16, June 21, 1972, 3, in Box 851, National Security Files, Nixon Presidential Materials; and Howe to Kissinger, "China Trip," June 24, 1972, Box 97, National Security Files, Nixon Presidential Materials, both available at the Nixon Presidential Library and cited in Evelyn Goh, "Nixon, Kissinger, and the 'Soviet Card' in the U.S. Opening to China, 1971–1974," *Diplomatic History* 29, iss. 3 (June 2005): 475–502, 485, footnote 43.

34. Mao–Kissinger Memcon, February 17, 1973, in William Burr, *Kissinger Transcripts: The Top Secret Talks with Beijing and Moscow* (Collingdale, PA: Diane Publishing, 1999), 88–89, also available at the Nixon Presidential Library and cited in Goh, "Nixon, Kissinger, and the 'Soviet Card,'" 475–502, 485, footnote 44.

35. Xiong Xianghui, "The Prelude to the Opening of Sino-American Relations," *Zhonggong Dangshi Ziliao* (*CCP History Materials*), no. 42 (June 1992): 81, as excerpted in Burr, "New Documentary Reveals Secret U.S., Chinese Diplomacy behind Nixon's Trip."

36. Kissinger to Nixon, "My Trip to China," March 2, 1973, Box 6, President's Personal Files, Nixon Presidential Materials, 2–3, available at the Nixon Presidential Library and cited in Goh, "Nixon, Kissinger, and the 'Soviet Card,'" 475–502,

37. Kissinger, *Diplomacy*, 72.

38. Memorandum of Conversation, Participants: Henry Kissinger, Winston Lord,

Huang Hua, and Shih Yen-hua (interpreter), Friday, August 4, 1972, 5:15–6:45 p.m., New York City, in "Foreign Relations, 1969–1976, Volume E-13, Documents on China, 1969–1972," released by the Office of the Historian of the U.S. Department of State, available at http://2001-2009.state.gov/r/pa/ho/frus/nixon /e13/72605.htm.

39. Kissinger to PRCLO Chargé Han Xu, Memcon, May 15, 1973, Box 238, Lord Files, 7.

40. Kissinger to Huang Zhen, Memcon, May 29, 1973, Box 328, Lord Files.

41. Nixon to Zhou, June 19, 1973, Box 328, Lord Files.

42. Kissinger to Huang Zhen, Memcon, July 6, 1973, Box 328, Lord Files and July 19, 1973, Box 328, Lord Files.

43. Winston Lord to Henry Kissinger, National Archives, RG 59, Policy Planning Staff (S/P), Director's Files (Winston Lord) 1969–1977, Entry 5027, Box 370, Secretary Kissinger's Visit to Peking, October 1973, S/PC, Mr. Lord, vol. I, National Archives, College Park, MD.

44. Kissinger–Zhou Memcon, November 10, 1973, in Burr, *Kissinger Transcripts*, 171–72. Zhou–Kissinger Memcon, November 13, 1973, Digital National Security Archives Online, Document 283. Memorandum, Fred Iklé to Henry Kissinger, National Archives, RG 59, Policy Planning Staff (S/P), Director's Files (Winston Lord) 1969–1977, Lot 77D112, Entry 5027, Box 370, Secretary Kissinger's Visit to Peking, October 1973, S/PC, Mr. Lord, vol. II, National Archives, College Park, MD.

45. Goh, *Constructing the U.S. Rapprochement with China*, 242. See also Kissinger–Zhou Memcon, November 10, 1973, in Burr, *Kissinger Transcripts*, 171–72.

46. Zhou–Kissinger Memcon, November 14, 1973, National Security Archive Online, Document 284.

47. Luo Guanzhong, *Romance of the Three Kingdoms*, chapter 21: "In a Plum Garden, Cao Cao Discusses Heroes," trans. C. H. Brewitt-Taylor (Beijing: Foreign Languages Press, 1995), available at http://kongming.net/novel/events/liubei-and -caocao-speak-of-heroes.php. I have slightly modified this long translation.

48. For more on American and Chinese threat perceptions in the Taiwan Strait, see Michael Pillsbury, "China and Taiwan—the American Debate," *RUSI Journal* 154, no. 2 (April 2009): 82–88.

49. "Guns for Peking," *Newsweek*, September 8, 1975; Reagan gave a press conference on May 28, 1976. According to the *Los Angeles Times*, "Reagan said he thought American arms sales to mainland China would be a natural development in the light of certain common interests the two nations have in dealing with the Soviet Union." Kenneith Reich, "Reagan Tells of Rumors Administration Plans to Renounce Taiwan After Election," *Los Angeles Times*, May 29, 1976. See Yuri Dimov, "Commentary," *Moscow Radio Peace and Progress*, October 29, 1975, trans. by U.S. Foreign Broadcast Information Service, Washington, DC, October 31, 1975. See also Ivan Broz, "American Military Policy and Its China Factor," *Rude Pravo*, April 27, 1976, which states that "one of the spokesmen of these most reactionary U.S. circles is Michael Pillsbury of the RAND Corporation. . . . It is extremely reprehensible. . . . Allegedly American military assistance

to China would reward the pragmatic leaders in Peking and be a guarantee that their development would not head elsewhere when Mao dies."

50. Edward Slingerland, *Effortless Action: Wu-Wei as Conceptual Metaphor and Spiritual Ideal in Early China* (New York: Oxford University Press, 2003).

51. Deng Xiaoping, "Realize the Four Modernizations and Never Seek Hegemony," May 7, 1978, available at http://dengxiaopingworks.wordpress.com/2013/02/25/realize-the-four-modernizations-and-never-seek-hegemony/.

52. Ezra F. Vogel, *Deng Xiaoping and the Transformation of China* (Cambridge, MA: Harvard University Press, 2011), 323 (Kindle edition).

53. Kissinger, *On China*, 366–68.

54. Presidential Directive/NSC-43, November 3, 1978, available at http://www.jimmycarterlibrary.gov/documents/pddirectives/pd43.pdf.

55. James Lilley and Jeffrey Lilley, *China Hands: Nine Decades of Adventure, Espionage, and Diplomacy in Asia* (New York: PublicAffairs, 2004), 214–15.

56. In NSDD 120, President Reagan ordered that the U.S. government "lends support to China's ambitious modernization effort, especially through our liberalized technology transfer policy." NSDD 120, "Visit to the US of Premier Zhao Ziyang," January 9, 1984, available at http://www.fas.org/irp/offdocs/nsdd/. NSDD 140 declared that a "strong, secure, and stable China can be an increasing force for peace." NSDD 140, "President's Visit to People's Republic of China," April 21, 1984, available at http://www.fas.org/irp/offdocs/nsdd/nsdd-140.pdf.

57. Kenneth Conboy, *The Cambodian Wars: Clashing Armies and CIA Covert Operations* (Lawrence: University Press of Kansas, 2013). See also Andrew Mertha, *Brothers in Arms: Chinese Aid to the Khmer Rouge, 1975–1979* (Ithaca, NY: Cornell University Press, 2014).

58. George Crile, *Charlie Wilson's War: The Extraordinary Story of the Largest Covert Operation in History* (New York: Atlantic Monthly Press, 2003).

59. Kissinger, *Years of Renewal*, 819.

60. Tyler, *Great Wall*, 284.

61. Ibid., 285. Tyler cites President Carter and eight others in note 97.

62. The full details of the massive United States–China covert action programs in Afghanistan and Cambodia have still not been declassified, or confirmed by either the U.S. or Chinese governments. My discussion of these programs here must be limited to describing these programs solely by reference to the unauthorized interviews contained in two books, *Charlie Wilson's War* and *The Cambodian Wars*.

63. Conboy, *Cambodian Wars*, 228.

64. Ibid., 226–27.

65. Mary Louise Kelly, "Intelligence Veteran Focuses on North Korea," NPR, October 13, 2006, available at http://www.npr.org/templates/story/story.php?storyId=6259803.

66. Crile, *Charlie Wilson's War*, and Conboy, *Cambodian Wars*.

67. NSDD 166, US Policy, Programs, and Strategy in Afghanistan, March 27, 1985, available at http://www.fas.org/irp/offdocs/nsdd/nsdd-166.pdf.

68. Steve Coll, *Ghost Wars: The Secret History of the CIA, Afghanistan, and Bin Laden, from the Soviet Invasion to September 10, 2001* (New York: Penguin Press, 2004), 66.

69. Ibid., 137.

70. Ibid. My role in all this has been previously revealed in three books. According to Raymond L. Garthoff, "Michael Pillsbury first floated the idea of arms sales and a broad range of American military security relationships with China in a much-discussed article in *Foreign Policy* in the fall of 1975. Not known then was that Pillsbury had been conducting secret talks with Chinese officials . . . his reports were circulated to a dozen or so top officials of the NSC, Department of Defense and Department of State as secret documents." Raymond L. Garthoff, *Détente and Confrontation: American-Soviet Relations from Nixon to Reagan* (Washington, DC: Brookings Institution, 1983), 696. According to Mahmud Ali, "Michael Pillsbury, a China analyst at the RAND Corporation . . . spent the summer of 1973 secretly meeting PLA officers stationed under diplomatic cover at China's UN mission. . . . The DoD managed Pillsbury." Mahmud Ali, *US-China Cold War Collaboration, 1971–1989* (New York: Routledge, 2005), 81. According to Diego Cordovez, the UN undersecretary general who negotiated with the Soviets about their withdrawal from Afghanistan, "Initially, the Stinger campaign was spearheaded by Undersecretary of Defense for Policy Fred Iklé and his aggressive Coordinator for Afghan Affairs, Michael Pillsbury. . . . The Stinger proponents won their victory in the face of overwhelming bureaucratic resistance that persisted until the very end of the struggle." Diego Cordovez, *Out of Afghanistan: The Inside Story of the Soviet Withdrawal* (New York: Oxford University Press, 1995), 195. President Clinton's deputy attorney general Philip Heymann wrote, "The covert action committee met every three to four weeks. Its existence was not officially acknowledged, although such a committee had operated in every administration since Eisenhower. In the Kennedy administration, for example, it was known as the Forty Committee. Any information on covert actions was protected under a compartmentalized security system given the name VEIL." Philip Heymann, *Living the Policy Process* (New York: Oxford University Press, 2008), 44.

71. Karl D. Jackson, Memorandum for the Interagency Group on U.S.-China Military Relations, Subject: U.S.-China Military Relations: A Roadmap, September 10, 1986, Department of Defense, International Security Affairs, Douglas Paal file, Reagan Presidential Library.

72. Ibid. See also Feigenbaum, *China's Techno-Warriors*.

CHAPTER 4: MR. WHITE AND MS. GREEN

1. Pillsbury, *Chinese Views of Future Warfare*. The photo of Deng shaking hands appears on page 2, under another photo on that page I took of a famous military hawk and the author of five books, General Peng Guangqian.

2. As a Senate committee staffer and consultant to the Pentagon, I had depended on

Peter's reports for seven years since we first met in 1982 when he was a leading analyst at the U.S. embassy in Beijing.

3. George H. W. Bush, Address on Administration Goals before a Joint Session of Congress, February 9, 1989, available at http://www.presidency.ucsb.edu/ws/?pid=16660.

4. Mann, *About Face*, 158.

5. Liu Xiaobo survived the massacre and would go on to receive the Nobel Peace Prize twenty years later, in 2009, for his work on a prodemocracy effort in China called Charter 08.

6. Minxin Pei, *From Reform to Revolution: The Demise of Communism in China and the Soviet Union* (Cambridge, MA: Harvard University Press, 1994), 152.

7. Ibid.

8. George H. W. Bush, diary entry, June 5, 1989, in George H. W. Bush and Brent Scowcroft, *A World Transformed* (New York: Alfred A. Knopf, 1998), 98.

9. Ibid.

10. George H. W. Bush, Memorandum of Conversation, Subject: "Meeting with Wan Li, Chairman of the Standing Committee of the National People's Congress and Member of the Politburo, People's Republic of China," May 23, 1989, 2:30 p.m.–3:45 p.m., Oval Office, Cabinet Room, and Residence, available at http://www2.gwu.edu/~nsarchiv/NSAEBB/NSAEBB16/docs/doc07.pdf.

11. Hu Qiaomu's death in 1992 received international coverage, including an obituary in the *New York Times*: "Hu Qiaomu, a Chinese Hard-Liner, Is Dead at 81," *New York Times*, September 29, 1992, available at http://www.nytimes.com/1992/09/29/obituaries/hu-qiaomu-a-chinese-hard-liner-is-dead-at-81.html.

12. Deng Xiaoping, *Selected Works*, vol. III (1982–92) (Beijing: Renmin chubanshe, 1983), 108.

13. Ezra Vogel, *Deng Xiaoping and the Transformation of China* (Cambridge, MA: Harvard University Press, 2012), 659–63.

14. Zhao Ziyang, *Prisoner of the State: The Secret Journal of Premier Zhao Ziyang*, trans. and ed. Bao Pu, Renee Chiang, and Adi Ignatius (New York: Simon & Schuster, 2009). In this book, the editors explain that "There are many who must remain unnamed who have worked behind the scenes from inside China. They took unimaginable risks to safeguard, preserve, and transport Zhao Ziyang's secret tapes to safety outside the country" (306). See also Michael Wines, "A Populist's Downfall Exposes Ideological Divisions in China's Ruling Party," *New York Times*, April 6, 2012, and *The Tiananmen Papers*, comp. Zhang Liang, ed. Andrew J. Nathan and Perry Link (New York: PublicAffairs, 2001).

15. Robert L. Jervis, *Why Intelligence Fails: Lessons from the Iranian Revolution and the Iraq War* (Ithaca, NY: Cornell University Press, 2010), 15. On page 25, Jervis explains that one of the four major reasons for intelligence failure in the cases he examines was that "the role of nationalism and its twin, anti-Americanism, was missed and misunderstood."

16. James P. Harrison, *The Long March to Power: A History of the Chinese Communist Party, 1921–72* (Bethesda, MD: International Thomson Publishing, 1972).

17. Yan Jiaqi, *Toward a Democratic China: The Intellectual Autobiography of Yan Jiaqi* (Honolulu: University of Hawaii Press, 1992), 252–70, contains the ten points, which Yan states were published on December 28, 1989.
18. Ruan Ming, with Nancy Liu, Peter Rand, and Lawrence R. Sullivan, eds., *Deng Xiaoping: Chronicle of an Empire* (Boulder, CO: Westview Press, 1994), 140–50.
19. "The President's News Conference," June 5, 1989, George Bush Presidential Library, available at http://bushlibrary.tamu.edu/research/public_papers.php ?id=494&year&month.
20. Mann, *About Face*, 262.
21. See, for example, Constantine Menges, *China: The Gathering Threat* (Nashville, TN: Nelson Current, 2005), 124–25.
22. Tyler, *Great Wall*, 381–416.
23. Elisabeth Rosenthal, "Envoy Says Stoning Will End, Ties Won't," *New York Times*, May 11, 1999, available at http://partners.nytimes.com/library/world /europe/051199kosovo-china-sasser.html.
24. Erik Eckholm, "China Raises Then Lowers Tone in Anti-U.S. Protests at Embassy," *New York Times*, May 11, 1999, available at http://www.nytimes.com /1999/05/11/world/crisis-balkans-china-china-raises-then-lowers-tone-anti-us -protests-embassy.html.
25. Ibid.
26. Transcript: Clinton opens youth violence summit, May 10, 1999, CNN, available at http://www.cnn.com/ALLPOLITICS/stories/1999/05/10/youth.violence.summit /transcript.html.
27. "America vs. Japan and Germany," Jin Dexiang, 3, cited in Pillsbury, *China Debates the Future Security Environment*, 99.
28. Eckholm, "China Raises Then Lowers Tone in Anti-U.S. Protests at Embassy."
29. However, for China's foreign policy decision making, it is more important to find out how the Chinese leaders interpreted the Belgrade bombing. For this, *Zhu Rongji in 1999*, published in *Chinese Law and Government* 35, nos. 1–2 (2002), a narrative account of secret decision making in which Zhu participated in that year based on documents smuggled out of Chinese archives, was particularly illuminating. These documents reveal what top Chinese decision makers were thinking in 1999, especially during the American bombing of the Chinese embassy in Belgrade. As a *New York Times* report comments, the text's appearance suggests there is a growing movement by a group of powerful Communist Party insiders to rewrite Party history and influence China's future by leaking information to the West. Craig S. Smith, "Tell-All Book Portrays Split in Leadership of China," *New York Times*, January 17, 2002, available at http://www.nytimes.com/2002/01/17 /world/tell-all-book-portrays-split-in-leadership-of-china.html.
30. The organization's name in those days was the Foreign Broadcast Information Center. Larry Chin had worked there for many years, according to Hoffman, *Spy Within*, 54–55.
31. Bill Gertz, *Enemies: How America's Foes Steal Our Vital Secrets—and How We Let It Happen* (New York: Crown Forum, 2006), 52–53.

32. See Glenn P. Hastedt, "Leung, Katrina (May 1, 1954–)," in Glenn P. Hastedt, ed., *Spies, Wiretaps, and Secret Operations: An Encyclopedia of American Espionage, Volume I* (Santa Barbara, CA: ABC-CLIO, 2011), 468–69; Charles Feldman and Stan Wilson, "Alleged Chinese Double Agent Indicted," CNN.com, May 9, 2003, available at http://www.cnn.com/2003/LAW/05/08/double.agent.charges/; and "A Review of the FBI's Handling and Oversight of FBI Asset Katrina Leung (Unclassified Executive Summary)," Special Report, U.S. Department of Justice, Office of the Inspector General, May 2006, available at http://www.justice.gov /oig/special/s0605/index.htm.

33. Gertz, *Enemies*, 52–53.

CHAPTER 5: AMERICA, THE GREAT SATAN

1. Jimmy Carter's China expert on the NSC, the late Stanford professor of political science Michel Oksenberg, wrote, "China's leaders are naturally suspicious of foreign powers. They believe that foreign leaders tend to be reluctant to welcome China's rise in world affairs and would prefer to delay or obstruct its progress. They fear that many in the outside world would prefer to divide China if given the opportunity. . . . China's leaders retain in their minds a strategic map of the points on their periphery that make them vulnerable to foreign influence." Michel Oksenberg, *Taiwan, Tibet, and Hong Kong in Sino-American Relations* (Stanford, CA: Institute for International Studies, 1997), 56.

2. For Chinese interpretations of the history and evolution of Sino-U.S. relations, see, for example, Qiao Mingshun, *The First Page in Chinese-US Relations* (Beijing: Social Sciences Academic Press, 2000); and Shi Yinhong and Lu Lei, "The U.S. Attitude Toward China and China's Entrance to the International Community: An Overview of 150 Years of History," in Tao Wenzhao and Liang Biyin, eds., *The United States and Modern and Contemporary China* (Beijing: CASS Press, 1996).

3. For further discussion of these "patriotic" education programs, see Wang Zheng, *Never Forget National Humiliation: Historical Memory in Chinese Politics and Foreign Relations* (New York: Columbia University Press, 2012); Peter Hays Gries, *China's New Nationalism: Pride, Politics, and Diplomacy* (Berkeley: University of California Press, 2005); Christopher R. Hughes, *Chinese Nationalism in the Global Era* (New York: Routledge, 2006); and Suisheng Zhao, *A Nation-State by Construction: Dynamics of Modern Chinese Nationalism* (Stanford, CA: Stanford University Press, 2004).

4. The source of the claim that this book will be reprinted is the CASS website. Wang Chun, *A History of the U.S. Aggression in China* (Beijing Workers' Press, 1951). For more, see Andrew J. Nathan and Andrew Scobell, "How China Sees America: The Sum of Beijing's Fears," *Foreign Affairs* (September/October 2012), available at http://www.foreignaffairs.com/articles/138009/andrew-j-nathan -and-andrew-scobell/how-china-sees-america.

5. The Chinese version of the CASS website is available at http://www.cssn.cn/; the English version can be found at http://bic.cass.cn/english/index.asp.

6. For more on the Boxer Rebellion, see Larry Clinton Thompson, *William Scott Ament and the Boxer Rebellion: Heroism, Hubris, and the "Ideal Missionary"* (Jefferson, NC: McFarland, 2009).

7. For more on the impact of Deng's rule, see Vogel, *Deng Xiaoping and the Transformation of China*.

8. *Selected Works of Mao Tse-tung, Volume IV* (Beijing: Foreign Languages Press, 1961), 450.

9. Xiong Zhiyong, "A Diplomatic Encounter between China and America Reviewed from the Signing of the Treaty of Wangxia," *Modern Chinese History Studies*, no. 5 (1989); Qiao Mingshun, *First Page in Chinese-U.S. Relations*, 200, 33–34, 38, 147, 171; Li Jikui, "Chinese Republican Revolutions," 41–42, in Tao Wenzhao and Liang Biyin, eds., *The United States and Modern and Contemporary China* (Beijing: CASS Press, 1996).

10. Shi Yinhong, Lu Lei, "U.S. Attitude toward China and China's Entrance to the International Community," 6.

11. Mei Renyi, Center for American Studies, Beijing Foreign Languages University, "American Reporting on China's Reform and Opening Up," 422 (Beijing: Foreign Languages University Press, 1995).

12. *The Thirty-Six Stratagems*, chapter 1, available at http://wengu.tartarie.com/wg/wengu.php?l=36ji&&no=3.

13. Deng Shusheng, *Meiguo Lishi yu Meiguo Ren* [*American History and Americans*] (Beijing: Peoples' Press, 1993), 55.

14. Tang Qing, "U.S. Policy toward Japan Before the Outbreak of the Pacific War," in *Jianghandaxue Xuebao* [*Jianghand University Journal*] (April 1997): 105–9.

15. Deng Shusheng, *Meiguo Lishi yu Meiguo Ren* [*American History and Americans*], 169.

16. Stefan Verstappen, *The Thirty-Six Strategies of Ancient China* (San Francisco: China Books and Periodicals, 1999).

17. Xiong Xianghui, "The Prelude to the Opening of Sino-American Relations," *Zhonggong Dangshi Ziliao* (*CCP History Materials*), no. 42 (June 1992): 81, as excerpted in Burr, "New Documentary Reveals Secret U.S., Chinese Diplomacy behind Nixon's Trip."

18. An English-language translation of *Silent Contest* is available at NNL, ZYH, and AEF, "Silent Contest" (Part I), *Chinascope*, available at http://chinascope.org/main/content/view/6168/92/; and NNL, ZYH, and AEF, "Silent Contest II," *Chinascope*, available at http://chinascope.org/main/content/view/6281/92/. Benjamin Carlson, "China's Military Produces a Bizarre, Anti-American Conspiracy Film (VIDEO)," *GlobalPost*, November 2, 2013, available at http://www.globalpost.com/dispatch/news/regions/asia-pacific/china/131101/china-military-produces-bizarre-anti-american-conspiracy-video. See also J. Michael Cole, "Does China Want a Cold War?," *Diplomat*, November 5, 2013, available at http://thediplomat.com/2013/11/does-china-want-a-cold-war/; and Jane Perlez, "Strident Video by Chinese Military Casts U.S. as Menace," *New York Times*, October 31, 2013, available at http://sinosphere.blogs.nytimes.com/2013/10/31/strident-video

-by-chinese-military-casts-u-s-as-menace/?_php=true&_type=blogs&_r=0&
gwh=6063CDDF0357954CDBF51A49E3DC10EB&gwt=pay.

19. "U.S.-China Economic and Security Review Commission Annual Report, 2002,"
release date: July 15, 2002, available at http://china.usc.edu/ShowArticle.aspx
?articleID=686#below.

20. Ibid.

21. Ibid.

22. Ibid.

23. Mark Landler and David E. Sanger, "China Pressures U.S. Journalists, Prompting Warning from Biden," New York Times, December 4, 2013, available at http://
www.nytimes.com/2013/12/06/world/asia/biden-faults-china-on-foreign-press
-crackdown.html?_r=2&.

24. Ibid.

25. Ibid.

26. Ibid.

27. Miles Yu, "Inside China: PLA Strategist Reflects Military's Mainstream," Washington Times, April 11, 2013, available at http://www.washingtontimes.com/news
/2013/apr/11/inside-china-pla-strategist-reflects-militarys-mai/?page=all#page
break.

28. "U.S.- China Economic and Security Review Commission Annual Report,
2002."

29. Ibid.

30. Kevin Spacey, The Usual Suspects, directed by Bryan Singer. Los Angeles: Spell-
ing Films International, Gramercy Pictures, and PolyGram Filmed Entertain-
ment, 1995.

CHAPTER 6: CHINA'S MESSAGE POLICE

1. Anne-Marie Brady has pioneered the scholarly study of the Chinese government's propaganda efforts, including Anne-Marie Brady, ed., China's Thought
Management (New York: Routledge, 2012). See also Anne-Marie Brady, "Chinese Foreign Policy: A New Era Dawns," Diplomat, March 17, 2014, available at
http://thediplomat.com/2014/03/chinese-foreign-policy-a-new-era-dawns/; and
Brady's Marketing Dictatorship: Propaganda and Thought Work in Contemporary China (Lanham, MD: Rowman & Littlefield, 2009); David Shambaugh, China's Communist Party: Atrophy and Adaptation (Berkeley: University of California
Press, 2008), 106–11. See also David Shambaugh, China Goes Global: The Partial
Power (New York: Oxford University Press, 2013).

2. Keith B. Richburg, "Chinese Artist Ai Weiwei Arrested in Ongoing Government
Crackdown," Washington Post, April 3, 2011, available at http://www.washing
tonpost.com/world/chinese-artist-ai-wei-wei-arrested-in-latest-government
-crackdown/2011/04/03/AFHB5PVC_story.html.

3. "State Enemies: China," Reporters Without Borders, Special Edition: Surveillance, available at http://surveillance.rsf.org/en/china/.

4. Patrick E. Tyler, "Who's Afraid of China?," *New York Times*, August 1, 1999, available at http://www.nytimes.com/1999/08/01/magazine/who-s-afraid-of -china.html.

5. Qiao Liang and Wang Xiangsui, *Unrestricted Warfare: Assumptions on War and Tactics in the Age of Globalization* (Beijing: PLA Literature and Arts Publishing House, 1999). A summary translation of *Unrestricted Warfare* is available online at http://www.fas.org/nuke/guide/china/doctrine/index.html.

6. For more on Chinese sensitivity to America, see: Andrew J. Nathan and Andrew Scobell, *China's Search for Security* (New York: Columbia University Press, 2012). See also Andrew J. Nathan and Andrew Scobell, "How China Sees America," *Foreign Affairs* (September/October 2012), available at http://www.foreignaffairs .com/articles/138009/andrew-j-nathan-and-andrew-scobell/how-china-sees -america.

7. Harvard University's Alastair Johnston noted in "Beijing's Security Behavior in the Asia-Pacific: Is China a Dissatisfied Power?" in J. J. Suh, Peter J. Katzenstein, and Allen Carlson, eds., *Rethinking Security in East Asia: Identity, Power, and Efficiency* (Stanford, CA: Stanford University Press, 2004), 34–96, that the authors of *Unrestricted Warfare* were "not strategists, but political officers," whose primary responsibility was "to write reportage about life in the military." The book, he adds, "was highly controversial inside China" and was "criticized in internal meetings in the military." Yet "none of this contextual information was part of the U.S. discourse" (68).

8. Erik Eckholm, "After the Attacks: In Beijing; Waiting Nervously for Response," *New York Times*, September 16, 2001, available at http://www.nytimes.com/2001 /09/16/us/after-the-attacks-in-beijing-waiting-nervously-for-response.html.

9. Wang Jiang, Li Xiaoning, Qiao Liang, Wang Xiangsui, *Xin Zhanguo Shidai [The New Warring States Era]* (Beijing: Xinhua chubanshe, 2003).

10. Wu Rusong, "Rou wu lun—Zhongguo gudian zhanlue zhiyao" ["On Soft Fighting— The Quintessence of China's Classical Strategy"], *Zhongguo Junshi Kexue [China Military Science]* 34, no. 1 (Spring 1996): 118.

11. Li Bingyan, ed., *Zhongguo lidai da zhanlue [The Grand Strategy of China's Past Dynasties]* (Beijing: Kunlun chubanshe, 1998), 51.

12. Huang Zhixian, Geng Jianzhong, and Guo Shengwei, *Sun Zi Jingcui Xinbian [A Concise New Edition of Sun Tzu]* (Beijing: Junshi kexue chubanshe, 1993), 70.

13. Chai Yaqui, *Moulue lun [On Deceptive Strategy]* (Beijing: Lantian chubanshe, 1996), 97.

14. Chai Yuqiu, ed., *Moulue ku [A Storehouse of Deceptive Strategy]* (Guangxi: Guangxi Renmin chubanshe, 1995), 152.

15. Nick Mulvenney, "China to Meet Dalai Lama Aides amid Tibet Tension," Reuters, April 25, 2008, available at http://in.reuters.com/article/2008/04/25/idINIndia -33236220080425.

16. Brian Duffy and Bob Woodward, "FBI Warned 6 on Hill about China Money," *Washington Post*, March 9, 1997, available at http://www.washingtonpost.com /wp-srv/politics/special/campfin/stories/cf030997.htm.

17. Bill Gertz, *The China Threat: How the People's Republic Targets America* (Washington, DC: Regnery, 2000), 45.

18. *China's Propaganda and Influence Operations, Its Intelligence Activities That Target the United States, and the Resulting Impacts on U.S. National Security: Hearing before the U.S.-China Economic and Security Review Commission*, 111th Cong. 88 (Apr. 30, 2009), statement of Dr. Jacqueline Newmyer, president and CEO, Long-Term Strategy Group, Cambridge, MA, available at http://origin.www .uscc.gov/sites/default/files/transcripts/4.30.09HearingTranscript.pdf. Quotations from a February 2009 *Reference News* (*Cankao Xiaoxi*) article, translated by the American Open Source Center, that Newmyer cited in her statement.

19. Friedberg, *Contest for Supremacy*, 194–95.

20. *China's Propaganda and Influence Operations, Its Intelligence Activities That Target the United States, and the Resulting Impacts on U.S. National Security: Hearing before the U.S.-China Economic and Security Review Commission*, 111th Cong. 67 (Apr. 30, 2009), statement of Dr. Ross Terrill, associate in research, John K. Fairbank Center for Chinese Studies, Harvard University, Cambridge, MA, available at http://origin.www.uscc.gov/sites/default/files/transcripts/4.30.09HearingTranscript.pdf.

21. Confucius Institute/Classroom website, available at http://english.hanban.org /node_10971.htm.

22. D. D. Guttenplan, "Critics Worry about Influence of Chinese Institutes on US Campuses," *New York Times*, March 4, 2012, available at http://www.nytimes .com/2012/03/05/us/critics-worry-about-influence-of-chinese-institutes-on-us -campuses.html?pagewanted=all&_r=0.

23. "China's Confucius Institutes: Rectification of Statues," *Economist*, January 20, 2011, available at http://www.economist.com/blogs/asiaview/2011/01/china%E2 %80%99s_confucius_institutes.

24. Daniel Golden, "China Says No Talking Tibet as Confucius Funds U.S. Universities," Bloomberg News Service, November 1, 2011, available at http://www.bloom berg.com/news/2011-11-01/china-says-no-talking-tibet-as-confucius-funds-u-s -universities.html.

25. Guttenplan, "Critics Worry About Influence of Chinese Institutes on U.S. Campuses."

26. Josh Dehaas, "Talks End Between Confucius Institutes and U Manitoba," *Maclean's*, June 21, 2011, available at http://www.macleans.ca/education/uniand college/talks-end-between-confucius-institutes-and-u-manitoba/.

27. Marshall Sahlins, "China U.," *Nation*, October 29, 2013, available at http://www .thenation.com/article/176888/china-u.

28. Golden, "China Says No Talking Tibet as Confucius Funds U.S. Universities."

29. Ibid.

30. Guttenplan, "Critics Worry About Influence of Chinese Institutes on U.S. Campuses."

31. Golden, "China Says No Talking Tibet as Confucius Funds U.S. Universities." Indeed, the subject of Tibet is not mentioned at all on the institute's website,

which is available at http://ealc.stanford.edu/confucius_institute/. In a January 10, 2013, interview of Professor Ban Wang by Stanford University's Office of International Affairs, Wang stated that, "For the past two years, whenever we had a difference of opinion with the Hanban or PKU counterparts, Professor Chao, Dean Saller and I would go to Beijing for face-to-face negotiations. Each time, we remind them that Stanford University has the control on how to manage the Institute. The situation turned out in our favor . . ." The Confucius Institute at Stanford University, available at https://oia.stanford.edu/node/14779. See also Wise, *Tiger Trap*, chapter 14.

32. "Sydney University Criticised for Blocking Dalai Lama Visit," *Guardian*, April 18, 2013, available at http://www.theguardian.com/world/2013/apr/18/sydney-university-dalai-lama.

33. Dehaas, "Talks End Between Confucius Institutes and U Manitoba."

34. Sahlins, "China U."

35. Don Starr, "Chinese Language Education in Europe: The Confucius Institutes," *European Journal of Education, Research, Development and Policy* 44, no. 1 (March 2009): 65–82, available at http://onlinelibrary.wiley.com/doi/10.1111/j.1465-3435.2008.01371.x/full.

36. Ibid.

37. "Profs Worry China Preparing to Spy on Students," *Maclean's*, April 27, 2011, available at http://www.macleans.ca/education/uniandcollege/profs-worry-china-preparing-to-spy-on-students/.

38. TGS and AEF, "People's Daily: The Rise of an Awakening Lion," *Chinascope*, last updated February 10, 2011, available at http://chinascope.org/main/content/view/3306/106/.

39. Tania Branigan, "Chinese Ambassador Attacks 'Cold War' Fears over Confucius Institutes," *Guardian*, June 15, 2012, available at http://www.theguardian.com/world/2012/jun/15/confucius-institutes-universities-chinese-ambassador.

40. Justin Norrie, "Confucius Says School's In, but Don't Mention Democracy," *Sydney Morning Herald*, February 20, 2011, available at http://www.smh.com.au/national/education/confucius-says-schools-in-but-dont-mention-democracy-20110219-1b09x.html.

41. Fred Hiatt, "Chinese Leaders Control Media, Academics to Shape the Perception of China," *Washington Post*, November 17, 2013, available at http://www.washingtonpost.com/opinions/fred-hiatt-chinese-leaders-control-media-academics-to-shape-the-perception-of-china/2013/11/17/1f26816e-4e06-11e3-9890-a1e0997fb0c0_story.html.

42. Ibid.

43. Ibid.

44. Neil King Jr., "Inside Pentagon: A Scholar Shapes Views of China," *Wall Street Journal*, September 8, 2005, available at http://online.wsj.com/news/articles/SB112613947626134749.

45. Ibid.

46. "UN Experts Warn of Severe Restrictions on Tibetan Monasteries in China," *UN*

News Centre, November 1, 2011, available at http://www.un.org/apps/news/story
.asp/story.asp?NewsID=40269&Cr=China&Cr1#.Uxi2dumPLVI.

47. "Q&A: Paul Mooney on Reporting in China," Bob Dietz, Committee to Protect Journalists, CPJ Blog, November 12, 2013, available at http://www.cpj.org/blog /2013/11/qa-paul-mooney-on-reporting-in-china.php.

48. Harrison Jacobs, "Chinese Censorship Is Spreading All Over the World," *Business Insider*, November 5, 2013, available at http://www.businessinsider.com/chi nese-censorship-is-spreading-all-over-the-world-2013-11.

49. Ibid.

50. "State Enemies: China."

51. U.S. State Department, Bureau of Democracy Human Rights and Labor, "2013 Human Rights Report: China (includes Tibet, Hong Kong, and Macau)," available at http://www.state.gov/j/drl/rls/hrrpt/2013/eap/220186.htm.

52. Will Sommer, "Post's Chinese Visa Fight Ends with a Whimper," *Washington City Paper*, September 17, 2012, available at http://www.washingtoncitypaper .com/blogs/citydesk/2012/09/17/posts-chinese-visa-fight-ends-with-a-whimper/.

53. Peter Ford, "Report on China's 'Jasmine Revolution'? Not if You Want Your Visa," *Christian Science Monitor*, March 3, 2011, available at http://www.csmoni tor.com/layout/set/r14/World/Asia-Pacific/2011/0303/Report-on-China-s-Jas mine-Revolution-Not-if-you-want-your-visa.

54. Harrison Jacobs, "Journalist Paul Mooney on Why He Was Blocked from China and How Things Could Get 'Much, Much Worse,'" *Business Insider*, November 21, 2013, available at http://www.businessinsider.com/paul-mooney-on-being-denied -chinese-visa-2013-11#ixzz2n5iYadYX.

55. Evan Osnos, "What Will It Cost to Cover China?" *New Yorker*, November 19, 2013, available at http://www.newyorker.com/online/blogs/comment/2013/11/what-will -it-cost-to-cover-china.html. See also Robert Dietz, "Foreign Reporters on Report ing in China," for the Congressional-Executive Commission on China Roundtable, "China's Treatment of Foreign Journalists," December 11, 2013, available at http:// www.cecc.gov/sites/chinacommission.house.gov/files/CECC%20Roundtable%20 -%20Foreign%20Journalists%20-Robert%20Dietz%20Written%20Statement.pdf.

56. Keith B. Richburg, "China Expels Al-Jazeera Reporter as Media Relations Sour," *Washington Post*, May 8, 2012, available at http://www.washingtonpost.com/world /asia_pacific/china-expels-al-jazeera-reporter-as-media-relations-sour/2012/05 /08/gIQAlip49T_story.html.

57. "Never in American history has this country been so influenced by a foreign dictatorship [as by China]" said A. M. Rosenthal, the late opinion columnist who had formerly served as executive editor of the *New York Times*. "In fact, possibly excluding Britain, never in my memory has any country at all had so much influ ence in American political, economic, and academic life." Quoted in Gertz, *China Threat*, 40–41.

58. Osnos, "What Will It Cost to Cover China?"

59. "Syria, China Worst for Online Spying: RSF," *Daily Star* (Lebanon), March 12, 2013, available at http://www.dailystar.com.lb/Article.aspx?id=209739&link=Technology

/Regional/2013/Mar-12/209739-syria-china-worst-for-online-spying-rsf.ashx
#axzz2rFONYvA9.

60. "State Enemies: China."
61. Ibid.
62. Ibid.
63. Jacobs, "Chinese Censorship Is Spreading All Over the World."
64. Ibid.
65. Laurie Burkitt and Paul Mozur, "Foreign Firms Brace for More Pressure in China," *Wall Street Journal*, April 4, 2013, available at http://online.wsj.com/news/articles/SB10001424127887323916304578400463208890042.
66. Jacobs, "Chinese Censorship Is Spreading All Over the World."
67. For more on the Chinese government's media control practices, see, for example, "How Officials Can Spin the Media," China Media Project, June 19, 2010, available at http://cmp.hku.hk/2010/06/19/6238/; "Media Dictionary: 'Propaganda Discipline,'" China Media Project, January 5, 2007, available at http://cmp.hku.hk/2007/01/05/145/; Frank N. Pieke, *The Good Communist: Elite Training and State Building in Today's China* (Cambridge, UK: Cambridge University Press, 2009); Yanmin Yu, "The Role of the Media: A Case Study of China's Media Coverage of the U.S. War in Iraq," in Yufan Hao and Lin Su, eds., *China's Foreign Policy Making: Societal Force and Chinese American Policy* (Burlington, VT: Ashgate, 2005). See also Anne-Marie Brady and He Yong, "Talking Up the Market," in Anne-Marie Brady, ed., *China's Thought Management* (Oxford, UK: Routledge, 2012); Min Jiang, "Spaces of Authoritarian Deliberation: Online Public Deliberation in China," in Ethan J. Lieb and Baogang He, eds., *The Search for Deliberative Democracy in China* (New York: Palgrave Macmillan, 2006); Ying Chan, "Microblogs Reshape News in China," China Media Project, October 12, 2010, available at http://cmp.hku.hk/2010/10/12/8021/; and Christopher R. Hughes, "Controlling the Internet Architecture within Greater China," in Françoise Mengin, ed., *Cyber China: Reshaping National Identities in the Age of Information* (New York: Palgrave Macmillan, 2004).

CHAPTER 7: THE ASSASSIN'S MACE

1. Sources include Victor N. Corpus, "America's Acupuncture Points. Part 2: The Assassin's Mace," *Asia Times Online*, October 20, 2006, available at http://www.atimes.com/atimes/China/HJ20Ad01.html; Michael Pillsbury, "The Sixteen Fears: China's Strategic Psychology," *Survival: Global Politics and Strategy* 54, no. 5 (October/November 2012): 149–82; "SteelJaw," "Required Reading: *Naval War College Review* Articles on China's DF-21/ASBM," *U.S. Naval Institute blog*, November 15, 2009, accessed March 2, 2014, available at http://blog.usni.org/2009/11/15/required-reading-naval-war-college-review-articles-on-chinas-df-21asbm; Bill Gertz, "China Building Electromagnetic Pulse Weapons for Use against U.S. Carriers," *Washington Times*, July 21, 2011, available at http://www.washingtontimes.com/news/2011/jul/21/beijing-develops-radiation-weapons

/?page=all; David Crane, "Chinese Electromagnetic Pulse (EMP) and High-Powered Microwave (HPM) Weapons vs. U.S. Navy Aircraft Carrier Battle Groups: Can the U.S. Military Effectively Counter 'Assassin's Mace'?," *DefenseReview.com*, July 22, 2011, available at http://www.defensereview.com/chinese-electro magnetic-pulse-emp-and-high-powered-microwave-hpm-weapons-vs-u-s-navy -aircraft-carrier-battle-groups-can-the-u-s-military-effectively-counter-assassins -mace/; Editors of *New Atlantis*, "The Assassin's Mace," *New Atlantis* 6 (Summer 2004): 107–10, available at http://www.thenewatlantis.com/publications/the-assas sins-mace; U.S. Department of Defense, Office of the Secretary of Defense, *Military Power of the People's Republic of China* (Washington, DC, 2005); Pillsbury, *China Debates the Future Security Environment*; David Hambling, "China Looks to Undermine U.S. Power with 'Assassin's Mace,'" *Wired*, July 2, 2009, available at http://www.wired.com/dangerroom/2009/07/china-looks-to-undermine-us -power-with-assassins-mace/; "China Developing EMP 'Assassin's Mace': Report," *China Post*, July 25, 2011, available at http://www.chinapost.com.tw/taiwan/china -taiwan-relations/2011/07/25/310981/China-developing.htm; Leonard David, "Pentagon Report: China's Growing Military Space Power," *SPACE.com*, March 6, 2008, available at http://www.space.com/5049-pentagon-report-china-growing-military -space-power.html; Shaun Waterman, "U.S. Slow Learner on Chinese Weaponry," *Washington Times*, April 5, 2012, available at http://www.washingtontimes .com/news/2012/apr/5/us-slow-learner-on-chinese-weaponry/?page=all; Mark L. Herman, Mark D. Frost, and Robert Kurz, *Wargaming for Leaders: Strategic Decision Making from the Battlefield to the Boardroom* (New York: McGraw-Hill, 2009); Robert Mandel, "Political Gaming and Foreign Policy Making During Crisis," *World Politics* 30, no. 4 (July 1977): 610–25. Mandel wrote that scenarios in earlier games included a Soviet invasion of China, tensions between India and Pakistan, island disputes between China and Vietnam, Chinese infiltration of Burma (now Myanmar), and insurgency in India.

2. For more information, see Bill Gertz, "China's High-Tech Military Threat," *Commentary*, April 1, 2012, available at http://www.commentarymagazine.com /article/chinas-high-tech-military-threat/; and Jan van Tol, Mark Gunzinger, Andrew F. Krepinevich, and Jim Thomas, "AirSea Battle: A Point-of-Departure Operational Concept," Center for Strategic and Budgetary Assessments, May 18, 2010, available at http://www.csbaonline.org/publications/2010/05/airsea-bat tle-concept/.

3. Gertz, "China's High-Tech Military Threat."

4. For an excellent survey of Chinese antiaccess strategies and investments, see James C. Mulvenon, Murray Scot Tanner, Michael S. Chase, David Frelinger, David C. Gompert, Martin C. Libicki, and Kevin L. Pollpeter, *Chinese Responses to U.S. Military Transformation and Implications for the Department of Defense* (Santa Monica, CA: RAND, 2006); Roger Cliff, Mark Burles, Michael S. Chase, Derek Eaton, and Kevin L. Pollpeter, *Entering the Dragon's Lair: Chinese Antiaccess Strategies and Their Implications for the United States* (Santa Monica, CA: RAND, 2007); and Ronald O'Rourke, "China Naval Modernization: Implica-

tions for US Navy Capabilities—Background and Issues for Congress," *CRS Report for Congress*, RL33153, May 29, 2007.

5. Shen Zhongchang, Zhang Haiying, and Zhou Xinsheng, "21 Shiji Haizhan Chutan" ["21st Century Naval Warfare"], *Zhongguo Junshi Kexue [China Military Science]*, no. 1 (1995): 28–32, in Pillsbury, *Chinese Views of Future Warfare*, xxxviii.

6. Bill Gertz, *The China Threat: How the People's Republic Targets America* (Washington, DC: Regnery, 2013), introduction to the paperback version, page ix.

7. Michael Raska, "Scientific Innovation and China's Military Modernization," *Diplomat*, September 3, 2013, available at http://thediplomat.com/2013/09/scientific-innovation-and-chinas-military-modernization/.

8. For classic examples, see Edward Timperlake and William C. Triplett II, *Red Dragon Rising: Communist China's Military Threat to America* (Washington, DC: Regnery, 2002); Gertz, *China Threat*; Steven W. Mosher, *Hegemon: China's Plan to Dominate Asia and the World* (San Francisco: Encounter Books, 2000); and Jed Babbin and Edward Timperlake, *Showdown: Why China Wants War with the United States* (Washington, DC: Regnery, 2006); Ted Galen Carpenter, *America's Coming War with China: A Collision Course over Taiwan* (New York: Palgrave Macmillan, 2005); and Richard C. Bush and Michael E. O'Hanlon, *A War Like No Other: The Truth About China's Challenge to America* (Hoboken, NJ: John Wiley & Sons, 2007).

9. Keith Crane et al., *Modernizing China's Military: Opportunities and Constraints* (Santa Monica, CA: RAND Corporation, 2005).

10. "U.S. Asia-Pacific Strategic Considerations Related to PLA Naval Forces Modernization," Hearing before the Subcommittee on Seapower and Projection Forces, House Armed Services Committee, December 11, 2013, available at http://armedservices.house.gov/index.cfm/hearings-display?ContentRecord_id=FA9EE283-A136-4C44-B489-F1814AFAB9EA. The witnesses called to testify at this hearing included Seth Cropsey, senior fellow, the Hudson Institute; Andrew Erickson, associate professor, U.S. Naval War College; Ronald O'Rourke, specialist in naval affairs, Congressional Research Service; and Jim Thomas, vice president and director of studies, Center for Strategic and Budgetary Assessments. For background, see Seth Cropsey, *Mayday: The Decline of American Naval Supremacy* (New York: Overlook, 2013).

11. For more on AirSea Battle, see, for example, Jose Carreno, Thomas Culora, George Galdorisi, and Thomas Hone, *Proceedings* (vol. 136/8/1,290, U.S. Naval Institute, August 2010); J. Noel Williams, "Air-Sea Battle: An Operational Concept Looking for a Strategy," *Armed Forces Journal* (September 2011); and Adam Segal, "Chinese Computer Games: Keeping Safe in Cyberspace," *Foreign Affairs* 91, no. 2 (March/April 2012).

12. Gertz, *Enemies*, 54; and Wise, *Tiger Trap*, 216–17. As Wise writes, "With Chi Mak convicted, the rest of the family pleaded guilty in rapid succession. In March 2008, Chi Mak was sentenced to twenty-four years in federal prison" (217).

13. For more on Chinese threat perceptions of the United States, see, for example, Yawei Liu and Justine Zheng Ren, "An Emerging Consensus on the U.S. Threat:

The United States According to PLA Officers," *Journal of Contemporary China* 23, no. 86 (2014): 255–74.

14. See Chen Youwei, "China's Foreign Policymaking as Seen Through Tiananmen," *Journal of Contemporary China* 12, no. 37 (November 2003): 715–38.

15. Gao Fugang and Sun Mu, "Study of Operational Effectiveness of Blockade Running of Escorted Submarine," *Junshi Yunchou Yu Xitong Gongcheng* [*Military Operations Research and Systems Engineering*] (September 3, 2006): 39–42. For additional details and references, see Pillsbury, "Sixteen Fears."

16. Such blockade methods are described in articles such as Tai Feng, "Multipronged Blockade of the Ocean: Japan's Measures after the Offshore Submarine Incident," *Xiandai Wuqi* [*Modern Weapons*] (March 2005): 51 (trans. Toshi Yoshihara, U.S. Naval War College); Li Zuyu, "Combat Uses of Japan's Airpower," *Shipborne Weapons* (March 2007): 48 (trans. Toshi Yoshihara); Wu Peihuan and Wu Yifu, "Acting with a Motive: The Japan–US Island Defenses Exercises," *Modern Weaponry* (February 2006): 8 (trans. Toshi Yoshihara).

17. The references cited in this study include Ge Genzhong, "Submarine Operation in Informatized Warfare," *Qianting Xueshu Yanjiu* [*Submarine Research*] 22, no. 1 (2004); Mao Chuangxin et al., *Case Study of Submarine Warfare* (Qingdao: Naval Submarine Academy, 1997); Zhang Wenyu et al., "Introduction to Asymmetric Operations of Submarines," *Qianting Xueshu Yanjiu* [*Submarine Research*] 22, no. 1 (2004); Rong Haiyang et al., *Submarine Tactics* (Qingdao: Naval Submarine Academy, 2001); Qin Gang, *Submarines in Naval Warfare* (Nanjing: Naval Command Academy, 1997); Wan Chun, *Surface Warship Tactics* (Nanjing: Naval Command Academy, 2004); Cheng Wangchi et al., "A Method to Estimate Force Required for Submarine to Run a Blockade," *Junshi Yunchou Yu Xitong Gongcheng* [*Military Operations Research and Systems Engineering*] 18, no. 1 (2004): 21–23.

18. Quoted in Toshi Yoshihara and James R. Holmes, "China's New Undersea Deterrence," *Joint Force Quarterly*, issue 50 (2008), 37. See also Andrew Erickson and Lyle Goldstein, "Gunboats for China's New 'Grand Canals'?: Probing the Intersection of Beijing's Naval and Oil Security Policies," *Naval War College Review* 62, no. 2 (Spring 2009), available at https://www.usnwc.edu/getattachment/f655705e-0ef3-4a21-af5a-93df77e527fa/Gunboats-for-China-s-New-Grand-Canals-Probing-t. See also J. Michael Cole, "China's Maritime Surveillance Fleet Adds Muscle," *Diplomat*, January 3, 2013, available at http://thediplomat.com/2013/01/chinas-maritime-surveillance-fleet-adds-muscle/; Mark Landler, "A New Era of Gunboat Diplomacy," *New York Times*, November 12, 2011; and "China Adds Destroyers to Marine Surveillance: Report," *Straits Times*, *Asia Report*, December 31, 2012, available at http://www.straitstimes.com/the-big-story/asia-report/china/story/china-adds-destroyers-marine-surveillance-report-20121231.

19. Zhang Dengyi, "Guanhao Yonghao Haiyang, Jianshe Haiyang Qiangguo" ["Manage and Use the Ocean Wisely, Establish a Strong Maritime Nation"], *Qiushi*, no. 11 (2001), 46; Feng Liang and Zhang Xiaolin, "Lun Heping Shiqi Haijun de Zhanlue Yunyong" ["A Discussion of the Navy's Strategic Use in Peacetime"], *Zhongguo Junshi Kexue* [*China Military Science*], no. 3 (2001): 78; and Lu Rude, "Zai Da

Zhanlue zhong gei Zhongguo Haiquan Dingwei" ["Defining Sea Power in China's Grand Strategy"], *Renmin Haijun* [*People's Navy*] (June 6, 2007).

20. Gao Fugang and Sun Mu, "Study of Operational Effectiveness of Blockade Running of Escorted Submarine."

21. Ibid. See also Da Wei, "Zhongguo de Haiyang Anquan Zhanlue" ["China's Maritime Security Strategy"], in Yang Mingjie, ed., *Haishang Jiaodao Anquan yu Guoji Hezuo* [*Sea Lane Security and International Cooperation*] (Beijing: Shishi chubanshe, 2005), 365.

22. Zhang Wenmu, "Jingji Quanqiuhua yu Zhongguo Haiquan" ["Economic Globalization and Chinese Sea Power"], *Zhanlue yu Guanli* [*Strategy and Management*] 1 (2003): 96.

23. He Jiacheng, Zou Lao, and Lai Zhijun, "Guoji Junshi Anquan Xingshi ji Woguo de Guofang Jingji Fazhan Zhanlue" ["The International Military Situation and China's Strategy of National Defense Economic Development"], *Junshi Jingji Yanjiu* [*Military Economic Research*] 1 (2005): 12.

24. Shi Chunlun, "A Commentary on Studies of the Last Ten Years Concerning China's Sea Power," *Xiandai Guoji Guanxi* [*Contemporary International Relations*] (April 20, 2008); and Liu Jiangping and Zhui Yue, "Management of the Sea in the 21st Century: Whither the Chinese Navy?," *Dangdai Haijun* [*Modern Navy*] (June 2007). See details in Pillsbury, "Sixteen Fears."

25. Da Wei, "Zhongguo de Haiyang Anquan Zhanlue," 119. See also Gabriel B. Collins and William S. Murray, "No Oil for the Lamps of China?" *Naval War College Review* 61, no. 2 (Spring 2008): 79–95; Erickson and Goldstein, "Gunboats for China's New 'Grand Canals'?"; "Chinese Admiral Floats Idea of Overseas Naval Bases," Reuters, December 30, 2009, http://www.reuters.com/article/2009/12/30/us -china-navy-idUSTRE5BT0P020091230. China's fear about its sea lines of communication is heightened by its concerns that global "peak oil" production has been reached, increasing China's future vulnerability to a blockade. See Cao Kui and Zou Peng, "Discussion of China's Oil and Energy Security," *Teaching of Politics* (November 2005); "A Study of Energy Security," Chinese Academy of Social Sciences, December 5, 2007, available at http://www.cass.net.cn/file/20071205106095 .html; and "The Real Meaning of 'Energy Security,'" Office of the National Energy Leading Group, September 18, 2006, available at http://www.chinaenergy.gov.cn/.

26. Erickson and Goldstein, "Gunboats for China's New 'Grand Canals'?"

27. *Zhanyi Xue* [*The Science of Campaigns*] (Beijing: NDU Press, 2000); Xue Xinglin, *Zhanyi Lilun Xuexi Zhinan* [*A Guide to the Study of Campaign Theory*] (Beijing: National Defense University Press, 2002); *Zhongguo Renmin Jiefangjun Lianhe Zhanyi Gangyao* [People's Liberation Army Outline on Joint Campaigns] (Beijing: Central Military Commission, 1999). The text of the outline for China's future military was issued in 1999 and is secret, but its existence is discussed in *A Guide to the Study of Campaign Theory* [*Zhanyi Lilun Xuexi Zhinan*] and in many other places. Its issuance was announced in "Zhongyang Junwei Zhuxi Jiang Zemin Qianshu Mingling Wojun Xinyidai Zuozhan Tiaoling Banfa" ["CMC Chairman Jiang Zemin Signs Order Implementing Our Army's New Generation

of Operational Regulations"], *Renmin Ribao* [*People's Daily*], January 25, 1999, available at http://www.people.com.cn/item/ldhd/Jiangzm/1999/mingling/ml0003 .html.

28. Zhang Yuliang, ed., *Science of Campaigns* (Beijing: National Defense University Press, 2006), 297–303.

29. Quoted in Gabriel B. Collins, Andrew S. Erickson, Lyle J. Goldstein, and William S. Murray, eds., *China's Energy Strategy: The Impact on Beijing's Maritime Policies* (Annapolis, MD: China Maritime Studies Institute and the Naval Institute Press, 2008), 320.

30. Xu Genchu, *Lianhe Xunlian Xue* [*Science of Joint Training*] (Beijing: Military Science Press, 2007). This volume, like many of the others cited here, is marked *junnei faxing*, which literally means "military internal dissemination." They are not "secret" in the sense of being actually classified, but in Chinese military bookshops, they are kept in special rooms that only officers of the People's Liberation Army may enter. They do not have ISBN numbers on their covers. The U.S. government has made many such volumes available to scholars at the Harvard University and University of California, Berkeley, libraries, though it is not known how they were originally obtained.

31. Guang Tao and Yao Li, *Zhongguo Zhanqu Junshi Dili* [*China's Theater Military Geography*] (Beijing: People's Liberation Army Press, 2005).

32. See chapter 2 of Dennis Blasko, *The Chinese Army Today*, 2nd ed. (New York: Routledge, 2012), 16–46.

33. Guang Tao and Yao Li, *Zhongguo Zhanqu Junshi Dili*.

34. "CCTV-7 Shows North Sword 2005 Exercise, PLA's Li Yu Meeting Foreign Observers," Beijing CCTV-7, September 28, 2005; "Chinese Military Paper Details North Sword 2005 PLA Exercise," *PLA Daily*, September 28, 2005; "PLA Airborne in '1st Live' Drill vs. 'Digitized' Armor Unit in 'North Sword,'" *Kongjun Bao* [*Air Force Daily*], September 29, 2005; "Xinhua Article Details 'North Sword 2005' Exercise Held at Beijing MR Base," *Xinhua Domestic Service*, September 27, 2005; and "China Launches Its Biggest-Ever War Exercises," *People's Daily Online*, September 27, 2005, available at http://english.people.com.cn/200509/27 /eng20050927_211190.html.

35. For an overview of this issue, see Murray Scot Tanner, "How China Manages Internal Security Challenges and Its Impact on PLA Missions," in Roy Kamphausen, David Lai, and Andrew Scobell, eds., *Beyond the Strait: PLA Missions Other Than Taiwan* (Carlisle, PA: U.S. Army War College Strategic Studies Institute, 2009), available at http://www.isn.ethz.ch/Digital-Library/Publications/Detail /?ots591=0c54e3b3-1e9c-be1e-2c24-a6a8c7060233&lng=en&id=99803. See also "2030: China Faces the Fate of Dismemberment: The U.S. Strategy for a Global Empire and China's Crisis," a 2009 speech by PLA Colonel Dai Xu at a meeting at the Nanjing-based PLA Institute of International Relations Studies, in Miles Yu, "Inside China: PLA Strategist Reflects Military's Mainstream," *Washington Times*, April 11, 2013, available at http://www.washingtontimes.com/news/2013/ apr/11/inside-china-pla-strategist-reflects-militarys-mai/?page=all#pagebreak.

36. The official was identified as Yu Hongjun, deputy director of the research division of the Central Committee Liaison Department, who gave an interview to the Qinghua University World Affairs Forum, according to *Shijie Zhishi [World Knowledge]* 23 (December 1, 2002): 34–39.

37. Li Xinqi, Tan Shoulin, and Li Hongxia, "Precaution Model and Simulation Actualization on Threat of Maneuver Target Group on the Sea," *Qingbao Zhihui Kongzhi Xitong Yu Fangzhen Jishu [Intelligence Control Systems and Simulation Methods]* (August 1, 2005); Pillsbury, *China Debates the Future Security Environment*, 83–85. Additional sources include Major General Guo Xilin, "The Aircraft Carrier Formation Is Not an Unbreakable Barrier," *Guangming Ribao Online*, December 26, 2000; Zhou Yi, "Aircraft Carriers Face Five Major Assassins," *Junshi Wenzhai [Military Digest]* (March 1, 2002): 4–6; Feng Changsong, Xu Jiafeng, and Wang Guosheng, "Six Aircraft Carrier Busters," *Zhongguo Guofang Bao [China Defense News]*, March 5, 2002, 4; Dong Hua, "Aircraft Carrier's Natural Enemy: Antiship Missiles," *Junshi Wenzhai [Military Digest]* (July 1, 2002): 50–52; Xiao Yaojin and Chang Jiang, "China's Existing Tactical Missiles Can Fully Meet the Need of a Local War Under High-Tech Conditions," *Guangzhou Ribao [Guangzhou Daily]*, October 21, 2002; and Wang Jiasuo, "Aircraft Carriers: Suggest You Keep Out of the Taiwan Strait!" *Junshi Wenzhai [Military Digest]* (April 1, 2001): 58–59.

38. For examples of operations-research analysis on antiaircraft-carrier methods, see "Preliminary Analysis on the Survivability of a U.S. Aircraft Carrier," *Zhidao Feidan [Guided Missiles]* 5 (2000): 1–10; "Study of Attacking an Aircraft Carrier Using Conventional Ballistic Missiles," *Dier Paobing Gongcheng Sheji Yuanjiuyuan [Second Artillery Corps Research Institute of Engineering Design]*, Xian, 2002; "Concept of Using Conventional Ballistic Missiles to Attack a Carrier Fleet," *Keji Yanjiu [Science and Technology Research]* 1 (2003); *Movement Forecast Model and Precision Analysis of Maneuvering Targets at Sea* (Beijing: Second Artillery Engineering Academy, 2005), cited in Pillsbury, "Sixteen Fears"; "Research on Optimization Methods for Firepower Allocation Plans in Joint Strike Fires," *Junshi Yunchou Yu Xitong Gongcheng [Military Operations Research and Systems Engineering]* (2005), cited in Pillsbury, "Sixteen Fears."

39. For a comprehensive discussion of Chinese Air Force doctrinal developments and new operational concepts, see Kevin M. Lanzit and Kenneth Allen, "Right-Sizing the PLA Air Force: New Operational Concepts Define a Smaller, More Capable Force," in Roy Kamphausen and Andrew Scobell, eds., *Right-Sizing the People's Liberation Army: Exploring the Contours of China's Military* (Carlisle, PA: Strategic Studies Institute, U.S. Army War College, 2007), 437–79.

40. Michael D. Swaine and Zhang Tuosheng, eds., with Danielle F. S. Cohen, *Managing Sino-American Crises: Case Studies and Analysis* (Baltimore: Johns Hopkins University Press, 2006). See also Michael D. Swaine, *America's Challenge: Engaging a Rising China in the Twenty-First Century* (Washington, DC: Carnegie Endowment for International Peace, 2011); G. John Ikenberry, "The Rise of China and the Future of the West," *Foreign Affairs* (January/February 2008); Fred C. Bergsten et al., *China's Rise: Challenges and Opportunities* (Washington, DC: Peterson Institute

for International Studies and Center for Strategic and International Studies, 2008); and Michael D. Swaine, "Chinese Crisis Management: Framework for Analysis, Tentative Observations, and Questions for the Future," in Andrew Scobell and Larry M. Wortzel, eds., *Chinese Decisionmaking under Stress* (Carlisle, PA: Strategic Studies Institute, U.S. Army War College, 2005), 5–53.

41. As viewed by Thomas C. Schelling, *Arms and Influence* (Santa Barbara, CA: Praeger, 1966), 55, n. 11, "It is not easy to explain why the Chinese entered North Korea so secretly and so suddenly. Had they wanted to stop the United Nations at the level, say, of Pyongyang, to protect their own border and territory, a conspicuous early entry in force might have found the UN Command content with its accomplishments and in no mood to fight a second war against Chinese armies for the remainder of North Korea. They chose instead to launch a surprise attack, with stunning tactical advantages *but no prospect of deterrence*" (italics mine). According to China's top commander in Korea, General Peng, "The enemy had boasted the ability of its air force to cut off our communication and food supply. This gave us an opportunity to deceive the enemy about our intention. By releasing some POWs, we could give the enemy the impression that we are in short supply and are retreating." Hao Yufan and Zhai Zhihai, "China's Decision to Enter the Korean War: History Revisited," *China Quarterly* 121 (March 1990): 94–115. Multiple deceptions were used to encourage MacArthur's arrogance and complacency. Russell Spurr, *Enter the Dragon: China's Undeclared War Against the U.S. in Korea, 1950–1951* (New York: Henry Holt, 1989); Jonathan R. Pollack, "Korean War," in Harry Harding and Yuan Ming, eds., *Sino-American Relations, 1945–1955: A Joint Reassessment of a Critical Decade* (Wilmington, DE: Scholarly Resources, 1989), 213–37; Sergei N. Goncharov, John W. Lewis, and Xue Litai, *Uncertain Partners: Mao, Stalin, and the Korean War* (Stanford, CA: Stanford University Press, 1993).

42. Susan L. Shirk, *China: Fragile Superpower: How China's Internal Politics Could Derail Its Peaceful Rise* (New York: Oxford University Press, 2007), 5.

43. Ibid., 269.

44. Robert L. Suettinger, *Beyond Tiananmen: The Politics of U.S.-China Relations 1989–2000* (Washington, DC: Brookings Institution Press, 2003).

45. "DoD Annual Report to Congress—Military Power of the People's Republic of China, 2002," U.S. Department of Defense (July 2002), available at http://www.defense.gov/news/Jul2002/d20020712china.pdf.

46. Quoted in Andrew Scobell and Larry Wortzel, eds., *Civil-Military Change in China: Elites, Institutes, and Ideas After the 16th Party Congress* (Carlisle, PA: Strategic Studies Institute, U.S. Army War College, September 2004), 315, available at http://www.strategicstudiesinstitute.army.mil/pdffiles/pub413.pdf.

47. Ibid., 324.

48. Jason E. Bruzdzinski, "Demystifying Shashoujian: China's 'Assassin's Mace' Concept," in Scobell and Wortzel, *Civil-Military Changes in China*, 324.

49. Cary Huang, "Jiang Zemin Reportedly Urges the Development of Strategic Weapons," *Hong Kong iMail*, August 5, 2000, cited in Scobell and Wortzel, *Civil-Military Change in China*, 359.

50. "Jiang Zemin Orders Effectual Preparations for Use of Force," *Ching Chi Jih Pao*, November 29, 2000, cited in Bruzdzinski, "Demystifying Shashoujian."

51. Wang Congbiao, "Studying Jiang Zemin's 'On Science and Technology,'" Guangzhou Yangcheng Wanbao, February 13, 2001, in Foreign Broadcast Information Service (FBIS). FBIS was an open-source intelligence component of the Central Intelligence Agency's Directorate of Science and Technology. It monitored, translated, and disseminated within the U.S. government openly available news and information from media sources outside the United States. In November 2005, it was announced that FBIS would become the newly formed Open Source Center, tasked with the collection and analysis of freely available intelligence. See http://en.wikipedia.org/wiki/Foreign_Broadcast_Information_Service.

52. James R. Lilley and David Shambaugh, *China's Military Faces the Future (Studies on Contemporary China)* (Washington, DC: American Enterprise Institute, 1999), 66.

53. "U.S.-China Economic and Security Review Commission 2013 Report to Congress: China's Military Modernization, U.S.-China Security Relations, and China's Cyber Activities," Hearing before the Armed Services Committee, U.S. House of Representatives, 113th Cong. 10 (November 12, 2013), testimony of Dr. Larry M. Wortzel, commissioner, U.S.-China Economic and Security Review Commission, available at http://docs.house.gov/meetings/AS/AS00/20131120/101510/HHRG-113-AS00-Wstate-WortzelL-20131120.pdf.

54. Ibid.

55. Dawn S. Onley and Patience Wait, "Red Storm Rising," *Government Computer News*, August 17, 2006, available at http://gcn.com/articles/2006/08/17/red-storm-rising.aspx.

56. "U.S.-China Economic and Security Review Commission 2013 Report to Congress," testimony of Dr. Larry M. Wortzel.

57. Ellen Nakashima, "Confidential Report Lists U.S. Weapons System Designs Compromised by Chinese Cyberspies," *Washington Post*, May 27, 2013, available at http://www.washingtonpost.com/world/national-security/confidential-report-lists-us-weapons-system-designs-compromised-by-chinese-cyberspies/2013/05/27/a42c3e1c-c2dd-11e2-8c3b-0b5e9247e8ca_story.html.

58. Nathan Thornburgh, "The Invasion of the Chinese Cyberspies," *Time*, August 29, 2005, available at http://content.time.com/time/magazine/article/0,971,1098961,00.html.

59. "U.S.-China Economic and Security Review Commission 2013 Report to Congress," testimony of Dr. Larry M. Wortzel.

60. Jim Finkle, "Hacker Group in China Linked to Big Cyber Attacks: Symantec," Reuters, September 17, 2013, available at http://www.reuters.com/article/2013/09/17/us-cyberattacks-china-idUSBRE98G0M720130917.

61. "Hidden Lynx—Professional Hackers for Hire," Symantec, September 17, 2013, available at http://www.symantec.com/connect/blogs/hidden-lynx-professional-hackers-hire.

62. Shaun Waterman, "China 'Has .75M Zombie Computers' in U.S.," United Press International, September 17, 2007, available at http://www.upi.com/Emerging

_Threats/2007/09/17/China-has-75M-zombie-computers-in-US/UPI
-73941190055386/.

63. Lilley and Shambaugh, *China's Military Faces the Future*, 71.

64. Chang Mengxiong, *"21 Shiji Wuqi He Jundui Zhanwang"* [*Weapons of the 21st
Century*], *Zhongguo Junshi Kexue* [*China Military Science*] 30, no. 1 (Spring 1995):
19–24, 49, in Pillsbury, *China Debates the Future Security Environment*, 292.

65. Ibid., 254.

66. Zhang Shouqi and Sun Xuegui, *Jiefangjun Bao*, May 14, 1996, cited in Louis
M. Giannelli, *The Cyber Equalizer: The Quest for Control and Dominance in
Cyber Spectrum* (Bloomington, IN: Xlibris, 2012), 147.

67. Corpus, "America's Acupuncture Points. Part 2: The Assassin's Mace."

68. "Annual Report to Congress: Military Power of the People's Republic of China
2008," U.S. Department of Defense, March 2008, available at http://www.defense
.gov/pubs/pdfs/China_Military_Report_08.pdf.

69. Joan Johnson-Freese, "China's Antisatellite Program: They're Learning," *China-
U.S. Focus*, July 12, 2013, available at http://www.chinausfocus.com/peace-secu
rity/chinas-anti-satellite-program-theyre-learning/.

70. Emily Miller, "Officials Fear War in Space by China," *Washington Times*, January 24, 2007, available at http://www.washingtontimes.com/news/2007/jan/24
/20070124-121536-8225r/?page=all.

71. Shirley Kan, *CRS Report for Congress: China's Antisatellite Weapon Test*, April
23, 2007.

72. Miller, "Officials Fear War in Space by China."

73. Bill Gertz, "China Conducts Test of New Antisatellite Missile," *Washington Free
Beacon*, May 14, 2013, available at http://freebeacon.com/china-conducts-test-of
-new-anti-satellite-missile/. See also Andrea Shalal, "Analysis Points to China's
Work on New Antisatellite Weapon," Reuters, March 17, 2014, available at http://
www.reuters.com/article/2014/03/17/us-china-space-report-idUSBRE
A2G1Q320140317.

74. Bill Gertz, "China Launches Three ASAT Satellites," *Washington Free Beacon*,
August 26, 2013, available at http://freebeacon.com/china-launches-three-asat
-satellites/.

75. Leonard David, "Pentagon Report: China's Growing Military Space Power."

76. Corpus, "America's Acupuncture Points. Part 2: The Assassin's Mace."

77. "Annual Report to Congress: Military Power of the People's Republic of China,"
U.S. Department of Defense, July 28, 2003, 51, available at http://www.defense
.gov/pubs/2003chinaex.pdf.

78. Corpus, "America's Acupuncture Points. Part 2: The Assassin's Mace."

79. Scobell and Wortzel, *Civil-Military Change in China*, 342.

80. "Annual Report to Congress: Military Power of the People's Republic of China,"
U.S. Department of Defense, July 28, 2003, 21, available at http://www.defense
.gov/pubs/2003chinaex.pdf.

81. See, for example, President Obama's first public speech about the U.S. pivot to
Asia, "Remarks by President Obama to the Australian Parliament," Canberra,

Australia, the White House, Office of the Press Secretary, November 27, 2011, available at http://www.whitehouse.gov/the-press-office/2011/11/17/remarks-pres ident-obama-australian-parliament. See also Hillary Clinton, "America's Pacific Century," *Foreign Policy*, October 11, 2011, available at http://www.foreignpolicy .com/articles/2011/10/11/americas_pacific_century.

CHAPTER 8: THE CAPITALIST CHARADE

1. The course used a translation of Angus Madison's *Dynamic Forces and Capitalist Development: A Long-Run Comparative View* (New York: Oxford University Press, 1991); a study by Thomas K. McCraw called "Government, Big Business, and the Wealth of Nations," in Alfred D. Chandler, Franco Amatori, and Takashi Hikino, eds., *Big Business and the Wealth of Nations* (Cambridge, UK: Cambridge University Press, 1999); and a book by Alfred D. Chandler, *The Visible Hand: The Managerial Revolution in American Business* (Cambridge, MA: Harvard University Press, 1993). The class also used a translation of a book by Chalmers Johnson called *MITI and the Japanese Miracle: The Growth of Industrial Policy, 1925–1975* (Stanford, CA: Stanford University Press, 1982). A related book was a translation of a book edited by Thomas K. McCraw, *America vs. Japan: A Comparative Study* (Cambridge, MA: Harvard Business School Press, 1986). They also had translated McCraw's edited volume *The Essential Alfred Chandler: Essays toward Historical Theory of Big Business* (Cambridge, MA: Harvard Business School Press, 1988) as well as Michael Porter's *The Competitive Advantage of Nations* (New York: Free Press, 1990).

2. Allison Watts, "The Technology That Launched a City," *Minnesota History Magazine* 57 (Summer 2000): 86–97, available at http://collections.mnhs.org/MNHis toryMagazine/articles/57/v57i02p086-097.pdf. According to Watts, the founder of the Pillsbury Company in 1874 decided to send the Austrian engineer William de la Barre to Hungary in search of this new technology. "The Hungarians were very secretive about their processes, and de la Barre had to disguise himself in order to take notes on their machinery. . . . This new method of gradual reduction soon completely replaced grist stones because the steel rollers could do more work with less power, lasted much longer, and yielded more flour. The innovation also prevented heat discoloration, minimized the crushing of the bran husk that speckled the flour, and utilized equipment that was easier to maintain than millstones or porcelain rollers." See also John W. Oliver, *History of American Technology* (New York: Ronald Press, 1956); William J. Powell, *Pillsbury's Best: A Company History from 1869* (Minneapolis: Pillsbury Publishing, 1985); John Reynolds, *Windmills & Watermills* (New York: Praeger, 1970); and George D. Rogers, "History of Flour Manufacture in Minnesota," in *Collections of the Minnesota Historical Society* 10, pt. 1 (St. Paul: Minnesota Historical Society, 1905).

3. This was done by obtaining technology for the vulcanizing process and machines to mold and extrude finished rubber to produce boots, gloves, rainwear, industrial hoses, and insulating materials.

4. This enabled DuPont to produce Styrofoam as well as nylon and other artificial fibers. By 1985, these man-made fibers accounted for more than 70 percent of total artificial fibers used in the United States.

5. Charles H. Ferguson and Charles R. Morris, *Computer Wars: How the West Can Win in a Post-IBM World* (New York: Times Books, 1993).

6. *The Economist Pocket World in Figures*, 2014 ed. (London: Profile Books, 2013), 24.

7. "Fortune Global 500," *CNN Money*, available at http://money.cnn.com/magazines /fortune/global500/index.html.

8. In rank order these include Sinopec, China National Petroleum, State Grid, the Industrial & Commercial Bank of China, and the China Construction Bank.

9. For more on China's robust economic growth, see, for example, "China Aims to Quadruple GDP, Build a Well-Off Society, and Become the World's Largest Economy by 2020," *China Economic Times*, December 17, 2002, FBIS CPP20021217000175, cited in Shirk, *China: Fragile Superpower*, 275. See also Joel Andreas, *Rise of the Red Engineers: The Cultural Revolution and the Origins of China's New Class* (Stanford, CA: Stanford University Press, 2009); Yongnian Zheng, *Will China Become Democratic?: Elite, Class, and Regime Transition* (New York: Cavendish Square Publishing, 2004); Robert Lawrence Kuhn, *How China's Leaders Think: The Inside Story of China's Past, Current, and Future Leaders* (Hoboken, NJ: John Wiley & Sons, 2010); Eamonn Fingleton, *In the Jaws of the Dragon: America's Fate in the Coming Era of Chinese Dominance* (New York: St. Martin's Press, 2008); and Dambisa Moyo, *Winner Take All: China's Race for Resources and What It Means for the World* (New York: Basic Books, 2012).

10. *The Economist Pocket World in Figures*, 2014 ed., 14. These efforts, begun shortly after the formation of the People's Republic of China in 1949, were largely ineffective until 1979, when the "One Child per Family" policy was mandated nationwide. Chairman Mao is said to have thought "about six hundred million" was the right population for China. Susan Greenhalgh, *Just One Child: Science and Policy in Deng's China* (Berkeley: University of California Press, 2008), 46–53. Mao said in 1958, "In the past, I said that we could manage with eight hundred million. Now I think that one billion-plus would be no cause for alarm" (52).

11. For more background, see "China 2030: Building a Modern, Harmonious, and Creative Society," Washington, DC: World Bank, DOI: 10.1596/978-0-8213-9545-5, License: Creative Commons Attribution CC BY 3.0.

12. Annalyn Censky, "World Bank to China: Free Up your Economy or Bust," *CNN Money*, February 27, 2012, available at http://money.cnn.com/2012/02/27/news /economy/china_world_bank/.

13. For more on China's "national champions," see Accenture Consulting, "China Spreads Its Wings: Chinese Companies Go Global" (2007), available at http:// www.accenture.com/NR/rdonlyres/1F79806F-E076-4CD7-8B74-3BAF BAC58943/0/6341_chn_spreads_wings_final8.pdf; Geoff Dyer and Richard McGregor, "China's Champions: Why State Ownership Is No Longer a Dead Hand," *Financial Times*, March 16, 2008, available at http://www.ft.com/intl/cms /s/0/979f69c8-f35b-11dc-b6bc-0000779fd2ac.html; Andrew Szamosszegi and

Cole Kyle, "An Analysis of State-owned Enterprises and State Capitalism in China," U.S.-China Economic and Security Review Commission, October 26, 2011, Annual Report to Congress (Washington, DC: U.S. Government Printing Office, 2011); and Joseph Casey, "Patterns in U.S.-China Trade Since China's Accession to the World Trade Organization," U.S.-China Economic and Security Commission, November 2012, available at http://origin.www.uscc.gov/sites/default/files/Research/US-China_TradePatternsSinceChinasAccessionto theWTO.pdf.

14. Ronald Coase and Ning Wang, *How China Became Capitalist* (New York: Palgrave Macmillan, 2012), x.

15. Deng Xiaoping said in a meeting in Beijing with German chancellor Helmut Kohl in October 1984 that farmers and the rural majority of China already had a free market. "Deng's statement was a masterpiece of concealment," Coase and Wang wrote. "China had not lifted its ban on private farming at all, but had rejected this idea." Ibid., 162.

16. This issue is part of the congressional mandate to the U.S.-China Economic and Security Commission to explore in its annual reports. The commission's annual reports are available at http://www.uscc.gov/Annual_Reports.

17. Pillsbury, *China Debates the Future Security Environment*, chapter 6.

18. Xiao Lian, CASS Research, Global Economy and Politics Research Center, "Prospect and Measures for China-U.S. Energy Cooperation," *Yafei Zongheng* (2008): 4.

19. Wang Xianglin, ed., "The Influence of Somali Pirates on China's Maritime Security," *International Relations Academy Journal* (2009): 5.

20. The Third Plenum of the 11th Central Committee Congress of the Communist Party of China, December 18–22, 1978, approved this transition.

21. Thomas L. Friedman, *The Lexus and the Olive Tree: Understanding Globalization* (New York: Farrar, Straus and Giroux, 1999), 195.

22. University of California, Santa Cruz Atlas, "Gross Domestic Product," last updated February 24, 2003, available at http://ucatlas.ucsc.edu/gdp/gdp.html.

23. Carol Lee Hamrin, a State Department senior research analyst focused on China, writes in *China and the Challenge of the Future: Changing Political Patterns* (Boulder, CO: Westview Press, 1990) that the Chinese used a long-term plan called *Global 2000 Report to the President: Entering the Twenty-First Century* (60). The Chinese invited the author of this report, Gerald Barney, to China to create a "China 2000" team (47). I believe that this contributed to the Marathon strategy. A second China 2000 study was drafted between 1983 and 1985 by China's State Council research center. Hamrin states that this was "an internal effort to parallel the external World Bank study commissioned by Deng Xiaoping that summer [of 1983]" (123). More than four hundred experts participated. The study used quantitative forecasting to create mathematical models to project trends to 2050 and 2080 using the "system dynamics national model" developed at MIT by Professor Jay Forrester (126). Hamrin quotes from a Chinese document that states, "In the middle of the next century, our country might approach or attain the economic development level of the advanced countries, and that, by

the end of the next century, we might even surpass them" (127). The Chinese report concluded that if China surpasses them, "then the long-cherished wish of numerous people with lofty ideals, and of the heroes and martyrs over the centuries, will be fulfilled. In this sense, the twenty-first century can be called a century of China!" (127). For Barney's account of these events that led to the Chinese drafting a twenty-year development plan, see Gerald O. Barney, ed., *The Future of China: Collected Papers* (Arlington, VA: Global Studies Center, 1985). See also Carol Lee Hamrin and Suisheng Zhao, eds., *Decision-Making in Deng's China: Perspectives from Insiders* (Armonk, NY: M.E. Sharpe, 1995). For more on Hamrin, see her Global China Center profile page at http://www.globalchinacenter .org/about/scholars/senior-associate/dr-carol-lee-hamrin.php.

24. See, for example, Shujie Yao, *Economic Growth, Income Distribution, and Poverty Reduction in Contemporary China* (London: Routledge Curzon, 2012), 9.

25. "Report of the Working Party on the Accession of China," World Trade Organization, October 1, 2001, 8, available at http://unpan1.un.org/intradoc/groups /public/documents/apcity/unpan002144.pdf. For a broader discussion of China's accession to the WTO, see Supachai Panitchpakdi and Mark L. Clifford, *China and the WTO* (New York: John Wiley & Sons, 2002); and Testimony of Calman J. Cohen, president, Emergency Committee for American Trade (ECAT), before the U.S.-China Economic and Security Review Commission, "Hearing on Evaluating China's Past and Future Role in the World Trade Organization," June 9, 2010.

26. This issue is discussed in Elizabeth C. Economy and Michael Levi, *By All Means Necessary: How China's Resource Quest Is Changing the World* (New York: Oxford University Press, 2014).

27. Chen-ya Tien, *Chinese Military Theory: Ancient and Modern* (Lanham, MD: Mosaic Press, 1992), chapter 6.

28. See recorded vote on H.R. 4444, May 24, 2000, available at http://thomas.loc.gov.

29. See Senate roll call vote on H.R. 4444, Sept. 19, 2000, available at http://www .senate.gov.

30. Minxin Pei, "Intellectual Property Rights: A Survey of the Major Issues," a report for the Asia Business Council, September 2005, available at http://www .asiabusinesscouncil.org/docs/IntellectualPropertyRights.pdf. See also Andrew Mertha, *The Politics of Piracy: Intellectual Property in Contemporary China* (Ithaca, NY: Cornell University Press, 2005).

31. See, for example, Jamil Anderlini, "Justin Lin Criticises China Growth Pessimists," *Financial Times*, July 29, 2013, available at http://www.ft.com/intl/cms/s /0/3e62c9de-f83e-11e2-b4c4-00144feabdc0.html#axzz2vZMIjwOr.

32. Lin made headlines again in 2002 when, upon the death of his father, he asked the Taiwanese government for permission to return to the island nation for the funeral. The Taiwanese government approved his application—and issued a warrant for his arrest. Rich Chang and Chris Wang, "Justin Lin Faces Arrest If He Returns: MND," *Taipei Times*, March 15, 2012, available at http://www.taipe itimes.com/News/taiwan/archives/2012/03/15/2003527832.

33. Justin Yifu Lin, *Benti Changwu: Dialogues of Methodology in Economics* (Singa-

pore: Cengage Learning, 2005); Justin Yifu Lin, Fang Cai, and Zhou Li, *The China Miracle: Development Strategy and Economic Reform* (Hong Kong: Chinese University Press, 2003); and Justin Yifu Lin, *Economic Development and Transition* (New York: Cambridge University Press, 2009).

34. Wang Jisi, "China's Search for a Grand Strategy," *Foreign Affairs* (March/April 2011), available at http://www.foreignaffairs.com/articles/67470/wang-jisi/chinas-search-for-a-grand-strategy.

35. Hamrin, *China and the Challenge of the Future*, chapter 3.

36. Writing in 2002, Joseph Stiglitz noted that he "had also been involved for nearly twenty years in discussions concerning transitions from Communist to market economies. My experience with how to handle such transitions began in 1980, when I first discussed these issues with leaders in China, as it was beginning its move toward a market economy. I had been a strong advocate of the gradualist policies adopted by the Chinese, policies that have proven their merit over the past two decades." Joseph Stiglitz, *Globalization and Its Discontents* (New York: W.W. Norton & Company, 2002), x–xi.

37. World Bank, "China—Long-term Development Issues and Options," World Bank country economic report (October 31, 1985), available at http://econ.world bank.org/external/default/main?pagePK=64165259&theSitePK=469372& piPK=64165421&menuPK=64166093&entityID=000178830_98101911363148.

38. Ibid., 16.

39. For a discussion of the effect of years of credit expansion on China's banking sector, see, for example, Lingling Wei and Daniel Inman, "Chinese Banks Feel Strains After Long Credit Binge," *Wall Street Journal*, August 15, 2013, available at http://online.wsj.com/news/articles/SB10001424127887323446404579010781178659564.

40. "Mao Yushi: Winner of the 2012 Milton Friedman Prize for Advancing Liberty," Cato Institute, available at http://www.cato.org/friedman-prize/mao-yushi.

41. U.S.-China Economic and Security Review Commission, *2013 Annual Report to Congress* (Washington, DC, November 20, 2013), available at http://www.uscc .gov/Annual_Reports/2013-annual-report-congress; Andrew Szamosszegi and Cole Kyle, *An Analysis of State-Owned Enterprises and Capitalism in China: A Report Submitted to the U.S.-China Economic and Security Review Commission* (Washington, DC: Capital Trade, 2011).

42. Peter Harrold, ed., "Macroeconomic Management in China," World Bank Discussion Paper no. 222, Washington, DC: The World Bank, 1993. See also Peter Harrold and Rajiv Lall, "China: Reform and Development in 1992–1993," World Bank Discussion Paper no. 215, Washington, DC: The World Bank, 1993.

43. World Bank, "China—Long-term Development Issues and Options"; Harrold, "Macroeconomic Management in China"; "China 2030: Building a Modern, Harmonious, and Creative Society," Washington, DC: World Bank, DOI:10.1596/978-0-8213-9545-5, License: Creative Commons Attribution CC BY 3.0.and 2013.

44. U.S.-China Economic and Security Review Commission, *Annual Report to Congress 2009* (Washington, DC: U.S. Government Printing Office, 2009), 57–65; World Bank and the Development Research Center of the State Council, P. R.

China, 2013; "China 2030: Building a Modern, Harmonious, and Creative Society." See also John B. Sheahan, "Alternative International Economic Strategies and their Relevance for China," World Bank, Staff Working Paper 759 (February 28, 1986): 1, 7–8, 14, available at http://documents.worldbank.org/curated/en/1986/02/1554704/alternative-international-economic-strategies-relevance-china.

45. "China's Banks by the Numbers," *Wall Street Journal*, November 26, 2013, available at http://online.wsj.com/news/articles/SB10001424127887324823804579013190828816938?mg=reno64-wsj&url=http%3A%2F%2Fonline.wsj.com%2Farticle%2FSB10001424127887324823804579013190828816938.html.

46. China has recently begun to allow foreign banks as local corporations. There were twenty of these as of March 2014.

47. "PBOC Says No Longer in China's Interest to Increase Reserves," Bloomberg, November 20, 2013, available at http://www.bloomberg.com/news/2013-11-20/pboc-says-no-longer-in-china-s-favor-to-boost-record-reserves.html.

48. Foreign exchange reserves held by countries include such things as gold, dollars, pounds, special drawing rights, and other liquid assets. These reserves are typically held by governments to cover shortfalls in the balance of trade between the home country and other trading partners.

49. A few other countries have used SOEs to good advantage in the early stages of their development. This usually occurs when free markets are weak or do not exist, when new industries are small, when possible foreign competitors are much stronger, or when scarce national resources must be husbanded carefully. Japan, South Korea, and the other so-called Asian Tigers are examples of countries that have taken this route.

50. Fraser J. T. Howie and Carl E. Walter, *Red Capitalism: The Fragile Financial Foundation of China's Extraordinary Rise* (Hoboken, NJ: John Wiley & Sons, 2011), 10.

51. Ibid., 163.

52. Ibid., 178.

53. David Fazekas, "Stocks Rise to New Record Highs on Strong Economic, Corporate News; Apple Strikes Deal in China; Facebook Joins the S&P 500," *Yahoo! Finance*, December 23, 2013, available at http://finance.yahoo.com/blogs/hot-stock-minute/stocks-rise-to-new-record-highs-on-strong-economic—corporate-news—apple-strikes-deal-in-china—facebook-joins-the-s-p-500-161042521.html.

54. Beth Gardiner, "B-Schools Embrace China," *Wall Street Journal*, June 15, 2011, available at http://online.wsj.com/news/articles/SB100014240527023043927045763759301027778602.

55. "China failing WTO Pledge on State-Owned Firms," *Asia Today Online*, March 17, 2012, available at http://www.asiatoday.com.au/archive/feature_reports.php?id=560.

56. Stephen McDonell, "Chinese Telco Huawei Tries to Shake Off Spy Image After NBN Ban," *ABC News 24*, June 11, 2013, available at http://www.abc.net.au/news/2013-06-10/chinese-telco-huawei-tries-to-shake-off-spy-image/4744886.

57. See Office on the National Counterintelligence Executive, "Counterintelligence Security: Foreign Spies Stealing US Economic Secrets in Cyberspace," Report to Congress on Foreign Economic Collection and Industrial Espionage, 2009–2011, October 2011, available at http://www.ncix.gov/publications/reports/fecie_all /Foreign_Economic_Collection_2011.pdf.

58. As the journalist Michael Schuman wrote in December 2013, "Policymakers in Beijing must be feeling warm and fuzzy these days. For years, they have railed against the dominance of the U.S. dollar in global trade and finance, complaining that it leaves the world at the mercy of erratic Washington politics and questionable economic management. . . . China's policymakers have been talking up a storm for years about internationalizing the renminbi, but progress has been glacial." Michael Schuman, "China's Quest to Take on the U.S. Dollar Has a Long Way to Go," *Time*, December 10, 2013, available at http://world.time.com /2013/12/10/chinas-quest-to-take-on-the-u-s-dollar-has-a-long-way-to-go/. Melissa Murphy and Wen Jin Yuan note that "speculation has focused on the future of the U.S. dollar, largely due to comments by senior Chinese officials that have led some observers to conclude that the renminbi (RMB) is 'set to usurp the US dollar' as the world's reserve currency." Melissa Murphy and Wen Jin Yuan, *Is China Ready to Challenge the Dollar?: Internationalization of the Renminbi and Its Implications for the United States* (Washington, DC: Center for Strategic and International Studies, 2009), 1. See also Nile Bowie, "Renminbi Rising: China's 'de-Americanized World' Taking Shape?" *RT*, October 29, 2013, available at http://rt.com/op-edge/china-leadership-alternative-dollar-916/; Wang Jiang, Li Xiaoning, Qiao Liang, Wang Xiangsui, *Xin Zhanguo Shidai* [*The New Warring States Era*] (Beijing: Xinhua chubanshe, 2003). In 2013, the World Bank released a report, *China 2030: Building a Modern, Harmonious, and Creative Society*, which referenced six reports that explained how China could move to transform the yuan into an international reserve currency. These reports are: Yiping Huang, "RMB Policy and the Global Currency System," Working Paper 2010-03, Peking University, China Center for Economic Research, Beijing, 2010; Markus Jaeger, "Yuan as a Reserve Currency: Likely Prospects and Possible Implications," Deutsche Bank Research, 2010; Jong-Wha Lee, "Will the Renminbi Emerge as an International Reserve Currency?" Asian Development Bank, Manila, 2010, available at http://aric.adb.org/grs/papers/Lee.pdf; John H. Makin, "Can China's Currency Go Global?" Economic Outlook, American Enterprise Institute for Public Policy Research, Washington, DC, January 2011; Friedrich Wu, Rongfang Pan, and Di Wang, "Renminbi's Potential to Become a Global Currency," *China and World Economy* 18, no. 1 (2010): 63–81; and Xiaochuan Zhou, "China's Corporate Bond Market Development: Lessons Learned," BIS Papers 26, Bank for International Settlements, Basel, 2005.

59. Ma Lianhua, "Gongxinbu Buzhang Li Yizhong: Mingnian Jiang Jiakuai Tuidong Jianbing Chongzu" ["Minister of the MIIT Li Yizhong: Will Accelerate Merger and Restructure Next Year"], *Zhongguo Qingnian Bao*, December 24, 2009.

60. See Jack Freifelder, "Pollution-Reporting Move a 'Turning Point' in Smog Battle:

Official," *China Daily USA*, January 21, 2014, available at http://usa.chinadaily
.com.cn/us/2014-01/21/content_17247647.htm.

61. U.S.-China Economic and Security Review Commission, *2013 Annual Report to Congress*, 11.

62. Usha C. V. Haley and George T. Haley, *Subsidies to Chinese Industry: State Capitalism, Business Strategy, and Trade Policy* (New York: Oxford University Press, 2013), especially the detailed synopsis on pp. xx–xxv.

63. Mark Litke, "China Big in Counterfeit Goods," ABC News, April 21, 2002, available at http://abcnews.go.com/WNT/story?id=130381, cited in Oded Shenkar, *The Chinese Century: The Rising Chinese Economy and Its Impact on the Global Economy, the Balance of Power, and Your Job* (Upper Saddle River, NJ: Pearson Prentice Hall, 2006), 100.

64. For example, the economist James Kynge estimated that American, European, and Japanese firms lost $60 billion in 2004 alone because of Chinese counterfeiting. "Modern China: The Promise and Challenge of an Emerging Superpower," *World Savvy Monitor*, no. 2 (June 2008), available at http://worldsavvy.org/monitor/index.php?option=com_content&id=157&Itemid=174.

65. Shenkar, *Chinese Century*, 102.

66. Office of the National Counterintelligence Executive, "Foreign Spies Stealing US Economic Secrets in Cyberspace: Report to Congress on Foreign Collection and Industrial Espionage," 2009–2011, October 2011.

67. Ibid., Executive Summary.

68. "Foreign Spies Stealing U.S. Economic Secrets in Cyberspace: Report to Congress on Foreign Economic Collection and Industrial Espionage, 2009–2011," Office of the National Counterintelligence Executive, October 2011, page 2, available at http://www.ncix.gov/publications/reports/fecie_all/Foreign_Economic_Collection_2011.pdf.

CHAPTER 9: A CHINA WORLD ORDER IN 2049

1. Robert Fogel, "$123,000,000,000,000," *Foreign Policy*, January 4, 2010, available at http://www.foreignpolicy.com/articles/2010/01/04/123000000000000.

2. Mark O. Yeisley, "Bipolarity, Proxy Wars, and the Rise of China," *Strategic Studies Quarterly* (Winter 2011): 75–91, available at http://www.au.af.mil/au/ssq/2011/winter/yeisley.pdf; and "After You," *Economist*, June 15, 2013, available at http://www.economist.com/news/books-and-arts/21579430-will-bipolar-world-be-peaceful-after-you.

3. Arvind Virmani and Ashley J. Tellis, "Tripolar World: India, China, and the United States in the 21st Century," Carnegie Endowment for International Peace, February 9, 2011, available at http://carnegieendowment.org/2011/02/09/tri-polar-world-india-china-and-united-states-in-21st-century/247d; and Arvind Virmani, "A Tripolar World: India, China, and U.S.," ICRIER (Indian Council for Research on International Economic Relations), May 18, 2005, available at http://www.icrier.org/pdf/TripolarWrld_IHC5.pdf.

4. "Global Development Horizons, Multipolarity: The New Global Economy," World Bank, 2011, 7.

5. Lydia Liu, "The Translator's Turn," in Victor Mair, ed., *Columbia History of Chinese Literature* (New York: Columbia University Press, 2001), 1057. The missionary W. A. P. Martin rendered the book *Elements of International Law* into Chinese in 1864. Liu states, "He and his fellow Chinese translators had great difficulty in trying to come up with suitable Chinese equivalents for 'rights' and other terms."

6. James A. Ogilvy and Peter Schwartz with Joe Flower, "China's Futures: Scenarios for the World's Fastest-Growing Economy, Ecology, and Society," *Foreign Affairs* (July/August 2000): 13, available at http://www.foreignaffairs.com/articles/56128 /richard-n-cooper/chinas-futures-scenarios-for-the-worlds-fastest-growing -economy-.

7. See Edward Wong, "Reformers Aim to Get China to Live Up to Own Constitution," *New York Times*, February 3, 2013, available at http://www.nytimes.com /2013/02/04/world/asia/reformers-aim-to-get-china-to-live-up-to-own-consti tution.html.

8. Wen said his Twitter account was "tweet bombed" with trash information. The heaviest attack occurred on April 25, 2012, when 590,000 spam messages were posted within twenty-four hours. He added, "Unidentified persons also posted viciously defaming information about me online at a rate of over 10,000 times per day." The rate, frequency, and size of the attack could not have been carried out by anyone other than the military. "Chinese Hacking: Impact on Human Rights and Commercial Rule of Law," Hearing before the Congressional-Executive Commission on China, 113th Cong., 2 (June 25, 2013), statement of Wen Yunchao (online alias "Bei Feng"), independent journalist and blogger, visiting scholar, Institute for the Study of Human Rights, Columbia University, available at http://www.cecc.gov/sites/chinacommission.house.gov/files/CECC%20Hearing %20-%20Chinese%20Hacking%20-%20Wen%20Yunchao%20Written%20State ment.pdf.

9. "Chinese Hacking: Impact on Human Rights and Commercial Rule of Law," Hearing before the Congressional-Executive Commission on China, 113th Cong. (June 25, 2013), available at http://www.cecc.gov/events/hearings/chinese -hacking-impact-on-human-rights-and-commercial-rule-of-law. An online video purporting to show a public execution in the Chinese countryside has reignited debate about the death penalty in a country consistently singled out by human rights groups for executing vastly more people than any other. "Video Reignites Death Penalty Debate in China," *Wall Street Journal*, August 13, 2013, available at http://blogs.wsj.com/chinarealtime/2013/08/13/death-penalty-debate-resur faces-in-china/.

10. Willy Lam, "Chinese State Media Goes Global," *Asia Times Online*, January 30, 2009, available at http://www.atimes.com/atimes/China/KA30Ad01.html.

11. See, for example, Edward Wong, "Human Rights Advocates Vanish as China Intensifies Crackdown," *New York Times*, March 11, 2011.

12. Hearing, "Chinese Hacking: Impact on Human Rights and Commercial Rule of Law," Congressional-Executive Commission on China, June 25, 2013.

13. "Chinese Hacking: Impact on Human Rights and Commercial Rule of Law," Hearing before the Congressional-Executive Commission on China, 113th Cong. 3 (June 25, 2013), statement of Louisa Greve, Vice President, Asia, Middle East and North Africa, and Global Programs, National Endowment for Democracy, available at http://www.cecc.gov/sites/chinacommission.house.gov/files /CECC%20Hearing%20-%20Chinese%20Hacking%20-%20Louisa%20Greve %20Written%20Statement.pdf.

14. Ibid.

15. Employees of this "business" include cyberpolice, hardware engineers, software developers, and Web monitors that watch, filter, and censor Chinese Internet users. "A Giant Cage," Special Report: China and the Internet, *Economist*, April 6, 2013, available at http://media.economist.com/sites/default/files/sponsorships /TM19/20130406_China_and_the_Internet.pdf. Just recently, when Zhang Qianfan, a liberal legal scholar at Peking University, tried to equate the Chinese dream with constitutionalism, censors deleted his comments on the importance of the constitution. "Xi Jinping's Vision: Chasing the Chinese Dream," *Economist*, May 4, 2013, available at http://www.economist.com/news/briefing/21577063-chinas -new-leader-has-been-quick-consolidate-his-power-what-does-he-now-want-his /comments?page=8.

16. Callahan, *China Dreams*, 51.

17. Peter Ford, "Tiananmen Still Taboo in China After All these Years," *Christian Science Monitor*, June 4, 2013, available at http://www.csmonitor.com/World/Global -News/2013/0604/Tiananmen-still-taboo-in-China-after-all-these-years-video.

18. Alexander Abad-Santos, "How Memes Became the Best Weapon against Chinese Internet Censorship," *Atlantic Wire*, June 4, 2013, available at http://www .thewire.com/global/2013/06/how-memes-became-best-weapon-against-chinese -Internet-censorship/65877/.

19. Ibid. Other examples include censored words such as "Tibetan independence," "brainwash," and "Ai Weiwei." David Bamman, Brendan O'Connor, Noah A. Smith, "Censorship and Deletion Practices in Chinese Social Media," *First Monday* 17, no. 3 (March 2012), available at http://firstmonday.org/ojs/index.php/fm /article/view/3943/3169. When the dissident Chinese author Yu Jie published a book criticizing the Chinese premier, he was taken into custody by police for reasons that were unclear, according to his wife. This wasn't the first time he had been taken. Some of the questioning sessions lasted twelve hours. His books have been banned from publication inside the country. He is an advocate for freedom of expression, publication, and religious freedom. "Yu Jie: Dissident Chinese Author Taken Away by Police," *Huffington Post*, July 6, 2010, available at http:// www.huffingtonpost.com/2010/07/06/yu-jie-dissident-chinese_n_636115.html.

20. "The Economist Explains: How Does China Censor the Internet?," *Economist*, April 21, 2013, available at http://www.economist.com/blogs/economist-explains /2013/04/economist-explains-how-china-censors-Internet.

21. Peter Navarro with Greg Autry, *Death by China: Confronting the Dragon—A Global Call to Action* (Upper Saddle River, NJ: Pearson Prentice Hall, 2011), 189; "Freedom on the Net 2012: A Global Assessment of Internet and Digital Media," Freedom House, September 24, 2012, 2, available at http://www.freedomhouse .org/report/freedom-net/freedom-net-2012#.Uu_6rOmPLmI. My Chinese visionary colleagues describe this as the "China effect," "Beijing consensus," "the spirit of Chinese culture," "China's peaceful rise," "yellow man's burden to civilize," and "rejuvenation of the Chinese nation."

22. "Freedom on the Net 2012: A Global Assessment of Internet and Digital Media," 2.

23. Ibid. China is rapidly expanding Chinese media team outlets across the continent to counter negative images of China with upbeat stories. They are training journalists and implementing exchange programs for African journalists. Claire Provost and Rich Harris, "China Commits Billions in Aid to Africa as Part of Charm Offensive—Interactive," *Guardian*, April 29, 2013, available at http:// www.theguardian.com/global-development/interactive/2013/apr/29/china -commits-billions-aid-africa-interactive.

24. For example, while China was sending its condolences to the United States following the September 11 attacks, it was encouraging anti-American rhetoric on the Internet. Anne-Marie Brady, *Marketing Dictatorship*, 99.

25. The Office of Foreign Propaganda was created to monitor the Internet, both inside and outside China. Western countries, they claim, use their control of the world's media to demonize China under the cover of promoting human rights and freedom. Ibid., 9, 13, 99.

26. Javier Corrales, Daniel Kimmage, Joshua Kurlantzick, Perry Link, Abbas Milani, and Rashed Rahman, *Undermining Democracy: 21st Century Authoritarians* (Washington, DC: Freedom House, June 2009), 3. Curiously, the only places China is avoiding are the four countries that maintain diplomatic relations with Taiwan: Burkina Faso, Gambia, São Tomé and Príncipe, and Swaziland. Provost and Harris, "China Commits Billions in Aid to Africa as Part of Charm Offensive— Interactive."

27. Chris Hogg, "China Banks Lend More Than World Bank—Report," BBC, January 11, 2011, available at http://www.bbc.co.uk/news/world-asia-pacific-12212936.

28. Stefan Halper, *The Beijing Consensus: How China's Authoritarian Model Will Dominate the Twenty-First Century* (New York: Basic Books, 2010), 38.

29. Corrales et al., *Undermining Democracy*, 4.

30. Halper, *Beijing Consensus*, 85. See also Joshua Eisenman, "Zimbabwe: China's African Ally," *China Brief* 5, no. 15 (2005).

31. Halper, *Beijing Consensus*, 85–86. Most of China's projects are transport, storage, and energy initiatives. China has poured millions toward health, education, and cultural projects. For example, it installed solar traffic lights in Liberia, and built a school for visual arts in Mozambique and an opera house in Algeria. Provost and Harris, "China Commits Billions in Aid to Africa as Part of Charm Offensive—Interactive."

32. Navarro with Autry, *Death by China*, 103.

33. James George, "China Arms Africa: Ignores UN Sanctions," *Examiner.com*, August 26, 2012, available at http://www.examiner.com/article/china-arms-africa -ignores-un-sanctions.

34. Halper, *Beijing Consensus*, 39.

35. Ibid. See also Arvind Subramanian, *Eclipse: Living in the Shadow of China's Economic Dominance* (Washington, DC: Peterson Institute for International Economics, 2011).

36. "Chinese Firms Helping Put Phone System in Kabul," *Washington Times*, September 28, 2001, available at http://www.washingtontimes.com/news/2001/sep /28/20010928-025638-7645r/.

37. Ibid.

38. Bill Gertz, *Treachery: How America's Friends and Foes Are Secretly Arming Our Enemies* (New York: Three Rivers Press, 2004), 117.

39. Ibid., 118.

40. Ibid., 119.

41. "Text: President Bush's News Conference," *WashingtonPost.com*, February 22, 2001, available at http://www.washingtonpost.com/wp-srv/onpolitics/tran scripts/bushtext022201.htm.

42. Maggie Farley, "U.S. Pushes for Response from China," *Los Angeles Times*, February 22, 2001, available at http://articles.latimes.com/2001/feb/22/news/mn-28550.

43. Gertz, *Treachery*, 121.

44. Ibid., 124.

45. Ibid., 125.

46. "China and the Environment: The East Is Grey," *Economist*, August 10, 2013, available at http://www.economist.com/news/briefing/21583245-china-worlds -worst-polluter-largest-investor-green-energy-its-rise-will-have.

47. Ibid.

48. Ibid.

49. "Executive Summary," in *OECD Environmental Outlook to 2050: the Consequences of Inaction*, OECD Publishing, 2012, 24.

50. Philip Bump, "China Air Pollution Already up 30 Percent," *Atlantic Wire*, April 3, 2013, available at http://www.theatlanticwire.com/global/2013/04/china-air -pollution-2013/63836/. "The new normal in Beijing is sending your kids to school wearing gas masks ($60 each) and for those who can afford it, stocking up on IQAirHealthPro indoor air filters (about $1,000 per room). Another sought-after product: pressurized canopies to cover school sports fields so school children can play outside.... There's also pressurized fresh air in a can ... flavors include 'pristine Tibetan' and 'postindustrial Taiwan.'" Christina Larson, "China's Autos Need to Emit Less Pollution," *Bloomberg Businessweek*, February 4, 2013, available at http://www.businessweek.com/articles/2013-02-04/chinas -autos-need-to-emit-less-pollution.

51. Edward Wong, "Beijing Takes Steps to Fight Pollution as Problem Worsens," *New York Times*, January 30, 2013, available at http://www.nytimes.com/2013/01 /31/world/asia/beijing-takes-emergency-steps-to-fight-smog.html?_r=0.

52. *Developing Countries Subsidize Fossil Fuels, Artificially Lowering Prices*, Institute for Energy Research, January 3, 2013, available at http://www.instituteforener gyresearch.org/2013/01/03/developing-countries-subsidize-fossil-fuel-con sumption-creating-artificially-lower-prices/.

53. Wong, "Beijing Takes Steps to Fight Pollution as Problem Worsens." According to one study, free coal policies in the 1990s caused China to lose 2.5 billion life years. Charles Kenny, "How Cleaning China's Dirty Air Can Slow Climate Change," *Bloomberg Businessweek*, August 5, 2013, available at http://www.busi nessweek.com/articles/2013-08-05/how-cleaning-china-s-dirty-air-can-slow -climate-change.

54. Elizabeth C. Economy, "China's Water Pollution Crisis," *Diplomat*, January 22, 2013, available at http://thediplomat.com/2013/01/forget-air-pollution-chinas-has -a-water-problem/.

55. Ibid.

56. Ibid.

57. Ibid.

58. According to Chinese fishermen, a decade ago it was possible to catch fish about 90 nautical miles from the coast but now they have to go out 130 to 160 nautical miles, and the catch has dropped by three quarters during the same time period. The number of types of marine products with commercial value has dropped from seventy to ten in recent years. *China's Water Challenge: Implications for the U.S. Rebalance to Asia: Hearing before the Senate Foreign Relations Subcommittee on East Asian and Pacific Affairs*, 113th Cong., 5 (July 24, 2013), statement of Elizabeth C. Economy, C. V. Starr senior fellow and director for Asia Studies, Council on Foreign Relations, available at http://www.foreign.senate.gov/imo /media/doc/Economy_Testimony.pdf.

59. Ibid.

60. For more on China's large-scale dam projects—and opposition to them—see Andrew Mertha, *China's Water Warriors: Citizen Action and Policy Change* (Ithaca, NY: Cornell University Press, 2008).

61. "Executive Summary," in *OECD Environmental Outlook to 2050: The Consequences of Inaction*, OECD Publishing, (2012), 20, available at http://www.oecd .org/environment/indicators-modelling-outlooks/oecdenvironmentaloutlook to2050theconsequencesofinaction.htm.

62. "State-Owned Enterprises: The State Advances," *Economist*, October 6, 2012, available at http://www.economist.com/node/21564274.

63. Jonathan Watts, "China's 'Cancer Villages' Reveal Dark Side of Economic Boom," *Guardian*, June 6, 2010, available at http://www.theguardian.com/envi ronment/2010/jun/07/china-cancer-villages-industrial-pollution.

64. By 2020, cancer deaths will climb from 2.5 million to 3 million annually. Christina Larson, "China Releases Grim Cancer Statistics," *Bloomberg Businessweek*, April 9, 2013, available at http://www.businessweek.com/articles/2013-04-09 /grim-cancer-statistics-from-china.

65. David McKenzie, "In China 'Cancer Villages' Is a Reality of Life," CNN, May 29,

2013, available at http://www.cnn.com/2013/05/28/world/asia/china-cancer-vil
lages-mckenzie/.

66. *Food and Drug Safety, Public Health, and the Environment in China: Hearing
    before the Congressional-Executive Commission on China*, 113th Cong., 2 (May 22,
    2013), statement by Senator Sherrod Brown, chair, Congressional-Executive
    Commission on China, available at http://www.cecc.gov/sites/chinacommission
    .house.gov/files/documents/hearings/2013/CECC%20Hearing%20-%20Food
    %20Safety%20-%20Chairman%20Brown%20Written%20Statement.pdf.

67. Watts, "China's 'Cancer Villages' Reveal Dark Side of Economic Boom." They have
    accessed resources and created a dumping ground for poor-quality products that
    would be unacceptable in Western markets. Navarro with Autry, *Death by China*.

68. Watts, "China's 'Cancer Villages' Reveal Dark Side of Economic Boom." The EU
    banned imports from China of animal origin after finding residues of veterinary
    medicines. Japan banned frozen spinach because pesticides were found to be 180
    times higher than Japanese standards. The United States banned pet food and
    toys with lead paint. Several East Asian countries discovered farmed fish inun-
    dated with carcinogenic antifungal agents and veterinary drugs.

69. *The IP Commission Report: The Report of the Commission on the Theft of American
    Intellectual Property* (Seattle: National Bureau of Asian Research, 2013), 12, avail-
    able at http://www.ipcommission.org/report/IP_Commission_Report_052213.pdf.

70. Ibid., Executive Summary, 3.

71. *IP Commission Report*. In 2012, Verizon, in cooperation with eighteen other pri-
    vate institutions and government agencies, found that 96 percent of the world's
    cyberespionage, including stealing trade secrets and intellectual property, come
    from China, 18. See also "U.S. Government, Industry Fed Up with Chinese Cyber
    Theft; What's Being Done?," *PBS Newshour*, July 8, 2013, available at http://www
    .pbs.org/newshour/bb/military-july-dec13-cybercrime_07-08/.

72. Reduced barriers to international trade allowed less-developed countries to
    manufacture lower-technology products and services for sale to more-developed
    countries, and allowed more developed countries to close entire industries and
    convert their labor forces to work on more advanced products. Prosperity
    increased broadly and allowed countries to move up the technology ladder. From
    1950 to 2012, global economic output increased more than sixteenfold and stan-
    dards of living rose for populations worldwide. *IP Commission Report*, 9.

73. Ibid., 25.

74. Ibid., 12.

75. Angela Huyue Zhang, "The Single Entity Theory: An Antitrust Time Bomb for
    Chinese State-Owned Enterprises," *Journal of Competition Law & Economics* 8,
    no. 4 (2012).

76. Ibid.

77. "Perverse Advantage: A New Book Lays Out the Scale of China's Industrial Sub-
    sidies," *Economist*, April 27, 2013, available at http://www.economist.com/news
    /finance-and-economics/21576680-new-book-lays-out-scale-chinas-industrial
    -subsidies-perverse-advantage/comments?page=2.

78. Ibid. Energy subsidies are provided to all industries. Rivals must overcome these economic titans with subsidized inputs and free money in markets that are heavily protected.
79. Zhang, "Single Entity Theory."
80. "State-Owned Enterprises: The State Advances."
81. Ibid.
82. "Chinese State-Owned Enterprises under the Microscope: Increased Antitrust Scrutiny by the EU and Chinese Authorities," Herbert Smith Freehills LLP, October 3, 2011, available at http://www.herbertsmithfreehills.com/-/media/HS/L-031011-5.pdf.
83. Joy C. Shaw and Lisha Zhou, "China Sets Antitrust Milestone with Investigation into Large SOE," *Financial Times*, November 5, 2011, available at http://www.ft.com/intl/cms/s/2/94fc97c6-0f73-11e1-88cc-00144feabdc0.html.
84. China was supposed to open its payments markets by 2006, according to their accession protocol, but Unionpay has retained its virtual monopoly on domestic payment systems. "State-Owned Enterprises: The State Advances."
85. "Market Access: Barriers to Market Entry," *AmCham China News*, April 29, 2011, available at http://www.amchamchina.org/article/7938.
86. The SCO's observers include Afghanistan, India, Iran, Mongolia, and Pakistan; its dialogue partners are Belarus, Sri Lanka, and Turkey.
87. Julie Boland, *Ten Years of the Shanghai Cooperation Organization: A Lost Decade? A Partner for the U.S.?* (Washington, DC: Brookings Institution, 21st Century Defense Initiative policy paper, June 20, 2011), 4, available at http://www.brookings.edu/~/media/research/files/papers/2011/6/shanghai%20cooperation%20organization%20boland/06_shanghai_cooperation_organization_boland.
88. Ibid., 8.
89. Amit Baruah, "Can Brics Rival the G7?" BBC News India, March 28, 2012, available at http://www.bbc.co.uk/news/world-asia-india-17515118.
90. Xiaoyu Pu and Randall L. Schweller, "After Unipolarity: China's Visions of International Order in the Era of U.S. Decline," *International Security* 36, no. 1 (Summer 2011): 41–72.
91. Wendy Friedman, *China, Arms Control, and Nonproliferation* (New York: RoutledgeCurzon, 2005), 94.
92. Bill Gertz, *Betrayal: How the Clinton Administration Undermined American Security* (Washington, DC: Regnery, 2001), 99.
93. Ibid.
94. "Helms Outlines China's Broken Promises," *Washington Times*, July 23, 2001, available at http://www.washingtontimes.com/news/2001/jul/23/20010723-024410-3938r/.
95. Gertz, *Treachery*, 136.
96. *The Administration's Perspective on China's Record on Nonproliferation: Hearing before the U.S.-China Economic Security Review Commission*, 109th Cong., 11 (September 14, 2006), statement of Paula DeSutter, assistant secretary for

verification, compliance, and implementation, available at http://2001-2009.
state.gov/t/vci/rls/rm/72302.htm.

97. Hu Jintao, "Build Toward a Harmonious World of Lasting Peace and Common
Prosperity" (speech, UN summit, New York, September 15, 2005), available at
http://www.un.org/webcast/summit2005/statements15/china050915eng.pdf.

98. Callahan, *China Dreams*, 44. Hu's concept of a "harmonious world" was spelled
out in two official documents that emphasized the diversity of civilizations and
China's history as a peaceful country, thereby ignoring the many periods of
violent expansion and contraction in its history, 47–48.

99. Hu Jintao, "Build Toward a Harmonious World of Lasting Peace and Common
Prosperity."

100. Yang Lina, "President Vows to Bring Benefits to People in Realizing 'Chinese
Dream,'" *Xinhua*, March 17, 2013, available at http://news.xinhuanet.com/eng
lish/china/2013-03/17/c_132240052.htm.

CHAPTER 10: WARNING SHOTS

1. For more on the design of the Chinese space station, see Leonard David, "China's
First Space Station Module Readies for Liftoff," *SPACE.com*, July 24, 2011, available at
http://www.space.com/12411-china-space-station-tiangong-readied-launch.html.

2. Joan Johnson-Freese, "China's Antisatellite Program: They're Learning,"
China-US Focus, July 12, 2013, available at http://www.chinausfocus.com/peace
-security/chinas-anti-satellite-program-theyre-learning/.

3. In 2011, MGM made changes to its movie *Red Dawn*, which had shown the Chinese
army invading to protect China's investments in the United States. MGM removed
references to China as a powerful overlord and replaced them digitally with North
Koreans. See Ben Fritz and John Horn, "Reel China: Hollywood Tries to Stay on
China's Good Side," *Los Angeles Times*, March 16, 2011, available at http://articles.
latimes.com/2011/mar/16/entertainment/la-et-china-red-dawn-20110316.

4. Jonathan Watts, "Copenhagen Summit: China's Quiet Satisfaction at Tough Tactics and Goalless Draw," *Guardian*, December 20, 2009, available at http://www
.theguardian.com/environment/2009/dec/20/copenhagen-climate-summit-china
-reaction.

5. Tobias Rapp, Christian Schwägerl, and Gerald Traufetter, "The Copenhagen
Protocol: How China and India Sabotaged the UN Climate Summit," *Der Spie-
gel*, May 5, 2010, available at http://www.spiegel.de/international/world/the
-copenhagen-protocol-how-china-and-india-sabotaged-the-un-climate-summit
-a-692861.html.

6. John Pomfret, "Many Goals Remain Unmet in 5 Nations' Climate Deal," *New
York Times*, December 18, 2009, available at http://www.nytimes.com/2009/12
/19/science/earth/19climate.html?pagewanted=all&_r=0.

7. John Pomfret, "U.S. Sells Weapons to Taiwan, Angering China," *Washington
Post*, January 30, 2010, available at http://www.washingtonpost.com/wp-dyn
/content/article/2010/01/30/AR2010013000508.html.

8. Mark Landler, "No New F-16s for Taiwan, but U.S. to Upgrade Fleet," *New York Times*, September 18, 2011, available at http://www.nytimes.com/2011/09/19/world/asia/us-decides-against-selling-f-16s-to-taiwan.html. For more on U.S. arms sales to Taiwan at about this time, see Helene Cooper, "U.S. Arms for Taiwan Send Beijing a Message," *New York Times*, February 1, 2010; Helene Cooper, "U.S. Approval of Taiwan Arms Sales Angers China," *New York Times*, January 30, 2010; and Keith Bradsher, "U.S. Deal with Taiwan Has China Retaliating," *New York Times*, January 31, 2010.

9. Shirley A. Kan, "U.S.-China Military Contacts: Issues for Congress," Congressional Research Service, November 20, 2013, 4, available at https://www.fas.org/sgp/crs/natsec/RL32496.pdf.

10. For more on China's use of metrics for measuring comprehensive national power, see, for example, Huang Shoufeng, *Zhonghe Guoli Lun* [*On Comprehensive National Power*] (Beijing: Zhonggou shehui kexue chubanshe, 1992); Yan Xuetong and Huang Yuxing, "The Hegemonic Thinking in Zhanguo Ce and Its Intellectual Enlightenment," *Quarterly Journal of International Politics* [*Guoji Zhengzhi Kexue*] 16, no. 4 (2008); Wang Songfen, ed., *Shijie Zhuyao Zonghe Guoli Bijiao Yanjiu* [*Comparative Studies of the Comprehensive National Power of the World's Major Nations*] (Changsha: Hunan chubanshe, 1996); Zhu Liangyin and Meng Renzhong, "Deng Xiaoping Zonghe Guoli Sixiang Yanjiu" ["A Study of Deng Xiaoping's Comprehensive National Power Thought"], in Li Lin and Zhao Qinxuan, eds., *Xin Shiqi Junshi Jingji Lilun Yanjiu* [*Studies of New Period Military Economic Theory*] (Beijing: Junshi kexue chubanshe, 1995); Eric S. Edelman, "Understanding America's Contested Primacy," Center for Strategic and Budgetary Assessments, October 21, 2010; Hu Angang and Men Hongua. "The Rising of Modern China: Comprehensive National Power and Grand Strategy," available at http://www.irchina.org/en/pdf/hag.pdf; and Lei Xiaoxun, "Yellow Book Ranks China 7th in Overall Strength," *China Daily Online*, December 25, 2009. For a broader discussion of assessments of national power, see, for example, Jeffrey Hart, "Three Approaches to the Measurement of Power in International Relations," *International Organizations* 30, no. 2; and Ashley J. Tellis, Janice Bially, Christopher Layne, and Melissa McPherson, *Measuring National Power in the Postindustrial Age* (Santa Monica, CA: RAND, 2000).

11. Gregory Chin and Wang Yong, "Debating the International Currency System: What's in a Speech?," *China Security* 6, no. 1 (2010): 3–20.

12. David C. Gompert and Phillip C. Saunders, *The Paradox of Power: Sino-American Strategic Restraint in an Age of Vulnerability* (Washington, DC: National Defense University, 2012).

13. Ibid., 21.

14. Ibid., Executive Summary, xxiii.

15. For a discussion of why national power is inherently difficult to measure, see Robert A. Dahl, "The Concept of Power," *Behavioral Scientist* 2, no. 3; David A. Baldwin, "Power Analysis and World Politics: New Trends versus Old Tendencies," *World Politics* 31, no. 2; and Joseph S. Nye Jr., "The Changing Nature of World Power," *Political Science Quarterly* 105, no. 2 (Summer 1990): 177–92.

16. Andrew W. Marshall, "A Program to Improve Analytic Methods Related to Strategic Forces," *Policy Sciences* 15 (November 1982): 47–50, 48, cited in Pillsbury, *China Debates the Future Security Environment*, 359.

17. Quoted in Michael Pillsbury, *China's Progress in Technological Competitiveness: The Need for a New Assessment* (Washington, DC: Report Prepared for the U.S.-China Economic and Security Review Commission, April 21, 2005), 5–6, available at http://www.uscc.gov/sites/default/files/4.21-22.05pillsbury.pdf.

18. Michael Beckley, "China's Century: Why America's Edge Will Endure," *International Security* 36, no. 3 (Winter 2011/12): 41–78.

19. Ibid., 44.

20. For more on the balance of power, see, for example, Edward Vose Gulick, *Europe's Classical Balance of Power: A Case History of the Theory and Practice of One of the Great Concepts of European Statecraft* (New York: W. W. Norton, 1955); and Brian Healy and Arthur Stein, "The Balance of Power in International History: Theory and Reality," *Journal of Conflict Resolution* 17, no. 1 (March 1973).

21. For more on how misperception can lead to war, see Jack S. Levy, "Misperception and the Causes of War: Theoretical Linkages and Analytical Problems," *World Politics* 36, no. 1 (October 1983): 76–99; and Stephen Van Evera, *Causes of War: Power and the Roots of Conflict* (Ithaca, NY: Cornell University Press, 1999).

22. Edward Wong, "China Hedges over Whether South China Sea Is a 'Core Interest' Worth War," *New York Times*, March 30, 2011, available at http://www.nytimes.com/2011/03/31/world/asia/31beijing.html?_r=0. See also Harry Kazianis, "Senkaku/Diaoyu Islands: A 'Core Interest' of China," *Diplomat*, April 29, 2013, available at http://thediplomat.com/2013/04/senkakudiaoyu-islands-a-core-interest-of-china/.

23. Tessa Jamandre, "China Fired at Filipino Fishermen in Jackson Atoll," *VERA Files*, ABS-CBN News, June 3, 2011, available at http://www.abs-cbnnews.com/-depth/06/02/11/china-fired-filipino-fishermen-jackson-atoll; Huy Duong, "The Philippines and Vietnam at the Crossroad," *Manila Times*, June 8, 2011; "Vietnam Says Chinese Boat Harassed Survey Ship; China Disputes," Bloomberg News, June 9, 2011, available at http://www.businessweek.com/news/2011-06-09/vietnam-says-chinese-boat-harassed-survey-ship-china-disputes.html; and "Vietnam Accuses Chinese Troops of Attack on Fishermen," *Voice of America*, July 14, 2011, available at http://blogs.voanews.com/breaking-news/2011/07/14/vietnam-accuses-chinese-troops-of-attack-on-fishermen/.

24. Keith Bradsher, "Philippine Leader Sounds Alarm on China," *New York Times*, February 4, 2014, available at http://www.nytimes.com/2014/02/05/world/asia/philippine-leader-urges-international-help-in-resisting-chinas-sea-claims.html.

25. "China Decries U.S. Comments on South China Sea as 'Not Constructive,'" Reuters, February 8, 2014, available at http://www.reuters.com/article/2014/02/09/us-china-southchinasea-idUSBREA18O1O20140209.

26. See Martin Fackler, "Japan Retreats with Release of Chinese Boat Captain," *New York Times*, September 24, 2010; and Martin Fackler and Ian Johnson, "Arrest in Disputed Seas Riles China and Japan," *New York Times*, September 19, 2010.

27. Wenran Jiang, "New Twists over Old Disputes in China-Japan Relations," James-

town Foundation, *China Brief* 10, no. 20 (October 8, 2010), available at http://www.freerepublic.com/focus/news/2604249/posts.

28. See Malcolm Foster, "6 Chinese Ships Near Islands in Dispute with Japan," Associated Press, September 14, 2012, available at http://bigstory.ap.org/article/6-chinese-ships-near-islands-dispute-japan; and Austin Ramzy, "Tensions with Japan Increase as China Sends Patrol Boats to Disputed Islands," *Time*, September 14, 2012, available at http://world.time.com/2012/09/14/tensions-with-japan-increase-as-china-sends-patrol-boats-to-disputed-islands/.

29. Mu Xuequan, "Chinese Surveillance Ships Start Patrol Around Diaoyu Islands," *Xinhua*, September 14, 2012, available at http://news.xinhuanet.com/english/china/2012-09/14/c_131849375.htm.

30. Martin Fackler, "Chinese Patrol Ships Pressuring Japan over Islands," *New York Times*, November 2, 2012, available at http://www.nytimes.com/2012/11/03/world/asia/china-keeps-up-pressure-on-japan-over-disputed-islands-with-patrols.html?pagewanted=all&_r=0.

31. See Jane Perlez, "China Accuses Japan of Stealing After Purchase of Group of Disputed Islands," *New York Times*, September 11, 2012, available at http://www.nytimes.com/2012/09/12/world/asia/china-accuses-japan-of-stealing-disputed-islands.html?_r=0.

32. Ian Johnson and Thom Shanker, "Beijing Mixes Messages over Anti-Japan Protests," *New York Times*, September 16, 2012, available at http://www.nytimes.com/2012/09/17/world/asia/anti-japanese-protests-over-disputed-islands-continue-in-china.html?_r=0.

33. "Anti-Japan Protests Spread Across China," *Financial Times*, September 18, 2012, available at http://www.ft.com/intl/cms/s/0/85f4f7a2-0138-11e2-99d3-00144feabdc0.html#axzz2t8p2UTpy. See also Ian Johnson, "China and Japan Bristle over Disputed Chain of Islands," *New York Times*, September 8, 2010.

34. Hou Qiang, "Announcement of the Aircraft Identification Rules for the East China Sea Air Defense Identification Zone of the PRC," *Xinhua*, November 23, 2011, available at http://news.xinhuanet.com/english/china/2013-11/23/c_132911634.htm.

35. Yan, "China Refutes Japan's Protest at ADIZ over East China Sea," *Xinhua*, November 25, 2013, available at http://news.xinhuanet.com/english/china/2013-11/25/c_132917199.htm.

36. "Echoing the Guns of August," *Economist*, January 23, 2014, available at http://www.economist.com/blogs/banyan/2014/01/china-japan-and-first-world-war.

37. Odd Arne Westad, "In Asia, Ill Will Runs Deep," *New York Times*, January 6, 2013, available at http://www.nytimes.com/2013/01/07/opinion/why-china-and-japan-cant-get-along.html?_r=0.

38. Ibid.

39. Zheng Wang, "China and Japan REALLY Don't Like Each Other," *Diplomat*, August 26, 2013, available at http://thediplomat.com/2013/08/china-and-japan-really-dont-like-each-other/. The 2013 survey is available at http://www.genron-npo.net/english/index.php?option=com_content&view=article&id=59:the-9th-japan-china-public-opinion-poll&catid=2:research&Itemid=4.

40. Michael Pillsbury, "A Japanese Card?," *Foreign Policy* 33 (Winter 1978–79): 3–30.

41. Liu Jiangyong, ed., *Kua shiji de riben—Zhengzhi, jingji, waijiao xin qushi* [*Japan across the century—new political, economic, and foreign relations trends*] (Beijing: Shishi chubanshe, 1995). The editor of this major collection is the CICIR director for Japan studies. See also Chen Shao, "Zhanhou Riben zonghe guoli de fazhan ji pinggu" ["An assessment of Japan's postwar comprehensive national power development"], *Taipingyang xuebao* [*Pacific Journal*] 3 (December 1995): 96–101. Chen is on the staff of IWEP at CASS, 16.

42. See Huan Xiang, "Sino-US Relations over the Past Year," *Liaowang* (January 11, 1988), in FBIS-CHI, January 15, 1988, cited in Pillsbury, *China Debates the Future Security Environment*, 114, n. 16.

43. Liu Jiangyong, "Distorting History Will Misguide Japan," *Contemporary International Relations* 5, no. 9 (September 1995): 1–11, cited in Pillsbury, *China Debates the Future Security Environment*, 122.

44. Liang Ming, "A New Trend That Merits Vigilance," no. 2 in series, "Experts Comment on the Strengthening of the Japanese-U.S. Military Alliance," *Jiefangjun bao* [*Liberation Army Daily*], June 5, 1999, 125, in FBIS-CHI-1999-0616, June 17, 1999.

45. Cited in Pillsbury, *China Debates the Future Security Environment*, 135.

46. Cited in ibid., 131.

47. Lu Guangye, "Going Against the Tide of History, Threatening World Peace," no. 3 in series, "Experts Comment on the Strengthening of the Japanese-U.S. Military Alliance," *Jiefangjun bao* [*Liberation Army Daily*], June 6, 1999, 4, in FBIS-CHI-1999-0617, June 18, 1999. See also Zhang Jinfang, "Serious Threats to China's Security," no. 1 in series, "Experts Comment on the Strengthening of the Japanese-U.S. Military Alliance," *Jiefangjun bao* [*Liberation Army Daily*], June 4, 1999, 4, in FBIS-CHI-1999-0616, June 17, 1999; and Liang Ming, "A New Trend That Merits Vigilance."

48. Lu Zhongwei, "On China-U.S.-Japan Trilateral Relations—a Comment on Their Recent Exchanges of Top-Level Visits," *Contemporary International Relations* 7, no. 12 (December 1997): 3, 5, 7, cited in Pillsbury, *China Debates the Future Security Environment*, 128, n. 52.

49. Yang Bojiang, "The Trans-Century Tendencies of Japan," *Contemporary International Relations* 8, no. 8 (August 1998): 17; Gao Heng, "Dongbei Ya de anquan geju ji weilai qushi" ("Northeast Asia's Security Structure and Future Trends"), *21 Shiji* (*The 21st Century*), no. 6 (1995): 35–36. For an extensive study on the Japanese Constitution and efforts to revise it, see Song Zhangjun, *Riben guo xianfa yanjiu* [*Studies on Japan's Constitution*] (Beijing: Shishi chubanshe, 1997), cited in Pillsbury, *China Debates the Future Security Environment*, 126, n. 48.

50. Xu Zhixian, "Xin shiqi Riben waijiao zhanlue de tiaozheng" ("Readjustment of Japan's foreign policy in the new era"), *Xiandai guoji guanxi* (*Contemporary International Relations*) 74, no. 12 (December 1995): 13. "Japan may fall short of its desire to become the permanent member of the UN Security Council for lack of the necessary support from China. . . . [I]f by any chance the development of

Japan-China economic relations cannot be rationalized, Japan will lose its geo-economic superiority." Xu Zhixian, Zhang Minqian, and Hong Jianjun, "On the Foreign Strategy and Trends in the China Policy of the United States, Western Europe, and Japan at the Turn of the Century," *Contemporary International Relations* 8, no. 3 (March 1998): 16; Shen Qurong, "Postwar Asia Pacific—Historical Lessons and Common Efforts for a Bright Future," *Contemporary International Relations* 5, no. 11 (November 1995): 5, 7, cited in Pillsbury, *China Debates the Future Security Environment*, 129, n. 54.

51. See Nicholas D. Kristof, "China, Reassessing Its Strategy, Views Japan Warily," *New York Times*, October 23, 1993.

52. Xu Weidi, "Post–Cold War Naval Security Environment," *World Military Trends* (Beijing: National Defense University, 1996).

53. Li Jiansong, "Continued Naval Developments in Nations on China's Periphery" (in Chinese), *Bingqi zhishi [Ordinance Knowledge]* (May 12, 1997): 17–20.

54. Ding Bangquan, "Adjustments and Trends in Japan's Military Strategy," *World Military Trends* (Beijing: Academy of Military Science, n.d.).

55. Wang Jisi, "China's Search for a Grand Strategy."

56. Parris Chang, "Beijing Copes with a Weakened Ma Administration: Increased Demands, and a Search for Alternatives," Jamestown Foundation, *China Brief* 14, no. 2 (2014), available at http://www.jamestown.org/programs/chinabrief /single/?tx_ttnews%5Btt_news%5D=41869&tx_ttnews%5BbackPid%5D=25& cHash=ce2455e039c0219fbcd4804a30a87105#.Uxcw_-mPLVJ.

57. Cited ibid.

58. In sum, as Parris Chang, a member of the Taiwan Democratic Progressive Party, notes, "Beijing's strategy toward Taiwan under Chairman Xi Jinping and his predecessor Hu Jintao has yielded positive results. The approach not only avoids possible military conflict with the United States, but receives support from Washington.... Beijing's economic means ... have enhanced Taiwan's economic integration with China and greatly increased the PRC's control over Taiwan's economy and society, helping to lock Taiwan into the mainland's orbit." Ibid. China's approach to its relations with Taiwan embodies the notion that military might is not the critical factor for winning a long-term competition. It also represents a successful attempt by China to co-opt others so that they will do its bidding.

59. Christian Gomez, "Communist China's Cold War," *New American*, December 3, 2012, available at http://www.thenewamerican.com/world-news/asia/item/13796 -communist-chinas-cold-war/13796-communist-chinas-cold-war?tmpl=com ponent&print=1&start=3.

60. Qin's triumph was carried out over seven generations of leaders, and was not at all preordained. See Victoria Hui, *War and State Formation in Ancient China and Early Modern Europe* (Cambridge, UK: Cambridge University Press, 2005). In Yan Xuetong, "Pre-Qin Philosophy and China's Rise Today," in Yan Xuetong, *Ancient Chinese Thought, Modern Chinese Power*, Daniel A. Bell and Sun Zhe, eds., trans. Edmund Ryden (Princeton, NJ: Princeton University Press, 2011),

204, Yan argued, "From China's point of view, we can draw on the experience of success or failure of rising powers from pre-Qin thought." Yan also writes on page 220, "Even though research into pre-Qin interstate political philosophy has attracted attention among scholars within China, it has not yet attracted the notice of international colleagues." Yan Xuetong and Huang Yuxing, "Hegemony in the Stratagems of the Warring States," in Yan Xuetong, *Ancient Chinese Thought, Modern Chinese Power*, 122–23. Additional studies include Gerald Chan, "The Origin of the Interstate System: The Warring States in Ancient China," *Issues and Studies* 35, no. 1 (1999): 147–66; Shih-tsai Chen, "The Equality of States in Ancient China," *American Journal of International Law* 35, no. 4 (1941): 641–50; Victoria Hui, "Toward a Dynamic Theory of International Politics: Insights from Comparing the Ancient Chinese and Early Modern European Systems," *International Organization* 58, no. 1 (2004): 175–205; and Richard Walker, *The Multistate System of Ancient China* (Westport, CT: Greenwood Press, 1953).

61. Alastair Iain Johnston, "How New and Assertive Is China's New Assertiveness?," *International Security* 37, no. 4 (Spring 2013): 7–48.

62. For background, see Yuan Peng, "Shifts in International System, China's Strategic Options," *Xiandai Guoji Guanxi [Contemporary International Relations]*, November 30, 2009, cited in Bonnie Glaser, "A Shifting Balance: Chinese Assessments of U.S. Power," Capacity and Resolve: Foreign Assessments of U.S. Power (Washington, DC: CSIS, 2011).

63. "China FM: Japan-U.S. Security Treaty a 'Relic,'" *CCTV English*, September 5, 2012, available at http://english.cntv.cn/program/china24/20120905/101987.shtml.

CHAPTER 11: AMERICA AS A WARRING STATE

1. Paul Hopper, *Understanding Development* (Cambridge, UK: Polity Press, 2012), 208.

2. Deloitte Touche Tohmatsu Limited and the Council on Competitiveness, "2013 Global Manufacturing Competitiveness Index," November 29, 2012, available at http://www.deloitte.com/assets/Dcom-UnitedStates/Local%20Assets/Documents/us_pip_GMCI_11292012.pdf.

3. Kent Hughes, *Building the Next American Century: The Past and Future of American Economic Competitiveness* (Washington, DC: Woodrow Wilson Center Press, 2005).

4. David R. Francis, "U.S. Still Leads the Pack; Only Japan Closes Gap," *Christian Science Monitor*, January 11, 1993, available at http://www.csmonitor.com/1993/0111/11071.html.

5. Ralph Gomory, "It Takes More Than Economics 101 to Compete with China," *Huffington Post*, October 24, 2013, available at http://www.huffingtonpost.com/ralph-gomory/economic-competition-china_b_4144822.html.

6. "U.S.-China Commissioner Expresses Concern over Whether Multinationals Are Good for the United States," *Manufacturing News* 13, no. 21 (November 30,

2006): 8, available at http://www.manufacturingnews.com/subscribers/users_orig
.cgi?mfgnews_username=mbg&flag=read_article&id_title=1&id_article=3344
&id_issue=207&id_sub=459&id_sl.

7. Robert D. Atkinson and Stephen J. Ezell, *Innovation Economics: The Race for Global Advantage* (New Haven: Yale University Press, 2012), 364.

8. Edward Wong, "Dalai Lama Says China Has Turned Tibet into a 'Hell on Earth,'" *New York Times*, March 10, 2009, available at http://www.nytimes.com/2009/03
/11/world/asia/11tibet.html?ref=dalailama&_r=0.

9. Rebiya Kadeer, "China's Second Tibet," *Wall Street Journal*, July 2, 2012, available at http://online.wsj.com/news/articles/SB10001424052702303561504577496930351770466?mod=rss_opinion_main&mg=reno64-wsj&url=http%3A%2F%2Fonline.wsj.com%2Farticle%2FSB10001424052702303561504577496930351770466.html%3Fmod%3Drss_opinion_main.

10. For example, Tim Gardam wrote in September 2011, "It is impossible to say how many Christians there are in China today, but no one denies the numbers are exploding. The [Chinese] government says 25 million, 18 million Protestants and six million Catholics. Independent estimates all agree this is a vast underestimate. A conservative figure is 60 million." Tim Gardam, "Christians in China: Is the Country in Spiritual Crisis?," BBC News, September 11, 2011, available at http://www.bbc.co.uk/news/magazine-14838749. See also Donata Hardenberg, "Christianity: China's Best Bet?," Al Jazeera, July 1, 2011, available at http://www.aljazeera.com/programmes/101east/2011/06/2011629646319175.html, who writes, "According to China Aid, a U.S.-based human rights group, the number of Christians in China has increased 100-fold since the PRC was founded. Current estimates range from 80 million to 130 million active Christians, including members of so-called house churches."

11. For more on Chen, see Jane Perlez and Sharon LaFraniere, "Blind Chinese Dissident Leaves U.S. Embassy for Medical Treatment," *New York Times*, May 2, 2012, available at http://www.nytimes.com/2012/05/03/world/asia/chen-guangcheng-leaves-us-embassy-in-beijing-china.html?pagewanted=all&_r=0.

12. Yang also advocates the idea that the path to democracy in China lies in the kindling of a united "citizen power" among all Chinese citizens.

13. Mary Kissel, "Bob Fu: The Pastor of China's Underground Railroad," *Wall Street Journal*, June 1, 2012, available at http://online.wsj.com/news/articles/SB10001424052702303640104577438562289689498?mg=reno64-wsj&url=http%3A%2F%2Fonline.wsj.com%2Farticle%2FSB10001424052702303640104577438562289689498.html.

14. David E. Sanger, "U.S. Blames China's Military Directly for Cyberattacks," *New York Times*, May 6, 2013, available at http://www.nytimes.com/2013/05/07/world/asia/us-accuses-chinas-military-in-cyberattacks.html?pagewanted=all&_r=1&.

15. *IP Commission Report*, Executive Summary, 2.

16. Jeffrey Mervis, "Spending Bill Prohibits U.S.-China Collaborations," *Science Magazine*, April 22, 2011, available at http://news.sciencemag.org/technology/2011/04/spending-bill-prohibits-u.s.-china-collaborations.

17. "Cybersecurity," Office of Congressman Frank Wolf (accessed February 15, 2014), available at http://wolf.house.gov/cybersecurity#.UwIUYOmPJMs.

18. William Pesek, "Chinese Should Beg Gary Locke to Stay on as U.S. Ambassador," *Seattle Times*, November 27, 2013, available at http://seattletimes.com/html /opinion/2022349457_williampesekcolumngarylocke28xml.html.

19. See the Institute of Public and Environmental Affairs website at http://www.ipe .org.cn/en/pollution/.

20. Andrew Jacobs, "Chinese Journalist Is Released on Bail," *New York Times*, July 8, 2013, available at http://www.nytimes.com/2013/07/09/world/asia/chinese-jour nalist-is-released-on-bail.html.

21. Andrew Jacobs, "Chinese Police Said to Fire on Tibetans," *New York Times*, July 9, 2013, available at http://www.nytimes.com/2013/07/10/world/asia/tension -flares-as-tibetans-celebrate-dalai-lamas-birthday.html. For another prominent instance of China shutting down a website to stifle debate, see "China Closes Unirule Web Site," *Radio Free Asia*, May 1, 2012, available at http://www.rfa.org /english/news/china/web-05012012142516.html.

22. David Barboza, "Billions in Hidden Riches for Family of Chinese Leader," *New York Times*, October 26, 2012, available at http://www.nytimes.com/2012/10/26 /business/global/family-of-wen-jiabao-holds-a-hidden-fortune-in-china.html ?ref=davidbarboza&gwh=75CDA070439118F7215E6E3CE22A8E5B&gwt=pay.

23. Palash Ghosh, "China Blocks Bloomberg Web Site After Story Details Xi Jinping's Family's Vast Wealth," *International Business Times*, June 29, 2012, available at http://www.ibtimes.com/china-blocks-bloomberg-website-after-story -details-xi-jinpings-familys-vast-wealth-704969.

24. Riva Gold, "Wikipedia Cofounder Refuses to Comply with China's Censorship," *Wall Street Journal*, August 9, 2013, available at http://blogs.wsj.com/digits/2013 /08/09/wikipedia-co-founder-refuses-to-comply-with-chinas-censorhip/.

25. Shawn Healy, "The Great Firewall of China," *Social Education* 71, no. 3 (April 2007): 158–62.

26. David Smith and Jo Revill, "Wikipedia Defies China's Censors," *Guardian*, September 9, 2006, available at http://www.theguardian.com/technology/2006/sep /10/news.china.

27. See, for example, Ye Xiaowen, "Common Interests Prevent 'Cold War' Between China and U.S.," *People's Daily Overseas Edition*, December 26, 2011, available at http://english.peopledaily.com.cn/90780/91342/7688092.html. See also Geoff Dyer, "U.S. v China: Is This the New Cold War?," *Financial Times*, February 20, 2014, available at http://www.ft.com/intl/cms/s/2/78920b2e-99ba-11e3-91cd -00144feab7de.html#axzz30CHWru3D; and Ambassador Cui Tiankai, "China's Policy Toward the Asia-Pacific," speech at Harvard University, April 25, 2014, distributed by the Chinese embassy, Washington, DC.

28. For a general discussion of this subject, see Michael Pillsbury, "The Sixteen Fears: China's Strategic Psychology," *Survival: Global Politics and Strategy* 54, no. 5 (October/November 2012): 149–82.

29. Robert M. Gates, *Understanding the New U.S. Defense Policy through the Speeches*

of Robert M. Gates, Secretary of Defense, December 18, 2006–February 10, 2008, Department of Defense (Rockville, MD: Arc Manor, 2008), 143.

30. The theme of Chinese resistance to foreign influences is discussed in detail in Jonathan Spence, *To Change China: Western Advisers in China* (New York: Penguin, 1969), and Anne-Marie Brady, *Making the Foreign Serve China: Managing Foreigners in the People's Republic* (Lanham, MD: Rowman & Littlefield Publishers, 2003).

31. Carlson, "China's Military Produces a Bizarre, Anti-American Conspiracy Film (VIDEO)."

32. Miles Yu, "Inside China: PLA Hawks Decry Sellout by Leaders," *Washington Times*, June 20, 2012, available at http://www.washingtontimes.com/news/2012/jun/20/inside-china-pla-hawks-decry-sellout-by-leaders/?page=all.

33. Menges, *China: The Gathering Threat*.

34. Most U.S.-funded programs in China aim to promote the rule of law and civil society using special allocations from the Department of State's Human Rights and Democracy Fund. Thomas Lum, "U.S.-Funded Assistance Programs in China," Congressional Research Service, April 24, 2009, available at http://www.au.af.mil/au/awc/awcgate/crs/rs22663.pdf.

35. The EU's assistance efforts in China, especially in the area of legal development, have reportedly been more robustly funded than similar American efforts. Thomas Lum, "U.S. Assistance Programs in China," Congressional Research Service, May 9, 2013, available at http://www.fas.org/sgp/crs/row/RS22663.pdf.

36. Swaine, *America's Challenge*, 283–88.

37. http://english.unirule.org.cn/.

38. Robert Zoellick has noted—and I agree—that any prospective "high-quality" U.S.-Chinese investment treaties should meet the following conditions: equal treatment of foreign and domestic companies, prohibiting unfair treatment of foreign investors, a ban on trade-distorting measures, the ability to transfer funds without delay into or out of the country, and a system of international arbitration to resolve disputes. Robert Zoellick, "International Treaties Can Once Again Help China Advance," *Financial Times*, March 10, 2014, available at http://www.ft.com/intl/cms/s/0/b8b391ec-a634-11e3-8a2a-00144feab7de.html#axzz2xeDm-lUqa. Meeting these conditions would shrink the advantages of China's state-owned enterprises, including the so-called national champions. This is just one of the reasons why China's leaders are unlikely to acquiesce to such terms anytime soon.

39. Another NED-funded journal is the *China Labor Bulletin*. A nongovernmental organization founded in Hong Kong in 1994, *China Labor Bulletin* has grown from a small monitoring and research group into a proactive outreach organization that seeks to defend and promote the rights of workers in China. See http://www.clb.org.hk/en/content/who-we-are.

40. Evan S. Medeiros, *Reluctant Restraint: The Evolution of China's Nonproliferation Policies and Practices, 1980–2004* (Palo Alto, CA: Stanford University Press, 2007), 40. Medeiros wrote that "The U.S. strategy . . . was to explicitly and publicly link

progress on a nuclear cooperation agreement to China's adoption of nonproliferation controls. This strategy had an immediate, albeit limited, effect on Chinese nonproliferation policies and practices."

41. Ibid.

42. Question for the Record Submitted to Mary Ann Casey by Senator Biden, June
25, 1971, unclassified, in "The Algerian Nuclear Problem, 1991: Controversy
over the Es Salam Nuclear Reactor," National Security Archive, edited by William Burr, posted September 10, 2007, Document 17b, available at http://www2
.gwu.edu/~nsarchiv/nukevault/ebb228/Algeria-17b.pdf.

43. The Ford Foundation, which does not receive U.S. government support, offered
grants worth $220 million for programs in China during 1988–2006. Ford Foun-
dation funding in China has supported governance, democracy, and civil society
programs, followed by health, education, and cultural activities and economic
development and environmental projects. The Ford Foundation offered grants
worth $275 million for activities to promote civil society; transparent, effective,
and accountable government; civil and criminal justice system reform; greater
access to secondary and higher education; community rights over natural
resources; and education in the areas of sexuality and reproductive health. See
"Results That Change Lives," Ford Foundation 2012 Annual Report, available at
http://www.fordfoundation.org/pdfs/library/AR12-complete.pdf.

44. For more on the growth of China's proliferation activities, see Shirley A. Kan,
"China and Proliferation of Weapons of Mass Destruction and Missiles: Policy
Issues" (Washington, DC: Congressional Research Service, January 3, 2014), avail-
able at http://www.fas.org/sgp/crs/nuke/RL31555.pdf. See also John R. Bolton, U.S.
Under Secretary of State, "Coordinating Allied Approaches to China," speech,
Tokyo American Center and Japan Institute for International Affairs, Tokyo, Feb-
ruary 7, 2005, available at www.Tokyo.USembassy.gov/E/P/TP-20050207-67.html.

45. Robert L. Suettinger, "United States and China: Tough Engagement," in Richard
Haass and Megan L. O'Sullivan, eds., *Honey and Vinegar: Incentives, Sanctions,
and Foreign Policy* (Washington, DC: Brookings Institution Press, 2000), 41.

46. Edward Wong and Jonathan Ansfield, "Reformers Aim to Get China to Live Up
to Own Constitution," *New York Times*, February 3, 2013, available at http://
www.nytimes.com/2013/02/04/world/asia/reformers-aim-to-get-china-to-live
-up-to-own-constitution.html?_r=0.

47. Ibid.

48. In 2000 Congress did establish two congressional commissions that supposedly
would act as institutionalized safeguards to protect American interests in our
dealings with China: the Congressional-Executive Commission on China (CECC)
and the U.S.-China Economic and Security Review Commission (USCC). The
USCC annual report, for example, contained up to fifty recommendations: among
them, to pursue more fair trade relations with China, to enforce WTO rulings, to
end currency manipulation, to help U.S. firms better understand export controls,
and to develop a national competiveness strategy. For more on Chinese factional
debates, see Jing Huang, *Factionalism in Chinese Communist Politics* (Cam-

bridge, UK: Cambridge University Press, 2000); and Victor C. Shih, *Factions and Finance in China: Elite Conflict and Inflation* (Cambridge, UK: Cambridge University Press, 2008).

49. Oksenberg to Brzezinski, April 4, 1980, *Foreign Relations of the United States*, vol. 13, 1146–47, available at http://static.history.state.gov/frus/frus1977-80v13/pdf/frus1977-80v13.pdf.

50. Hearing of the Commission on the Roles and Capabilities of the United States Intelligence Community, Room SD-106, Dirksen Senate Office Building, Washington, DC, January 19, 1996, available at http://www.fas.org/irp/commission/testlill.htm.

51. Ambassador Lilley makes this observation two-thirds of the way into a three-hour-long hearing, while questioning me as a witness in front of the China Security Review Commission. See also "Security Issues: Panelists Talked about the Ongoing Relationship between the U.S. and China, Focusing on China's Perceptions of the U.S. Strategically, Regionally, and Militarily," C-SPAN, August 3, 2001, available at http://www.c-span.org/video/?165505-1/security-issues.

52. Jane Perlez, "Myanmar Reforms Set U.S. and China in Race for Sway," *New York Times*, March 30, 2012.

53. "Derek Mitchell Named Myanmar Ambassador by Obama Administration," Associated Press, May 17, 2012.

54. See, e.g., Fareed Zakaria, "A Conversation with Lee Kuan Yew," *Foreign Affairs*, March/April 1994.

55. Graham Allison, Robert D. Blackwill, and Ali Wyne, *Lee Kuan Yew: The Grand Master's Insights on China, the United States, and the World* (Cambridge, MA: MIT Press, 2013), xxvii.

56. Ibid., xxvii, 3, 14, 15–16.

57. Ibid., 4.

58. Quoted in Shambaugh, *China Goes Global*, 248.

59. Wang Jiang, Li Xiaoning, Qiao Liang, Wang Xiangsui, *Xin Zhanguo Shidai* [*The New Warring States Era*] (Beijing: Xinhua chubanshe, 2003).

60. Martin Jacques, *When China Rules the World: The End of the Western World and the Birth of a New Global Order*, 2nd ed. (New York: Penguin Books, 2012).

61. Ansuya Harjani, "Yuan to Supersede Dollar as Top Reserve Currency: Survey," CNBC, February 26, 2014, available at http://www.cnbc.com/id/101450365.

62. Shambaugh, *China Goes Global*.

63. The literature on this subject has grown. For the authoritative view, see the Department of Defense's "Background Briefing on Air-Sea Battle by Defense Officials from the Pentagon," November 9, 2011, available at http://www.defense.gov/transcripts/transcript.aspx?transcriptid=4923. See also the scholarly debates: Sean Mirski, "Stranglehold: The Context, Conduct and Consequences of an American Naval Blockade of China," *Journal of Strategic Studies* 36, no. 3 (June 2013): 385–421; Terence K. Kelly, Anthony Atler, Todd Nichols, and Lloyd Thrall, *Employing Land-Based Anti-ship Missiles in the Western Pacific* (Santa Monica, CA: RAND Corporation, 2013); Marc Lanteigne, "China's

Maritime Security and the 'Malacca Dilemma,'" *Asian Security* 4, no. 2 (2008): 141–61; Douglas C. Peifer, "China, the German Analogy and the New AirSea Operational Concept," *Orbis* 55, no. 1 (Winter 2011): 114–31; Robert Potter, "The Importance of the Straits of Malacca," *e-International Relations*, September 7, 2012, available at http://www.e-ir.info/2012/09/07/the-importance-of-the-straits-of-malacca/; Jason Glab, "Blockading China: A Guide," *War on the Rocks*, October 1, 2013, available at http://warontherocks.com/2013/10/blockading-china-a-guide; Aaron L. Friedberg, *Beyond Air-Sea Battle: The Debate over U.S. Military Strategy in Asia* (London: International Institute for Strategic Studies, 2014); Elbridge Colby, "Don't Sweat AirSea Battle," *National Interest*, July 31, 2013, available at http://nationalinterest.org/commentary/dont-sweat-airsea-battle-8804; Joshua Rovner, "Three Paths to Nuclear Escalation with China," *National Interest*, July 19, 2012, available at http://nationalinterest.org/blog/the-skeptics/three-paths-nuclear-escalation-china-7216; Raoul Heinrichs, "America's Dangerous Battle Plan," *Diplomat*, August 17, 2011, available at http://thediplomat.com/2011/08/17/americas-dangerous-battle-plan; Christopher Ford, "'Air/Sea Battle,' Escalation, and U.S. Strategy in the Pacific," *PJ Media*, January 6, 2013, available at http://pjmedia.com/blog/airsea-battle-escalation-and-u-s-strategy-in-the -Pacific.

64. Amitai Etzioni, "Who Authorized Preparations for War with China?," *Yale Journal of International Affairs* (Summer 2013): 37–51.

65. Warren Zimmerman, *First Great Triumph: How Five Americans Made Their Country a World Power* (New York: Farrar, Straus and Giroux, 2002).

66. Wu Chunqiu, *On Grand Strategy* (Beijing: Current Affairs Press, 2000).

67. Anne Orde, *The Eclipse of Great Britain: United States and British Imperial Decline, 1895–1956* (Basingstoke, UK: Palgrave Macmillan, 1996); Aaron L. Friedberg, *The Weary Titan: Britain and the Experience of Relative Decline, 1895–1905* (Princeton, NJ: Princeton University Press, 1988); and Lanxin Xiang, *Recasting the Imperial Far East: Britain and America in China, 1945–1950* (Armonk, NY: M.E. Sharpe, 1995).

68. Feng Yongping, "The Peaceful Transition of Power from the UK to the U.S.," *Chinese Journal of International Politics* 1, no. 1 (2006): 83–108.

AFTERWORD TO THE PAPERBACK EDITION

1. Edward Wong, "Chinese Colonel's Hard-Line Views Seep into the Mainstream," *New York Times*, October 2, 2015, available at http://www.nytimes.com/2015/10/03/world/asia/chinese-colonels-hard-line-views-seep-into-the-mainstream .html.

2. Ibid.

3. Ibid.

4. Robert Burns, "Pentagon Chief Takes Jab at China with Aircraft Carrier Stop," *Navy Times*, November 5, 2015, available at http://www.navytimes.com/story

/military/2015/11/05/pentagon-chief-takes-jab-china-aircraft-carrier-stop
/75204754/.

5. Ian Storey, "China's Terraforming in the Spratlys: A Game Changer in South China Sea?—Analysis," *Eurasia Review,* June 26, 2015, available at http://www .eurasiareview.com/26062015-chinas-terraforming-in-the-spratlys-a-game -changer-in-south-china-sea-analysis/.

6. Felix K. Chang, "Strategic Intentions: China's Military Strategy White Paper," *Geopoliticus: The FPRI Blog, Foreign Policy Research Institute,* May 2015, available at http://www.fpri.org/geopoliticus/2015/05/strategic-intentions-chinas-military -strategy-white-paper.

7. Simon Denyer, "Chinese Military Sets Course to Expand Global Reach as 'National Interests' Grow," *Washington Post,* May 26, 2015, available at https:// www.washingtonpost.com/world/asia_pacific/chinese-military-sets-course-to -expand-global-reach-as-national-interests-grow/2015/05/26/395fff14-3fb1 -4056-aed0-264ffcbbcdb4_story.html.

8. Ibid.

9. Bill Gertz, "New Details of Chinese Space Weapons Revealed," *Washington Times,* October 14, 2015, available at http://www.washingtontimes.com/news/2015/oct /14/inside-the-ring-details-of-chinese-space-weapons-r/.

10. Ibid.

11. Jeffry Bartash, "Third-Quarter GDP Tracking Below 2%, Complicating Fed Decision," *MarketWatch,* September 23, 2015, available at http://www.market watch.com/story/bumpy-us-economy-hits-more-turbulence-2015-09-23; Kevin Yao, "China Third-Quarter GDP Growth Seen at Five-Year Low of 7.3 Percent, More Stimulus Expected," *Reuters,* October 10, 2014, available at http://www.reuters.com/article/2014/10/10/us-china-economy-gdp-idUSKCN0 HZ0GE20141010.

12. Joseph E. Stiglitz, "The Chinese Century," *Vanity Fair,* December 31, 2014, available at http://www.vanityfair.com/news/2015/01/china-worlds-largest-economy.

13. Charles Riley, "China Now Has More Billionaires Than U.S.," CNN Money, October 15, 2015, available at http://money.cnn.com/2015/10/15/investing/china -us-billionaires/.

14. Scott Cendrowski, "China's Global 500 Companies Are Bigger Than Ever—and Mostly State-Owned," *Fortune,* July 22, 2015, available at http://fortune.com /2015/07/22/china-global-500-government-owned/.

15. Ibid.

16. Gabriel Wildau, "Renminbi Overtakes Japanese Yen as Global Payments Currency," *Financial Times,* October 6, 2015, available at http://www.ft.com/intl/cms /s/0/bb54b4f0-6bf2-11e5-aca9-d87542bf8673.html#axzz3oyfwmfkr.

17. National Committee on United States-China Relations, "Justin Yifu Lin: China's Mid- and Long-term Economic Growth Prospects after the Third Plenum," January 7, 2015, available at https://www.ncuscr.org/content/video-justin-yifu-lin -chinas-mid-and-long-term-economic-growth-prospects-after-third-plenum.

18. Ibid.

19. "China's Economy Will Be Larger Than U.S. by 2028," *The Globalist,* September 27, 2015, available at http://www.theglobalist.com/china-economy-larger -united-states/#; Akshat Kaushal, "Crisis Unlikely to Affect China's Economic Power: Arvind Subramanian," *Business Standard,* August 31, 2015, available at http://www.business-standard.com/article/economy-policy/crisis-unlikely-to -affect-china-s-economic-power-arvind-subramanian-115090100026_1.html; Tham Tuck Seng, PricewaterhouseCoopers, China Desk, available at http://www .pwc.com/sg/en/services/china-desk.html.

20. Robert Atkinson, "Stop China's Plan to Weaken American Innovation," *Christian Science Monitor,* April 1, 2015, available at http://www.csmonitor.com/Technology /Breakthroughs-Voices/2015/0401/Stop-China-s-plan-to-weaken-American -innovation.

21. Stiglitz, "Chinese Century."

22. Ibid.

23. Michael Pillsbury. "How China's Generals Already Gamed Xi's Meeting with Obama," *Defense One,* September 24, 2015, available at http://www.defenseone .com/ideas/2015/09/how-chinas-generals-already-gamed-xis-meeting-obama /121904.

24. Ibid.

25. Ibid.

26. Ibid.

27. Wendell Minnick, "China's 'One Belt, One Road' Strategy," *Defense News,* April 12, 2015, available at http://www.defensenews.com/story/defense/2015/04/11/taiwan -china-one-belt-one-road-strategy/25353561.

ACKNOWLEDGMENTS

This book has been five decades in the making. It would have been impossible had I not been accorded the unusual opportunity to discuss and debate ideas with thirty-five Chinese "scholar-generals." Most have published books and articles about Chinese strategy. Some I have known for more than twenty years. None ever violated his or her oath to protect national secrets and uphold the Party line. However, all of them have lively intellects and a desire to enlighten those of us considered "friends from afar," as Confucius might say. Their insights proved instructive, even if they do not agree with all of my conclusions. Henry Kissinger assisted directly and indirectly with understanding the context of ideas the Chinese put forward.

Most of the generals have worked their entire careers at the prestigious Academy of Military Science. They include: Chen Zhou, Gao Rui, Huang Shuofeng, Li Jijun, Li Qingshan, Liu Jingsong, Liu Tinghua, Liu Yuan, Luo Yuan, Mi Zhenyu, Pan Junfeng, Peng Guangqian, Wang Pufeng, Wu Chunqiu, Wu Rusong, Yao Youzhi, Yao Yunzhu, Zhang Shiping, Zhao Xiaozhuo, and Zheng Minxia. I also appreciate the advice and publications provided by seven scholar-generals in military intelligence headquarters, all former military attachés: Chen Xiaogong, Gong Xianfu, Zhang Naicheng, Zhang Tuosheng, Zhang Wutang, Zhao Ning, and Zhen

Zhiya. I have benefited from suggestions and books provided by eight scholar-generals at the National Defense University in Beijing: Liu Mingfu, Liu Yazhou, Pan Zhengqiang, Wang Zhongchun, Yang Yi, Yu Guohua, Zhang Zhaozhong, and Zhu Chenghu. Major General Zhai Yuqiu, dean of the military academy in Nanjing, contributed ideas from his three volumes on ancient stratagems. I am heavily indebted to Professor Shi Yinhong, a counselor to the State Council, who once taught today's generals in Nanjing. Shi relishes his iconoclastic role as a candid, prolific author on China's strategy, but always stays within the limits of Party and military discipline dealing with foreigners.

To protect the identity of a few other important sources, I have used pseudonyms or otherwise disguised them.

I also acknowledge my debt to two professors of Chinese philosophy, Roger Ames and François Jullien, for providing the proverbial key to unlocking the Chinese concept of *shi*. In addition, I acknowledge the decisive role of Andy Marshall, the legendary director at the Office of Net Assessment in the Department of Defense, who allowed me the opportunity to study Chinese strategy and share my insights with successive administrations.

Many Western specialists on Chinese strategic thinking contributed ideas to this book: not all will agree with my interpretations, and they certainly do not all agree among themselves. They are: Roger Ames, Dennis Blasko, Dan Blumenthal, Anne-Marie Brady, Richard Bush, Dean Cheng, Thomas Christensen, Warren Cohen, John Culver, Robert Daly, Daniel de Mots, David Dorman, Elizabeth Economy, Andrew Erickson, Evan Feigenbaum, David Finkelstein, Rick Fisher, Rosemary Foot, Christopher Ford, Aaron Friedberg, Banning Garrett, John Garver, Bonnie Glaser, Paul Godwin, Carol Hamrin, Paul Heer, David Helvey, Charles Horner, Iain Johnston, François Jullien, Robert Kagan, Roy Kamphausen, Henry Kissinger, Stephanie Kleine-Ahlbrandt, David Lai, Michael Lampton, Richard Lawless, Deborah Lehr, Cheng Li, Kenneth Lieberthal, Thomas Mahnken, Mark Mancall, James Mann, Evan Medeiros, Alice Miller, Frank Miller, James Mulvenon, Andrew Nathan, Douglas Paal, Robert Ross, Gilbert Rozman, Phil Saunders, Ralph Sawyer, Andrew Scobell, David Shambaugh, James Shinn, Randy Shriver, Abram Shulsky, Mark Stokes, Michael Swaine, Jay Taylor, Ashley Tellis, Timothy Thomas, Drew

Thompson, John Tkacik, Peter Tomsen, Christopher Twomey, Jan Van Tol, Arthur Waldron, Thomas Welch, Allen Whiting, Dennis Wilder, Larry Wortzel, Lanxin Xiang, Michael Yahuda, Maochun Yu, and Xiaoming Zhang.

This book would not exist without the genius of its editor, Paul Golob, who I suspect knows mysteriously how to channel his role models, like the great editor Maxwell Perkins, to inspire, discipline, reward, and persuade authors to produce something beyond what anyone realistically thought possible. My thanks as well to my gifted agents, Keith Urbahn and Matt Latimer of Javelin, who shaped and guided this effort from the start. Two brilliant graduate students assisted with the research and editing: Nick Bellomy and Ashley Frohwein. I also thank graduate students Jon-Michael LaGray and Mark Hanson, who helped start the draft. Chris O'Connell, a production editor at Henry Holt, contributed to the final draft.

The Hudson Institute's esteemed founder, Herman Kahn, taught me how to think critically and strategically and look beyond the conventional wisdom of the day. I benefited greatly from reading a selection of Kahn's work in a 2006 volume written by the Hudson Institute's president, Ken Weinstein. "History," Herman Kahn advised, "happens in straight lines and curves."

Most important, my everlasting appreciation to my wife, Susan Pillsbury. Susan contributed specific ideas to this book based on her eight visits to China, all of which were taken before she married me. We were introduced in London, as I was en route to Beijing in April 1989 to interview the Tiananmen Square student demonstrators. Back then, she had a premonition that Beijing's leaders were not going to live up to our wishful thinking about democracy, free trade, and human rights. As always, she proved both wise and prescient.

INDEX

ABOUT THE AUTHOR

MICHAEL PILLSBURY is the director of the Center for Chinese Strategy at the Hudson Institute and has served in presidential administrations from Richard Nixon to Barack Obama. Educated at Stanford and Columbia Universities, he is a former analyst at the RAND Corporation and research fellow at Harvard and has served in senior positions in the Defense Department and on the staff of four U.S. Senate committees. He is a member of the Council on Foreign Relations and the International Institute for Strategic Studies. He lives in Washington, D.C.